PUBLIC

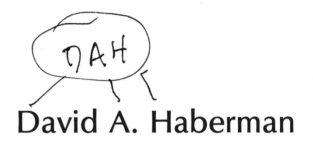

David A. Haberman

Public Relations

THE NECESSARY ART

RELATIONS

THE NECESSARY ART

(HAD)

Harry A. Dolphin, APR

88

 IOWA STATE UNIVERSITY PRESS / AMES

DEDICATION

To all those public relations practitioners
who insist actions must speak louder than words,
images must reflect reality, and communications
must inform rather than manipulate—
and to the students who will follow in their footsteps.

David A. Haberman is Professor and Chairman, Department of Journalism and Mass Communication, Creighton University, Omaha, Nebraska.

Harry A. Dolphin is a public relations consultant and former Chief of Public Affairs, Missouri River Division, U.S. Army Corps of Engineers.

©1988 Iowa State University Press, Ames, Iowa 50010

Printed in the United States of America

First edition, 1988

Library of Congress Cataloging-in-Publication Data

Haberman, David A.
  Public relations.

  Includes index.
    1. Public relations.   I. Dolphin, Harry A.
  II. Title.
  HM263.H22   1988   659.2   87–17139
  ISBN 0–8138–1457–X

Contents

Foreword

What is PR—public relations? It's the sum total of all the impressions made by every person associated with a company, organization, or institution. It's projecting the most accurate and honest image of an organization or firm—and living up to that image. It's applying common sense to the obvious. It's doing good and getting credit for it.*

My young children think public relations is Dad standing on the street corner meeting the public; my older children think it's Dad attending one cocktail party after another. I can assure you it's neither. More accurately, it's 10 percent inspiration and 90 percent perspiration—the formula written by Thomas Edison.

You must alternately and even concurrently be . . . writer . . . photographer . . . media specialist . . . marketing expert . . . financial analyst . . . protocol officer . . . recruiter . . . exhibitor . . . interviewer . . . speech maker . . . publisher . . . image maker . . . editor . . . psychologist. It's interesting, challenging, and ever-changing.

Public relations is an important function in today's world.

---

*William E. Ramsey is a member of the national task force on chapter extension, national awards committee, national membership committee of the Public Relations Society of America; former Midwest district chairman, PRSA; first person accredited by PRSA examination in Nebraska; former president of Nebraska PRSA chapter and first "Public Relations Professional of the Year" selected by the chapter; recipient of national Paul Lund Award for service, conferred by PRSA. Director of public relations for private schools and universities; vice president of Bozell & Jacobs, Inc., major national advertising and public relations agency; director of public relations and development at Father Flanagan's Boys Home (Boys Town) after Pulitzer Prize story revealed institution's accumulated wealth in 1971; currently president of Bill Ramsey Associates, Inc.

We must communicate better within our organizations and with the public; we must tell the good news of our firm's accomplishments—and level with the public about our firm's or our institution's shortcomings. Credibility is the key.

I once saw a sign: "Absolutely no deliveries to be made through this door." Wouldn't it have been friendlier and just as effective to say: "Please make deliveries to the rear door. Thank you!"?

That's where Public Relations begins—with the obvious. It is a collection of seemingly small things, the total of which equals clear, concise, friendly, and honest communication and understanding.

Public relations starts with you. A business firm, a school, any organization or institution is judged by each person who works for it. Everyone has to be a part of the action, not criticizing on the sidelines. Public relations involves being a doer, not a talker—telling a story clearly and honestly while helping management shape policy and plan programs.

William E. Ramsey, APR

Preface

Bill Ramsey has directed public relations in education, in business, and at an internationally famous child-care institution with assets worth hundreds of millions of dollars. In fact, he helped Boys Town re-establish its credibility, arriving in the wake of reports that raised serious questions about its financial policies.

With this background, he describes his work, and the work of public relations practitioners everywhere, very simply and straight-forwardly: "projecting an honest image and living up to that image . . . applying common sense to the obvious . . . doing good and getting credit for it."

In writing this textbook, we have tried to be direct and straightforward too, saying what public relations is and what it is not. We have tried to face head-on, rather than ignore, the widespread distortions of public relations found in a lot of pop culture and stereotypes that have attached themselves to the term "public relations." And we have tried to be candid rather than complacent or defensive in our effort to dispel both the false hopes and the false suspicions that public relations arouses in many people.

We have also placed our emphasis on the "deeds" in the "good deeds well told" mini-definition of public relations. Our theme, which we have tried to reprise often, is that action is the first and foremost element in public relations. We have stressed that action is itself a form of communication—often the most effective form. "Actions speak louder than words" is our byword. It is a principle we believe in and a principle we have found too often neglected or even ignored, not only in the performance of some practitioners but in the writings of some professionals and in some textbooks as well.

For the student examining public relations for the first time, we have tried to write a book that provides a clear, uncluttered picture of what public relations is—as a concept, a function, and a career field. We have tried to come up with a truly helpful alternative to the books and monographs that tend to get bogged down in social science jargon. (Some of this may be the result of public relations' understandable aspiration to the status of a profession, and some of it, of course, may be necessary to reflect the complexities of human beings and their dealings with each other.)

For the professional, we have tried to provide detailed practical material in areas that other texts do not explore in what we consider sufficient detail. Our experience and observations tell us that these areas—speech-writing, effective use of audiovisual materials, exhibitry, photography, and legal aspects of public relations—are continuing to increase in importance for seasoned as well as beginning practitioners. Obviously they will also be important to students who hope soon to enter public relations.

In attempting to be straightforward, we have discussed both the "good news" and the "bad news" about public relations. The good news we have underscored is the deep personal satisfaction that public relations provides the practitioners who can see an employer or client credited for good deeds. It is also the satisfaction of communicating effectively with important publics, of winning and holding their support and confidence, and even at times regaining their trust.

Another bit of good news for students, incidentally, is that public relations is a growing field that rewards talent and enterprise. Offering a forecast for the current decade, a leading practitioner, Robert K. Gray, has said: "Public relations will experience a metamorphosis shedding old conceptions, acquiring new responsibilities and garnering an increasing amount of power, prestige and pay." We think he is correct, and we have written from this strongly positive perspective.

Students should also know that the annual surveys of college and university journalism enrollments published by *Journalism Educator* indicate increasing numbers enrolling in public relations programs. More importantly, the annual studies of journalism graduate placements by the Newspaper Fund, Inc., evidence a growing portion of those graduates going into public relations positions. The more limited data available on salaries indicate that beginning public relations practitioners are paid somewhat more than entry level salaries paid in other areas of journalism and significantly more than their classmates in many other areas of journalism as the years go by.

Along with Gray's stimulating forecast for public relations and these career prospects, it is only realistic to remind practitioners as well as students that the responsibilities of public relations will continue to include hundreds of daily situations in which misunderstandings fester, confrontations occur, disputes erupt, jobs don't get done, and productivity lags because of breakdowns in human relations. Often this can be connected with some of the bad news about public relations: Public relations can't perform miracles. (Who says it can? Lots of people, like all those who say, "That's just a PR problem" or "All we have to do is improve our image.") Despite myths and misinformation, there is no public relations magic that can assure success for a business—any more than there is a foolproof public relations formula that can guarantee a political candidate victory at the polls. The bad news includes the reality that, inevitably, some of those exciting challenges will turn into frustrations and failures, even when the practitioner has done all that could or should reasonably be expected.

Often, however, such bad news is self-inflicted. Public relations efforts sometimes are not all they ought to be. Some are unplanned, poorly organized, and ineptly administered. Beyond that, some people continue to operate outside the mainstream of public relations professionalism and responsibility. Their efforts are shoddy, hokey, and sometimes downright dishonest. They continue to generate that distorted image that feeds the popular identification of public relations with flackery, press-agentry, image-building, and attitude manipulation.

We hope that thoughtful readers of this book will be inoculated against such self-inflicted sicknesses!

Public Relations

THE NECESSARY ART

1 The role of public relations

It is true that you may fool all of the people some of the time; you may even fool some of the people all of the time; but you can't fool all of the people all the time.

—ABRAHAM LINCOLN

Show us your works!

—The challenge hurled by nonbelieving Sorbonne students at Frederic Ozanam, turning him from debate over the needs of the poor to founding the St. Vincent de Paul Society, which now aids the poor worldwide.

Defining public relations

When Michael B. arranged a reception for a distinguished alumna visiting the university where he is public relations director, it was one of the duties of his office.

When Mark S. wrote and sent out a news release about two new restaurants to be opened by one of his agency's clients, he was practicing public relations.

When Owen T. met with the administrator of the hospital where he works to discuss providing patients with a handbook even before they are admitted, he was doing public relations too.

When Pat C. recruited captains for the United Way campaign and sent them invitations to the campaign's kickoff breakfast, she also was performing a public relations function.

So was Steve K. when he edited last month's issue of the magazine sent to the 1,726 people who work for his employer.

These are real public relations settings. They demonstrate the variety of functions performed by practitioners of public relations. But they also suggest that it is not easy to fashion an umbrella that will cover such

a spread of activities. Yet defining public relations is obviously important as a first step in learning about this vibrant and growing field.

Unfortunately, professionals in the field have yet to arrive at a consensus definition. Even the task force appointed by the Public Relations
Society of America to consider the stature and role of public relations
wrestled with the problem. In its report at the end of 1980, however, it
simply recommended that the society establish an official definition
and noted several suggestions.

Many others have already tried their hand at defining public relations, and their efforts are helpful. Their definitions range from the
somewhat "heavy," like that of the respected practitioner, Rex F. Harlow:

> Public relations is a distinctive management function which
> helps establish and maintain mutual lines of communication,
> understanding, acceptance and cooperation between an organiza-
> tion and its publics; involves the management of problems and
> issues; helps management to keep informed of and responsive to
> public opinion; defines and emphasizes the responsibility of man-
> agement to serve the public interest; helps management to keep
> abreast of and effectively utilize change, serving as an early warning
> system to help anticipate trends; and uses research and sound and
> ethical communication techniques as its principal tools.

—to the "light" and delightfully simple: Public relations is good deeds
well told.

Edward Bernays, widely considered one of the founding fathers of
public relations as a profession, posed serious problems with his definition. He is reputed to be the first person to use the term "public relations
counsel," which is certainly an improvement over "press agent." But his
choice of words in defining public relations as "the engineering of consent" was an easy target for critics. He meant doing things and providing
information and persuasion that would move key persons and groups to
accept or "consent" to programs and policies. But many found that
word "engineering" something that could have come right out of the
ominous doublespeak of George Orwell's *1984* and therefore dis-
missed this attempt at defining public relations.

Louis J. Wolter and Stephen B. Miles, writing in the *Public Relations
Journal* in 1982, said, "(T)he best three-word definition of postmodern
[mid-1980s and beyond] public relations would be 'management of
interdependence.'" Their definition focused on the growing realization
that not only individual persons but even large nations are not fully

independent of the rest of humankind. (Americans quickly learned this during the Arab-imposed oil embargoes of the 1970s!) People and countries need the help of others, and they need to work peacefully and productively with others. Public relations, say Wolter and Miles, is the "flywheel" that hitches up the energy, talent, and resources of individuals and societies with the energy, talent, and resources of other individuals and societies. The result is a coordinated system that serves the needs of all those "hitched up" individuals and groups.

Two other definitions are in wide use. One is that used by Scott M. Cutlip and Allen H. Center in their textbook, *Effective Public Relations*:

> Public relations is the planned effort to influence opinion through good character and responsible performance based upon mutually satisfactory two-way communication.

The other was provided by the editors of *Public Relations News*:

> Public relations is the management function which evaluates public attitudes, identifies the policies and procedures of an individual or organization with the public interest, and executes a program of action to earn public understanding and acceptance.

Public relations educator John Marston suggests that "and communication" ought to be inserted after "of action" in this latter definition.

When the definitions speak of public relations as a management function, they are saying:

1. Public relations policies and actions are the responsibility of management—the top leaders and decision makers in a corporation, institution, or organization.

2. Those top decision and policy makers have to involve themselves in public relations. They not only have to make major public relations decisions (e.g., "We will give time off to employees who volunteer to assist the United Way campaign" or "We will never try to cover up or minimize injuries or the mishandling of toxic materials at any of our plants"); they also have to "do" public relations (e.g., making themselves available to inquiring reporters, serving on community betterment organizations, maintaining personal contact with middle managers and on-the-line employees).

3. Top leadership has to be as aware of the needs of good public relations as corporate directors are of the need to make a profit, a hospi-

tal administration is of the need to keep drawing sufficient patients, and the leaders of a relief agency of the need to keep contributors donating.

4. Managers and leaders cannot totally delegate public relations to subordinates or hired agencies, acting as if public relations staffers are some sort of laundry service or clean-up crew whose work is peripheral to the overall success of the business, organization, or institution.

The beauty of the ". . . good deeds well told" definition is that it gets to what we consider the heart of public relations. It emphasizes the essential ingredient in effective, ethical public relations—an ingredient that is too often neglected—action or performance that is good for all of society. This little definition also places that ingredient first—before any attempt to obtain approval or "engineered consent."

A manufacturer that establishes a carefully planned and alertly monitored safety program is performing good deeds for its employees. This is action that speaks clearly of company concern for employees' welfare. This manufacturer is practicing genuine good public relations with its employees.

Contrast this with another firm that puts up signs and posters by the dozen and runs all kinds of articles on safety in the employee magazine during National Safety Week but does not have a quality safety program or allows its safety program to become a paper program that is not enforced or supervised. This company, despite all its communication on safety, is not practicing good public relations. Its action—or inaction—speaks louder than its words.

However, despite its excellent insight, ". . . good deeds well told" leaves much unsaid. It seems to assume that deeds or actions that are truly good for an entire society are easily identified and easily accepted as good by all the individuals and groups existing in human communities. Yet identifying those good-for-everybody activities is obviously one of the most complex tasks facing public relations practitioners, especially if they are to be "managers of interdependence."

The brief definition also does not say anything about how those good deeds are to be well told—and how the practitioner finds out whether even the well-told story has been heard, or understood, or remembered. It does not suggest to whom (special "publics" or all of society) the telling should be addressed. Certainly it seems to ignore the fact that it may be extremely difficult for practitioners to decide how to word their messages most understandably and convincingly—and even to determine the most effective ways to get the message out in the first place.

Nonetheless, with a simple definition we can emphasiz
that acceptable performance is the cornerstone of public
Practitioners must be deeply involved in determining what
actions are good. Next, they must see to it as managers that those
actions are undertaken. Then, and only then, can they take up the
problems involved in communicating the fact that good deeds have
been performed.

To look at it another way, good deeds or acceptable actions themselves can be a form of communication. Often they are the most effective
form of communication: Actions speak louder than words. The food flown
to starving Ethiopians in the mid-1980s spoke far more eloquently than
scores of sympathetic diplomatic messages of other peoples' concern for
the citizens of that war-torn, drought-ravaged land.

As Lincoln indicated to a White House caller more than a century
ago, a well-worded expression of neighborly concern from someone
who really is causing trouble or hardship might be accepted gratefully at
first. But eventually its insincerity will become evident—when, as with
the Ethiopians, for example, words from some countries were not
accompanied by food.

ANALYSIS

Although there is no consensus definition of public relations, those
definitions most widely cited can be helpful in understanding what
public relations is and does. The definitions can help in constructing a
useful overview of public relations. The key factors or elements in those
definitions are:

1. Public relations consists, in the very first instance, of good deeds
or actions that are beneficial to all of society. This suggests a recognition
of human interdependence, the reality that what each one of us does
affects others. This is the point that Wolter and Miles stress in their
three-word definition, "management of interdependence."

2. Public relations must also consist of efforts to determine what
those beneficial actions should be in particular circumstances, both
now and for the future.

3. Public relations practitioners must then work at successfully
communicating to others ("publics") that their business, agency, or institution really is acting for the good of society and not for its own
short-term advantage.

4. Public relations requires that the management or leadership of
organizations share fully with PR practitioners the awareness that

acceptance by society is of highest priority if the organizations are to function successfully now and in the future.

5. Public relations obviously then will include on-going planning, analysis, and evaluation; skillful, persuasive communication; and constant study of conditions and attitudes in the larger society within which practitioners and their organizations function.

If those elements were universally accepted and applied, the Public Relations Society of America probably would not have had to appoint its task force on the stature and role of public relations mentioned earlier. In addition to the need for a widely acceptable definition of public relations, the task force found that many people still see public relations as something aimed at them rather than as something done for them.

The task force also found that too many euphemisms—titles that seem to have been chosen to avoid using the term public relations—are used to describe public relations functions. The result is that people tend to wonder about the motives of practitioners who seem ashamed of the name of their profession.

ACTION AND DECISION. Students taking their first formal look at public relations in this textbook will undoubtedly be aware of this "image problem" the task force found. But that should not get in the way of understanding what authentic, ethical public relations is. No profession should be defined or understood on the basis of its least qualified or most shoddy practitioners.

Yet too many people persist in thinking of public relations as essentially an image-making or image-refurbishing business, and they think of image here as a mask, the artificial smiling face that covers a frown or leer. Even some influential leaders seem to persist in thinking of PR practitioners as "pros" who can make a bad situation look good, that all they have to do is go into their media manipulation act and their client's misdeeds will be ignored or forgotten.

There are still some too who call themselves public relations practitioners and think they can work such magic. Every now and then some temporary or partial success bolsters that myth and feeds the misconception of what public relations truly is. But talk without deeds is just talk, and that is what it eventually is seen to be. Furthermore, to cite Lincoln again, "If you once forfeit the confidence of your fellow citizens, you can never regain their respect and esteem."

COMMUNICATION. Though public relations is performance above all, it is also communication. The light of good deeds is not to be hidden under a bushel basket. Communication lifts the basket and puts a reflector behind the light. Performance (e.g., what a business manufactures or sells) will never be acceptable unless someone finds out about it and can make a judgment based on what has been learned.

While it is true enough that some actions do speak for themselves, others do not. Even those that seem to speak for themselves may have to be explained. The careful testing of a product before it is marketed goes on in a laboratory, not in front of a network television camera that transmits a picture message about the product to an entire nation live and in color. If the laboratory testing is to be appreciated as a good action, someone has to tell about it. For the telling to be effective, knowledge and skill in communication are essential; public relations people must be able to write and speak effectively. They must also have knowledge and skill in the use of the mass media—newspapers, magazines, radio, and television. This has made people with journalistic or mass communication skills sought after in the practice of public relations. It explains why those who have worked for a print or broadcast medium continue to be sought by public relations departments and firms. Businesses, institutions, and organizations are willing to pay well for communications knowledge and skills.

In emphasizing the role of communication, however, we must immediately stress that informing people or publics about acceptable performance is not the only kind of communication of significance for public relations. To know that their clients' and employers' performance really is acceptable, practitioners must receive communication as well as they send it. They must hear what their publics are saying. They must establish and maintain communication lines that receive as well as transmit.

Just being a listener is not enough. They must be good listeners. They must not only know what society thinks and feels; they must be understanding and receptive. Otherwise society's feedback will be no better than background music; you are aware of it, but it does not say a thing to you.

MANAGEMENT INVOLVEMENT. Thoughtful public relations practitioners and educators alike acknowledge that many managers and leaders still look upon PR people as organizational firefighters or troubleshooters. When disaster strikes, the public relations firefighters, otherwise left to play checkers, are summoned by an alarm to speed to the rescue.

The correct perception of the public relations staff's role, much more widely accepted today, is that of providing continuous evaluation, planning, and counsel, much more than even "fire prevention."

As Lew Riggs has written in *Public Relations Quarterly*, executives will be looking to their public relations people when they need "peer-level thinkers," people who have a broad view of the business or organization and have developed wide-ranging problem-solving abilities.

Riggs also foresees PR practitioners as "totally immersed in management strategy" in the years ahead. This, of course, will mean that professionals will have to develop competence in basic management functions beyond communication. Other professionals have cited the need for practitioners to be "management-oriented," meaning public relations people must know how top managers think and act and what they expect from their staffs.

Philip Lesly, also writing in *Public Relations Quarterly*, says that often top management demands measurability and accountability. Executives deal with the tangible and concrete—production, sales, and bottom-line profits in business. Public relations professionals must meet managers' needs for measurability and accountability but not stop there. They have to inform executives about human values and attitudes as they affect production, sales, and profits. In other words, PR people have to be able to mix the intangible with the tangible.

PUBLIC RELATIONS VERSUS ADVERTISING. In developing a clear concept of public relations, it is important to avoid the error of lumping PR with advertising. People who have little direct contact with these two fields or with the media sometimes do this, uncertain about the distinction between publicity or promotion and advertising.

Publicity is a part, but only a part, of public relations. Acceptable performance, dialogue, and interaction with the publics affected by that performance are the heart of public relations. Nonetheless, both publicity and advertising do tell about business and organizations and what they do or produce. In addition, much of paid advertising uses an indirect approach to selling. Its aim is to build confidence and respect for the product or its producer rather than to sell individual units to consumers. That is the type of ad or commercial that says, "If it's a XXX, it's got to be good" or "XXX, a name that stands for quality."

Other factors may contribute to blurring the line between advertising and public relations. For instance, public relations staffs will some-times buy space in print publications or air time on broadcast stations to convey promotional or point-of-view messages. A common example is the company message published as a paid advertisement during a labor dispute, often in response to a paid message placed by the union to give its side of the dispute.

That example itself shows that it is a misleading oversimplification to say that the essential difference between advertising and public relations is that one pays to use the media (advertisers buy time and space) while the other does not (PR releases are published and aired without charge). In addition to the paid point-of-view message, public relations people may pay for publication of their messages in other ways. In major publishing centers, for instance, there are firms that perform a service not unlike that of a literary agent. For a fee, these firms will help place informational articles in key publications. The information articles may describe the activities of a public relations practitioner's employer or client. When published, such articles are undeniably paid publicity.

Although the practice is widely rejected as unethical, some news-papers still publish special sections with "news features" that just happen to focus on the activities, background, products, and services of those advertisers. In some instances, such sections are published with full notice to readers that all the contents, advertisements and feature copy, have been provided by the advertisers. In either case, the public-ity is certainly not "free" though it was written by public relations people.

Truly unpaid publicity, on the other hand, can be effective adver-tising. When news reports told of Procter & Gamble's Crest tooth-paste winning the approval of the Council on Dental Therapeutics of the American Dental Association, not only did P & G stock soar in value, so did the sales of Crest, which still displays this approval state-ment on every tube (as do other dentifrices that have subsequently won endorsement).

Newspaper editors still fume in their trade publications over all the "free advertising" public relations people manage to get into their news-papers under the guise of news releases. Such editors seem to forget that information favorable to a product or its producer can be legitimate news as well as effective unpaid advertising.

With all these important qualifications in mind, advertising can be defined as a paid sales message, usually conveyed through the mass media, designed to persuade people to purchase certain goods or serv-ices. Those sales messages, we must remember, are most often informational as well as persuasive. They provide facts about the product or service ("More than a century of continuous service") or even the production process ("Brewed the Old World way with water from God's country"), even though the information is combined with claims of desirability or superiority.

Another significant distinction between advertising and publicity involves control over the content of the message. Unless advertising copy is unacceptable because of the type of product or the unsubstantiated claims made for it, the advertiser in most cases has complete control over the paid advertising message. The advertiser can say what it wants to say in the way it wants to say it.

On the other hand, publicity, in the form of news releases, will face news and editorial judgments by the staff of a newspaper or broadcast station. Experts estimate that fewer than one-third of all releases sent out are published at all. Those that are published are usually edited; the message is changed and shortened. An editor will consider the amended version an improvement; however, the public relations writer may be keenly disappointed that the published story does not say quite what it was meant to.

Advertising generally is tied directly and immediately to sales, even if it uses a subtle or "soft-" rather than "hard-sell" approach. Public relations has a wider and longer-range concern, even if sales or profits are a major objective. The goal of public relations is acceptable performance and the recognition of that acceptable performance by all the concerned publics. Public relations efforts may not, and most often do not, result in an immediate, obvious increase in sales. A business or organization has a right to expect that over time good public relations will have a positive though indirect effect on profits or organizational success. But the business or organization cannot gauge the effectiveness of its public relations effort by immediate response to its products, services, or mission in the great majority of cases.

Even in pointing out these differences between public relations and advertising, it is apparent that there is considerable interplay between the two. A producer that has good relations with its publics should have an easier time selling its products in the atmosphere of acceptance its public relations program has achieved. On the other hand, an advertisement aimed at selling the idea that the producer is reliable, careful, quality-conscious, and fair can help form an attitude of acceptance in the minds of the producer's publics.

WHERE PUBLIC RELATIONS OPERATES

The general public is probably most aware of the existence of public relations practitioners in very large corporations and, perhaps, in the upper echelons of government. But that is the tip of the iceberg.

Anyone or any cause requiring the support or cooperation of others for achieving an objective is a candidate for public relations assistance. Many obtain this assistance from PR practitioners who are dispersed widely in contemporary American society.

BUSINESSES. Larger firms tend to have their own PR staffs, while some smaller businesses use the services of public relations agencies on a contract basis. Within a large business, public relations staffs may handle external and internal communication; publish external and internal pamphlets, brochures, and periodicals; coordinate interaction with the local communities where the business has plants and offices; give talks to civic and professional organizations, or prepare speeches that company executives deliver to such groups; and plan and coordinate special events, such as the opening of a new facility or the celebration of a special company anniversary or milestone.

ORGANIZATIONS. This category includes trade associations, professional associations (the American Medical Association, the American Bar Association, and hundreds of others along with their state and local affiliates); civic groups; issue-oriented interest groups; health-research organizations (e.g., American Heart Association, Multiple Sclerosis Society); churches and church-related organizations; labor unions; social organizations; and political parties.

INSTITUTIONS. Included here are schools at every level and of every kind; hospitals, clinics, and other health and rehabilitation centers; research and charitable foundations; child-care institutions; and service centers.

The number of public relations personnel employed by individual businesses, organizations, and institutions varies greatly, as you will see when specialized areas of public relations are discussed in Chapters 8 and 9. In larger public relations staffs, you will find more specialization. Some people may spend most of their time preparing external news releases, while others spend almost full time researching and writing speeches for company executives or officers of an international union, for instance. Fund raising may be a primary activity for the public relations staff of one of the health-related organizations. Everything during the year may be geared to the annual period when a direct appeal for public contributions is made.

In smaller public relations programs, the variety of work is almost limitless, as we will see. It will include news releases, speech writing, and fund raising plus everything from setting up visitor tours to lobbying members of Congress.

A brief history of public relations

Throughout history, successful leaders and groups achieved their goals by carefully cultivating support from key people. Even though the terminology would have been strange to them, and even though in many cases they may not have been conscious of using a special process, in a sense they were all practitioners of successful public relations.

Yet it was only when the United States was no longer a rural nation with little more than home industry and had emerged from the first stages of the Industrial Revolution that we developed an awareness of something we now call public relations. The name came even later, the profession developed only after the name provided some sort of identity for practitioners, and the importance and full scope of the field are still unfolding today.

In one sense then, public relations is as old as the human race. In another sense, it is still in its adolescence.

EARLY PUBLIC RELATIONS

No doubt political public relations had been employed even before the Industrial Revolution came to the United States. Historians tell us that one-third of the English colonists in the thirteen colonies initially supported the American Revolution, another third opposed it, and the final third fell in the undecided column. Yet the powerful rhetoric of Thomas Paine, the fiery oratory of Patrick Henry, and the marvelous pen of Thomas Jefferson certainly broadened the acceptance that the new nation finally enjoyed when a peace treaty acknowledging its independence was signed in 1783.

A few decades later, Andrew Jackson's "image" as the hero of the

Battle of New Orleans in 1814 was used to help him win the presidency in 1828. He even employed Amos Kendall as a ghost writer for his political speeches and used Kendall's sharp political sense in other ways as well.

Even a modern public relations person envies a slogan as effective as William Henry Harrison's 1840 "Tippecanoe and Tyler too" and "Honest Abe's" log cabin birth and rail-splitter image.

In the business sphere, public relations in some form undoubtedly existed for decades before it had a name or an identity. In fact, it is sometimes said that it was raw promotion, often exaggerated and sometimes thoroughly misleading, that brought hundreds of thousands of Europeans to our shores. It started with the Spaniards who played up the handful of gold Columbus was able to scrape up in the West Indies, and it continued with the ship owners who touted America as a land of promise to so many central and eastern European peasants throughout the nineteenth century.

This might suggest that public relations simply grew out of advertising and promotion. But if you remember the discussion of the nature of modern public relations, promotion is just one aspect; and misleading promotion does not fit the description of effective, ethical public relations at all. Nonetheless, we cannot ignore the fact that the tout and the promoter are all a part of Americana, and they are still with us today— often cloaking themselves in the respectability of a public relations-related title.

Public relations as it is known today probably began to develop as industrialists ran into the political, economic, and social reform movements of the late nineteenth and early twentieth centuries. Many of the industrialists saw that the negative picture the reformers painted of them could not be ignored. These giants of finance and industry, the Morgans, Vanderbilts, and Rockefellers, were for the most part shrewd enough to learn that economic power had to be wielded carefully or it could be lost. If the famed statement attributed to Vanderbilt, "The public be damned," was actually uttered, its speaker was perceptive enough to deny it when he realized its impact.

ENCOUNTERING PUBLIC OPINION

Little by little the major figures of American business and industry accepted the wisdom of employing people who had earned the reputation of being able to influence public opinion. More correctly, these first public relations practitioners may be described as skilled in communicating material that put their employers in a favorable light. Some of these early practitioners were working before the turn of the century, of course, but their activities spread and increased in the years before and after World War I.

It was that war, too, that demonstrated that promotional public relations activities and techniques could work. They could sell war bonds, recruit volunteers for the Red Cross and other patriotic organizations, and get young men to enlist in the army and navy. With the war's end, there still were causes for which public support was essential. Money was raised in America for the victims of the fighting in Europe—for rebuilding French cathedrals and for feeding hungry children in defeated Germany.

Within their own borders, Americans saw the labor union movement growing. They also saw business and industry vigorously fight that growth. The battle was often violent and bloody. The more perceptive business leaders learned that violence could be used to break strikes and crush unions, but only at the cost of growing public hostility.

The full brunt of that hostility toward business was yet to come. The collapse of the economy after the stock market crash of 1929 began to focus antibusiness feelings. The election of 1932, with the sweeping economic regulations that followed, gave it voice. For many Americans "business" became a bad word because they were convinced that business had performed badly in bringing economic ruin to the country. The reputation of American business could not be laundered or rehabilitated overnight. It would require acceptable performance to achieve that. When business was unable to end the country's economic stagnation, the long decade of the Great Depression simply reinforced that truth.

Public relations during the Depression Era saw the emergence of such people as Ivy L. Lee; his one-time partner, George F. Parker; the leader of the Committee on Public Information during World War I, George Creel; and Creel's protégés, Carl Byoir and Edward L. Bernays.

Lee, like thousands of other practitioners today, came into public relations from journalism. His work as a business reporter apparently led him to realize business's need to get its side of the economic story told when critics were attacking it from all sides. Although he had trouble at first persuading business leaders of this need, he eventually was signed on by the coal industry, a major railroad, the Rockefeller interests, and, in the twilight of his career, the Nazi-controlled I. H. Farben dye cartel.

Lee adopted the term "public relations" somewhere around the middle of a career that ran from 1906 to 1934. More importantly, in a pronouncement sent to newspaper editors, he set forth some basic principles of modern public relations:

1. The public is to be informed, not kept in the dark.
2. Information provided the news media must be honest and accurate.
3. Reporters' questions are to be answered promptly and fully.
4. Public relations information must be recognized as distinct from advertising.

Despite—or maybe because of—his success, Lee had bitter critics. The famed American muckraker Upton Sinclair hung the label Poison Ivy on him. Another public relations pioneer, Creel, played on that epithet by saying Lee was a "poisoner of public opinion."

Parker, another one-time newspaperman, entered public relations as a publicity writer for politicians. Among his clients was Grover Cleveland, whose presidential campaigns Parker handled. It was while working with the Democrats in 1904 that Parker was assisted by Lee, and the two formed a short-lived partnership after the campaign. While other publicists were still looked upon with contempt by many in the newspaper field, Parker in his later partnership with C. A. Bridge drew respect with the motto, "Accuracy, Authenticity, and Interest."

Creel's fame as a public relations practitioner came during World War I, when he headed the federal government's Committee on Public Information, America's first avowed propaganda agency, promoting support for the war effort at home and attacking the actions of the Central Powers abroad. Considering the significant extent to which the United States was able to contribute to Germany's defeat during just the last 18 months of the war, Creel's committee must certainly be credited with a major achievement in motivating the national effort.

Byoir and Bernays got their public relations training largely as members of the Committee on Public Information. Byoir went on after the war to start what was for some years the largest public relations agency in the United States. Bernays became the unofficial prophet of public relations and a highly successful practitioner as well. Bernays wrote what is considered the first book on public relations, *Crystallizing Public Opinion*, in 1923. For more than half a century he has retained the prophet's mantle, campaigning for changes in public relations education and speaking out on the need for greater professionalism.

WORLD WAR II

In the United States, the Depression did not end until arms production began with the outbreak of World War II in Europe. In the minds of many people this, not the efforts of business and industry, ended economic stagnation. Such a perception did little to refurbish the reputation of corporate business.

But the new war did give new impetus to public relations. Major companies—automobile manufacturers are a prime example—saw an opportunity to tell of their contribution to the war effort. The federal government itself used well-developed public relations campaigns to mobilize citizen support for the war. These campaigns included everything from persuading citizens to conserve and donate materials considered valuable in making weapons and military equipment (rubber, scrap metal, etc.) to discouraging absenteeism in war-production plants and protecting military secrecy.

Public relations techniques were also used in internal and external propaganda. Even before the United States entered the war, the excesses of the Nazi propaganda ministry under Josef Goebbels cost Germany a fatal loss of credibility in the international community. The United States wisely labeled its principal propaganda office the Office of War Information and recruited a highly respected journalist, Elmer Davis, to head it. Under Davis, the agency achieved a reputation for reliability. People saw that it was willing to admit American setbacks and difficulties and unwilling to make claims of imaginary military successes.

Those immersed in the fledgling field of public relations had known it all along, but by the war's end, a significantly greater number of Americans were also aware that effective public relations was necessary for the success of any effort requiring the cooperation of many people. Public relations programs and departments multiplied in business and industry. Sometimes they grew out of personnel or publicity offices. Sometimes they were created without any predecessor in the management structure. Organizations and institutions across the country formalized their public relations efforts. Government, still shying away from admitting it was involved in "public relations" activities, added many public information and public affairs officers and public liaison personnel.

PROFESSIONALISM

A new respectability and a new professionalism far removed from the negative style of early press agentry came to public relations as colleges and universities began offering courses in this new field. While the first such courses, often labeled "Publicity" or "Press Relations," appeared in the 1920s, the real growth occurred in the late 1940s and after, with more than 300 institutions reportedly offering public relations study by the 1970s. Today it is estimated that nearly 500 schools offer courses in this field. The term "public relations counsel," coined by Bernays back in 1923, or "public relations practitioner," came into vogue at this time.

Indicative of what was happening, the Public Relations Society of America was founded in 1948, just three years after World War II. PRSA was the successor to the National Association of Public Relations Counsel and the American Council of Public Relations. The former began in 1936 as the National Association of Accredited Publicity Directors, and the latter was formed in 1939 primarily as a West Coast organization. The Washington-based American Public Relations Association, founded in 1944, merged with PRSA in 1961. About a dozen specialized national public relations groups also developed significantly during this period. Some of them, like the American College Public Relations Association, organized in 1917, dated back to the World War I era, however.

The Public Relations Society of America has been a major contributor to the professionalizing of public relations through its accrediting program, publication of the *Public Relations Journal*, and adoption of a code of ethics for practitioners. The accrediting program encourages members to prepare for a detailed examination covering their knowledge of public relations principles and practices as well as the special ethical and legal aspects of public relations and mass communication. Once they have passed the examination, members are given a special "accredited in public relations" status within the society and are authorized to designate themselves "APR."

PRSA has also been active in maintaining a keen interest in public relations education in America's colleges and universities. The society has outlined a recommended curriculum for students who intend to major in public relations at a four-year college or university. PRSA has also become an active, contributing member of the Accrediting Council on Education in Journalism and Mass Communication. The council evaluates communications programs, including public relations sequences, in four-year institutions.

Another important contributor to the professional status of the field is the International Association of Business Communicators, headquartered in San Francisco. As its name suggests, IABC brings together practitioners whose efforts are directed at one of the most significant aspects of public relations. IABC too has formulated a comprehensive examination for members who wish to achieve accredited status within the organization. It publishes its own magazines, *Communication World* and the *Journal of Communication Management*, and it also supports and has been represented on the Accrediting Council on Education in Journalism and Mass Communications.

THE FUTURE

As new issues and problems confront America, there is broad agreement that the role of public relations will grow and become more critical.

In the 1980s, Americans continue to focus their attention on the national economy, an area where public relations has a major role. They considered the economy the central issue in at least two presidential elections. They worried about the impact of large federal deficits on business and their own individual welfare. They saw the deterioration of America's competitive position in world markets, with chronic and even terminal unemployment for thousands in basic industries such as steel and auto manufacturing. These conditions provided public relations opportunities.

When people saw Japanese imports successfully challenge their own automobile industry, they were willing to take a serious look at the Japanese industrial model. What they saw was a highly motivated work force with a life-long commitment to its employers. When they compared this with the discord characterizing relations between the United Auto Workers and General Motors, Ford, and Chrysler, they began to realize the tremendous potential for improvement in labor-management relations alone in the United States.

Yet a survey by the International Association of Business Communicators in the early 1980s, after nearly 40 years of growth for employee communications programs, found that the "grapevine" still outranked handbooks, bulletin boards, small group meetings, and employee publications as a source of employees' information about their jobs and employer. This led Lew Riggs to write, "Employee communications has become, as a result, one of the hottest new roles for public relations and one requiring considerable acumen."

Riggs and the Public Relations Society of America task force on which he served also saw these challenges awaiting public relations in the coming years:

1. To provide an early warning system to alert business executives and organization leaders to the issues and movements that are going to affect them.

2. To involve businesses, institutions, and organizations much more actively in the public issues that affect them. Public relations practitioners will become more activist. In its first official statement in 1982 on the role of public relations, PRSA itself said practitioners must see that public relations encompasses "planning and implementing the organization's efforts to influence or change public policy."

3. To help clients and employers cope with the splintering of viewpoints that seems to be growing in American society. The expanded role and political clout of so-called interest groups with their political action committees (PACs) are evidence of this. Public relations practitioners will have to keep alert to the changing social and political environment and use their professional skills in guiding businesses, institutions, and organizations in adjusting to these changes promptly and wisely.

In a sense, this future is already upon us. As the controversy over costs and alternate sources of energy continues (despite a temporary easing of the oil crisis in the mid-1980s), the importance of public support for compromises in some areas and sacrifices in others is emerging more clearly. This means that environmentalists and industrialists will have to tell their stories more effectively and persuasively, and some middle ground will have to be found to accommodate the interests of both camps. The social and political leaders who strive for compromises and solutions that demand sacrifices in this and other controversies will have to be more effective in winning widespread acceptance. All will inevitably require the assistance of public relations practitioners.

What we say about energy can be said for the problem of national productivity in the face of increasingly competitive world markets and the corrosive effects of inflation and the problem of restructuring education and social welfare programs to meet the changing growth patterns and ethnic makeup of America's population.

Doubt and cynicism may be widespread in the years ahead. After all, people have long been confused by the conflicting claims of energy producers and environmentalists and consumer advocates. They have been affronted by unexpected foreign hostility and worried by both military threats and what appears to be the inordinate cost of military defense. They have been disheartened by the inability of government and business to solve major economic problems.

In the face of this, the public relations of the future will call for greater candor and honesty, more involvement in policy planning and implementation, greater emphasis on acceptable performance, and more sophisticated management techniques to plan, effect, oversee, and evaluate acceptable performance. In addition, there will always be the need for genuine skill and insight in telling the story of acceptable performance and in maintaining dialogue with all those asked to approve that performance.

The social and economic contributions of public relations

Like old soldiers, some stereotypes never die. Unfortunately, they don't fade away either. To many news people today, a public relations practitioner is still a "flack." Even when it is said with a smile, it stings. The man or woman who leaves news work to enter public relations is still a deserter or traitor, according to some former colleagues. Those terms are not used with 100 percent seriousness, of course, but they do reveal a traditional prejudice.

A graduate student at a state university recently did a thesis on the attitudes of news people toward public relations practitioners. Some old epithets were included in multiple-choice questions asked of the news people. When they learned this, some public relations practitioners called for the study to be stopped. They thought it breathed new life into old stereotypes and demeaned them and their work.

A bit too defensive? Or unconscious evidence that practitioners themselves believe a negative attitude toward their work is still alive and kicking? (The student's thesis, incidentally, later reported that a significant number of PR practitioners themselves agreed that some people in their field deserved a few of those epithets!)

What is far more important than the needling and name calling that afflict every professional group is the realization that public relations practitioners can and do make significant contributions to the society in which they work. As we've seen in considering its immediate future, public relations is destined to make an even greater contribution to solving major problems. Competent, ethical practitioners have every reason to feel very positive about their profession and the work they do. And it is our observation that the best practitioners do feel this way. They know that they, as well as the businesses, organizations, and institutions they serve and advise, are "doing good deeds."

PROVIDING VALUABLE COUNSEL

From a negative standpoint alone, PR people can prevent or undo bad decisions, and they can do this without a hint of do-goodism. They can very realistically point out that these bad decisions and poor policies invariably end up being bad in terms of the business or organization's long-term success.

For example, a large manufacturer discovers an engineering flaw in one of its products. The flaw could cause serious injury to those who use the product. The old "public be damned," profits-are-all-that-count thinking might suggest the manufacturer simply weigh the cost of correcting the defect against the cost of defending lawsuits filed by injured customers. On that basis, the decision might be, "Forget the flaw. It will cost less to settle the lawsuits than it would to recall and revamp the product." Sad to say, situations like this still happen.

However, the reaction was just the opposite in 1980 when Procter & Gamble did not wait for government or consumer demands before withdrawing a tampon product from the market. Preliminary studies had indicated the product might be a factor in toxic-shock syndrome, a serious illness that struck a number of users. Around the same time a quick-service chain, Speedylube, invited customers back for a free motor oil change when it got word that some of the crankcase oil it had been using might have been part of a faulty batch that jellified at extremely low temperatures.

These cases could be multiplied. They show ethical, effective public relations in action. Responsible public relations counselors will not condone the "forget the flaw" approach. The ethical, responsible public relations person immediately points out the blatant wrongheadedness of such a decision and its total insensitivity to those who are among the seller's most important publics. Even if the advice is not expressed in terms of morality, it can properly be framed in terms of human relations, something every business needs to consider as a check on pure profit-loss thinking. It can be seen like this: Write off those injured or short-changed customers and we will lose the respect of thousands of others, including potential customers, for years to come.

Public relations people can help create a more responsive, humane approach to social change, too, not just remedy spot product failures like the Procter & Gamble and Speedylube situations. Delayed retirement provides an exemplary opportunity. Managements with sound counsel have not tried to "get" senior employees whose ability to perform has been lessened by age. They have seen senior employees as loyal partners in their success over the past decades, not worn-out production units. As a result, they have reassigned and reclassified such people where their experience and mature judgment can still provide a valuable contribution to the employer's mission.

TELLING IMPORTANT STORIES

The premier accomplishment and satisfaction for the journalist is obtaining important information and putting it in the hands of the general public, which has a real need for the information. Public relations people who provide their publics with reports on what their business, organization, or institution is doing can share in the same type of satisfaction.

A large percentage of the news in newspapers and on the air originates with public relations staffs. In a study of newspapers, Scott Cutlip concluded that about a third of the news columns were filled with information that had come from public relations sources. The reporters in any community—and that includes media centers like Washington, New York, Chicago, and Los Angeles—are too few to cover "all the news that's fit to print," as the *New York Times* boasts it does. The news media actually rely on public relations people to help them cover the news.

There is a double contribution and satisfaction for public relations practitioners who get a news release in print or on the air. Not only have they helped inform the public; they have also furthered the objectives of an employer or client.

CONTRIBUTING TO EMPLOYER/CLIENT SUCCESS

If the objective of a PR practitioner's employer or client is to cure the sick and injured (the goals of a hospital), or to educate young people for life and responsible citizenship (the hope of a college or university), or to assist the handicapped and economically dependent (the task of government and private social agencies), just about anyone would agree that these employers and clients are contributing to the good of society. Then anyone who helps a hospital, college, or social agency is participating in that contribution and can enjoy genuine personal career satisfaction. That, of course, is exactly what public relations people are doing each day, helping their employers and clients achieve highly laudable goals.

The same can be said of business. Producing a safe, efficient, dependable automobile at a fair price, for instance, is definitely contributing to the good of society. Our present life-style needs such a product.

The principle applies to a host of products and services we use in feeding, clothing, and housing ourselves and our families. We are, or should be, grateful that they are being made and provided and that someone has told us about them.

Philosophers and psychologists will agree that our mental, emotional, and physical health needs periods of leisure and recreation. Therefore, the principle applies as well to many so-called non-necessities—products and services designed to make leisure and recreation more refreshing and enjoyable. The manufacturing and marketing of these and the providing of services in those areas are definite, valuable contributions to a healthy, happy, well-adjusted society. Public relations practitioners who assist in the overall success of the producers of the products and the providers of the services certainly join in this valuable contribution, and they have good reason to be proud and satisfied.

Summary

A dozen perceptive definitions of public relations can be found, starting with those in good dictionaries. Some tend to be complex and rather technical, while others are neat summaries or deft insights into part of what public relations encompass.

You can take your choice of definitions. But you should always remember that public relations is essentially acceptable performance and dialogue, not monologue, with all the publics affected by and interested in that performance. Remember that an authentic concept of public relations must include each of these elements:

1. Recognizing and accepting the importance of winning the approval of others for the long-term success of your business, organization, or institution.
2. Resolving that you will therefore act acceptably, for the common good, rather than for your own short-term advantage.

3. Planning how you can attain and maintain acceptable performance.

4. Implementing those plans and monitoring performance regularly to see that they stay implemented.

5. Keeping in touch with those segments of society—your special publics—most directly concerned with your performance. This implies not only telling them about your performance but seeking their responses and reactions.

6. Assuring top management's awareness of the need for effective public relations in this full sense, and getting management to involve itself and accept responsibility for a sound, day in, day out public relations program.

The identification of these elements and their synthesizing by what we now know as the public relations profession has taken place through the centuries of recorded history. But it was the Industrial Revolution, particularly in America, that seems to have led to the formal development of our modern concepts of public relations.

The promotional aspects of public relations were practiced successfully by early nineteenth century politicians and then by promoters of many sorts. Reform movements at the turn of the century, often targeting industrialists, seem to have compelled the barons of business to realize the need for public acceptance. Public relations was seen as the means to achieve that acceptance.

The two world wars, which required universal citizen support, brought government the realization that it too must inaugurate strong public relations programs. Some of the important figures in the history of public relations in America achieved fame through their roles in these programs. They include George Creel, Carl Byoir, and Edward Bernays.

Many others among the early practitioners came from journalism. Most notable among this group is Ivy Lee, who adopted the term "public relations" to describe his work.

While the offering of a smattering of college courses on some aspects of public relations afforded the field a bit of respectability earlier, professionalism made its greatest strides after World War II, particularly with the organization of the Public Relations Society of America. This society, through various mergers, eventually became the central, unified force for professionalism, setting high standards for education and practice. It has been joined in this continuing effort by a sister organization, the International Association of Business Communicators.

At present, public relations continues to mature and grow as the importance of and need for sound programs becomes more widely recognized. Nonetheless, critics of the field often challenge the social contribution of "PR."

As you examine the field, however, you should be conscious of the very real contribution that public relations practitioners can make to their society through valuable counsel and effective communication.

Exercises

1. Identify an accessible public relations practitioner and a manager or administrator with whom the practitioner works. Then ask them, separately, how they would define public relations. Compare the definitions with those presented in this chapter to see if they add anything. Then write your own evaluation of all the definitions, telling which you think is best and why you think so.

2. Talk to two students who are not in your public relations class. Ask them what they think of when they hear the term "public relations." Compare their informal definitions or descriptions with those you have already obtained. Has the concept of "flackery" turned up in the student comments?

3. If public relations-type activities have been going on for centuries, as this chapter suggests, what reasons can be offered for the fact that individuals were not recognized as public relations practitioners until the late nineteenth and early twentieth century? Discuss why you think these reasons are valid or not.

4. Though he is considered a public relations prophet, Edward L. Bernays apparently has so far not changed the pattern of most public relations education programs. At least surveys indicate that 95 percent of the public relations courses taught in American colleges and universities are offered in schools and departments of communication. Recalling the way public relations has been defined and described, discuss the reasons that may exist for reluctance to identify public relations solely with business. Discuss the reasons for associating public relations with journalism and mass communication. Do you accept these reasons as valid?

Case study

A very popular network television "magazine" program airs a story on political corruption and lawlessness in a mineral-rich western state. The state's second largest source of income, after minerals, is tourism. The governor is furious over the television coverage, fearing it will ruin many businesses in the state that depend upon both summer and winter tourists. The governor wires the network, demanding an opportunity to respond to the program. He is turned down.

"No problem," says his top aide. "This is just a public relations problem. We can just get us one of those big New York or Los Angeles advertising agencies to renew our image as a tourist paradise and forget about the network program."

Based on what you've learned about the meaning and role of public relations, evaluate the aide's prescription for the tourism industry's obvious problem. Are you able to offer any positive suggestions to the governor, using the general concepts of public relations we've covered so far?

Suggested readings

Cutlip, Scott M., and Allen H. Center. *Effective Public Relations.* 5th ed. Englewood Cliffs, N.J.: Prentice-Hall, 1982.

"Emerging Issues for Public Relations." *Public Relations Journal,* February 1980.

Golden, L.L.L. *Only by Public Consent.* New York: Hawthorne Books, 1968.

Greyser, Stephen A. "Changing Roles for Public Relations." *Public Relations Journal,* January 1981.

Hiebert, Ray Eldon. *Courier to the Crowd: The Story of Ivy Lee.* Ames, Iowa: Iowa State Univ. Press, 1966.

Hill, John W. *The Making of a Public Relations Man.* New York: David McKay, 1963.

Jackson, Patrick. "Tomorrow's Public Relations." *Public Relations Journal* March 1985.

Lesly, Philip. "The Stature and Role of Public Relations." *Public Relations Journal,* January 1981.

Marston, John E. *Modern Public Relations.* New York: McGraw-Hill, 1979.

McKee, Blaine K. "P. T. Barnum: Master Publicist." *Public Relations Journal,* October 1972.

Newman, Lloyd N. "PR Phase II: Adviser Becomes Decision-Maker." *Public Relations Journal,* December 1980.

"The New Public Relations." *Public Relations Journal,* January 1981.

Newsom, Doug, and Alan Scott. *This Is PR.* 3d ed. Belmont, Calif.: Wadsworth Publ. Co., 1984.

Reilly, Robert T. *Public Relations in Action.* Englewood Cliffs, N.J.: Prentice-Hall, 1980.

Riggs, Lew. "Present and Future Trends in Public Relations." *Public Relations Quarterly,* Summer 1982.

Schmertz, Herbert. "Advocacy Has Its Rewards." *Communicator's Journal,* May/June 1983.

Wolters, Louis J., and Stephen B. Miles. "Toward Public Relations Theory." *Public Relations Journal,* September 1982.

2 How public relations functions

Myth versus fact: recognizing PR reality

Public relations performs no miracles. It comes without a "success or your money back" warranty. It requires work in order to work.

To attain its objectives, it also requires logic and order, qualities too infrequently associated with public relations in the minds of many people. But the failure of too many public relations campaigns, and even comprehensive programs, can be attributed to a rush-in-where-angels-fear-to-tread or fly-by-the-seat-of-the-pants approach. Assumptions are made and hunches are played: "This seems to be wrong, but I bet if only we did . . ., everything would be okay, so let's do it." Some practitioners themselves misperceive public relations as an area where intuition or insight, unburdened by evidence, can get the job done. They seem to think that way you can avoid the need for time-consuming fact-finding, attitude ascertainment, and on-going dialogue with important publics.

Of course there is a place for intuition, insight, and creativity in public relations. But these elements cannot substitute for less glittering items like humility (admitting you do not know everything intuitively, so you have to do some investigating and researching) and patience (accepting that you have no quick solution so you have to keep trying longer and harder.)

The successful practitioner must also be sophisticated enough to acknowledge the reality that even acceptable performance and well-planned and executed give-and-take communication cannot be programmed to produce favorable responses and attitudes automatically. People may have honest differences over what is acceptable performance. Communication and persuasion are not controlled processes like those an elementary chemistry textbook might describe, where one takes so much of X and Y, mixes, and, Presto!, there is Z. We have to take people as they are, with all their preexisting ideas, values, and attitudes. They cannot be isolated from competing communication and persuasion, and they cannot be neatly shorn of their preexisting ideas of what is good or acceptable and what is not.

But if it is true that doing all the right things will not guarantee public relations success, there is a consoling flip side: Sometimes the objective of a public relations effort is attained because of some uncontrolled or even unanticipated nonpublic relations factor. A practitioner must recognize this reality, however, and not go bragging that PR work did it all. Next time when the critical nonpublic relations factor is absent, the practitioner may have a hard time explaining why the sure-fire process did not work.

In at least two political campaigns in which we were closely concerned, truly attractive candidates—intelligent, articulate, candid, honest, experienced, and hard-working—ran campaigns that were almost textbook perfect. And each lost by a narrow margin. The possible explanations are many: A majority of the voters may just have disagreed with the loser's stand on key issues. Our candidates may not have been able to overcome their opponents' name identification advantage despite vigorous campaigning. Or, the favorite, the voters simply made a big mistake. At any rate, the lesson of public relations' no-guarantee nature was affirmed.

We have also seen a superbly organized fund-raising campaign run into recession and unemployment, failing to achieve its goal. Again the flip side: An inept drive may exceed its quota simply because a major contribution comes from a wealthy donor who planned on giving long before the campaign began.

The necessary steps

If you accept that there is no magic in public relations and that uncontrollable factors can sometimes account for both apparent success and failure, we can examine the logic, order, and effort that are needed if a public relations program is to function as effectively as possible. This will be discussed in terms of these essential steps:

1. Determine goals and the intermediate objectives leading to them.

2. Learn everything possible pertaining to the present public relations climate in which the program will operate, particularly in relation to its goals and objectives.

3. Know what resources you will have to attain your goals, including your budget.

4. Identify the publics to be affected.

5. Consider carefully the best means and techniques to use in employing resources to achieve your goals with the key publics. (This includes formulating some alternatives so that unexpected obstacles can be overcome.)

6. Act according to your plan and timetable but be willing to make modifications if conditions warrant.

7. Evaluate results and make a record for the future.

DETERMINING GOALS

Like many human activities, public relations can be "bureaucratized," that is, made into an activity weighted down with goals or mission statements to which intermediate objectives have been related, augmented by policies and procedures, all of which are set forth in great detail in handbooks and manuals, which are regularly updated or thoroughly rewritten, according to a periodic evaluation process set forth elsewhere but carefully calendared by the appropriate staff member, etc., . . .

A suffocating atmosphere of sterile unreality will always hover over such a public relations operation. Problems will often have a way of being dealt with, for good or for ill, long before the correct public relations procedure for dealing with them can be located in the proper handbook or manual. So much time and effort are expended on articulating goals, objectives, procedures, policies, and practices that there is no time left to DO SOMETHING to achieve those goals. That is one extreme but it is one Thomas Peters and Robert Waterman found common in businesses they did *not* include in their best-seller, *In Search of Excellence*, listing America's best-run companies.

The other extreme is the seat-of-the-pants or "drift" approach to public relations, which merely reacts to bad situations. Its advocates may think of themselves as doers who do not waste time with theoretical nonsense. "We deal with real situations and real people in the here-and-now," they might tell you. "We can't waste time thinking about our job. Our role is simply to *do* it!"

Those are caricatures—but barely. In public relations, too much time can be spent theorizing and too little time in practical thinking, especially about what should be accomplished and how. Without some fairly well-defined goals, all human activity, public relations included, will be undirected and effective only by accident. Before you start up the engine, know where you want to go.

Determining goals for a special public relations campaign is usually much simpler than determining goals for an over-all public relations program. The goal of a fund drive for a voluntary social agency, for example, may be to raise enough money for the agency to carry on its services during the coming year. Ordinarily it is not too hard to put that into words.

Determining goals for a comprehensive public relations program to be undertaken by a large corporation, a multi-campus university, a worldwide religious organization, or an international labor union obviously is more difficult and complex. For one thing, many more publics may be involved, internally and externally, and conflicting interests may disagree on particular goals. To skirt the issue by formulating empty generalities hardly solves the problem.

Sometimes so much time and effort are put into goal formulation that the formulators think the job of public relations is as good as accomplished now that it is all down on paper. That is a real danger in a large public relations program and among large staffs, especially in non-crisis times. The words on paper are only a beginning, and they have to be disseminated, read, reread, understood, and applied if they are to have any real value.

Here are some practical guidelines for goal setting to keep the process from undoing itself and becoming removed from reality:

1. *Examine the existing statement of fundamental purposes.* Look at a corporation's Articles of Incorporation; according to the logic of the law, the purposes set forth in the Articles are what the state has chartered the corporation to do. Substitute the constitution or charter for a noncorporate agency or organization. The preamble as well as the first article or section of a constitution ordinarily contain statements of mission or goals.

2. *Look at what the corporation, agency, institution, or organization has become and what it is currently doing.* These aspects give more substance than the verbal assertions of purpose in the Articles or constitution.

3. *Relate the role of public relations to these purposes and activities.* List the ways public relations can assist in achieving the purposes and supporting the activities.

Any statement of goals is going to imply some underlying values, of course. Public relations staffers who are tackling the job of stating goals might well spend some time thinking about the most important values they see their employer or client advocating. These values may be the basis for listing additional goals, or they may be seen as contributing to the goals and thus be labeled intermediate goals or objectives.

To illustrate, let's go through the process for a particular public relations employer or client—a large, electrical appliance manufacturer.

Typically, the statement of purpose in such a corporation's Articles of Incorporation would read something like this:

> The purposes of this Corporation shall be: manufacturing, buying, selling, trading, repairing, altering, letting, dealing in, and marketing electrical appliances, devices, and machinery of all kinds and descriptions, including wireless and general electrical supplies and parts; buying and selling the same on commission or as owner; installing the same in facilities appropriate thereto; buying, selling, dealing in, and manufacturing all other kinds of goods, products, and merchandise; transacting all other business necessary or convenient in connection therewith; taking, acquiring, and holding stock in any other corporation; purchasing, leasing, acquiring ownership of, constructing, building, and operating manufacturing plants, warehouses, offices, distribution centers, and other facilities of every kind and nature for the manufacture, distribution, repair, and storage of such products and the performing of services in connection therewith; performing services of every kind and nature whatsoever not inconsistent with the law that are necessary, suitable, proper, expedient, or convenient to the manufacture and distribution of electrical appliances, devices, and machinery as aforesaid; and doing all other things incidental thereto not forbidden by law or these Articles of Incorporation.

If you are asked to use this legal description of purpose as a starting point in drafting public relations goals, how would you begin?

Like too many practitioners, you might be strongly inclined to start with the idea that public relations must gain acceptance for the manufacturing, marketing, wholesaling, retailing, etc., of the various products. Recalling our defining of public relations, however, that would be putting the cart before the horse.

The first and primary goal of a public relations program must be acceptable performance. Then you seek to assure acceptance.

The public relations program's goals might be stated something like this:

1. The production of quality electrical appliances that are efficient, safe, dependable, and fairly priced.

2. The establishment and maintenance of employee support for and conscientious participation in the manufacturing and marketing of quality electrical appliances.

3. The adoption of policies and practices that retain customer satisfaction with the corporate product and with the methods by which that product is marketed at both the wholesale and retail levels.

4. The protection of shareholder investment while at the same time obtaining the best possible return on capital.

5. The inauguration and maintenance of policies and programs that contribute to the general welfare of the communities and regions in which the corporation's manufacturing plants, offices, and other facilities are located.

(Additional goals would be drafted for each of the publics that the public relations staff is able to identify.)

There are still some in business, and in public relations itself, who would object that such goals statements describe general management functions or relate to general management concerns and prerogatives. This is a correct observation but not a valid objection. Public relations, as we have defined and described it, is a management function. To be truly successful, public relations must be a function of top management. That point cannot be overemphasized.

Remember that for many years General Motors has had a large and highly professional public relations staff. When its product was criticized by Ralph Nader in his famous *Unsafe at Any Speed* appraisal of the Corvair, did that staff have a role in determining the corporate response? Should ethical, professional public relations practitioners counsel the use of private detectives and other forms of personal harassment to deal with a critic if they had a voice in top management decisions? If public relations objectives are to be restricted to support for predetermined goals, public relations will be limited, forever picking up the pieces, issuing the statements of denial, explanation, or apology after suspicions have been aroused or the damage has been done.

SETTING OBJECTIVES

That is why public relations goal setting involves a *second* stage— determining intermediate goals or *objectives*. These must try to say how public relations will play its role in achieving the corporate goals. For example:

1. To encourage, by providing counsel and appropriate assistance, and by facilitating feedback wherever possible, the production of quality electrical appliances.

2. To assist in the planning and drafting of programs that are designed to win and retain employee support for and participation in the manufacturing of quality appliances.

3. To recommend and evaluate policies and practices for maintaining customer acceptance of the company's products at all points in the marketing process.

4. To provide counsel and afford means of effective communication in retaining the confidence of shareholders.

5. To alert corporate leaders to the special needs of the communities in which the company operates, suggesting ways the company can conduct itself as a responsible, contributing citizen of those communities, and communicating to the community the role of the company in community betterment.

It should be apparent that what we have thus far are thoughts and words. Public relations functions as action, however. So each of these objectives must be spelled out daily by the company's public relations staff.

For instance, how can a public relations staff "encourage . . . the production of quality appliances"? What kind of counsel will promote that?

Example: We have found, through our investigations and through feedback from customers, dealers, and members of the general public, that there is a widespread opinion that our automatic washers tend to break down after about 20 months of ordinary family use. People say our washers are attractive, efficient, and dependable, until they pass the year-and-a-half mark. Then owners feel they have to spend too much money on service calls and major repairs.

Checking with our sales department, we find that we have lost a significant number of laundromat accounts because of this reputation. The laundromat operators need durable and dependable machines. Some of them say they have to replace our machines after six months because it is not economical to repair them after that.

The major consumer organization's reports also criticize our automatic washers on the same grounds, and we have evidence that more and more young families are reading these reports before purchasing major appliances.

Our gas and electric clothes dryer sales may be affected by the reputation of our washers. Our marketing people tell us that many customers buy dryers at the same time they buy automatic washers, and usually they buy the same brand. Our dryers get a high rating in the consumer publications, but when someone buys another brand in an automatic washer, the same brand of dryer is often purchased even though our dryer may be superior.

If we want to improve the reputation of our automatic washers, we must redesign for greater durability. Otherwise not only will sales suffer in this line but our overall corporate reputation for quality products will falter as well.

Now clearly the engineering and marketing divisions of the manufacturer should have been aware of this situation and should have dealt with it. That is the way businesses are supposed to operate. But the consumer movement has provided too much evidence that this often just does not happen. The record of product recalls over the past decade is there for all to read. Moreover, the engineers and marketing experts may not have the comprehensive perspective that public relations counsel must have. It is precisely because the first function of public relations is to assure acceptable performance that a public relations staff must be supersensitive to public attitudes (in this case, customers' opinions about a major product) even if other departments within the corporate structure should be aware of the situation first. It is also because public relations' functional first step is to discover everything it can about performance and perception of that performance that public relations staffs are in an excellent position to provide this kind of counsel.

LEARNING THE BACKGROUND

Whether a public relations person hopes to establish an overall public relations program for an employer or a client aims at a much narrower goal—raising more money for lung disease research and treatment this year than last—the starting point is the same. It is the present setting, the way things are and have been. A public relations practitioner must therefore make a comprehensive study of the existing situation.

To illustrate, imagine that you are given an important public relations assignment to improve police-community relations in your city.

Following the "rush-in" path, you might come up with the suggestion to change the police image, give officers a more "with-it" image, modernize the uniforms, emphasize the youth of a lot of the officers, etc.

Without any attempt to discover prevailing attitudes toward police, this could be disastrous. What if a good segment of the community is already worried about inexperienced personnel on the police force? What if influential citizens feel they can support more rigorous law enforcement only if it is supervised by mature officers, those with a few flecks of gray in their not-too-long sideburns? What if the traditional uniform is popularly associated with traditionally trustworthy civil servants rather than with young "products of a permissive society"? And what about that bit of folk wisdom that advises "If it works, don't fix it"? Maybe police-community relations are generally quite good, so that only minor tinkering or fine tuning are called for.

To avoid the dangers of a shot in the dark, public relations must perform a second major function, finding out how the employer or client is performing now and how the publics concerned are reacting to that performance. That includes researching what those publics know about the employer or client's performance, what they think or feel about the performance on the basis of what they do or do not know, and what they are doing on the basis of their knowledge and feelings.

After setting reasonable goals, a practitioner working in police-community relations would (1) observe the operation of the police department, particularly its contacts with its various publics; and (2) observe members of those publics in their relations with police and ask detailed questions about their attitudes toward the police.

Certainly, there is still a role in the fact-finding function for intuition and insight. A practitioner could surely have the insight that many people feel intimidated by police officers, no matter how innocent these people are; the "long arm of the law" just makes them nervous. They start thinking about things they might have done unconsciously or duties they may have forgotten to perform. (Just a little thing like neglecting to signal for that last lane change on the drive to work this morning perhaps.) The public relations counsel for the police would then be interested in seeing how officers deal with these average innocents, a special public of citizens police routinely question or deal with when its members come seeking information or assistance.

The public relations person would also know intuitively that police officers, as human beings, will be on their best behavior if they know they are under observation, and that they will resent the observation if it feels as if they are being spied on. Some reasonable accommodation must be found, and that may not be easy.

To discover community attitudes toward the police, residents of the community and people who have dealt with the police must be interviewed. Include those who have run afoul of the law as well as citizens in need of assistance. In addition, a sampling of the entire community should be taken; even people who have had no direct contacts with the police will have attitudes toward them. Where those attitudes come from may be as important for formulating a successful public relations program as what those attitudes are.

Implicit in this discussion of the intelligence-gathering function of public relations is the ingredient of foresight. Good public relations cannot be limited to one-shot efforts, to reacting to emergencies and crises as they occur. It cannot wait until there is a call for facts before it commissions research. A sound program will be gathering information and encouraging feedback continually.

This information gathering will not be done as if the public relations office is simply a repository either. The information coming in will be analyzed and passed along to those outside the public relations staff who should be alerted so they can act accordingly.

Illustrating this is a type of incident occurring from time to time on college and university campuses—the food riot. The reason most often cited for these eruptions is the poor quality of the meals served to boarding students by the institution's food service. Effective intelligence gathering, incidentally, would investigate whether that is the real and sole reason.

Typically, administrators are jolted by the unexpectedness of the disturbance. Food service personnel are shocked, too, and usually hurt and indignant.

The rest of the scenario is almost trite. Food service personnel are shuffled or maybe a new service is brought in. A few amenities (cloth tablecloths or seconds on dessert) are provided temporarily, maybe a few students are disciplined, and then everything returns to normal, with another slow buildup of student dissatisfaction and resentment just waiting for another explosion to relieve it.

For the college trying to portray itself as a place of serious learning by mature young people, the food riot is hardly helpful when administrators approach the legislature or major nongovernment benefactors for more money. It is hard to conceive of any amount of immediate after-the-fact publicity fully erasing the negative impact of a food riot.

A situation with some similarities can exist with the company-run cafeteria in a large corporation's office building. Typically such cafeterias are installed to encourage employees to eat on the premises to reduce off-the-job time each day or to provide a generous fringe benefit. If the cafeteria loses considerable money rather than breaking even as planned because employees find its menus unattractive or the quality of the food unacceptable, there is a very real public relations problem here, too, even if it does not include cleaning up after a riot.

From the comfort of a theoretical vantage point, we can easily see that the best solution to the food riot or company cafeteria problem is prevention. Yet before such situations can be prevented, a public relations staff must know about student and employee attitudes toward food services. Members of the public relations staff have to eat where students or employees eat and listen to their comments. These comments, especially if they are strongly negative, must be passed along to those who can do something to improve the food.

Some food service contractors and colleges have ended the potential for disruptions by establishing permanent lines of communication with the students, consumers of that institutional cooking that never quite matches Mom's. They have encouraged student governments and dormitory councils to appoint food committees that meet regularly with food service managers. Together the groups and managers survey students periodically on their attitudes toward the food service and its product; act on responses promptly rather than simply filing them; encourage student employees to pass along less structured student response. And, like successful restaurateurs everywhere, food service managers with good public relations sense get out from behind their desks and counters to mingle with the customers regularly for first-hand feedback.

Information gathering encompasses activities like this and many more. To find out if and how news releases are used, a public relations staff clips newspapers or subscribes to a clipping service and monitors newscasts. To ascertain community opinion, public relations staffers meet regularly with community leaders and community members. They dust off and even change the color of suggestion boxes periodically so the boxes do not become fixtures no one sees after a while. They encourage reader response to publications and brochures sent to their internal and external publics. They also keep informed on developments beyond their corporation, institution, or organization, alert to the impact those other events may have on their employer or client.

When technical difficulties arose at the Three Mile Island nuclear power plant in Pennsylvania in 1979, the situation was seized by many opponents of nuclear energy as an occasion for dramatizing their point of view. The alert public relations staff for a public power district in another part of the country, aware that local demonstrations were probable at its nuclear power plant in the wake of Three Mile Island, actually invited local antinuclear power leaders to a meeting to discuss how and where a demonstration might be carried on. The staff sat down with its critics and worked out a plan that would put demonstrators near enough to the nuclear plant to make their point and draw the news media coverage they sought but that would also maintain security and employee access to assure uninterrupted operation. As a beneficial side effect for the local controversy, each side saw that nobody on the other side had horns or cloven hoofs. Contrast that with the panicky overreaction that greeted so many demonstrations during the late 1960s and early 1970s, often with unnecessarily tragic results.

INVENTORYING RESOURCES

When the Mutual of Omaha Insurance companies decided to make a special event of their 75th anniversary, their public relations and advertising staffs set an objective of obtaining the widest possible awareness that the parent company was three-quarters of a century old. Among the resources at hand was the existence of a nationally distributed Mutual television program, "Wild Kingdom"; the existence of advertising contracts with many nationally circulated magazines; and the existence of many broad direct-mail sales programs. Though this was only the beginning of a careful inventory, it did make it clear that there were effective means available for conveying the anniversary theme to a national public.

Company X might have a 75th anniversary too and want nationwide publicity. But when it lists its resources, it will see it has no television program and its advertising contracts are with specialized publications that reach a fairly narrow readership across the country.

Both Mutual of Omaha and Company X will have to consider the money available to them in promoting their anniversary observance. For Mutual of Omaha, piggybacking on existing media access will cut costs. For Company X, the expense of prime time television network exposure may simply be unaffordable.

In both instances, the inventorying of resources and estimating of costs must go hand in hand. Sometimes public relations people are given a predetermined budget for a special observance like an anniversary. Then the money allotted can be treated as a resource and, after completing its inventory, the staff can move to its next function.

More often, however, the inventorying of resources function is more complicated. With goals, information, and a list of existing resources, a public relations staff will move to the planning function. With a definite plan in hand, it will be ready to discuss costs. If management decides that the plans will cost too much to implement, the plan must be revised and the inventory of nonmonetary resources must be reviewed. A less expensive plan, using the available resources, is then devised.

Of course, knowing how much money, how many people, and how much time you have is not enough. The experienced practitioner understands that it is also essential to know what you can get with the money, what your people are capable of accomplishing, and what it is reasonable to expect to get done in the time allotted.

This is an area where creativity and experience can work well together. Big budgets do not guarantee public relations success, and limited budgets do not doom practitioners to frustration and failure. In judging newspaper and magazine competitions over the years, we have seen smaller publications edited with intelligence, creativity, and frugality outshine the big and elaborate. Four-color reproduction on expensive coated paper can be arresting but not necessarily effective. Well-written copy in a simple but neat and appealing black-and-white layout on relatively inexpensive paper stock can lack glitter but communicate superbly. Editors and news directors will think more of a careful, thorough news release typed on ordinary newsroom copy paper than they will of padded puffery printed on quality bond with a fancy engraved logo.

Finally, resources are more than money, staff, physical tools, and facilities. They include time, talent and creativity, preexisting attitudes, and the opportunities afforded by the mix of current events and movements that are part of the setting for any public relations effort. An inventory that does not take these elements into consideration is incomplete.

DETERMINING PUBLICS AND MEANS

In determining goals and setting objectives, public relations practitioners think of publics. In inventorying resources, they will have considered preexisting attitudes, and this implies assessing publics. But when it comes down to determining exactly how objectives will be attained, it is time to pinpoint publics, to decide who constitutes them, where they are, how they can be reached, and how two-way communication can be established with them.

The concept of *public* is fairly simple but extremely important. In the context of public relations, a public is a group of persons with a common background and a common interest in the performance of a business, organization, or institution. A public can be as intimate and well delineated as the parents of the 23 second graders at Springhill Elementary School or as broad as the registered voters in the United States of America.

Public relations people have frequently been accused of ignoring such guides as census reports and documents as well as public opinion studies when they reach the point of identifying specific publics. Another criticism of PR planning voiced by practitioners themselves is the failure of many to keep informed on case studies of previous public relations programs and campaigns, suggesting the lesson that "those who ignore history are condemned to repeat it."

This critical stage in planning cannot proceed effectively without reference to the information already gathered and to data on other public relations efforts. Then publics can be identified and means for establishing real give-and-take relations with them can be selected.

Of course, experience (including that of other practitioners) and existing data are not enough; logical thought, critical analysis, and innovativeness are essential too. Reference to the experience of others keeps us from reinventing the wheel, but it poses the peril of rut thinking, opting to do things the way we have always done them.

If the community public needs to be informed of an important accomplishment, a practitioner should use the standard news release form and established distribution, knowing that this has been the effective way to get the word out in the past. But if the message is really aimed at a public narrower than the local community, or if the message is too sensitive or complex to be communicated appropriately by means of a general news release, logical analysis will dictate another approach. Practitioners will rely on a mixture of experience and creativeness in asking, "Will a brochure be more appropriate? A personalized letter? Personal contacts or small group meetings?" Later will come questions of how much detail the message should include, which style and language will be appropriate, how the message will relate to the interests and concerns of the particular public, whether repetition will be needed for emphasis or clarity, etc.

Several years ago when a regional food product firm, Skinner Macaroni, was acquired by foods giant Hershey, the Skinner public relations staff had no experience with getting out the message that a merger was about to occur. The PR case histories of other corporate mergers are largely disaster stories, rumors and leaks, followed by panic, dismay, disaffection, and even bitterness. In dealing with the situation, Skinner's staff followed the steps of sound public relations practice, however. It analyzed the situation in terms of its company's primary goal, the production of quality food products, with such related objectives as employee cooperation, customer acceptance, and community goodwill.

The staff sensed that employees would immediately wonder about job security and working conditions under new ownership. It realized that customers would be concerned about product quality, identification, and costs. People in the community would be concerned about the merger's impact on local employment, the continued interest of company executives in civic projects, corporate financial support for local causes (everything from the United Way to non-tax-supported education).

Fortunately, the Skinner and Hershey managements were public relations conscious. They briefed the PR staff thoroughly, enabling it to anticipate questions and prepare authoritative responses, and, even more importantly, to get the facts of the merger to key publics promptly, before any rumor and panic stage could develop.

In each step the specific means employed related to the public relations staff's resources. If a general news release had to be disseminated immediately, was the staff able to do the job itself or would it have to engage an agency for assistance? Would the usual distribution list for local or regional releases suffice with a story of this magnitude? Were computerized employee home address mailing tapes available? Were lists and charts of management and supervisory personnel readily available so that proper groupings could be arranged for briefings? What other means besides such group sessions could be used to give members of key publics an opportunity for prompt feedback?

EXECUTING THE PLAN

TIMING. The Skinner case was a situation where timing meant *now!* But whenever possible, schedules should be planned and followed carefully to achieve maximum effect. If a brochure will be a valuable tool in personal solicitation in a fund drive, its printing must be timed so that copies can be distributed to division leaders, captains, and solicitors by the time they gather for their send-off session, even earlier if possible, but certainly not after they have been asked to contact prospects. If a news release is designed to build interest in a public appearance by an influential figure, it must be distributed in time to be published and broadcast when people can still decide to attend. If a news conference is called by a member of Congress to announce plans not to run for reelection, it should be scheduled after the legislator has decided on the candidate to be endorsed as successor if maximum impact is to be given the endorsement.

Just as disseminating information too soon may lessen its impact, waiting too long may bring a "What else is new?" response when the information is finally revealed, due to the job rumor and leaks have already done.

Timing is also extremely important as a factor in affecting attitudes. Events have a way of preparing people to accept what they rejected earlier. Opinion surveys indicated Americans were strongly opposed to any form of gasoline rationing in the 1970s. But when they encountered closed service stations during the Arab oil embargo, they quickly accepted rationing in the form of alternate-day access to the pumps. When American embassy personnel were taken hostage in Tehran and Iran cut off oil to the United States in 1979, polls indicated another upswing in acceptance of rationing. Contrast that with the reaction a proposal to ration would induce today.

Sometimes attitude-changing events have to be awaited. On rare occasions, such influential events can be promoted or even created. However they occur, the events must be recognized as a prerequisite to successful persuasion. Attempts at changing attitudes before such events occur may be futile, and premature attempts may even take the edge off efforts to change attitudes after the events do occur.

RETAINING FLEXIBILITY. Coaches and players often judge their team's performance by its game plan. While it is certainly important to have and use a plan, to keep it in sight as the action begins to unfold and to refer to it frequently, rigid adherence to a plan can cause problems.

Plans are plans, not inviolable orders. Plans can be changed, and sometimes they must be. A public relations consultant may have plotted a low-key campaign for a political candidate through the primary election with an intense thrust before the general election. That consultant better go back to the drawing board if the candidate unexpectedly encounters strong last-minute opposition in the primary. If there is no change in strategy, the consultant may need no plan at all for the general election because the candidate will not be in the running.

An intensive public relations campaign compressed into a period of weeks obviously runs less risk of straying from or ignoring its plan than a public relations program prepared for long-range use by a business, institution, or organization. In the long-range program, it becomes important to schedule periodic reviews of plans to make sure a public relations staff is doing all it is supposed to be doing on schedule.

At the same time, public relations people must continue their information-gathering function. They must be alert to what is happening while they are conducting their communication and persuasion activities. If they had planned to sponsor a televised debate on the school district budget limitation that is to be voted on in next month's referendum, they may find their television program competition overwhelming. Maybe the World Series is going into its seventh game three days late because of continuing rain. That bumps the championship game up against the debate on TV. A change of plans is a must. If it is impossible to reschedule the debate, the PR people will have to compensate in some way for the diminished TV impact on the community.

A public relations staff may launch an effort to have employees invite their neighbors to tour the company's new plant with them. When the employees do not seem to be responding to the promotion, an embarrassingly small turnout is in prospect. Then it is time for a change in plans, either a concentrated last-minute publicity effort that was not in the script or possibly a postponement of the open house.

EVALUATING THE RESULTS

Suitable evaluation is a must for a public relations campaign or program. How extensive the evaluation is will depend on available time and money as well as the conscientiousness of the PR staff. But some reasonable evaluation with a substantial foundation must be made—a feeling, an ill-defined impression, or a complimentary letter from Mother will not do. Yet it is amazing how insubstantial feedback is sometimes used by staffs with impressive resources when they have spent large amounts of money and effort on a program. It is almost as if they are afraid of learning the truth about their performance.

Employers and clients are entitled to facts from which they can evaluate the success and cost effectiveness of the money spent on a public relations program. Every truly professional practitioner will want such data too. We learn from experience, and that includes our mistakes; we have to realize them if we are not to repeat them.

Evaluation should also underline successes. This lets a practitioner know what works and can be tried again. Instead of a mere pep-talk letter, a campaign newsletter is sent to workers during a fund drive to remind them to complete their contacts, especially among less enthusiastic givers. Response to the newsletter is much more positive than it has been to reminder letters. That is a lesson that can be applied to future fund-raising projects.

The goals and objectives of a program or campaign should be used as measuring sticks in determining success or failure. A practitioner can say, "This is what we wanted to accomplish. This is what we did, and this is what happened." In addition to helping determine success or failure, a look at goals and objectives may show that they were unrealistic or perhaps poorly defined. That in itself is another lesson for the future.

Evaluations can show that while stated objectives were not achieved, other very positive effects were identified. Several years ago a large private high school undertook an evaluation of its recruitment program. To attract students, the school used mailings to prospective students and their parents, personal contacts, visits to the school, and a heavily promoted open house. The evaluation indicated most of the people who attended the open house reacted positively to the experience but they rated it low on the list of factors that led to enrolling at the school. In fact, many of the students who reacted negatively to the open house enrolled at the school.

One might conclude that the open house's primary objective, to encourage students to enroll, was not achieved. But one can also conclude that the open house did not have a negative effect. In terms of the persuasion process, it may very well have served as reinforcement of the potential students' preexisting favorable attitude toward the school, and reinforcement of favorable attitudes is essential for successful public relations. (That is one reason members of Congress make all those trips back to the home district, to repeatedly remind voters that their representative is devoted to them and their interests.) Thus, thoughtful evaluation may show that an apparent failure is really a success.

To obtain the greatest benefit then, a public relations evaluation should consist of:

1. A review of the goals and objectives of the program or project.
2. A thorough description of the actions taken to achieve those goals and objectives.

3. A careful comparison of conditions after the public relations actions were taken with the conditions sought (goals/objectives).

4. An objective attempt to connect the public relations activity with conditions afterward (an attempt to determine whether the public relations efforts actually caused what happened).

5. An analysis of how and why the public relations efforts caused or failed to cause the conditions sought.

6. A summary or case history of the public relations activity, describing what it tried to do, how it fared, and what changes might or must be made in a similar effort in the future. (This last step can also be the basis for a checklist or plan for a similar project in the future.)

Summary

Public relations is an art rather than a science, though it clearly uses the knowledge and techniques of the social sciences. It requires logic and order as well as creativity and enthusiasm for effectiveness. Unless public relations is practiced carefully, step by step, it is doomed to hit-and-miss success, and its practitioners will never know for sure whether it was their effort, the effort of others, or intervening events that contributed most to results.

Those steps that are to be followed are:

1. Set realistic goals and agree on objectives.

2. Gather enough information to give a clear picture of existing conditions.

3. Take an inventory of resources for achieving objectives.

4. Plan carefully how, when, and with whom resources will be used to reach those objectives.

5. Use those resources according to plan but be alert to the need to change the plan.

6. Survey conditions after the efforts have been concluded.

7. Take a critical look at what resulted from the efforts and record conclusions for future reference.

Exercises

1. Take the first four steps listed on pages 31–32 and apply them to the public relations program of a business, institution, or agency with which you are familiar. Determine what the goals are, what kinds of knowledge a public relations practitioner should have about the enterprise, what resources are available for a public relations program there, and what means are most appropriate for attaining goals. Make some lists.

2. What is the lesson of General Motors' effort to neutralize a critic like Ralph Nader by putting private detectives on his trail? (Read news accounts of this.) How should public relations deal with a highly influential critic who has attacked the quality of a major company product? Discuss.

3. Does your institution have any public relations problems? (If it does not, it is unique!) If you do not know what those problems are, what is the best way to find out? What are the areas of potential problems, and how do you think those areas should be monitored?

4. What public relations efforts undertaken by your institution are basically reinforcement of existing attitudes? Could any of these efforts be dropped or reduced without harm to the overall public relations program? On what basis can you make a judgment? Discuss.

5. If a fund drive to raise $1 million brings in $1.2 million in cash and pledges, has it been successful? If it brings in $890,000 in cash and pledges, has it been unsuccessful? (What do you need to know before rating the campaign a success or less-than-a-success that the dollar figures do not tell?) Discuss.

Case study

Jack R. has been a successful public relations practitioner with a large clothing manufacturer that had to weather a serious labor-management conflict. Its products were boycotted nationally as a result. But that was five years ago and employee relations have improved dramatically. Management now has to bargain with a strong international union, but production, sales, and net profits are up nonetheless. Aware of Jack R.'s role in resolving the clothing manufacturer's problems, Death Valley Petro-Chemical offers him a job as vice-president for public affairs.

DV Petro-Chemical has been under investigation by the Environmental Protection Agency for 18 months. Thirteen employees currently have lawsuits pending against the company, claiming they have been permanently disabled by inhalation and ingestion of toxic substances during their years of work. Two local communities and the state have brought criminal charges against DV Petro-Chemical for alleged violation of laws governing water and air pollutants.

If you were Jack R., what would you want to know before accepting the job? Are there any commitments from DV's top management that you would want to obtain? If you took the job, what are some of the first things you would strive to accomplish?

Suggested readings

Center, Allen H. "State of the Art: Is the Pyramid Upside Down?" *Public Relations Journal,* July 1980.

Close, H. W. "Public Relations as a Management Function." *Public Relations Journal,* March 1980.

Dilenschneider, Robert L. "Anticipation: A Key Weapon in Crisis Strategy." *Communication World,* April 1985.

Goldman, Elaine. "Dinosaur or Rocket?" *Public Relations Journal,* October 1984.

Ibarra, Karen, and Loretta Stagnitto. "PR's Role in Management." *Public Relations Journal,* October 1980.

Lesly, Philip. "The Changing Evolution of Public Relations." *Public Relations Quarterly,* Winter 1982.

Meadows, Edward. "Why the Oil Companies Are Coming Up Dry in Their Public Relations." *Fortune* 100 (July 1979): 54–57.

Pennington, Bruce. "How Public Relations Fits into the Puzzle." *Public Relations Journal,* March 1980.

Pimlott, J. A. *Public Relations and American Democracy.* Rev. ed. Princeton, N.J.: Princeton Univ. Press, 1971.

Roach, William J. "Taming the Planning Monster." *Communication World,* October 1984.

Rogers, Henry C. *Walking the Tightrope: The Private Confessions of a Public Relations Man.* New York: William Morrow, 1980.

Seitel, Fraser P. *The Practice of Public Relations.* Columbus, Ohio: Charles E. Merrill Publ. Co., 1979.

Simon, Raymond. *Public Relations: Concepts and Practice.* Columbus, Ohio: GRID, Inc., 1976.

Taft, Robert W. "How to Handle Negative Information." *Public Relations Journal,* April 1984.

3 Key qualifications for practitioners

To succeed in public relations, the practitioner need not be a Renaissance man or woman, but that capability would help. A variety of talents is asked of the individual, especially in smaller shops and departments. The qualifications necessary to perform a challenging assignment will depend on exactly what that assignment is, and in public relations, those assignments cover a wide spectrum. They can range from greeting visitors and conducting plant tours to producing sophisticated multimedia presentations for a mammoth stockholders meeting. Assignments also vary with the activities and needs of the client or employer.

Keeping this in mind, there are nevertheless a set of qualifications that are essential for every public relations practitioner. Not only are they basic, they are vital if the practitioner is to succeed.

Communication skills

Before delving into the specifics of communication and public relations, some fundamental observations about communication are in order. They are important.

1. Effective communication is the cornerstone of successful public relations; therefore, communication skill is the most important qualification for a public relations practitioner.

2. The most challenging aspect of communication in public relations is often internal rather than external—informing those who set policy and make decisions. These key people must be reached so that the quintessential ingredient of PR—acceptable performance—can be obtained.

3. Successful communication is not easy. Or, to turn it around, it is easy to fail.

4. Even good communication will not solve every problem or guarantee PR success.

To dispose of the last point first, everyone has heard and used, "Basically, it's just a matter of communication" so often that it has become a cliche. Whoever says it is suggesting that the conflict, regardless of what it is, is simply the result of misunderstanding.

But analyze that assumption. A friend asks to borrow your car. You say no. (The friend borrowed your car last month, dented a fender and did not repair it, ran your tank nearly empty and did not buy gas.) Your friend is miffed at the refusal. In other words, there is conflict, a problem in your relationship. Is it "basically, just a matter of communication?" Or, do you understand each other quite well?

Turn to corporate life. In collective bargaining, labor requests a 13 percent pay increase. Management says no. Productivity declined this past year, the company is in the red, and a cost increase would trigger a price increase that would give an advantage to competitors' products. Even assume that management opened its financial records to labor, so there is no dispute over the financial facts.

Here is a disagreement, a conflict. Can it be resolved by communication alone? Communication + persuasion + willingness to compromise, perhaps, but *not* by communication alone. Obviously, this is more than basically or solely a communication problem.

Back to our other observations. They state, unequivocally, that effective communication is an essential ingredient of success in public relations. Ability to communicate is a skill that practitioners must be willing to develop painstakingly and continually.

But, exactly what do we mean by *communication*, that term that people toss off so blithely? In its Latin form, *communicare*, it means to impart or share, literally "to make common." The idea, of course, is that one individual (the communicator) tries to make his or her thoughts "common" with the thoughts or perceptions of the person or persons to whom the communicator is speaking, writing, broadcasting, showing illustrations, etc.

Wilbur Schramm, a pioneer in communication theory, developed a diagram, or model, of the communication process that is helpful in analyzing the steps and recognizing the difficulties. In its simplest form, as shown in Figure 3.1, the model involves a sender at one end of a line and a receiver at the other end. Adapting this model to mass communication, the terms "communicator" and "audience" are occasionally substituted for "sender" and "receiver."

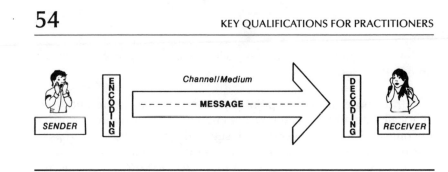

3.1 *Schramm communication model.*

What the communicator wants to "make common" with the person or persons at the other end of the channel, the message, must be put into the channel carefully. In communication theory, that process is referred to as "encoding." Think of this in terms of the old telegram. A telegrapher encoded the words of the message into dots and dashes of the Morse Code to send them by wire to the telegrapher-receiver.

Letter writing is another common example. We may communicate with a distant friend by letter, encoding our message by tracing out written representations of our words. Even in this rudimentary communication, skill is required. The writer-communicator (1) must have a vocabulary that permits expressing thoughts as fully and exactly as possible; and (2) must put those words together in a form (grammatically correct, properly punctuated, and logically developed) suitable for transmission through this particular medium or channel, a letter.

There is more. The writer-communicator must know the limitations of the medium. Can a letter transmit a smile? Can you subtly suggest you are not serious but only needling good-naturedly when the written word is your medium? Ink on paper can be a one-dimensional communication.

Ultimately, the writer-communicator and all communicators, no matter their medium, must fashion the message in terms readily understood by their target, the person to whom the message is addressed. The communicator must understand the receiver's ability to "decode" the message; can she read the handwriting? understand the words? get the drift of the sentence? And, finally, will that receiver get the same mental picture, the same concepts the sender had when the process began?

To fully appreciate the receiver's ability to decode or understand the message, the communicator also must be aware of experiences the receiver has had. If you describe something as "majestic as the Taj Mahal," that message will be understood clearly by someone who has seen that beautiful monument. It will be less effective if the receiver has seen only photographs. But it will be totally ineffective if the receiver neither has seen the Taj Mahal nor has any idea of what in the world it is.

Thus far we have talked about person-to-person or one-on-one communication. This is involved frequently in public relations, often in crucial situations such as when PR counsel must persuade decision makers to change policies that produce unacceptable performance. And we hope to have communicated that even this basic type of communication is challenging.

An even greater part of public relations communication, however, is so-called mass communication, although "mass" in this sense is not entirely accurate. The word connotes some sort of amorphous blob that is "out there" somewhere; whereas, "mass" in "mass communication" is simply people—lots of them, but each a unique, intelligent, feeling human person. It is not as tidy a phrase, but it would be more fitting and accurate to speak of "many-person" communication or a "large audience" or "many receivers with widely varying characteristics" in place of "mass communication" and "masses."

If person-to-person communication—even face-to-face—is not easy, communication with many people simultaneously, obviously, is much more difficult. Think of the different perceptions you have as a member of a small group. Someone addresses you, and a member of the group says, "Did you hear that putdown of X? I really object to it!" Another says, "I didn't take it that way at all. Actually I thought it was a compliment." (You? Maybe you were not sure which it was!)

This suggests that in communicating with a large audience, the public relations practitioner must consider many additional factors relating to people's ability to understand or decode—factors such as average educational level; age (which may relate to experience); vocational background (which may relate to education, experience, or both); residence or geographic background; and social, religious, and political heritage.

It would be easy to conclude that successful mass communication must be impossible, complicated as it is by all these factors. But remember the success of large newspapers, popular magazines, commercial television networks, and some of the excellent programming on public TV in reaching and communicating with large numbers. Communicators who use these mass media may not achieve precise and complete communication, but that is not always achieved in personal communication either.

The bottom line is that a PR practitioner must develop special skills to communicate with large audiences and must know a great deal about media that transmit this type of communication. First we will consider the particular skills that relate to communication.

WRITING

We are aware of the marked difference when we say one person "is capable of writing" but another "is a writer." The former is literate; he can put words from some language onto paper where they can be read by another person who knows the same language. But that is a long way from being a Shakespeare, a Dante, a Cervantes, or even a Zane Grey.

There is a vast gulf between someone who writes according to the rules (spelling, punctuation, capitalization, usage, and syntax) and a person who writes articulately, expressively, and compellingly. Lest anyone misunderstand, we are not saying the rules are unimportant. They are vital to good writing. The worst mistake a prospective PR person can make is to ignore the rules. Such a person is headed for a brief career in public relations, one blighted by unused or, at best, heavily edited news copy and public service announcements.

Moving from being able to write to being a writer is not a mysterious process. Popular wisdom has it that writers are born, not made, and there may be a grain of truth in that. An occasional person has a seemingly inborn feel and love for language, and a frustrated few will decide that writing cannot be taught. (After many years of trying, we will admit there is truth in that, too.) But a person who sincerely wants to write can learn to write, helped by a teacher who acts more as critic and guide than as instructor.

Writing, in the sense of effective expression, is learned by doing, by trying and then trying to do better, over and over again. It was the method of Ernest Hemingway and William Allen White, of Thomas Wolfe and Frank O'Connor. No matter their talent, or greatness, the best are humble enough to recognize the need to rewrite. Dorothy Parker said, "I can't write five words but that I change seven."

Writing is learned by reading and studying what good writers have written, analyzing that good writing to determine what gives it quality and attempting to develop and mold your own skills based on those you recognize in others.

Writing skill in the public relations sense also encompasses the ability to write at different levels for different audiences. The importance of this aspect is obvious when we study the many publics of a corporation, organization, or institution. Each is a different audience; each must be reached.

For example, as the winter cold and flu season approaches, a public health agency might prepare messages aimed at elementary school students and at employees of local businesses. The school children might be told:

> Catching cold is no fun. You can't play outside with your friends. You may even miss school and have to work hard to catch up with the other kids when you get back. So, dress warmly when the weather gets cold, and don't forget your rubbers and boots when it snows. Chills and wet feet are a great way to catch a cold— and miss all the fun of the season!

The same message tailored to adults might be written this way:

> Winter is delightful. Winter is rotten. It means white Christmas, sleigh bells, sledding, and skiing . . . and distressing colds, five varieties of flu, medical bills, and used-up sick leave. Science hasn't found the cause or cure for the common cold. But it has discovered that dressing warmly to prevent chills, getting rest, exercising reasonably, and following a sensible diet—one including fresh vegetables and fruit, especially citrus fruit—build resistance to colds. So, how about joining the Resistance Movement to guarantee a delightful winter?

Or, knowing that is a bit cute for some publications, the agency could provide an optional straight version:

> Three out of ten American employees lost as much as four days from work last winter because of respiratory ailments—colds and flu. It not only cost their employers an estimated $2.1 million, but it cost the victims almost half that amount in lost pay.
> Health experts say prevention is the most effective way to combat respiratory infections. They advise dressing warmly to avoid chills that lower body resistance to cold and flu viruses; getting seven to eight hours sleep regularly; eating vitamin-rich fresh fruits and vegetables; and keeping fit by following a pattern of regular exercise.

At whatever level or for whichever audience, the understandability of a message is tied to its interest factor because we work harder to understand that which interests us. Interest and understandability go hand in hand when we analyze effective writing.

Factors relating directly to understandability have been identified by a number of experts, and vocabulary leads the list. A word's length or the number of syllables is the basis for deciding whether it is difficult to understand; usually, a word with more than three syllables is more difficult than a word with three or fewer. But, this is not a perfect yardstick. For example, "community" has four syllables, but for most people it is not a difficult word. However, "keratose" with only three syllables would send most of us to the dictionary.

Sentence length is the second most cited factor in gauging understandability. Here experts prescribe in terms of averages. Sentences should average 19 to 20 words to maximize understanding. That means sentences can and should vary in length, but a writer must compensate with shorter sentences when using one of more than 20 words. It reminds us of the obvious: long, involved sentences, especially when unrelieved by shorter sentences, impede understanding.

Rudolf Flesch, renowned for his long battle for sound instruction in reading and writing, adds a third factor in his system of gauging understandability: personal words and personal phrases. He suggests that conveying information in terms of *people* makes it more interesting and compelling, and therefore more understandable.

College-level writing courses are one of the most effective tools available for sharpening writing skill, particularly if they are disciplined and demanding. Literature courses and studies in classical and modern languages are highly recommended; literature if the styles of the various writers are emphasized, and languages since even at the elementary level these require involvement in the nuts and bolts of vocabulary, grammar, and syntax. (The latter is true of a study of English as well as foreign languages.)

SPEAKING

A stereotype burdening public relations is that of the so-called typical practitioner—a 110 percent extrovert who not only can but will get up and whip through an enthusiastic extemporaneous speech at each lull in the conversation. Some of the most successful PR people we know are quite the opposite of this gregarious speech maker. Nonetheless, they are acceptable platform performers, even if they do not ooze charisma. They know, as anyone in public relations should know, that oral communication is an essential tool of the trade, including everything from informal conversation with individuals and small groups to formal speeches from a lectern.

Writing skill is the foundation for anyone who must address an audience. Regardless of delivery, to communicate effectively, the speech must have substance, and that substance must be well expressed. Thoughts must be presented understandably, even more understandably than when written because the spoken word has just one chance to be comprehended. There is no instant replay if the live audience misses the point the first time around. Success in this area is determined by the writing of the text, or the drafting of an outline if the speaker prefers to work from notes.

Even a masterful address is ineffective, however, if it is mumbled, read or recited in a monotone, or punctuated by awkward pauses as if the speaker were reaching constantly for the right word. Too often each of these weaknesses is a symptom of the same disease: inadequate preparation. The mumbling covers uncertainty, the reading betrays unfamiliarity with the text, and pauses reveal a lack of rehearsal.

Preparation includes more than the word message. You have heard of nonverbal communication and may have seen presentations on body language or paralanguage. An awareness of nonverbal communication is part of preparation to meet with an audience.

At the fundamental level, nonverbal communication involves additional dimensions, or ways, we communicate by our appearance or demeanor when speaking with someone face-to-face or even television screen-to-face. Unlike the simple letters formed in ink on paper, the in-person presentation provides an added dimension that permits us to suggest subtly that we are not serious when we say something, that our needling is friendly and not hostile. Remember, too, that the tools of this new dimension (facial expression, eye contact or eye aversion, posture, gestures, and various voice inflections) can give us away and cancel the effectiveness of our words if they are not in harmony with what we say. And, if our body language is unnatural like the patently coached gestures of the merchants who star in their own TV commercials, then our nonverbal communication is merely distracting rather than contributing to the communication of our message.

Writing skill requires practice. Speaking skill requires the same. Both require constant self-criticism and strong motivation for self-improvement; both are enhanced by positive criticism from others who have developed the skills themselves. For anyone planning a career in public relations, courses in public speaking should not only be taken but taken seriously. Drama courses and extracurricular forensics are also helpful. As with writing, much can be learned by observing the masters.

There is an appreciable difference, however, between conveying information of substance interestingly and merely entertaining or making a good impression. Always have something to say before making a speech. A smiling face, an artful gesture, and a charismatic manner may be useful political tools, but if the words are empty, it is a long time until the next election. And, it is poor public relations.

Integrity

> Good name in man and woman, dear my lord,
> Is the immediate jewel of their souls;
> Who steals my purse steals trash; 'tis something,
>   nothing;
> 'Twas mine, 'tis his, and has been slave to
>   thousands;
> But he that filches from me my good name
> Robs me of that which not enriches him,
> And makes me poor indeed.
>   —*Othello*, III, iii
>   William Shakespeare

The good name to which Shakespeare referred is what others think we are. Integrity is what we really are. Morals aside, these two—good name and integrity—can become so intertwined that under most circumstances they are the same; thus, the man or woman who would have a good name will act with high integrity. It is good business. The public relations practitioner does not deal directly in products; rather, the practitioner markets personal talent, knowledge of public relations, and personal integrity. The client or employer, the public, and media representatives with whom the practitioner interacts must believe in that person's integrity.

In its simplest terms, integrity is the consistent practice of a value system, even in the face of opposition. Defining integrity becomes more complex when we realize how difficult it is for each of us to identify and rank the values of the employer or client and relate personal values to those of that employer or client.

No vocation shelters a person from all value judgments and conflicts, but some require more confrontation with values than others. A laboratory technician or an assembly line worker faces fewer value decisions than a legislator; so too, the public relations practitioner cannot escape making value judgments daily. In employee relations, is the job assignment policy paternalistic and demeaning to employees? In community relations, is the company acting as a responsible citizen by seeking a tax reduction that could burden home owners with more taxes? In stockholder relations, is it fair for executives to spend so much time on a private hospital fund drive and so little time working directly for the corporation? In media relations, should we tell the entire story or just the good side and hope those reporters avoid probing questions?

If a public relations practitioner believes the ultimate value for a business is profit, there can be a certain logical integrity in answering many of those questions contrary to the interests of employees, community residents, and other important publics. For profits, we can substitute a successful fund drive for an institution or passage of favorable legislation for a special interest organization. PR people should recognize the shortsightedness of opting for profit now and trusting that future profits will not be affected by unhappy employees, hostile neighbors, and other antagonistic publics. Sacrificing long-term success for short-term profit not only shows a marked lack of integrity, it is also a poor business practice.

The crunch comes when the client or employer's values conflict seriously with those of the practitioner. A career may be on the line, along with food for the family, mortgage payments, Junior's braces, and the practitioner's ulcer medicine. It is naive and presumptuous to prescribe for every instance of moral conflict, but such conflicts can and do occur. When a situation arises, each practitioner must decide how critical that conflict is and whether to accept or reject a role in what the client or employer insists upon.

A friend once said much the same in the talk to PR practitioners. Afterward, a member of the audience confronted him, said he faced just such a crisis, and asked what he should do. On the spot, our friend said, "I think you should get out." When he had a chance to think about what further agonies he might have put his questioner through, our friend worried about whether he had said the right thing. After all, his job was secure.

But there was a happy ending. Months later, our friend again met his questioner. Smile wrinkles replaced the tension lines in his face. "I want to thank you for your advice," the man said. "Let me tell you about my terrific new job. . . ."

It would be naive to suggest that every conflict involving integrity will resolve itself so neatly. Integrity can involve sacrifice, but everything worthwhile has a price.

To reemphasize a point: call it what you will—your integrity, good name, or reputation—it is a vital ingredient in your every interaction with news media representatives. The public relations practitioner cannot succeed if the reporter, editor, or news director does not believe him. If in the past that practitioner has lied, twisted facts, or withheld information, the media representatives probably discovered the truth. Maybe not immediately. Perhaps not in time for publication. But, they learned. That practitioner's value to the employer or client has been destroyed. The truth on that one occasion might have caused discomfort for the client or employer and pain for the practitioner. The human tendency is to avoid that hurt, even the critical decisions that led to it. We all tend to be practical about such situations. Values and integrity can become so pragmatic, however, that we twist or ignore them with ease. We call it rationalizing. The persons who enter public relations must choose their brand of integrity early on and stick with it; otherwise, they will become the hired gun or flack others refer to so contemptuously.

Creativity

Connotations surrounding the term creative person are so strong we inevitably think of an artist (perhaps a painter, musician, or poet) when it is used. That is natural, but it is too narrow an association. People are creative in many fields other than painting, music, and poetry, and you need not master one of these fine arts to be creative in public relations.

Creativity in our context is the ability to develop interesting, even exciting and appealing ideas, ideas for dealing with unacceptable performance, inspiring or maintaining acceptable performance, attracting uninterested or apathetic publics, or conveying more effectively to those publics the performance of a client or employer. This is the most important type of creativity for a successful public relations practitioner. You may be a marginal artist, but if you have a good idea and can describe it well, you will find someone with the technical skill to depict that idea.

Native talent and skill potential are creative gifts, but to a degree, creativity can be developed through knowledge, experience, and an active, open, inquisitive mind. Knowledge and experience provide the bits and pieces of concepts and images that go into new ideas. The active mind will experiment with these bits and pieces. The open mind looks at them in new ways. And the inquisitive mind is driven to do both to find out how it will all work. Some examples:

1. There's that uninterested public, the community in which your client institution, a hospital, operates. Residents know about your institution, but they know it is just one of a half dozen hospitals. Because of the lack of community interest, your hospital has a low occupancy rate. It does not receive the donations it needs to underwrite new equipment or update facilities.

The noncreative PR approach is a shrug and a "well, we tried" attitude, or even a "let's do more of what we're already doing" proposal. A creative approach would look for the positive characteristics of the hospital and seek ways to communicate those characteristics to local residents. Your hospital may handle patient paperwork (admissions and insurance claims) more quickly than the national or even local norm. That is something patients and potential patients would like to know. If the hospital needs increased donations, a benefit involving "names" in the community might be planned. Not only would these people attract attention to the benefit, they also could draw attention to the hospital's need for a new heart-lung machine or a mental health wing.

2. A voluntary health agency has been on the telethon circuit in recent years, depending on a marathon of entertainment as its principal fund raiser, but pledges have declined each year. The novelty has worn off; even the performers act tired, at the beginning of the telethon. The noncreative approach? "We've made this our trademark, and it's helped in the past, so let's stick with it." The creative approach would press for a new attention-getting event, perhaps a live performance by a nationally known entertainer in a large arena with ticket prices scaled to the range of previous telethon pledges.

3. An employee publication won a number of awards. Other editors think it is great. There is a problem, however. Surveys show that employees pass over the contents that management thinks should be read carefully. The noncreative reflex might be, "We're giving them an award-winning magazine, and they don't appreciate it. Maybe some day they will." The creative person could take several tacks: a new writing style or a redesign of the way it appears in the publication, or another means of communication entirely.

Some belittle their own creativity, saying, "I'm not an idea person. Someone else always comes up with the innovations." They say this as if

(1) they are doomed forever to noncreativeness, and (2) new ideas are 100 percent original and have never surfaced before. Consider how Shakespeare borrowed plots. Consider the similarities of epic themes through the ages. Consider the critics' claim that every novel ever published employs one of only a half dozen basic plots. We suggest that human creativity normally uses the ideas of others, even their methods of embodying those ideas, in some different ways. You do not have to start from scratch.

In this sense, creativity is developed by being aware of what others are doing. Consider adapting what those others do to what you want to do or to what is appropriate for your purposes. If you see a brochure with an attractive layout, experiment with that design in your format. You will adapt what someone else created but most likely borrowed in idea form from still another person's work. Yet you will be adding something new. If a multiscreen presentation impresses you, experiment with several screens using available graphics. Maybe two rather than three screens work best. Maybe four, or eight. Create.

It is awareness of what others are doing, of what can be done with what you have, and a desire to experiment that provides the all-important creativity that means success in public relations.

Knowledge of the media

Important person-to-person relationships in public relations are too often neglected. For example, a bank launched a promotional campaign to establish its image as "Your Friendly Bank in Riverton." Someone forgot to bring employees into the campaign, and some tellers were just as grumpy as ever. The promotion was a bust because the one-on-one relationships were ignored, undermining the entire program.

Person-to-person is important, but to reach all their publics and the many individuals who make up those groups, public relations people must rely on mass media.

THE MEDIA CONNECTION

Theorists have made much of the varying effects different media have on audiences. Marshall McLuhan, the Canadian media philosopher, described media as "hot" or "cool," depending on audience reaction or involvement required. He, of course, gave us that invaluable insight, "The medium is the message," meaning that the characteristics of any communication medium color a message or give a message a specific setting. Clearly, this makes the message differ from what it would be if sent by another medium. As an example, consider the impact of hearing about an incident from a friend compared with the impact of learning about it from radio or a newspaper.

In only three generations the role of the mass media has taken a quantum leap in American life, largely because of the electronic media. Some segments of our population (e.g., television addicts) seem obsessed with the media. A series of Roper surveys spanning more than 20 years describe Americans' increasing dependence on television to learn of world events. Many argue persuasively that TV programming with its heroes and heroines has been a major force in winning acceptance for the "new morality" in our country.

So, the mass media are of surpassing importance to the public relations professional. They are the tools used to tell about good deeds or acceptable performance. Whether the practitioner would influence legislators, win stockholder approval, persuade employees, or gain customer approval, the media play a vital role.

Among the many techniques used by public relations people are interviews and news conferences and the dissemination of news releases, photographs, tapes, and films. Media contacts range from a simple telephone call to a major production involving hundreds of persons, but their very nature implies that the desired end result is transmission of information to the public through the mass media.

Moreover, the news media depend on public relations people as a major source of news. If all news were traced to its source, between one-fourth and one-third would have originated with a public relations staff. Without public relations input, the information in many cases would never become public. Imagine how much news from your campus would be reported if the college or university itself failed to supply a constant stream of information to the media. Not even a metropolitan daily has a large enough staff to stay on top of the happenings among the thousands of employees representing the many large businesses in a major city.

Mutual of Omaha is the world's largest provider of health insurance. In its headquarters city, employees carry home reports about company affairs. But outside their homes, most knowledge of the company has come from news stories published or broadcast by the media, including the highly successful television program, "Wild Kingdom."

Much of public relations success is measured by accomplishments in the media, the number of stories published or broadcast. Though a large volume is used, it is only a fraction of all news releases produced. Getting material in print or on the air is a highly competitive process.

Remember, however, that media exposure by itself does not insure success for a campaign. But without that exposure, chances of success are nil.

MASS MEDIA FUNCTIONS

In the United States, the mass media function (1) to provide information, particularly about current events; (2) to interpret issues of public concern and help shape an informed public opinion; (3) to provide inexpensive entertainment for large numbers; and (4) to assist in broad-based marketing of goods and services (advertising).

The news function (providing information on events as quickly as possible after they occur or sometimes as they occur) is the most important function media perform for society. When people are in need (starving Ethiopians, Americans held hostage in a foreign country, Central American earthquake victims, or the local family whose home has burned) most Americans learn about them within hours through the news media. The events are news and they have been covered extensively by newspapers, radio, and television. An informed public turns to help those in need.

In a democracy, people must have information about government affairs and public issues if they are to act responsibly. Our country is so large that it is impossible for each person to know what public officials say and do except at the community level and then probably only in smaller communities. Even at the local level, few attend each city council meeting or each meeting of the school board. Were it not for news coverage, most Americans would lack a constant, reliable source of information about conduct of governmental affairs.

While they readily accept the information function, some people object to the mass media assuming an interpretive role. They contend that interpretation is a misuse of media power, making media managers "unelected governors." But analyze the situation.

Interpretation includes explanation and backgrounding, a natural outgrowth of the information function. After all, few are better equipped to explain what happened than the reporter on the scene. Commenting on events is a natural outgrowth of explanation, and we have a right to hear the comments of those closest, noninvolved observers—the reporters covering that event.

It is a distinctly American trait of the media to separate information from interpretation, or at least to label interpretation or opinion as such. You have seen newspaper articles identified as "Interpretive Report" or "Opinion of Author." By and large, editorial comment is confined to editorial pages. Broadcast editorials, while less common than newspaper editorials, are identified carefully as the opinion of station management.

Another important aspect of the interpretive function of American media is the presentation of more than one point of view on issues. While media managers have their own opinions, they publish letters expressing differing views, and they broadcast forum and call-in programs with a variety of opinions.

Interestingly, through the years, broadcast programs offering interpretation, such as "Meet the Press" and "60 Minutes," have attracted some of the largest audiences, even though they originated on a medium known primarily for entertainment content. Of course, a superficial analysis of radio and television programming clearly shows that the main thrust is entertainment. Music—from country to classical—dominates radio, while soap operas, situation comedies, cops-and-robbers, sports, talk shows, and movies occupy most of the television day.

Critics, from Newton Minow to former media executives like Fred Friendly, expressed unhappiness with much that television airs as part of its entertainment function. It was Minow, a former Federal Communications Commission chairman, who termed television programming "a vast wasteland." Disinterested scholars agree, however, that lots of people watch lots of TV, and they enjoy what they watch. As a result, projectors chatter in far fewer movie theaters across the country than were operating only a generation ago. Some of the biggest names in general circulation magazines are part of history, like the theaters, victims of television's popular appeal.

A good word must be said about television, however. Entertainment is a real human need, as folk wisdom suggests in the old saying, "All work and no play makes Jack a dull boy." If television and radio failed to provide acceptable entertainment, people would turn elsewhere. Of course, the quality of television entertainment is open to criticism.

The one reason television can afford lavish entertainment packages like the Super Bowl, the Olympics, two-hour specials featuring top talent, mini-series based on best-sellers or made-for-TV movies is that the medium performs the fourth function—advertising. Neither radio nor television in their present forms could exist without commercial sponsors. Again, without arguing the apparent quality or taste of each commercial, we should recognize that advertising messages frequently provide valuable information for consumers, sometimes in a delightfully entertaining way. These messages, beamed to a national audience, create coast-to-coast markets for products and services. Many economists contend that national markets sustain mass production, thus lowering cost to consumers and contributing to the high economic standard Americans enjoy.

NEWSPAPERS

Newspapers are the oldest mass medium, growing out of the newsletters and essayists' papers published in the early days of printing in Europe. As is the case with radio and television, newspapers today are financed by advertising, although they have subscription income as well.

In the United States are approximately 1,750 daily and 9000 weekly newspapers. The numbers have remained fairly stable since the 1950s. While there is great reliance on television for news of major national and international events, newspapers remain the primary medium for reporting local news, and only newspapers provide the detailed reporting needed by the truly informed citizen. Take the word of television news' "father figure," Walter Cronkite, for this. He said this in an *Editor & Publisher* article years ago and has repeated the point since then.

Successful daily papers have deep penetration within their central markets. That means these dailies reach 70 to 80 percent of the homes within the cities in which they publish. Beyond question, therefore, newspapers are essential for any public relations program.

As a rule, smaller papers provide extensive, detailed coverage to local events; thus, they remain an excellent medium for reaching the local community. Although *USA Today* is the only truly national newspaper in the United States, several large papers also circulate and are read throughout the country (e.g., the *New York Times* and the *Wall Street Journal*), so they too are effective vehicles for reaching a widely diffused public like corporate shareholders or members of national associations.

Newspapers share with magazines (especially journals of opinion) most of the interpretation function of the media. Although their editorial pages are not as well read as the front pages and sports sections, editorials are followed carefully by community leaders and other influential citizens. Therefore, they often have influence far beyond their immediate readership. It is a serious mistake for the public relations practitioner to underestimate this influence. On the other hand, newspaper editorials influence but they certainly do not control public opinion. Public relations practitioners must remember this, too.

MAGAZINES

Many influential magazines died at the dawn of the television age, and some practitioners write off magazines as an important medium for public relations. Do not be one of them, even though many surviving periodicals suffered circulation losses attributable at least in part to competition from television.

But among periodicals, the major news magazines remain an important voice. They are read by millions. (*Time*, for example, has a circulation of 4.5 million.) And their readers are among the best educated and best informed citizens of the country. In addition, other magazines with relatively small circulations are read and heeded by leaders in government, business, education, religion, the various professions. New national programs often are discussed first or proposed in these magazines. So, news magazines and special interest periodicals must be known to any public relations practitioner whose employer or client will be affected by national programs and policies.

BOOKS

The influence of books, like the influence of magazines, is frequently underestimated. Social critics, for instance, point out that Americans, on the average, read fewer than one book a year, and that average includes students who may read a dozen textbooks. Nevertheless, the United States has millions of devoted, serious book readers. Without them, paperback publishing would not have grown exponentially since World War II. These readers are influential well beyond their numbers.

Books may be influential of themselves, even with limited circulation. Rachel Carson's *Silent Spring*, for example, led to nationwide restriction on use of pesticides. Another example, Ralph Nader's *Unsafe at Any Speed* launched the crusade that resulted in many of the safety features mandated on today's automobiles. The public relations practitioner unaware of current nonfiction best-sellers ignores a communication medium with great potential for shaping opinions and attitudes.

FILM

In the first half of the twentieth century, motion pictures grew into the most popular form of entertainment in the United States. They were pushed out of the limelight but not offstage by television. Fewer feature-length entertainment films are produced today than 35 years ago, but movie audiences have stabilized. For those of high school and college age, movies remain popular both as entertainment and as provider of role and behavior models. In fact, television adds to their influence by showing them after the motion pictures have run in theaters. Thus, their impact on thought and values remains high.

RADIO

The early radio receivers that followed the pioneer crystal sets were impressive, large pieces of furniture; today radio is identified with the ubiquitous transistor. In American society, we are rarely out of radio earshot. Along the way, radio became a significant information medium, especially when immediacy is vital, such as periods of national crisis or during natural disasters.

Radio is unique in that it reaches massive audiences during "drive time," commuting hours in the morning and late afternoon when America is on wheels going to and from work. To reach people quickly with an announcement or to remind them of an important event, radio is without peer as a medium for public relations messages. People turn to radio in emergencies. For example, Americans first learned of the assassination of Premier Indira Gandhi of India from radio. Affected citizens stay tuned for details on flood and fire, famine and pestilence.

TELEVISION

Television permeates American life so thoroughly that children during the 1970s and 1980s asked their parents, "What did you *do* before television?" Statistics on TV viewing are mind-boggling. Within certain age groups in the United States, primarily the young and old, viewing averages more than 20 hours a week.

Within a decade after television came on the American scene, it was a major factor in our life and culture, and much of that impact is positive. Television introduced many Americans to serious drama, music, and dance; theaters, symphonies, and ballet groups have benefited. Documentaries bridge distances between states and between nations.

Television created national figures overnight and introduced them to Mr. and Mrs. America right in their living rooms. For years, scholars will study the impact of television coverage of death and violence in Vietnam. That impact altered our national history.

MEDIA RELATIONS

If public relations people are to gain acceptance of important publics by successful use of mass media, they must establish solid working relations with media managers. Knowing what the various media strengths and weaknesses are is not enough. Practitioners must know media needs, what editors and news program directors want to print or broadcast.

The fast track to learning this is to work for a news medium, but that is not the only route. College courses on mass communication and the mass media, properly conducted, will prepare a person for a career involving media relations. And on-the-job training can succeed *if* it is accompanied by an eagerness to learn.

Several points to remember in establishing solid working relations with the media:

1. Meeting requirements. Many newspapers and some of the electronic media prepare manuals for nonprofessional contributors. Some hints are elementary, but public relations people can profit from any idea the manuals provide about the particular form the paper or station prefers news releases to follow.

For example, if an editor insists that reporters draw a square around each name in a story to indicate the spelling has been double-checked, the PR practitioner can reconfirm the spelling of each name in a news release (you should anyway) and square them before submitting the release. If a broadcasting outlet prefers news copy typed in all capitals to conform to wire service copy used in newscasts, the PR release will be more welcome if it is typed that way, too.

The knowledgeable PR writer understands that writing for newspapers is not the same as writing for radio and television. So, given the chance, separate releases should be written for print and broadcast. (See Chapter 10.)

Another important part of servicing news outlets is furnishing graphics. Public relations practitioners must know the photographic requirements and preferences of the media people with whom they deal. (A reminder: radio stations, despite technological advances, should not be sent photographs. It has happened!)

It should be unnecessary to provide this caution, but after seeing many bad examples, we must add: news stories must be prepared meticulously. An accurate story prepared correctly is the only acceptable story. A public relations writer destroys credibility with a news source and a news medium by misspellings, incorrect punctuation, wrong titles, and most heinous of all sins, making mistakes in names and crucial statistics.

2. Respecting deadlines. Like news people, PR practitioners face deadlines, so they must be fully sensitized to media deadlines and to their inflexibility. Yet, many are not. The Case of the Friendly Informer illustrates the point:

A major brewery strike neared settlement. The brewery's PR executive called the local daily to advise the editor that he was hand-carrying a release on the latest development. He arrived almost on deadline. Instead of rushing his story to the city editor, he exchanged pleasantries with several reporters on the fringe of the newsroom. He arrived at the editor's desk 10 minutes past deadline. The contrite PR man told the city editor, "I didn't know you had an early deadline on Saturday." It hardly cooled the editor's ire to discover the release reported a tentative strike settlement, a story radio and television would run long before his Sunday edition.

The PR executive learned an expensive lesson on establishing priorities. Visiting with reporters, editors, and media executives is an important part of the business. It is a solid way to learn the news outlet's needs and preferences, and such visits can lead to improved relations and cooperation. But be selective and judicious in your timing. Schedule calls with an eye on the clock and never on deadline.

3. Establishing credibility. Unfortunately, telling the truth does not automatically establish your credibility. Others must believe you are telling the truth and that you will continue to do so, especially when telling the truth is not easy.

But not telling the truth makes credibility impossible, and outright lying is the obvious way of not telling the truth. A tempting ploy for public relations people is to tell only part of the truth, to "put the best face on the situation" and "emphasize the positive." In all probability, such a course will be interpreted by news media representatives as deliberate distortion, another form of lying.

A difficult task for any PR practitioner is persuading an employer or client that maintaining credibility offsets the consequences of admitting the bad with the good. The employer or client too often takes the position, "That's the reason I hired you—to keep the public's eyes on the good we do and off the bad."

But getting management to "see the light" can be done, and results are gratifying. One of the nation's largest freight haulers is the Union Pacific Railroad. Any rail carrier faces occasional derailments that can result in extensive property damage, personal injuries, even death. Threats to the environment or to community safety may be involved, for example, if a tank car of corrosive liquids or poisonous gases is involved.

Yet, the Union Pacific public relations staff has earned the reputation of often being first to alert news media to such accidents and of giving accurate, objective accounts of damages and injuries. Of course, they emphasize the relative infrequency of derailments and the railroad's overall safety record, but certainly that is a legitimate part of the story.

Credibility is closely related to integrity, an absolute requirement for public relations, as noted earlier.

Sensitivity and judgment

In discussing communication, we emphasized that when drafting a message, a communicator must know the audience, its educational level, concerns, and experiences.

We suggest that the public relations practitioner also have a feel for the concerns, fears, hopes, and preferences of those audiences who are the client's or employer's publics. The practitioner must anticipate with a high degree of accuracy how those publics feel, think, and react when specific events occur and when messages are directed at them.

We do not imply that the PR practitioner must borrow a crystal ball. Rather, he must (1) be genuinely concerned about people who constitute those publics; (2) translate that concern into willingness to learn about them; (3) encourage feedback from them; and (4) based on this knowledge and the experience of working with members of these publics, be able to empathize with them. Ideally, the practitioner is like the husband or wife in a happy marriage: each knows and respects the other so that each can predict how the other will react to job frustrations, disruptions in family routine, unexpectedly large bills, or serious illness.

Developing this kind of sensitivity is not an occult art. A competent public relations person who attends stockholders meetings over the years can anticipate the reactions of outspoken leaders to varying profit pictures or to management proposals to sell unprofitable divisions or acquire mineral deposits and timberland. The veteran practitioner will make accurate predictions on how much play the media will give a merger, introduction of a new product, or the sudden resignation of the chief executive officer.

These situations all point to the importance of experience as a conscious learning process, one the practitioner thinks about and mentally keeps on file for ready reference.

But much more than experience is implied by the sensitivity being described. It involves respect and concern for others, and that means understanding their position and dealing with them fairly and openly. The self-centered individual who ignores others lacks this quality and will be a liability in public relations. Even if such a person avoids saying the wrong things, the lack of feeling is just below the surface and negative vibrations flourish. Murphy's Law of public relations is: "You can do as much damage accidentally as you can on purpose."

Sensitivity, the ability to think and feel as others do, is invaluable in developing that other important attribute for the successful public relations practitioner: judgment. But judgment is more. It involves choosing the right course based upon an appreciation for the ideas and the sensitivities of others.

A sensitive practitioner may know or sense that residents of the local community, an important public, have a feeling of civic inferiority. Their city is in the shadow of a nearby metropolis that is wealthier, more sophisticated, and much better known. The practitioner even senses that employees from the local community carry this complex with them to their jobs, so they lack pride in workmanship, pride in accomplishment, and pride in the company. Morale always sags. "Success" is with the bright lights and greener grass of the big neighbor.

As often happens, the big city does lure talented people from the local community, and many young people decide they can succeed only in the larger setting, so the situation can become more than a morale problem. It can threaten loss of the skilled work force and a first-rate management team.

Eventually a member of top management suggests moving part of company headquarters to the big city. "It will be good for company prestige and improved communications. We will establish closer contact with major customers. We'll be closer to our advertising agency, the banking community, even our major stockholders."

The public relations professional understands the detrimental impact the move will have on employee recruitment and retention as well as on company identity. And if that professional exercises judgment as well as sensitivity, she will know that the proposal calls for careful action: first, an objective study of the advantages and disadvantages, then a reasoned effort to show top management that the ill effects of the move would outweigh the possible gains.

Thus, the public relations practitioner is laboring in an area that is at least as important as media relations. The professional is serving as a vital part of the corporate staff and advising management on a serious public relations problem. This leads us to an investigation of the relationship of the public relations practitioner with the client or employer.

Knowledge of client or employer

The primary role of public relations is to promote acceptable performance. It is easy to lay down that principle; accomplishing it is the challenge. And deciding on the first step can be a mindbender, especially in a huge conglomerate, a national organization with hundreds of affiliates, or a government agency with offices and staff in a dozen or more states.

Scale the problem down by personalizing it. If you would win support from others for acceptable performance by a single person, you first must know quite a bit about that individual. Obviously you must observe that person's performance or behavior closely before assuring yourself that it *is* acceptable.

If you are to suggest means of improving performance, you must know about the client's business, profession, or service. You will learn of problems and how the client deals with them. Before you move to the next stage of public relations, gaining acceptance of the client's performance, you must know your client's publics as well, the people or organizations whose approval is important to the client.

Apply this same approach to a corporation, institution, or organization. As the first step, it is absolutely essential for a public relations practitioner to become thoroughly familiar with such an employer or client. It would be impossible, even for an experienced professional, to move into a new assignment and immediately "do public relations" for a client or employer without preparation.

Examine the situation practically. As an example, a practitioner who has worked for a soft drink manufacturer, receives an offer from a public relations agency whose major account is one of the country's largest private hospitals devoted to treating physically handicapped children. Imagine the practitioner's first day on the new job. No revamping publicity procedures for the hospital. No planning special events to draw attention to the institution's programs. No launching a nationwide direct mail solicitation for funds. No telling the hospital administrator how to correct a problem in employee relations.

Back at the bottling plant, this same practitioner had a marvelous program for publicizing the company. The practitioner had developed a successful hospitality plan for plant visitors. The practitioner's experience and corporate awareness contributed to an excellent employee relations program, an industry model. The practitioner designed and wrote promotional material mailed to potential customers, material copied by a half dozen competitors.

Despite all that knowledge, experience, and skill, our practitioner must "go back to school," thoroughly studying the new client before undertaking any projects or offering advice about situations peculiar to the client's activities.

Does this mean a practitioner must get "requalified" each time he changes jobs? In the sense that familiarization with the employer or client is concerned, it certainly does. But it is a process of self-education that can be interesting and stimulating. When you are doing this, you are not in a rut!

Remember, too, that much public relations wisdom and experience can be transferred from service with one employer or client to another. We can vouch for this: there are more similarities between public relations work for a non-tax-supported university and public relations work for a federal agency than most people imagine.

Exactly what questions the practitioner must answer concerning the new client or employer depend on the activities of that client or employer, of course. But some items apply generally:

1. What is the employer/client doing now in public relations? Does the company sell products and/or services? Is it in wholesale or retail markets? Both? What does the organization hope to achieve? What is the ultimate service or function the agency or institution wants to perform?

2. What are the principal activities of the employer/client? What types of products does the company make or sell? What are the major competing products within these classes? Where are most of the employees located? Where are the plants and offices?

3. What is the structure of the organization and the chain of com-

mand within the employer/client organization? Where does public relations fit in the command structure? Who sets policies? Who has the final word in decision making? Who has input into decision making? Are decisions based on consensus after consultation? Is the top public relations professional one of the decision makers and does the public relations staff have ready access to decision makers?

4. How is the employer/client performing currently? Are sales and profits acceptable? Is funding adequate for the organization's needs? What is the source of funding, public or private? Is the organization performing acceptably in serving its publics?

5. What publics concern the employer/client?

6. How are the publics or "target audiences" being reached and how successful have these efforts been?

7. What is the attitude of top management toward public relations?

8. What resources are available for the public relations program?

THE ROLE OF PUBLIC RELATIONS
IN THE ORGANIZATION

The role of public relations has grown, and public relations professionals have become increasingly visible in American organizations since the 1950s. Much of what might be termed public relations during the period between World Wars concentrated on organizing, writing, and placing publicity while orchestrating occasional multiphase programs to modify or burnish an organizational image.

The growing size and complexity of modern institutions plus explosive developments in mass communications led to change. Today's public relations professional must develop a working knowledge of organizational structure and understand human relations while constantly honing skills as a communicator.

The public relations function—known by titles, such as public affairs, institutional relations, and others—has multiple functions in today's organization. These include developing and maintaining communications with the organization's many publics, of course, but also designing programs that modify organizational behavior and/or perception of the organization by the various publics and, often the most important function, advising management concerning the perception of the organization by various publics, appropriateness of organizational behavior with any possible need to modify that behavior and, if necessary, developing the proper course for that modification.

Consequently, few modern public relations practitioners are

merely "hired guns," hitting targets designated by an executive higher in the corporate structure. In many progressive organizations, public relations is part of top management, reporting directly to the chief executive officer. Seldom is public relations relegated to a position lower than the second echelon, that is, responsible to an executive who in turn reports directly to the top.

Summary

Along with "good deeds" (action) public relations is communication, the effective telling of those good deeds. So communication skills are essential for the successful practitioner. Even the skills are not enough, however. A public relations person must know the limits of effective communication, that without good will and receptivity on the part of both sender and receiver, communication alone cannot resolve conflicts. Today's practitioner cannot be so naive as to believe that problems are always "basically, just a matter of communication."

Public relations people today need not only skills for interpersonal communication, but they need to be aware of the requirements for using mass communication effectively. Many of their messages will be designed for large, diffused publics that can best be reached through the mass media. The practitioner then must know the advantages and disadvantages of print and electronic media as well as their availability and their needs.

Even the effective communicator will lose an audience, however, if the communicator does not have credibility. The way to establish credibility, of course, is to be credible, a person of integrity, a person who can be trusted. If a public relations person is, first of all, to insure that employers and clients act honestly and for the common good, it is even more obvious that such a practitioner must also be a person of integrity.

Because public relations people perform so many functions and face such varied challenges, they must be open-minded, flexible, and creative. They must be aware of new possibilities, new and more appealing ways to accomplish longstanding objectives. They cannot be satisfied with doing things the same way simply because "that's the way we've always done it."

Exercises

1. Write a brief antilittering appeal aimed at (a) 3rd graders; (b) college students; and (c) a general adult audience in your community. You can make it a newspaper editorial, a radio public service announcement, or copy for a print advertisement. Explain the differences in the messages and the reasons for these differences.

2. Take a paper you have written for this or another course you are enrolled in. Calculate its rating according to the widely used formula developed by Robert Gunning. (Determine the average number of words per sentence; add that figure to the percentage of words that are three syllables or more but not combinations of words of two syllables or fewer [like "bookkeeper" or verbs made into three syllables by adding -*es*, -*ed*, or -*ing*] but treat the percentage as a whole number; then multiply the sum by 0.4. Example: 21 average words per sentence + 7% three-or-more-syllables words = 28; 28 × 0.4 = 11.2. That 11.2 is considered roughly equivalent to the number of years of formal education a typical reader would need to read the copy with ease.) Most popular publications that have used this formula strive to keep their material at the 9 or 10 level.

3. Pick out two television commercials that involve a person shown on the screen delivering a spoken message on behalf of the sponsor's product. One commercial may be for a nationally marketed product and one for a local sponsor. Read over the points on pages 58 and 60 with regard to oral communication (delivery, body language, etc.) and critique each commercial on the basis of these points.

4. What are some of the special events that organizations in your community employ to raise funds—entertainments, raffles, bake sales, etc.? Have any of these events been done so often that response is declining? Choose at least two of these events that are lagging and see if you can inject a little public relations creativity into them by suggestions for change or appropriate substitution that might revive the fund-raising effort.

Case study

Scott T. graduated from a state university with a degree in journalism. His minor was English literature, and he took quite a few social science courses, including the beginning course in economics. After college he landed a job as a reporter on a daily newspaper in a city of 100,000. His work was in general news, with a few business-related assignments.

Because of his passion for contemporary music, he was an avid radio listener and became acquainted with several deejays. One of them suggested Scott would really enjoy filling a part-time weekend slot at this station. To his surprise, Scott's editor had no objection to Scott's moonlighting as a part-time weekend deejay as long as Scott used a "radio name."

Scott pursued his dual career for several years, then was attracted by the opportunity to join the public relations staff of a large clothing manufacturing corporation in the community. The company had a program which paid for college-level courses its employees took during their off hours.

What is your assessment of Scott's qualifications for a public relations position with the manufacturing corporation? If he were to get the job, what courses would you advise him to take under the company's program to better prepare himself for advancement in a public relations career?

Suggested readings

Burton, Paul. *Corporate Public Relations*. New York: Reinhold Publ. Co., 1966.

Fenner, Freda D'Sousa. "How to Get the Right First Job in Public Relations." *Public Relations Journal,* April 1985.

Finding That First Job in Public Relations. Midland, Mich.: Dow Chemical Co., 1985.

Marshall, Larry. "The New Breed of PR Executive." *Public Relations Journal,* July 1980.

Muller, Jean R. "Why PR Counselors Get into the Business." *Public Relations Journal,* March 1980.

Newsom, D. A. "Realities, Questions and Challenges for Public Relations Education." *Public Relations Journal,* March 1984.

Parker, Robert A. "The Ladder to Success." *Public Relations Journal,* March 1981.

Simon, Raymond. *Public Relations: Concepts and Practice.* Columbus, Ohio: GRID, Inc., 1976.

Teahan, Frederick H. "New Professionals Profile." *Public Relations Journal,* March 1984.

4 Fact-finding and research

The need for information

Scene: The office of the executive director of a regional over-the-road trucking industry association.

Characters: The executive director, president of the association, a vice-president, and the association's deputy director for public affairs.

PRESIDENT: At the national convention last month, I learned that a number of other regional groups have been offering group insurance packages to members and their employees. Apparently they solicit proposals from a number of insurance companies, pick the one they think is best, and offer it to their members.

DIRECTOR: That sounds like a good fringe benefit. It shows that the association is looking out for its members.

VICE-PRES.: I don't know. If others are like me, they already have well-established insurance programs for their employees. If my company finds out this package is cheaper, we're going to be unhappy because we're paying too much. Or we'll feel we should break away from an insurer we've been getting good service from for a long time. I think a lot of members would be upset—maybe even consider it interference in their own businesses.

PR DIRECTOR: Why wonder? Why don't we ask our members what they prefer?

What the public relations director for the trucking association is applying are two fundamental principles of public relations: (1) establish a base of knowledge, and (2) act from that base of knowledge.

The heart of public relations is acceptable performance. But to help achieve it, practitioners must know what current performance is. They must also know if it is acceptable, and it it is unacceptable, they must know why and to whom it is unacceptable.

82

Practitioners must also send out messages telling about acceptable performance and know if those messages are being conveyed effectively, what the responses are, and how those responses affect the client or employer.

At each point, the practitioner needs facts. Failure to get the necessary facts can undermine an attempt to achieve good public relations. Ignorance of important facts can make further action futile or even harmful.

Information has to be current too. Today's facts may be outdated over the course of the next year or month or week. Fact-finding then is a never ending requirement for effective public relations.

Consider this little example of failing to keep a collection of data, a mailing list, up to date. One of us has been associated with a periodical that changed its name more than a decade ago. The top editor has been in the job more than half a dozen years. Yet the periodical still gets many news releases from public relations people whose mailing list carries the periodical's former name and the name of an editor who preceded the current editor's predecessor. Consider the first impression such news releases make on the current editor and the impact on the chances those releases will be published.

This situation is trivial, however, compared to the risk of failure and waste assumed by any comprehensive public relations campaign undertaken without adequate fact-finding. Like diving into a pool without checking its depth beforehand, the result may be disaster.

Civic leaders in a midwestern city once thought they had the answer to their community's future. It was an exciting package of improvements that would not only transform the image of the city but improve its quality of life and make it more attractive to new industry. These forward-looking advocates of change launched an overpowering public relations campaign to sell their package to voters. There was, after all, the need to get financing through voter approval of a large bond issue.

During the campaign for the bonds, civic leaders saturated the community with favorable arguments and responded quickly to questions and objections raised by opponents. They did everything right, or so it seemed.

When the votes were counted, the community improvement package was wiped out. For years afterward, city leaders tended to lick their wounds and the city seemed at a standstill. Little by little, however, it surfaced that local residents were not just narrow-minded and nonprogressive when they voted against the big package, although that is what many of the disappointed community leaders had been muttering. Most local citizens, it seems, were for parts of the package but against others. In succeeding years, virtually all of the improvements were gradually completed.

The community had, however, been unnecessarily on hold for several years. It was the result of failure to gather essential information on the attitudes of the most significant public that led to offering an unacceptable package.

The ways information is obtained

Fact-finding research is conducted in many ways. For the public relations practitioner, it includes especially:

1. *Observing and monitoring performance.* This can range from personal observation of people at work to a review of highly sophisticated product-testing results and complex production and profit figures. It will deal with the concrete (units produced, customers served, dollars earned) and also with the intangible (employee morale, stockholder confidence, executive vision).

2. *Identifying publics.* This may involve simply noting the groups with which the practitioner's employer or client comes in contact regularly and which have the ability to affect the success of the employer or client.

3. *Discovering the opinions and attitudes of those publics.* Here the social sciences can provide valuable guidance and excellent tools so that the public relations practitioner does not have to rely on unaided intuition. Essential in this area are two other kinds of research: (1) searching for the best means to communicate with those publics, and (2) discerning the effectiveness of communication with the publics.

OBSERVING PERFORMANCE

Thomas Peters and Robert Waterman passed along many valuable insights in their best-selling book, *In Search of Excellence: Lessons from America's Best-Run Companies.* One is the importance of visibility of top managers. But this visibility is not a one-way relationship.

Successful executives are not simply seeking adulation when they tour the plant or visit the field station. They not only want to know what their people have to say; they want to see what and how their people are doing.

First-hand, on-site visits are such an obvious, elementary type of fact-finding that they are too often overlooked, and maybe even looked down upon as hopelessly unsophisticated. But direct observation remains one of the most important means of fact-finding public relations practitioners can employ.

However, if it is to be truly informative, observation must not be totally casual. The supervisor who walks through the plant should discuss more than the weather or the latest sports event with the workers there. That supervisor should have a clear idea of what subjects employees should be directed to, develop skill in getting the employees to open up, and be a good listener.

The same goes for public relations people. They cannot afford to isolate themselves from production-line employees or any other public. They must include direct observation near the top of their research methods list; and their observations must be regular, planned, and thorough. That implies going so far as to schedule visits to offices, departments, or divisions at predetermined intervals; preparing an agenda or list of questions (maybe kept in the visitor's head but given previous thought nonetheless); and devoting some time afterward to studying what the visitor saw and heard.

To get the most from observation, whether it is a relatively short visit or a thorough, prolonged inspection, a record should be made. History researchers as well as news reporters take notes and tape interviews; accident investigators as well as construction engineers photograph sites extensively at various stages and from different angles. They know, as the PR person must, that the human memory is leaky, so valuable facts may escape it as time passes.

Besides, the results of observation can be shared with others through records. With records, trends can be discerned; cause-result relationships can be suggested.

USING REFERENCES. The record of others can augment the observation research of practitioners too. Such records include reference materials that public relations people, like the staff in a newsroom, keep at hand. The references will include such elementary items as telephone and city directories for all the communities in which the practitioner's employer or client carries on activities, state government directories ("blue books") for the states in which they operate, the *Congressional*

Directory, a good atlas, a current almanac, an encyclopedia, a diction-ary, a thesaurus, and a book of quotations.

In connection with their media relations work, practitioners will also want quick access to media directories and lists (e.g., *N. W. Ayer & Sons Directory of Newspapers and Periodicals* or the current *Editor & Publisher Yearbook*, Standard Rate and Data Services reports, the *Broadcasting Yearbook*).

Practitioners will also have a number of periodicals available for research in their office reference collection. They will include current newspapers published in the communities where the employer or cli-ent has facilities; back issues and clippings of stories from various periodicals dealing with the employer or client; magazines with infor-mation relating to the employer or client; magazines with information relating to the employer or client's business or activity, especially trade and organizational journals; and books that deal with such areas.

Another reference item is an idea file, with samples of the embod-ied idea whenever possible. The idea file is a collection of materials that catch the practitioner's eye because they may some day be adapted for use on behalf of the employer or client. Typically the file contains bro-chures (kept for their creative design perhaps), pamphlets that are good examples of effective promotion, programs prepared for special events, news releases that illustrate how others dealt with problem situations, and, undoubtedly, lots of quickly written notes when samples could not be obtained but an idea popped up in the course of observing someone else's public relations endeavors.

ESTABLISHING ARCHIVES. "Reinventing the wheel" has become a cliché, but it still is an apt analogy for the needless effort practitioners can expend if they do not produce some reference materials of their own. If you are called upon to provide some historical background for your company or institution, it does no good to recall that someone once wrote a history, but you did not think to keep a copy. Or if a reporter calls for some figures you put together a year or so ago, it can be pretty frustrating to start from scratch because you did not save them.

Build up your own collection of information about your employer or client. That way a practitioner is able to answer questions more read-ily and confidently, and the practitioner will not have to waste time retracing steps seeking facts searched out before.

Like any good library, the practitioner's archives should be well organized for quick access. Even more frustrating than failing to keep valuable information is knowing you kept it but having no idea where you can find it now that you need it. Efficient filing systems are a must.

Today, library researching is often aided by computer retrieval. Programs allow the information seeker to ask the computer to provide all the references keyed to names or terms. The public relations practitioner's own archives can use such systems too. Data can be stored in a computer and quickly found by asking the computer to search out the facts when they are needed. The tendency in business, government, and institutions is to have computer systems with more than adequate capacity for present needs. That means there often is ample capacity to serve the public relations staff.

One caution: if the type of information stored in the computer is important and may have to be called up quickly in emergency situations, public relations people must know that they will not bump into other users at such critical times. Access must be assured.

IDENTIFYING PUBLICS

Some publics are common to many public relations endeavors and are easily identified. Any enterprise that involves retail sales obviously finds customers a most important public. The management of a public utility is aware that the residents of the community or area it serves are a key public. A manufacturer is aware that suppliers of raw materials and parts are critical to its success.

But businesses, institutions, and organizations are distinctive as well as similar. Each may have publics that are not common in other settings; or some of the common publics may be segmented—actually several separate publics. For instance, the population characteristics of a metropolitan area often vary so much that the area lacks social unity. Instead of a single community public, public relations people have to realize that they have several community publics distinguished by ethnic, economic, or historical identity. Failure to recognize this can be a serious defect in the public relations program.

Relying too heavily on lists of standard publics is dangerous, too, because they may omit a public that is important in your circumstances. Years ago, when civic leaders proposed public improvements, they may have thought of local businesses and residential taxpayers as the significant publics whose approval they had to win. That accorded with traditional thinking. Today it would be inconceivable to ignore environmentalists as a significant public whose assent must be sought.

Practitioners have found the soundest approach is to consider carefully all the persons who will affect or be affected by an operation. These people can be grouped into publics. But the list of publics must always be recognized as tentative. It must always be left open for additions (new arrivals, customers for a new product, special interest groups that have just formed, etc.).

DISCOVERING OPINIONS AND ATTITUDES

Once publics have been identified, public relations practitioners want to know how these publics perceive performance. PR people will also want to know whether their messages directed to those publics are getting through, being understood, and influencing existing attitudes. This is why opinion measurement is taking on ever greater importance in public relations today.

In the United States with its private enterprise economic system, many others besides public relations practitioners have a stake in opinion measurement, of course. A great deal of talent, effort, and money has been devoted to opinion measurement by marketing people and politicians, two major users of opinion measurement. PR practitioners can benefit from the body of information they amassed by seeking data wisely and carefully. They can begin by noting that research has led a number of social scientists to agree that favorable or at least accepting public opinion is necessary for the long-term success of those who would lead or serve the general public. As political scientist Alan B. Monroe put it: "The public almost always gets its way."

ASSOCIATIONS AND EXPERIENCES. Sociologists and psychologists have identified factors that seem to influence opinion formation or at least offer a basis for predicting attitudes. Sociologists emphasize affiliations or group memberships as a strong influence on opinion formation, though they do not discount the impact of events and personal experiences. Psychologists focus on the relation between learning and attitude development. They also recognize the social influences that obviously exist in a teacher-pupil relationship. (Teacher, of course, can mean a parent, an older sibling, a playmate, or a friend.)

Parents are recognized as the first teachers, and infants learn what is good and bad, what is desirable and what is undesirable, in terms of what their parents approve or disapprove. Children also learn from direct experience. Some food tastes good, some bad. Hot things burn. Sharp edges cut.

Throughout the learning process, human beings associate new observations and new instructions with what they already know. They tend to classify new knowledge in the categories they have previously established, based on their previous learning. These categories are sometimes referred to as "stereotypes." That word unfortunately has acquired negative connotations. But if people refuse to modify their mental categories or form new ones in the face of new experiences, the negative connotation may be deserved.

For the public relations practitioner, this emphasis on group identity and the learning process as factors in attitude formation is valuable. It suggests, for example, that to persuade people you must talk to them in terms of their own experiences and mental categories. They must be asked to see the relation between what the persuader sees as good and desirable and their own preexisting categories of good and desirable. They must also be spoken to in terms of their group values.

Example: A food processor might attempt to win customer acceptance for a sizable price increase by appealing to stereotypes that potential customers have regarding everyday necessities:

> Like you, our employees were paying 79 cents for a loaf of bread seven years ago. Like you, they pay $1.10 today. That's a 39% increase.
> Our mainline appliance sold for $59.95 when bread was 79 cents. That appliance is priced at $67.75 today—only 13 percent more.

Or the approach to a blue-collar clientele might tie itself to the importance of the hourly wage:

> Five years ago when industrial workers were making an average of $7.50 an hour, our mainline appliance was sold for $299. Today those workers average $9.80 an hour—up 31%. Our price increases for the same period—including the figures we are announcing today—average under 27%.

As human beings mature, they spend more time communicating with others. Some of that communication is going to be carefully designed to influence their opinions and persuade them to action. The advertising message that says you should buy a product or the political appeal that asks you to vote for a candidate are examples. Thus, communication, as an experience designed by others, can affect opinions, as advertisers and political campaigners know so well. This premise is basic to much of what public relations practitioners do.

Persuasive messages are often not as direct and overt as the hard-sell advertisement or the straightforward campaign appeal. Indirect approaches may exert even stronger influences. They may, for instance, express approval or disapproval of particular people or stands on issues through persons we admire, suggesting that we ought to share the opinion because of our admiration for the person expressing it. The celebrity's testimonial or product endorsement in advertising is a prime example of this approach.

OPINION LEADERS. Within a formal group, leaders are selected to help group activity. The civic organization and the social club elect officers, for instance.

But leaders also emerge in an informal group—co-workers who eat lunch together, students who attend many of the same classes, residents of a neighborhood. The leaders are those whose thoughts come to be respected most by the others. Their reactions get attention in the various situations the group faces. The formal or informal leadership role also may confer on these people the role of "opinion leader."

This often happens in civic affairs. Anyone who wants to win community backing for a project seeks the approval of civic and social leaders, thinking that many in the community will tend to share these opinion leaders' views.

From such human interaction, sociologists have evolved the concepts of the opinion leader and peer influence. Communications scholars have also developed a related "two-step" or, more exactly, a "multistep flow" theory of communication and attitude influence that is especially helpful in understanding how attempts to communicate and influence through the mass media often work in practice. It can also be applied to a chain of non-media communication.

The multistep flow theory suggests that many people are affected indirectly rather than directly by information and persuasion messages transmitted by newspapers, magazines, and broadcasting stations. Even if people receive the messages directly from the media, by reading newspapers and watching television, the messages do not fully register or take effect. The messages do have impact, however, when the readers and viewers hear what their opinion leaders have to say about the messages. Opinion leaders may repeat the messages with their approval or disapproval; then the others are affected. Or opinion leaders may reshape the message so that it means more to others; until then, those others paid little heed to it, neither accepting or rejecting it.

Sometimes the mass media message does not reach members of a group at all. They may not read newspapers regularly or carefully. They may watch television but not newscasts, or they may watch newscasts inattentively. Opinion leaders, however, do receive the media message. Typically, they are a heavier consumer of mass media messages.

In the next step in the flow, the opinion leader gives others their first real knowledge of an event or their first report on an issue. If the report is colored by the opinion leader's approval or disapproval, as it usually is, it can be highly influential.

Even when people form opinions on the basis of direct communication through the mass media, they will ordinarily modify those opinions when they discuss them with families, friends, co-workers, neighbors, fellow club members, etc. The need for belonging, for getting along with others, exerts strong influence here. The pressure to conform is real, and it is not always deserving of scorn.

AGENDA SETTING. In recent years, the influence of the mass media on public opinion has been examined from the aspect of message choice rather than content. This approach considers the power that the media (particularly the news media) have in determining what people will consider the important questions and issues of the day. In other words, some scholars suggest that by giving or withholding coverage of events, the news media can "set the agenda" for public discussion.

If television, for example, preempts regular programming to cover a presidential primary election in tiny New Hampshire, it is saying this election is highly significant and worthy of everyone's attention. By implication, it may be telling voters throughout the country to take seriously the candidate who gets the most votes in a state with a tiny fraction of the country's voting population. The supportive or non-supportive effect such agenda setting had on candidates like Gary Hart, John Glenn, Walter Mondale, Jimmy Carter, and Edmund Muskie has alarmed many.

Negative agenda setting can be just as significant. Compare the news coverage of Vietnam before American forces withdrew in the early 1970s with coverage afterward. Compare the attention the media gave Iran while Americans were hostages there with coverage immediately afterward. Right after the Americans left, it was almost as if Vietnam and Iran had vanished. By implication, this noncoverage could be saying quite forcefully that these countries are no longer important.

OPINION MEASUREMENT. Along with knowing as much as possible about how attitudes and opinions are formed and what some of the significant influences on formation are, a public relations practitioner should know how to discover what pertinent attitudes and opinions are on issues relating to public relations success. The practitioner will also want to know how widespread an opinion is and, if possible, how firmly it is held. Obtaining this kind of information must precede the planning of any major public relations program.

Opinion research can be informal or quite complex. Practitioners may sometimes neglect opinion research with the excuse that "we can't afford all the expense of a high-powered survey, with all that computer involvement and such." It is important to remember that it can be informal—talking to people about their feelings toward the company or organization, undertaking the observation research discussed earlier.

That old stand-by, the employee suggestion box, is also an informal, inexpensive means for getting opinions, especially where employees are regularly encouraged to use it and their suggestions get sympathetic attention.

Telephone calls and letters are another informal gauge of opinion. They may not represent the opinions of an entire public with pinpoint accuracy, but they certainly indicate what some members of that public think. Often a bit of unstructured feedback that comes in the mail can alert a practitioner to a situation that can be corrected before it gets out of hand, if the practitioner is wise enough to read it and take it seriously.

Conversations or debriefings involving employees or agents who come into headquarters from distant facilities or branches are also a valuable means for gauging opinion. The messages may be secondhand and the messenger may be personally involved, but the information can be much better than total ignorance.

Often it is clear that informal procedures are inadequate, however. Let's say many people are involved in a particular matter, and the issues are highly sensitive so accuracy is critical in gauging opinion. A more formal approach to opinion measurement is called for. A carefully planned and administered set of questions is required to elicit specific information, and a carefully selected sample must be obtained if those whose opinions are sought constitute a group so large that each member cannot be questioned.

Sometimes public relations practitioners and others get so close to an opinion survey they do not appreciate the effects that can be produced by the way a questionnaire is administered. They might borrow a bit of wisdom from those who have studied student evaluations of courses and faculty members in colleges and universities. These people seem to agree on two points: (1) students generally are aware of how they are doing in a course (what grade they are going to get); and (2) students tend to be kind—even generous—in evaluating instructors unless they have developed a real antipathy toward an individual professor. This, researchers conclude, indicates that a course evaluation conducted soon after a very difficult test that many students unexpectedly did poorly on may bring quite different responses compared to one administered before that test.

Public relations people have to consider time and setting, too, when they decide to get into formal opinion measurement. Will employees' responses to questions about their physical working conditions be affected if they are surveyed soon after they receive a substantial pay raise? Or right after they are compelled to give up a cherished fringe benefit? And if they are interviewed individually, will the employees be as candid with a supervisor as with an outside interviewer?

TAKING THE PROPER STEPS. To avoid pitfalls in formal assessments of opinion, public relations practitioners have to follow procedures that have been developed and refined through years of study and experience.

Before discussing these steps we would like to emphasize that formal opinion measurement, if it is to be worthwhile, has to be appreciated as something more than getting a lot of people to talk about what they think of a business or organization. If it is to be useful and worth the time and effort it entails, PR practitioners must be confident that it is valid. That is, if 65 percent of the responses to a question are "Yes," practitioners must be able to feel certain that: (1) 65 percent of the people who actually responded to the survey did in fact answer "Yes," and (2) close to 65 percent of the entire population represented by the sample would also respond "Yes."

Furthermore, practitioners must be sure of the reliability of the survey. They must be confident that the questions are clear, unambiguous, and precise.

Now, examine each of the steps of formal assessment of opinion.

1. *Decide exactly what you want to find out and from whom.* This first step seems so obvious, but there is a big difference between wanting to find out something and finding out exactly what you need to know. When this step is not thought through carefully, practitioners have ruefully recognized the difference when their results were in and it was too late to make changes.

Say a corporation is interested in staggering work hours for some reason (to help employees cope with the overburdened public transportation system, ease the crowding in company parking lots, or save energy). That corporation wants to know how acceptable such a system would be. Without widespread cooperation, any staggered hours system could result in rampant tardiness, absenteeism, and resentment that is reflected in on-the-job performance.

There will be a world of difference between putting a form into the employee publication asking for a yes or no response to "Would you be in favor of a system of staggered working hours?" and a valid, reliable survey.

Consider these aspects: What exactly does "a system of staggered hours" mean to an employee? How will it affect this particular employee? What will her hours be under the new system? How will it affect the car pool, getting the children to school, having someone at home when the children return, making the weekly bowling or volunteer work schedule? How will it affect this employee's coordination with other departments that may be on a different schedule? What other employment and personal relationships will be affected? Until staggered hours is spelled out so that the employee can consider all these factors, a yes/no response is virtually meaningless.

Next, a public relations person would have to consider whether all employees actually would be involved in rescheduling work hours. Some positions that are staffed 24 hours by three shifts might not be included in the new schedule as a practical matter. Some levels of staff may not have regular eight-hour shifts assigned; others might not be involved because of location, etc. Therefore, including all workers in the survey would make results misleading.

2. *Determine the most effective and practical method for obtaining that information.* In the previous example, use of a form in the employee publication might be a quick and apparently economical way to survey opinion, but response might be so slight that the survey is ineffective.

Assuming all the particulars of the staggered scheduling were provided so that employees could make an informed response, there is no guarantee they all would respond. In fact, experience provides a virtual guarantee that many (perhaps up to 95 percent) will not respond. Any sort of voluntary response survey such as this faces the same problem.

What you want to find out, how important that information is, and your resources (time, money, personnel) should determine how you go about gauging opinion. If you have very little money and need only a general, informal sense of existing opinion, the form in the employee publication may suffice. If you need results quickly, a telephone survey will produce responses faster than a publication, mailed survey, or a personally administered questionnaire. But if you want respondents to spend at least 20 minutes providing in-depth answers, better not try to use the telephone or a mailed questionnaire. The personally administered survey may be necessary.

Similarly, if you want information from key people only, because they have the answers you need, the personal interview is most appropriate, assuming your respondents can be located and contacted individually. But if you want to test for responses after an event has occurred or a public relations campaign has been conducted, you might use a panel approach, selecting a group whose members agree to be surveyed beforehand and again afterward to check for effects. Market research frequently uses this technique in testing for product acceptability. Panelists may be interviewed about their tastes and preferences, then given one or more new products, and later reinterviewed to see if the new products affected their preferences.

In making decisions on the most effective and practical method for surveying opinion, the public relations practitioner should be guided by what other researchers have found:

• *Telephone interviews are less expensive and faster than face-to-face interviews.* Response is high. It is often easier to get the people you need as respondents by telephone than by personal visit. However, studies indicate respondents may tend to be less straightforward with a telephone interview than with an interviewer they are looking in the eye.

• *Mailed surveys are usually less expensive than telephone surveys.* But their response rates are low. Depending upon which study you read, the expected percentage of return on mailed surveys ranges between 5–25 percent. If the survey is mailed to people deeply involved in the subject or to a small group of highly motivated persons returns can be much greater.

Return rates are also increased by (1) simplifying the response form so that it does not require a lot of time and effort; (2) reducing the length of the questionnaire; (3) using response forms that can be answered easily by checking or circling choices, thus avoiding open-ended questions that require written answers; (4) writing a persuasive cover letter to accompany the questionnaire; (5) offering a reward for responding (a pen, pocket atlas, note pad, etc.); and (6) providing return postage.

Hearing from people who are more motivated and involved than the average person, as the practitioner who uses the mail questionnaire will, may be advantageous. Such people tend to be more influential than the average person. But their responses may not be typical and may overrepresent their segment of the entire population or universe being surveyed. Well-organized and methodical people are generally overrepresented in all self-return or voluntary surveys, mailed or not.

• *Personal interviews conducted by trained and qualified interviewers tend to have great reliability.* They are the best means for obtaining in-depth responses, and they may be the most practical means when particular respondents or types of respondents must be contacted to fill a sample.

But personal interviews are expensive. If a skilled interviewer is paid $10 an hour, has to travel from respondent to respondent, spends time with amenities before and after administering the questionnaire, and is compensated for preliminary processing of responses, the cost of 100 interviews is substantial.

In addition to cost, personal interviews are open to interviewer bias. The raised eyebrow, look of amusement, or frown can cue respondents to the interviewer's reaction to their answers. Even the apparent disparity between the economic and social standing or age of the interviewer and the interviewee can affect responses.

3. *If sampling is necessary, determine the procedure for selecting individual respondents.* Cost and time are again factors that lead practitioners to survey sample groups rather than the entire population whose views they want to learn. The number of persons in the population may make anything but sampling impractical too.

The concept behind sampling is that some members of a group or public, if selected properly, can provide a fairly good indication of how the entire group or public thinks or reacts. By finding how members of the sample respond, the practitioner has a usable measurement of how members of the entire population would respond.

Samples are formed in several ways. One major distinction is made between *accidental* and *purposive* samples.

Accidental samples are made up of individuals who are questioned or selected simply because they happen to be somewhere or to have done something at a particular time. A common example of the accidental sample is people emerging from a polling place on election day. They are questioned about their choices because they constitute a sample of those who voted. In no way have they been identified or selected ahead of time.

In recent years, however, television networks and other media have conducted purposive sampling of voters at polling places to analyze group support of candidates. The purposive sample is one in which respondents have been predesignated on the basis of some plan or rationale that suggests the particular respondents ought to be representative of segments of the total population. For example, CBS's interviewers might look for members of labor unions, Hispanics, or women who are not employed outside their homes among the persons selected for the exit polls conducted at voting places on election day. Someone will have decided that the labor union, Hispanic, and women's vote is significant in the balloting at that location.

Purposive sampling is usually divided into *probability* or *random* sampling and *quota* sampling.

Probability sampling is designed to make sure that every person in the entire population has an equal or at least a statistically known chance of being selected as a respondent. Quota sampling seeks out persons who have certain characteristics which are important aspects of many people in the entire population; the quota sample will select a number of people with these characteristics proportionate to the frequency the characteristic is found in the total population. For example, if census data indicate that the residents of an urban area are 75 percent white, 75 percent of the members of the quota sample will be white. If 32 percent of the population is made up of hourly wage earners, 32 percent of the sample must also be made up of hourly wage earners.

The approach in probability sampling differs radically. At its most elementary level, probability sampling begins with a list of all the persons in the population, say 10,000. The names of the individuals on the list must be arranged in an arbitrary or uncontrolled order by the researcher. Alphabetical order is a common form of arbitrary or uncontrolled order.

Next, the size of the sample is decided. Time and money are factors that play a role in determining size. How many people can be reached in time to tabulate the responses by the date we need to use the results? How many interviewers can we afford to engage, and how many interviews can we expect them to conduct before the results must be compiled? What funds are available for printing the questionnaires? For tabulating results? For running the cross tabulations needed?

If we decide we can do 200 interviews among the 10,000 persons in our population, then we will select each 50th name on our uncontrolled list or make our selection using the random numbers.

Validity will be a major consideration in our probability sampling. In somewhat oversimplified terms, the larger a probability or random sample is, the smaller the standard statistical margin of error there will be in the results. Mathematical formulas, based on experience and experiment, are used to calculate the *confidence level* and *standard error* percentage in survey results.

For instance, statisticians say a sample of 100 persons will have a standard error range of ±10 percent, with a confidence level of 95 percent. At a 50 percent confidence level, the probable error range would be ±3 percent. In layman's terms this means, in the first instance, you could expect that 95 times out of 100 your results with a sample of 100 would be within 10 percent of the results you would obtain by surveying the entire population from which the sample is drawn. In the second instance, it means that 50 percent of the time, your results with a sample of 100 would be just 3 percent above or below the results obtainable from the entire population.

If you increased your sample five times to 500, the standard error range would be ±4 percent; at a 50 percent confidence level, it would be ±2 percent. This shows that a large increase in the size of the sample will not produce a proportionate decrease in the standard error. It is because of this statistical phenomenon that national probability or random surveys can use samples of 1500 to 3000 respondents and obtain results that would not vary greatly if much larger samples were employed.

At a more sophisticated level, probability sampling begins with the use of *random numbers* rather than starting off by selecting every 50th or every ____nth name on a list. The random numbers are compiled on the basis of having no sequential relationship with each other. Today, statisticians use computers to compose tables of such random numbers. The numbers can then be used to select each respondent, or they can be used simply to start the process of selection. In the latter case, the additional selections follow an interval or every ____nth name process. The object is always to assure that the sample is truly random, that each individual in the population has an equal or statistically known chance of being selected as part of the sample.

Compared to probability sampling, quota sampling is generally conceded to be more open to biasing or skewing. It is based on a principle that is extremely difficult to achieve: the selection of respondents whose personal backgrounds and characteristics correspond proportionately to those of persons in the total population in every respect that influences opinion formation.

Difficulties inevitably arise in selecting sample respondents within the population. Years of study and experimentation have provided a list of some of the most important characteristics or demographics (age, sex, place of residence, education, economic status, religion, ethnic origin, political affiliation, etc.) that appear to relate to opinion formation. On the issues in which public relations people will be interested, the characteristics that relate to opinion formation may be tied more to other characteristics or factors, job status, work experience, etc. If these can be identified with certainty, quota profiles can be established.

National survey organizations, particularly when they take polls on public issues and political questions affecting the entire country, use a combination of probability and quota or *area* sampling as a matter of practical necessity. They will select geographic areas on a quota basis, choosing areas that have the significant characteristics of part of the general population. Then within those selected areas, they conduct probability sampling. Their experience over half a century has enabled them to make statistical adjustments and compensations that appear to make their final samples representative.

Most public relations practitioners will not be dealing with national samples. Then they can use some probability sampling procedure that produces usable results if all the prerequisites regarding the clear determination of objectives, careful formulation of questions, neutral administration of questionnaires, etc., are heeded. Practitioners must keep reminding themselves that unreliable or misleading information is dangerous, and that surveys are never a fully satisfactory substitute for first-hand contacts and on-site observation.

4. *Prepare a survey instrument suitable to your goals, respondents, and method of administration.*

5. *Pretest the questionnaire.* These two steps are closely related. In drafting a survey instrument or questionnaire, the practitioner's focus must obviously be to obtain as fully and clearly as possible the information that is the goal of the research. That information should be collected in a form that will make it easy to analyze and digest. Questions should be composed to suit the way they will be asked in a personal interview, individually administered questionnaire, mailed survey, etc.

It is always wise to start this phase by investigating to see if research seeking similar information has been undertaken previously and if its results have been reported. Social scientists sometimes refer to this as conducting a search of the literature, meaning the researcher tries to find out, through published articles and books, what other surveys have sought and what they have found.

This entails work in the library, where the PR practitioner's guide should always be: "Make friends with your reference librarian." Every casual library user will know how to locate books by author, title, or subject matter in the standard card catalog indexes. And most users should be aware of the special indexes of periodicals that avoid the overwhelming job of paging through endless issues of hundreds of individual publications. PR practitioners should be particularly aware of the indexes that will be most helpful to them (the *Humanities Index* and the *Social Sciences Index* in particular).

In addition, PR people should be aware of the periodicals that serve their profession and are therefore more likely than other publications to carry the type of reports they are interested in when planning a research project. These include *Public Relations Journal, Public Relations Quarterly,* and *Communication World. Public Opinion* and *Public Opinion Quarterly* report broadly on opinion research and issues. Additional indexes that may be helpful for the PR researcher include the *Business Periodicals Index* and the *Public Affairs Information Service Index.* For popular periodicals, there is the *Reader's Guide to Periodical Literature.* Also helpful are the *Humanities Index* and the *New York Times Index.* But to zero in on particular data and to save time, that friendly research librarian should always be consulted.

If practitioners would like to compare results of their surveys with previous research, it is important to use the same or very similar questions. Additional questions can be asked to try to obtain the distinctive information they may be seeking as well.

Sometimes the researchers who conducted the earlier study are candid in mentioning the problems they encountered with their particular questions and the shortcomings in their results attributable to question wording or sequence. Then the PR practitioner knows this is a model not to follow.

In all circumstances, the form of the questions should relate to the number of people to be surveyed. Open-ended questions, which permit the person questioned to give an individualized response not suggested by a list of alternatives, require much more time to answer. The responses may be difficult to tabulate because they require so many categories. On the other hand, open-ended questions can give more spontaneous and uncontrolled response. Their answers may be more truly informative than those to closed questions. When not administered individually, however, open-ended questions may get hurried, cryptic answers. They may also be skipped over or thrown away by busy people.

Closed or "direct response" questions ask the respondent to check yes or no, agree or disagree, or some other form of alternative answer. These questions may appeal to respondents because they can be answered quickly. Such questions may also be entirely adequate for measuring the opinions that are important. If what the practitioner wants to know is whether a wholesaler thinks it gets prompt service on orders placed with the practitioner's firm, a simple yes/no response may suffice.

If the question is not so straightforward, a multiple-choice response may be appropriate. The chief problem with multiple-choice questions is offering a wide enough spread of alternatives. If you ask respondents whether your service is (1) superlative, (2) excellent, (3) very good, or (4) fine, you may think responses show you are doing a great job. But they really tell you practically nothing because some obvious alternatives have been omitted. That is why so many multiple-choice questions use "none of the above," "all of the above," and "other" alternatives.

To gauge the strength of an attitude or opinion, questions asking for a continuum or scale response may be used. Statements are made, and the respondents are asked whether they (1) agree strongly, (2) agree, (3) are undecided or neutral, (4) disagree, or (5) disagree strongly. Sometimes numerical values are substituted for the descriptive words. "On a scale of 1 to 10, with 10 being 'best,' please rate the following. . . ."

Another approach employs what is widely referred to as a *semantic differential* technique. This presents respondents with word choices to describe their feelings and reactions. For example, respondents might be asked to indicate which word or phrase describes how they feel about current Social Security payments. The list might have "totally inadequate" at one extreme and "excessive" or "much too high" on the other, with "adequate" or "just about right" at the center of the semantic scale. The challenge with this approach is to select appropriate and sufficient alternatives.

Often similar questions are asked at different points in a questionnaire to test the consistency of responses. Again, the challenge is to find appropriate synonyms so that the questions truly reinforce each other and do not end up really asking different things. These similar questions are referred to as *clusters*. When the answers are in, responses are compared. If the answers consistently reflect an identifiable attitude or choice, this indicates the cluster is reliable. If the answers appear to be inconsistent, there is an indication of undecidedness, perhaps misunderstanding of some of the questions or issues, or faulty wording of the questions.

To make sure that questions are not faulty and that a survey will actually draw out the information a PR practitioner wants it to, pretesting is standard procedure. The questionnaire is tried out on people whose knowledge and background are similar to those of the ultimate respondents. If people in this pretest do not understand or simply misunderstand some questions, the public relations person goes back to the drawing board. Those questions must be rewritten to clarify their meaning and the response they seek.

People in the Gallup organization tell of a question they once had to throw out. It asked respondents, "Do you own stock?" They found that a disproportionately high number of farmers and ranchers in the Midwest and Plains states were answering "Yes." Say "stock" to a farmer or rancher and the word means livestock (cattle, sheep, hogs, horses) what else? What the Gallup people wanted to know about was the ownership of stock shares in corporations. Their revised question asked, "Do you own securities—like stocks and bonds issued by a business corporation?"

Open or undefined terms like "often," "many," "large," and "important" should be avoided in wording questions because they invite very subjective and widely differing interpretations. It may be a "great" game if your team wins, but that same game is "terrible" to the losers. "How was the game?" is a judgment question, open to highly individualized responses that may be impossible to tabulate.

The leading question is another danger. It is the type of question that leads respondents to a particular response. It suggests they are expected to answer in a certain way. It blocks an unprompted, candid response. Between "You've never been convicted of a felony, have you?" and "Have you ever been convicted of a felony?" it is obvious which is the leading question, is it not? (And yes, that was a leading question too!)

By using weighted or loaded words, a question can be leading even if the form of the question is not obviously directive. "Do you favor a limited period of public service by our young people to make it clear to nations that threaten our very way of life that we are not craven cowards?" might browbeat just a bit. (Note that the weighting can be positive, negative, or both.)

An introduction to a question or set of questions, if one is used, should be truly an explanation, not a subtle suggestion that can influence responses. A university recently included the following item in a survey of alumni: "A university's impact is measured not only by the business and professional achievements of its alumni, but their commitment to civic, church and community programs. Please list the programs and organizations in which you have been active." This was followed by four blank lines that ran the full width of the page. As a typical alumnus respondent, would you feel that your alma mater expected a pretty impressive list from you, even if you have to stretch your record just a bit? (Incidentally, there was but a single blank line on the survey form after the question, "What course or courses benefited you the most?" What does that suggest?)

Careful pretesting should uncover such faults and weaknesses. It should involve not only an analysis of responses but interviews with the pretest respondents to find out whether they felt any questions were leading questions, whether they had a sense of what the question drafter wanted to get in the responses, etc.

6. *Administer the survey as efficiently and neutrally as possible to assure unbiased responses.* To be efficient, a survey must be designed to produce the desired effect with a minimum of expense and effort. Following the prescribed steps, practitioners will have determined their desired product and the means to attain it. Now it is a matter of following through.

If a mail survey has been selected, measures promoting a high rate of response must be taken. If telephone interviews are to be used, interviewers must be carefully instructed regarding courtesy and objectivity. If personally administered questionnaires are planned, the interviewers will be further instructed regarding objectivity; not even facial expression should be allowed to indicate the interviewer's reaction to responses. In addition, with the telephone and face-to-face interviews, the interviewers will have to be carefully directed regarding the selection of respondents. If a selected telephone number does not answer, the interviewer must know when and how to substitute another number. The personal interviewer must likewise have a precise formula for identifying primary and secondary respondents.

7. *Tabulate results to make them as informative and useful as possible.* As discussed in step 4, PR practitioners should plan a questionnaire form that will facilitate tabulation. Since more and more surveys are

being tabulated with computer assistance today, it is common sense to confer with the computer people when putting a questionnaire together. This can make tabulation faster and less expensive. In addition, it can insure that the cross tabulations that PR people may want to make to check for variables can be done and done efficiently. For instance, a practitioner may want to know how length of employment related to employees' responses to staggered working hours or if there was a significant difference between men's and women's responses.

8. *Evaluate not only the results but the entire procedure.* Tabulated responses need study and discussion. Practitioners must be able to decide what they mean. The critical question is: What do the data tell us? And a second, often painful question must follow: Is this what we wanted to know or did we miss the mark?

Even if the research has successfully provided the information sought, practitioners should ask: Could we have done better? Are there ways we could have obtained more information without appreciably more effort? Specifically, can we tell now that some of our questions could have been improved? Are we satisfied that our sampling really covered the population we are interested in?" If the survey was somehow off target, if the questions could have been better, or if sampling had some failings, these weaknesses should be identified and recorded. A report should note the gaps and failings as well as the successes of the project.

And that record should not be buried deep in the files where it will never be found; it should be readily available for next time. Experience has to be recalled to be instructive.

9. *If the results are usable, use them.* Research should provide new information, but it is valuable only if it is used. Even if it tells practitioners that a current program is so successful that it does not need any changes whatsoever, which is highly unlikely, at least they can use the information to assure that the program continues in its present form. More likely, even favorable responses will include information that indicates the successful program can be fine tuned. Using that information means doing the fine tuning!

Some of the saddest conclusions to public relations projects are written by practitioners who say, "Well, it looks as if in general we're doing okay in this area. Let's get on to something else now." Or, "It seems we've got a lot of unhappiness out there, but we don't have the time or staff to do what ought to be done to correct the situation. We'll just have to forget about it." Reactions like that mean the research has been wasted. Why bother to learn something if you have already made up your mind you cannot, or will not, do anything about it?

The data should not be buried if top management is going to be dissatisfied with research results either. Management has a need and a right to know about those unfavorable responses. They should be presented thoughtfully and tactfully, of course, to avoid an emotionally defensive reaction. Practitioners should get used to saying, "We may have a problem here. . . ." They will be wise, too, to approach their chief executive officer with some practical remedies along with the bad news. But they must inform that CEO.

A brief reprise: Public relations research must never end.

A successful survey of attitudes, a comprehensive communications audit, or a careful monitoring of staff performance are all laurels the successful practitioner cannot rest on. People and the situations they create change; survey data become outdated.

Particularly when measures are taken to improve a situation, follow-up research is important. If a survey showed employees unhappy with lighting before a new system was installed, it is neither reasonable nor wise to assume that the change automatically resolved the problem. Do follow-up research by observation or survey. If the results are positive, do not forget to do more research after the "honeymoon effect" following the change has worn off!

Summary

You do not have to be an aviator to know what the expression "flying blind" means. Have you ever driven on a highway in dense fog? It is a dangerous and scary situation.

Yet public relations programs are sometimes flown blind. They are undertaken without sufficient effort to know the history, the people, the problems and the issues they will be running up against. Crashes result, with loss of time, effort, and sometimes credibility and confidence instead of loss of life and limb. But the losses are just as real.

Aircraft pilots can use radar and charts and weather reports to overcome heavy weather and low visibility. Public relations practitioners must use research.

Gathering information takes various forms. It ranges from the essential observation and monitoring of performance and careful identifying of publics to the more complex ascertaining of opinions and attitudes.

In undertaking opinion research, practitioners can benefit from the work of social scientists who have been working in this area for generations. The key, of course, is to follow the necessary steps, beginning with a clear determination of exactly what information is sought and from whom. Then the proper methods can be selected logically and appropriately. The process does not end until results and procedures have been critically evaluated, and those results have been put to use.

Exercises

1. In the example of incomplete alternatives for a multiple-choice question (see page 101), provide a proper spread of possible responses to guarantee usable results.

2. Select one of the publics of the institution you attend or of the employer for whom you work. Determine what opinions members of that public have that should be known by the administration or management. Then decide what the best means is for discovering those opinions. What are your reasons for your decision?

3. As a follow-up to Exercise 2, compose a list of questions that would elicit opinions of the members of that public. Check your questions for leading questions, weighted words, and ambiguous terms.

4. If you were to set up a quota sample of the students at your college or of the employees where you work, with what characteristics or demographics would you structure your sample? Why? Would those characteristics have any relation to the objective of your survey? Explain.

Case study

In March, 1981, President Ronald Reagan was wounded in an assassination attempt. The NCAA basketball championship game was scheduled for that evening. NBC had an exclusive contract for televising the game. The Academy Awards presentation was also scheduled on CBS.

The Academy Awards program was postponed and televised when it was held. The basketball game was played and televised as scheduled. The motion picture industry was widely praised for its decision to postpone the awards program; the NCAA was widely criticized for not postponing the game. A number of well-known sportswriters were among the most outspoken critics.

Turn back the clock. It is the day of the attempted assassination, and the big game is scheduled just seven hours after news of the shooting is first reported. Imagine you are the one person who will make the decision on whether the championship game will be postponed, and you want to decide on the basis of public opinion.

Given the time element, is there any way you can gauge public opinion among the sports fan public? Or are you trapped in one of those groping-in-the-dark situations? Does anything in this chapter offer an alternative to that?

Suggested readings

Baer, Daniel H. "Communication Audit: Getting Full Measure." *Public Relations Journal,* July 1979.

DeMaio, Theresa J. "Refusals: Who, Where, and Why." *Public Opinion Quarterly,* Summer 1980.

Ewing, Raymond P. "Evaluating Issues Management." *Public Relations Journal,* June 1980.

Gallup, George H. *The Sophisticated Poll Watcher's Guide.* Princeton, N.J.: Princeton Univ. Press, 1976.

Holsti, Ole R., and James N. Rosenau. "Does Where You Stand Depend on When You Were Born?" *Public Opinion Quarterly,* Spring 1980.

Jones, Wesley H. "Generalizing Mail Survey Inducement Methods." *Public Opinion Quarterly,* Spring 1979.

Jordan, Lawrence A., Alfred C. Marcus, and Leo G. Reeder. "Response Styles in Telephone and Household Interviewing." *Public Opinion Quarterly,* Summer 1980.

Kennedy, Laurel A. "How to Use Research to Prevent a Takeover." *Public Relations Journal,* May 1985.

Lindeman, Walter R. "Hunches No Longer Suffice." *Public Relations Journal,* June 1980.

Monroe, Alan D. *Public Opinion in America.* New York: Dodd, Mead & Co., Inc., 1975.

Presser, Stanley, and Howard Schuman. "The Measurement of a Middle Position in Attitude Surveys." *Public Opinion Quarterly,* Spring 1980.

Rivers, William. *Finding Facts.* Englewood Cliffs, N.J.: Prentice-Hall, 1975.

Robinson, Edward J. *Public Relations and Survey Research.* New York: Meredith Corp., 1969.

Smith, David L. "How to Buy Research Services." *Public Relations Journal,* June 1980.

Strenski, James B. "Techniques for Measuring Public Relations Effectiveness." *Public Relations Quarterly,* Spring 1982.

Wheeler, Michael. *Lies, Damn Lies and Statistics: The Manipulation of Public Opinion in America.* New York: Liveright, 1976.

Wright, Donald K. "Some Ways to Measure Public Relations." *Public Relations Journal,* July 1979.

5 Internal publics

A saying that has become part of PR folklore advises us that public relations is "treating the public better than we treat our relations." That may be all too true; but if it is, it is a poor way to run the store. It is like the husband who tells his friend, "You know, when she fixes me a fine meal and wears that fancy dress, I love my wife so blamed much it's all I can do to keep from tellin' her." That husband is guilty of poor internal relations because, at the most intimate level, family members are internal publics.

At the organizational level, when working with the family—internal publics—we might make an arbitrary division into two categories: (1) people or publics outside the acknowledged formal decision-making structure; and (2) people or publics who are part of that structure.

The actual divisions are unimportant, even equivocal. The vital point is that all of the members of the internal "family" be recognized as significant internal publics. The organization needs their goodwill, understanding, and support.

Make no mistake, the organization will have some type of internal relations, some image, with all these publics. Whether that image is good or bad depends largely upon how these audiences perceive the organization, not necessarily how it really is. The larger the total internal audience, the more important is a well-conceived, well-managed internal relations program.

Every organization (manufacturing plant, school, government agency, hospital, private club, political party, church, or even army) has a formal chain of communication and an informal chain or grapevine. Everyone has attended meetings where the grapevine operated and a hidden agenda could be sensed.

The thrusts of presidents, mayors, and baseball managers, for example, have been blunted by aggressive, energetic activists, organized groups, and outspoken outfielders. Presidents Johnson and Nixon contended with antiwar activists within their administrations. Misunderstandings between Jimmy Carter and his brother made frequent

109

headlines, and White House staff shuffles have indicated internal trouble for the Reagan administration. During her initial term as mayor of Chicago, Jane Byrne had difficulty communicating with city employees and even members of her own party. Billy Martin, that many-times manager of the New York Yankees, lost the job once after a series of confrontations with Reggie Jackson, Yankee slugging star at the time.

Often the internal publics that caused the disruptions were outside the formal decision-making structure, but they controlled or influenced the destiny of the nation, a large city, and a major league ball club nonetheless. An open communication line to these internal audiences might have caused them to act differently. The complete story, told accurately and promptly to the internal publics, is a powerful management tool.

Nonsupervisory members of the informal communication chain may be either blue-collar or white-collar employees, students or parents of students, hospital employees or patients, small stockholders, or soldiers in the ranks. However, the informal chain includes supervisors and managers, faculty and administrators, medical and technical staff, consultants and contributing patrons, elders and church members. In each case, they are integral organization members, and the organization, knowingly or unknowingly, depends upon them to represent it formally and informally in innumerable ways.

As examples, the college student hired as a summer ranger may be the only U.S. Forest Service employee a camper ever sees; the lathe operator from the midnight shift may be the only representative of a manufacturing corporation a potential customer ever sees; Aunt Sadie may be the only family member with first-hand knowledge of County Hospital, and that came from a visit to the emergency ward after a traffic accident; and the corner bartender, a well-known link in the grapevine, may depend on student customers for his entire understanding of the neighboring college. Thus regardless of title, the ranger, bartender, student, and Aunt Sadie wield considerable influence in molding the public's understanding of an organization. The Forest Service, plant, hospital, and college need their goodwill, understanding, fairness, and accuracy as disseminators of information. Each is either part of the internal audience or depends upon it for information about the organization.

If the organization makes no effort to inform its internal publics or if that effort is unsuccessful in conveying a complete and accurate story, the internal audience will obtain a story from some other source. If it picks up distorted or inaccurate information or "conventional wisdom" about the organization, the organization can be severely damaged.

Without a sound internal relations program, the rumor mill works overtime, and everyone loses.

Lack of a sound internal relations program created serious problems for an independent midwestern university shortly after World War II. In rapid succession, the university dropped football as too expensive, loaned part of its meager endowment to another university (at the prevailing interest rate), and announced a modest fund-raising campaign to meet operating costs. The climax came when the borrowing college hired the university's popular and successful basketball coach, and critics complained, "—with our money too!"

In view of the loan and absence of a published financial report, alumni and friends were convinced the university had an ample endowment. The fund-raising campaign was cancelled. Football gone; basketball deemphasized; students demonstrated.

The university president resigned to return to the classroom and laboratory. His successor enlarged the public relations staff and opened the university's books. Once they understood the situation, students, faculty, and staff helped the new president "set the record straight." The next fund drive was a marked success.

Everyone wants to know the facts. If primary sources are silent, internal audiences will listen to a secondary source, any secondary source. They listen to rumors and the organization suffers.

Get the word out

START 'EM YOUNG

Most organizations begin the process of informing new members of their internal public when those individuals come aboard. Colleges and universities have orientation week for freshmen and their parents, businesses generally count on their personnel departments to welcome new employees, military organizations provide briefings to incoming recruits. Each recognizes the need for the individual to understand what is expected in the way of personal performance, what the organization expects, and what the individual can expect from the organization, and the working conditions that will prevail, including the individual's rights, benefits, and privileges.

In the case of the employee, working hours in the particular department are detailed, or the number is set for the units to be produced in a given time. Salary is stated, including withholding for Social Security, retirement, insurance, union dues, taxes, etc. Vacation policy and sick leave are explained, along with the dress code, parking arrangements, eating facilities, etc. The supervisor and fellow employees are introduced. In short, anything that will touch directly on the new employee's day-to-day work life is detailed. The employee is even told where and how to seek redress of grievances if the organization does not live up to its part of the work bargain. And later perhaps, the new employee is told about promotion policies.

The average new employee begins a job with a certain amount of trepidation mixed with enthusiasm. So the employee should know that the organization reacts favorably and encourages fresh thinking if it leads to a better, more efficient way of doing business. "You're coming in with a fresh outlook, Johnson. We occasionally have trouble seeing the problems because we grew up with the organization. So we look to others for new ways of doing things. If you have a suggestion, here's the way our program works to get that idea to someone who will give it solid consideration, and here are the benefits you can get from our suggestion program." All of these points are made through an effective internal information program early in the employee's career.

But that is not enough. No employee is an automaton.

WHAT DO THEY DO?

At this point, supposedly, Johnson knows what happens in the immediate vicinity of his desk or machine. But unless Johnson is a machine, production from the unit named Johnson may still be unsatisfactory. "Why was this specification written this way?" Johnson wonders. "Why does this bolt go in this hole?" In brief, the employee wants to know, "What am I doing and why?" "Why should I work myself into an early grave? Ever watch old Smitty float around? People like that don't do nothin'."

Management experts have learned that greater job satisfaction results from increased knowledge, and increased production, quantitatively and qualitatively, results from greater job satisfaction. So Johnson should learn where that specification or that bolt fits into the overall operation of the organization. After learning the goals and objectives of a specific job, the employee must see how they fit into the goals and objectives of the department. Finally Johnson must understand how the department fits into the total organization. For the utmost understanding, Johnson, on the assembly line or in the executive suite, should have a basic understanding of the role played by other departments, too, including what Smitty is actually doing and how that fits into the departmental and organizational goal. Through a well-developed internal relations program, the employee learns what the organization seeks to accomplish and how that goal will be reached.

Thus, through a sound internal relations program, Johnson learns the importance of the role he plays in maintaining these standards:

"We make the best one-cylinder, four-cycle gasoline engine in the industry at a competitive price. It is durable because its short stroke and high torque provide greater output at lower operating speed than any of our competitors' models. Higher standards, enforced by Smitty's inspection team, push us above industry standards."

Incoming freshmen, through a solid internal information program, learn what the institution expects:

"A greater percentage of our graduates are accepted by professional schools than those of any other institution in the state, and the percentage is rising. Our immediate goal is to record the top percentage in the three-state area. Our success is the result of a top-flight faculty and a hard-working student body. We expect more from you here because we have more to give. You will work harder than some of your high school classmates in other colleges, but you will get more out of it. Here's how our system developed. . . ."

New employees learn that they play a vital role in the company's continued success, even though the job is an unsung role in the computerized baggage-handling division:

"Our airline flies the best equipment in the world but so do our competitors. Our edge comes in service. For the past three years, our record tops the industry when it comes to getting our passengers together with their luggage at the end of a flight. That's important to the passengers, to our airline, and to you."

The internal relations program has as one of its goals the building of esprit among new employees: "You work for the best newspaper in the area. Our readers get the latest news, the finest syndicated features, complete sports and social reporting, and entertaining comics. Top professionals provide this, and you are as important as any of them. Our readers expect to receive our newspaper before they get a copy of a competing paper. And they assume the paper will be safe from the weather, delivered by a helpful, friendly carrier. That is you. No matter how good the newspaper, if the reader doesn't get it on time and in good shape, the work everyone else does is wasted. That's why you must be the best newspaper carrier in this town."

Regardless of the position, the employee learns through a good internal relations program that the job is important to the organization's success.

History as public relations

Knowing the organization's past can enhance the employee's sense of the present and make being part of the future important and a matter of individual pride. An awareness of the roots of the organization can add to job satisfaction and help the employee better understand and accept organizational decisions. It further develops the sense of belonging, especially if the employee learns the complete story, warts and all. The employee knows the traditions and names, and their significance. They are part of the total story.

Most organizations have a prepared history. It may range from a one-page mimeographed broadbrush treatment by public relations staff members to hardcover and well-illustrated comprehensive efforts, prepared under contract or by organization historians hired for the specific task. Industrial giants like General Motors, AT & T and Colt have full-time historical divisions. The military services, NASA, and the U.S. State Department are government agencies that employ historians.

Public relations bonuses accrue occasionally when a history produced at the direction of an organization sells well in the general book market. Examples include *Vision* by Harold Mansfield (Duell, Sloan & Pierce), a history of the Boeing Airplane Company; *The Story of the New York Times* by Meyer Berger (Simon & Schuster); a number of histories produced by and for various government agencies, and occasional well-written college and university histories.

The new employee frequently is provided an introduction to the organization's history as part of the entrance briefing. The format may be straight lecture with printed handouts, a motion picture, a slide lecture, exhibits, or a combination of media forms.

Again, presenting history is an integral part of welcoming the individual as a member of the company or organization. In addition to obvious on-the-job benefits, the employee who understands the organization's history is a better public relations representative, on a formal or informal basis. The interested grocery clerk, barber, pastor, or civic club member will learn a more complete and accurate story from that employee. And quite certainly, the story will be told by a more enthusiastic representative of the business or agency.

No longer a one-on-one game

From the viewpoint of a communicator or public relations practitioner, the best of all possible worlds is one in which the person with the message sits across the table from the individual with whom she wishes to communicate. The system worked fine in the days of the self-sufficient village and the independent fiefdom. But when the forerunners of Florsheim, Budweiser, and Browning began selling shoes, beer, and weapons beyond the village limits and even national boundaries, their need for improved communications increased at an alarming rate. Two people and a table no longer handled the chore.

The system failed in communicating with potential customers who no longer could get word of quality shoes from satisfied users in the thatched roof cottage next door. Face-to-face exchange was equally inadequate in communicating with the individual who made innersoles for shoes in a village on the far side of the mountain and never saw the home plant or Mr. Florsheim.

To the Sheriff of Nottingham, a bow made in Sherwood Forest might have been a big deal, but it did not impress William Tell over on the continent unless communication improved even faster than the growth of industry and expansion of trade.

FACE-TO-FACE COMMUNICATIONS

The closer we remain to the two-people-across-the-table approach, the more effective our communication will be. The receiver not only hears the message but can interpret the body language used by the sender or communicator, and the receiver can ask for explanations of fuzzy phrasings or blanks that remain in the transmission. But the larger and more complex an organization or business becomes, the more difficult it is to use this method of communication.

Many creative managers strive for an "open door" policy. They invite employees, to the extent possible, to come directly to them with problems, rumors, suggestions and, in some organizations, even with personal problems.

The program can become self-defeating, however; it can require more time than the busy manager can spare. One solution is to "layer" the open door policy. That is, top level executives can open their doors to first-line supervisors, who in turn institute an open door policy for their staff members, and those staff members have a similar relationship with individuals who report to them.

The open door policy is not outlined here as a panacea, but as one approach used by some businesses and organizations. If it is to have any measure of success, the manager using the program must listen carefully to each visitor, not only to what is said but what is meant. Success depends upon the degree of human understanding exercised by the manager. That manager must really listen and must act on what is learned.

Another method of increasing, even multiplying opportunities for the face-to-face approach is staff meetings. The military is a great proponent of this device though it is used by many businesses and organizations too. Such meetings disseminate information to those with a need to know; they are particularly useful in organizations where contact between units is infrequent. Staff meetings emphasizing a free exchange with limited control by the ranking executive are most successful. Such meetings are the most time-consuming, however.

Generally, items affecting the whole business or agency are placed on the agenda. Staff members present items from their areas arising since the last meeting and outline coming events of general interest. Ideally, such exchanges result in improved cooperation within the organization or institution, and avoid unpleasant surprises for the boss.

Carried to its logical conclusion, the technique results in top executives or staff members scheduling subsequent meetings within their divisions and departments, assuring that the last persons in the chain receive the information that may affect them.

Two difficulties immediately apparent in the use of staff meetings are: (1) unless highly structured (a problem in itself), the meetings are extremely time-consuming, especially in organizations or businesses that schedule them periodically rather than only on occasions when significant events make them desirable, and (2) passing precise information through a series of carriers can, and often does, result in error or distortion.

Briefings are a variation or extension of the face-to-face communication that was used before mass communication was possible. Briefings educate an audience quickly, accurately, and as painlessly as possible. The complexity of the briefing and the technology used today depend on the size and/or prestige of the audience. An informal, conversational style is effective if the briefing is for one or two people, "briefer" and audience in close proximity exchanging ideas and information. If the facilities are compact and at hand, a tour can be a valuable part of the briefing. Printed handouts, desk-top flip charts, and self-contained rear screen slide projectors to show charts, sketches, and photographs of products or sites that cannot be visited as part of the briefing are valuable aids.

As audience size increases, the briefing technique may become more complex, because there will be fewer opportunities for interchanges between the briefer and the members of the audience. Tours by large groups are unwieldly and less productive, so a comprehensive presentation is an efficient substitute. Furthermore, with larger audiences, the briefer can devote less attention to each member, so boredom or distraction can occur more easily.

The effectiveness of a briefing is measured by the accuracy and completeness of the message received by the audience. Thus, the most effective briefing employs the best available technology within a reasonable budget. An increasing number of businesses and organizations use videotape recordings and multimedia presentations in which a self-contained rear projection module is replaced by multiple projectors, dissolve units, one or more projection screens and, occasionally, a taped message. Small flip charts give way to larger charts or an overhead projector.

The briefing is a valuable tool to acquaint new internal publics with a business or organization; to educate visitors, ranging from casual tourists to VIPs; to update stockholders at the annual meeting; and to periodically update staff and employees using a "State of the Union" approach.

Flexibility in the briefings permits concentration on a single subject. For example, general contractors like Peter Kiewit Sons and Massman Construction conduct lunchbox sessions on safety. Their safety engineers conduct concise, informal briefings for small groups of employees during scheduled breaks. Because the subject is mutually beneficial to management and employees, few objections are raised regarding the infringement on personal time.

Another example of the use of briefings: A new top executive was assigned to a complex government office. Employees included many highly skilled people representing a wide diversity of duties (accountants, attorneys, engineers, writers, research scientists, etc.). Although impressed by the obvious professionalism represented on the staff, the executive was surprised by the lack of understanding among disciplines. Because employees in the laboratory did not understand the duties of those in the comptroller's office and vice versa, some employees tended to belittle the work of others. Map makers, for example, thought the management specialists were goofing off. The management specialists looked upon the laboratory unit as overstaffed and underutilized. In all likelihood, some were convinced that the new top executive was grossly overpaid.

The solution was "Brownbag Briefings." Each Monday during the scheduled lunch period, a special presentation was made by the head of a different department or office. Each department and office was restricted to half an hour, and programs began promptly at noon in the agency's main conference room. All employees were invited to bring their lunches to the briefings. The managers explained the duties of their units, the technical backgrounds of staff members, and the results expected. The briefers concluded by outlining how their unit's production fit into the overall goals and objectives of the office.

The first such briefing was conducted by the top executive himself. He explained his job and the duties of other employees in the executive office. This guaranteed a large opening audience, set the tone for succeeding briefings, and secured the cooperation of managers who were to follow.

The series continued until presentations had been made by each department and office. Programs ranged from a straight oral presentation that included questions and answers to screening of a videotape prepared by a local commercial television station as a special. Yet another in the series included an overview by the supervisor and shorter briefings by four assistants.

THE PRINTED WORD

The tyranny of the clock and sheer numbers of people involved may severely limit the opportunities for effective face-to-face communication between management and employee today, however. So a time-honored substitute is the written word, taking many forms—bulletin board to engraved watch. In each instance, the sender tells the receiver: "We care. You are important, and you have the right to know what's going on in this company," or "We appreciate the role you play in the health and life of our organization."

The oft-maligned bulletin board has survived the test of time and cultural changes. Cave paintings pre-date writing; they were "bulletin boards." The form has survived through cuneiform signing in ancient Babylonia and Egyptian hieroglyphics found in the Pyramids to the variety of signs displayed everywhere today, from air terminals to subway walls. In each case, the author had a message to deliver, found a high traffic area, and delivered the message as effectively as possible.

One key to successful bulletin boards is a high traffic area. A second is attracting attention, by limiting the number of displays, providing a distinctive display, or offering information that is consistently of high interest to the audience. They do draw attention; sometimes more than the bulletin board "keeper" every imagined.

In a large Omaha office, the public relations department developed a single-subject board, "The Employee of the Month," to help employees get acquainted. An indiscriminate collection of informal photographs was taken of employees on the job. The person to be honored was chosen from the photo stack, sometimes simply because the photo was atop the stack. After almost two years, the public relations staff was disenchanted and considered the project a waste of time and materials. After all, who cared?

Obviously one man did, the current Employee of the Month. He was a dour, unassuming, unflappable little man who worked quietly with no fanfare. A guy who seemingly did not care. Except once.

Shortly after the new photo went on display, the public relations director, quite coincidentally, was stuck after hours finishing a speech due the next morning. At last he struggled into his coat and started for the elevator. He turned the corner, stopped dead, quietly retraced his steps, reentered the office and stayed another 15 minutes. The building was not deserted. Not quite.

The unflappable honoree had waited until the building was empty, returned with his camera, and took photos of the Employee of the Month bulletin board at the elevator bank.

The public relations director tore up the memo he had written to the president suggesting the Employee of the Month board be replaced by a product display. Today the board has been repainted, color prints have replaced the black-and-white photos, and the honorees receive a congratulatory letter from the president. The public relations director and the top executive are convinced the bulletin boards do draw attention. Careful consideration is given each item before exhibiting it on an official bulletin board. Employees of the Month must earn the honor.

Memoranda and reading files are additional means of keeping employees informed. Three cautions should be observed with office memos: (1) like Christmas nuts, a few memos are palatable and interesting, but too many become a pain and the recipient swears off for the duration; (2) keep them short; (3) avoid bureaucratic gobbledygook. The recipient expects to read and understand memos rapidly. If that is impossible, the intended audience will "file this thing until later," and later never comes.

Many organizations circulate a reading file, a collection of correspondence originated by offices and departments within the business or organization. If any correspondence is of interest to other offices and departments, a copy is placed in this circulating file.

Although markedly inefficient because of the inevitable tendency of some person in the chain to ignore the "Do Not Delay" stamp, the reading file can "get the word to the troops." Correspondence to be included should be selected carefully. Tabbing everything for the file lessens effectiveness because the busy individual eventually tires of scanning reams of "Your request of the fourth complied with" and "This negative reply is in compliance with your March 14 letter." Some organizations go a step further by tabbing items in the reading file that have particular significance for specific individuals on the circulation list. If used properly, the reading file is another in a long list of devices that keep employees well informed on company or organization matters.

Summary

Every organization or business, small or large, has some type of public relations. An image exists. As far as the organization is concerned, the public has an impression that is never neutral. A great part of the credit, or blame, is the result of interactions with internal publics. If the internal publics are well informed and think well of the organization, their attitudes frequently are transmitted well beyond the confines of the organization itself. And the better their understanding, the more accurate the picture transmitted, both in the formal and informal contacts made outside the organization by the internal publics.

The process of informing the individual begins quite properly when that person becomes part of the organization's internal publics. The process continues throughout the individual's association with the firm or agency.

All available tools are used by today's organizations in communicating with their internal publics. Because the most direct communication is the most effective, the ultimate is a one-on-one relationship as typified by the open door policy employed in many organizations. However, size, distance, and numbers preclude exclusive reliance on this approach in all internal relations situations. The organization with a sound internal relations program uses a broad range of media to reach internal publics.

An understanding of and open communications with the many internal publics are indispensable if a sound public relations program is to be developed.

Exercises

1. Identify the various internal publics affiliated with the local Chamber of Commerce.

2. Outline points to be covered in briefing a newly hired employee of the Chamber. Outline a briefing for a newly enrolled member of the Chamber. Comment on the differences in subject matter covered.

3. Identify in detail the sources that could be used in researching a history of the Chamber of Commerce.

4. Interview a public relations staff member from a local business or organization that has a well-developed internal relations program. List the various groups that are considered internal publics and the various methods used to communicate with them. Describe any awards or special events established to recognize the internal publics.

5. Clip a Sunday edition of a metropolitan newspaper, selecting items that resulted from internal relations activities by businesses, agencies, or organizations.

Case study

Acme Industries manufactures a full line of pleasure boats and is located in Riverview, a city of 3000 population. Acme employs 500 persons, many of whom are from the surrounding farms and work for Acme on a seasonal basis. The company has succeeded because it produced a quality product at a competitive price.

The Jones family founded the company and managed it until recently. Family members are almost universally liked and respected in Riverview. Consequently, Acme's internal relations program has been an informal one. If employees had a gripe, personal problem, or suggestion, they went right to one of the Joneses at the plant, in the local supermarket, or on the street.

But the family sold the business to a corporation with headquarters in the state capital, 150 miles away. Problems have arisen. Production is off. Three major Acme dealers complained in writing about small irregularities in the finish and poorly fitted panels on recently received top-of-the-line Wide-World Cruisers.

Unfounded rumors circulating among employees include stories that no more seasonal employment will be permitted, that one of four assembly lines will be closed and a foreign import substituted for the popular Wave Tamer model, that workers will be moved to Riverview from other corporate plants, and even that the Acme plant will be relocated outside the state.

You are hired to develop the first formal internal relations program in Acme history.
- Determine program goals and explain the need for each.
- Outline a program that will attain these goals and explain how the various elements will assist in attaining the goals.
- Develop a program to introduce new employees to the company in a way which will minimize repetition of the current problem or similar problems.

Suggested readings

Burton, Paul. *Corporate Public Relations*. New York: Reinhold Publ. Corp., 1966.

Fenderson, Kendrick. "Telling Is Out, Dialogue Is In." *Public Relations Journal*, July 1979.

Leeds, Gerard G. "The Personal Touch." *Communicator's Journal*, July/October 1984.

Lubliner, Murray. "Why You Should Level with Your Employees." *Public Relations Journal*, July 1979.

Sigband, Norman B. "Face to Face." *Communicator's Journal*, May/June 1983.

Simpson, Eugene L. "Participating Employees Produce." *Communicator's Journal*, July/August 1983.

Walters, Kenneth D. "Your Employees' Right to Blow the Whistle." *Harvard Business Review* 52(1975):4.

6 Internal communications

As with all aspects of public relations, the essence of an effective internal relations program is acceptable performance. People within the organization have to do their jobs and do them well. They also have to be directed, encouraged, appreciated, and informed if this is to be accomplished. This requires an internal communications system in which messages are transmitted and received accurately, completely, and rapidly. The larger the organization, the more difficult and involved the task.

Thus, this vital communication is a single task in an establishment with a work force of only four or five persons. But if the organization grows into a chain of outlets with hundreds of employees, the difficulty of maintaining communication has grown exponentially.

Because most successful organizations today recognize the need to communicate accurately with their internal audiences, they avail themselves of the best and most modern communication tools within budget. Trained professionals are employed to develop the messages. The organization uses the printed word, displays, broadcasting, telecasting, multimedia presentations, speakers, whatever medium or combination will provide the best coverage of the internal audiences. And tools are selected that will provide accurate feedback from those audiences.

Employee publications

Employee publications remain the premiere method of getting out the word in most businesses, institutions, and organizations. Well-produced and well-managed publications are seen by a greater percentage of the internal audience and have higher readership than any other medium. Any organization beyond the simplest (the one with

124

a manager-owner and two or three employees) can benefit from some type of organizational publication.

Designed to keep employees informed, it does much more. Organizational information is passed along to many who may not read bulletin boards, or the interoffice memos, and to those excluded from the staff meetings. The internal publication also shows these people what the new chief executive officer looks like, describes his background, thoughts, and goals. It shows them the new product line and describes how it works, where it will be marketed, and who contributed to its development. It alerts them to the new plant hours, shift changes, and cafeteria menus. It announces the safety campaign and the company or organization's attitude toward the communitywide charity drive. But it does even more.

The internal audience looks to the employee publication for word of promotions, awards, retirements, and new hirings. It reads about people, its people. It learns whose son was graduated from college, whose daughter passed the bar exam, who bowled the high individual game, who builds doll houses and shoots skeet as hobbies. It learns that Smitty is the same John R. Smith who was an all-conference guard on State University's memorable Whirling Dervishes of two decades ago. It reads that Johnson has registered beagle pups for sale. And increasingly important, the internal audience learns the corporate viewpoint of public issues.

In short, employee publications tell the internal audience about the organization and about each other. The medium is as informative as the old party line, and much more accurate. It is as friendly as the clannish lunch bunch that meets every noon.

Some internal publications have developed as a natural outgrowth of the many information bulletins produced by personnel offices. But the most professional and successful are those designed and developed by the professionals in the public relations department. Many large corporations and organizations have a full-time staff assigned to their internal publications.

One of an editor's first tasks in many organizations is to assemble a willing, reliable force of volunteers to assist in gathering news from various departments and offices. Frequently this involves a solid selling job, since the correspondents will find news gathering an added duty, with their only repayment being personal satisfaction. However, some organizations recognize the extra work by issuing an occasional bonus or scheduling a social event to reward the in-house correspondents. Generally, however, stringers must be content with an occasional credit line in the publication and an infrequent pat on the back from a fellow worker.

PROFESSIONALISM

Consistently high quality is more than a matter of pride for an editor. Professionalism is a matter of survival. Whether the medium is a weekly church bulletin or a multiedition metropolitan daily newspaper, a publication rises or falls because of its quality. If the publication is to realize its goal of informing and entertaining its readers, the editor must provide good writing, tight editing, and quality production.

The institution circulating the publication has a great deal riding on the project. Frequently management depends on employees' receiving specific information vital to the future of the organization and the well-being of employees. If the internal publication is poorly done, many in the audience may fail to read or understand the message. So, many of the same rules that pertain to a daily newspaper govern an internal publication produced by a business or organization.

Grammar, punctuation, spelling, and syntax must be correct. Since journalistic writing style was developed to facilitate reading, that style is used almost universally in newspapers. It is also a plus for the employee publication. The essence of this writing style is the arrangement of facts in order of descending importance, making certain that all the obvious, logical questions about an event are answered, especially the questions asked by the famous Five Ws of journalism: Who? What? When? Where? Why? plus an H, How?

Be assured that the internal publication is designed to offer something more than a printed record of the chief executive's social calendar and the company bowling league scores. Therefore, factors that determine news value recognized by general circulation newspapers are equally applicable here. The difference is only one of degree. An event is newsworthy because one or more of the following factors is present:

1. *Timeliness.* Modern news media have taught their audiences to expect immediacy. When they learn through the media that an accident has occurred, those audiences almost expect to open the window and hear a collision. To an extent, timeliness is demanded of the company or organization publication as well. Although it may not publish as frequently as a newspaper, its readers expect it to provide the latest available information.

2. *Proximity.* This is the real forte of the employee publication.

Economic news, for example, is carried regularly by the mass media. But the employee publication can localize the story, explain how recent changes in the economy will affect the company or organization and its employees. The local newspaper may run a bare-bones treatment of management changes in the corporation, but the employee publication will present the story in detail. The employee publication can localize events of internal significance, the *New York Times* and CBS cannot.

3. *Significance.* The decision or event that affects many people is newsworthy. A fuel shortage, inflation, weather, national elections, wars, and major crop failures rank as large headlines. Within the company or organization, a strike, cutoff of a major market, a change in top management, destruction of the main assembly plant, or a new salary plan are of major interest to readers of the employee publication because of the significance of those events to them. These internal events are news.

4. *Magnitude.* Sheer size can determine the newsworthiness of a story. The largest sapphire, the most destructive tornado, the tallest basketball player, the longest-playing Broadway show arouse curiosity. Conversely, the smallest computer, the tiniest racing plane, and the lightest defensive tackle interest the reader too.

Each of these factors draws the reader, and each helps an editor determine the news value of a story in the company publication no less than on the national news wire. But there is more.

Every editor worthy of the name insists on Pulitzer's "accuracy, accuracy, accuracy." Each name, date, and location, each fact must be checked and rechecked. It must be correct. Anything less diminishes the credibility of the publication and cannot be tolerated. In addition to causing embarrassment and the loss of credibility, inaccuracy can and does create legal problems. Libel and copyright laws apply to employee publications just as they do to the general circulation newspaper and magazine.

Many internal publications print editorials, and this is altogether proper. The unfortunate practice of permitting the publication to editorialize in news columns, however, should be discouraged. Editorializing in news columns is unprofessional, juvenile, dishonest, and misleading. Of course, editorializing should not be confused with interpretive reporting.

Thorough backgrounding of a story is sound journalistic practice and results in a more interesting story. Thus, in stories having several interpretations, it is quite proper to search them out and inform the reader. But the writer's personal opinion does not represent one of those interpretations. That is editorializing. Inserting personal opinion in news copy is poor journalism and unforgiveable public relations.

Hand in hand with editorializing is the all too frequent tendency on the part of some internal publications to serve simply as a voice of management. An old axiom of the political scientist is that he who pays, controls. In the case of a company publication, this may be true, but heavy-handed control is inadvisable. In publications where tight management control is exercised, the publication becomes a mere mouthpiece of management or the organization's leadership, to the exclusion of other legitimate functions. The publication can depend on losing credibility and readership. Of course the employee publication is a management tool. It is funded by the company or organization because management expects value received. Management expects to realize benefits from the internal publication, and rightly so.

But the major benefits for management come through the total work force. These benefits are better informed audiences with improved morale. They result when the individual becomes better acquainted with other employees, with the goals of the business or organization, with what the future holds, and with what is going on around the plant, the total organization, the campus, or the department. If the employee fails to read the publication because it is viewed as so much company propaganda, the entire effort is wasted. So avoid excessive organizational emphasis in the employee publication.

The employee publication that makes the greatest contribution is one representing two-way communication between employees and management. Such publications devote space to letters from readers, guest columns by employees and other staff members, action lines open to readers, etc. Readers look upon the publication as their publication, an open line to communicate with management concerning working conditions, a way to communicate ideas for changing and improving the operation of the company or organization. They look to the publication as another tool for getting things done.

An internal publication in a small engine manufacturing plant made that point. A question box feature made it clear the publication represented employees as well as management.

The organization already had an extensive suggestion program that was quite successful. Most executives employed an open door policy. But the question box added a new dimension; it guaranteed anonymity to the individual who might have a complaint or suggestion. The employee was assured that the subject under discussion would be explored fully by the person within the organization responsible for the area. The suggestion could be written, without signature, and slipped into a locked box located in a high traffic area next to the vending machines.

The program resulted in several policy changes, including change in plant working hours, clarification of practices employees did not understand (generally much to management's surprise), a revised parking system, and a chance for some employees to blow off steam. But most important, readers were convinced that the publication benefited employee-management relations.

FORMAT

In internal publications, format is a matter of taste and budget, probably more a determination based on budget. Formats range from simple one-page typewritten news sheets duplicated on office copiers or mimeographs to publications that feature full color reproductions on coated paper stock in a magazine style. The most common design, particularly in medium to large companies and organizations, uses regular newsprint and generally follows a newspaper tabloid style.

Publication frequency is determined by budget, the amount of activity within the organization, and, once again, taste. Some organizations and businesses, although their readership numbers only in the hundreds, publish a small daily news sheet (e.g., The Mutual of Omaha companies and several assembly plants for one of the major automobile manufacturers). The more common practice, according to figures compiled by the International Association of Business Communicators, is for organizational publications to publish less frequently (weekly, monthly, or bimonthly).

Two major factors determine the publication method used for employee publications: cost and coverage. In centralized operations, the obvious choice is the in-house mail system for distribution. However, in business, institutions, and agencies where a comprehensive internal mail system is not a necessary function, supplies of the publication may be placed at drop points throughout the plant or office area, high-traffic locations that can almost guarantee complete coverage. Still others, including the auto assembly plants with the daily news sheet, distribute their publication in the company cafeteria during breaks and at mealtimes. To enhance coverage and to reach employees' families, some internal publication staffs mail copies to employees' homes. This method provides the most complete coverage, but it is the most expensive circulation system. No best method of circulation has been found; the goal is total saturation within budget.

Some publications accept unpaid advertising, thereby establishing a free exchange for employees to advertise lawn services, babysitting and catering businesses operated by their children, worm farms and freshwater bait, football tickets and cabin rentals. Other services the publication may offer include recipe exchanges, theatrical reviews by the person at the next desk, travel tips, and safety hints. Services are as varied as the imagination of the editors and writers, professional public relations staffers and volunteers.

Employee publications are only one type of printed tool to assist in communicating with the internal publics. Others are frequently over-looked, however, because they were not designed specifically for this in-house audience.

Most large businesses and organizations, whether dealing in prod-ucts or services, publish brochures and pamphlets designed for potential customers. These represent the best the company can pro-duce from the standpoint of quality writing, layout, and illustration. These publications can be a useful tool for dealing with internal publics also, but all too seldom reach this in-house audience, primarily because they are expensive to produce.

However, the high production costs, the price paid for writing tal-ent, photography, art work, typesetting, negative and platemaking, etc., have been absorbed in the large printing run for the targeted audience, the customers. These costs will not be repeated regardless of the num-ber of copies produced. Thus, increasing the total production run to include a supply for distribution to employees could be accomplished for a relatively modest figure.

Examples: A four-color brochure was produced for distribution to customers. Fifty thousand copies were printed for $8500. So the indi-vidual brochures cost 17 cents each. Increasing the press run to 52,000 copies raised the total production cost to $8,737. Thus, each of the 2500 employees within the organization received a copy of the attrac-tive brochure at an added cost of less than 10 cents per employee.

On the occasion of its centennial, an organization developed a well-written story of its development and the role the organization's colorful founder played in regional history. The short, soft-cover book-lets were produced for distribution to 2000 select customers and business associates of the top executives. Total costs, excluding the author's fees, were approximately $3000—$1.50 a copy. Increasing the run to 2500, an adequate surplus to cover the organization's 400 employees, raised the cost to $3,454—less than 92 cents for the addition booklets.

The gesture was a significant public relations achievement. As far as most employees were concerned, the founder had been only a name under an oil painting in the main conference room. Now, however, the founder's exploits were table talk in the cafeteria, and several employees developed speeches based on the company history for delivery before their civic clubs.

Benefits are obvious. The need to keep internal publics informed has been discussed. Their information must be accurate, positive, and current. Once the internal publics have been grounded in what makes the company or organization tick, no better way can be found to keep them updated than to supply the latest product and service literature, the most recent material prepared for customers.

Employees should be told that new models feature four-wheel drive; the college now offers a major in celestial navigation; the agency will open a park with facilities for the handicapped; or the firm will specialize in portfolios for retired persons. Internal publics must be at least as well informed as external publics.

Literature made available to internal publics should also include annual reports, revised timetables, and new plant or campus tour guides. In short, this important audience should be on the distribution list for anything that can improve in-house education and make employees themselves active public relations representatives of the business or organization.

Internal electronic programming

Modern electronic technology contributes to the tools used effectively to inform internal audiences. The list begins with the simple public address system.

Particularly effective in reaching large concentrations of people, the public address system must be used in moderation for simple, brief announcements giving information that is important to the audience. Use of the PA system should be restricted to periods when the audience is free to hear (i.e., during scheduled breaks and lunch periods or immediately before or after shifts). The system's effectiveness diminishes markedly if it is used to reach the general audience more than six or eight times during the average work day. If the system is overused, the audience becomes irritated by the intrusion, and that irritation develops into an uncanny knack for shutting out the droning electronic voice.

System complexity ranges from a simple installation with a single microphone, amplifier, and all-weather speakers to the more sophisticated systems employing broadcast-quality microphones, powerful high-fidelity amplifiers, and banks of broad-range speakers.

The wired or wireless carrier-current broadcasting system is a natural refinement of the simple PA system. Improved quality of transmission permits broadcast of background music through the day. Because the system provides a measure of entertainment and is subject to greater control by the individuals or groups in its audiences, carrier-current broadcasting is more readily accepted by the audience. Occasional announcements delivered through the system are accepted more tolerantly than those delivered to the captive audience by the PA system.

Most major military installations and a number of private businesses provide newscasts over their carrier-current radio systems. The newscasts accepted most readily by audiences are those that blend general news copy with in-house stories. To enhance the appeal of such newscasts, the public relations practitioners responsible for their development follow many of the same guidelines that apply in development of organizational publications. They avoid ponderous company orientation in the newscasts, and they shun editorializing in the news copy. The newscasts are designed to provide information the audience needs to know, will enjoy knowing, or will profit from knowing.

The next logical step has been taken by some businesses and agencies that are oriented toward reaching their internal publics. They have incorporated a closed circuit television system into their internal information program. Because the audience sees and hears the message, closed circuit television (CCTV) is one of the most effective internal communication systems available with current technology. The messages are retained longer and in greater detail by the audience.

However, there are several limitations of the system: (1) unless a large number of receivers are situated throughout the organization's facilities, the audience will be limited; (2) the medium demands almost complete attention, so closed circuit TV cannot be used during times when the audience is expected to be productive, unlike judiciously employed closed circuit radio; and (3) equipment and production costs soar in comparison with other internal media.

Equipment for a basic closed circuit system will cost from 10 to 15 times as much as the electronic gear needed for a simple carrier-current radio system. Space requirements are far greater, and personnel costs for the simplest production are at least double those needed for an audio presentation.

Mutual of Omaha uses closed circuit television effectively in its home offices. The company produces a 15-minute in-house newscast shown in company cafeterias during lunch periods. The productions are a combination of live telecast and videotape. In addition to hard news concerning employees, company developments, and coming events, the public relations staff produces quality features on employees, places, and things connected with the company. The system also telecasts commercial program segments sponsored on network television by Mutual of Omaha. Furthermore, the in-house network is a powerful tool for presenting training programs to employees. An executive responsible for the company training program said, "Our people adapt readily to the television set as a training medium. They've grown up with it."

Firms using CCTV translate their programs to videotape for shipment to outlying field offices or for repeat use in the home office or plant system. Once all field offices are equipped with videotape players, shipping tapes from point to point is a simple, inexpensive method of guaranteeing that a precise, controlled, quality message is transmitted to the field.

Whether or not the organization uses closed circuit TV, videotape is a convenient method of communicating with field offices. A television receiver and a tape player (at approximately double the cost of the receiver) are the only pieces of equipment required in the field office, bringing costs within the reach of many firms and organizations.

Programs can be as inexpensive as a "talking head," a single-camera shot of the chief executive or some other figure familiar to employees delivering the message to the camera. Through videotape, each employee, regardless of location, can see and hear the boss deliver the annual state of the organization message, witness the periodic awards program, or see the safety engineer demonstrate proper operation of the latest equipment. The communication is effective, and it has the added dimension of being available for repeated use if warranted.

Electronic communication provides a valuable set of tools for the public relations practitioner who must deliver a message to internal publics. The depth of public relations involvement in electronic communications depends on the talents available on the public relations staff and the extent of the budgetary commitments to the medium. The practitioner may be restricted to a simple audio tape recorder, or involvement may include a complex TV system complete with studios and sophisticated equipment.

Summary

Size, distance, and numbers preclude exclusive reliance on the one-on-one relationship if the modern organization is to communicate completely, accurately, and quickly with its internal audiences. The organization with a sound internal relations program will use the broadest range of media, handbills to closed circuit television and satellite relays, to reach internal publics.

The public relations practitioner must be as professional in the methods and techniques employed when communicating with an internal audience as with the external publics. Because the basic tools are the same, many of the guidelines employed in working with and for the mass media apply equally when communicating with internal audiences.

The professional communicating with the internal audience, therefore, will use journalistic style, telling the readers what happened, to whom, when it happened, where, why, and how. When writing for internal publics, as for any audience, the professional evaluates the story by making certain it includes one or more of the factors that determine news value: timeliness, proximity, significance, and magnitude. And as in all dealings with any public, the PR practitioner makes every effort to guarantee accuracy.

The internal publics are among the most significant audiences with which any public relations practitioner communicates. They must be treated with the professionalism and respect their importance demands.

Exercises

1. Interview the editor of an employee publication. Determine publication frequency and format, target audiences, editor's impressions of the publication's effectiveness, and reasons behind the various types of material published. Describe the staffing arrangement.

2. What other media are used by the organization to communicate with internal audiences? What percentage of the total internal audience does each reach and with what frequency?

3. Use copies of the employee publication or samples from other media to demonstrate the impact of timeliness, proximity, significance, and magnitude upon the audience.

4. How does the internal communications program fit into the overall public relations effort of the organization? What percentage of total staff time is devoted to the internal relations program?

5. Is editorializing permitted in the internal media? In news copy? In special editorial comment or dedicated editorial columns? Why?

Case study

The Sun Master Company began ten years ago to manufacture and market a revolutionary solar cell invented by Dr. E. J. Franklin. The inventor is a humble person who failed to realize the impact the solar cell would have. The unit is the size of a home refrigerator and retails for less than $2000. A single unit converts solar power to enough electrical energy to supply a family residence of 1500 square feet, including heating and air conditioning. The unit is effective even on overcast, cold days.

Sun Master has grown from a single, small manufacturing plant employing 15 persons to a corporation with plants in six different cities (Portland, Oregon; Boise, Idaho; Topeka, Kansas; Waterloo, Iowa; Toledo, Ohio; and Bangor, Maine) and an employee payroll of 3500.

Problems came with growth. The rapid expansion spawned unfounded rumors of mergers, corporate takeovers, and outright sale of the patents. The most recent rumor is that Sun Master is negotiating with a foreign monopoly and that all fabrication will be moved overseas. As a result, although wages are among the highest in the nation, employees are restive, leaving for rival employers and making unreasonable demands on Sun Master. In fact, many of the most damaging rumors seem to originate from within the company.

Franklin retained complete control over the organization until recently when corporate naivete resulted in a threatened strike. Now, a management team has been hired to solve operational problems at Sun Master. The new corporate officers recognize the need for a solid public relations effort with emphasis on internal communications.

You have been hired to develop an employee publication or publications. Draft a proposal, including frequency, circulation, format, type of material to be published, and estimated costs. Explain what the publication or publications are designed to accomplish and problems that may be solved by the program.

What other media should be part of the internal relations program? How would the various elements complement each other?

Suggested readings

Allen, Fred T. "Ways to Improve Employee Communications." *Nation's Business,* September 1975.

Brush, Douglas P. "Internal Communications and the New Technology." *Public Relations Journal,* February 1981.

D'Aprix, Roger. "Communicating Critical Issues." *Communicator's Journal,* May/June 1983.

Gildea, Joyce Asher, and Myron Emmanuel. "Internal Communication: The Impact on Productivity." *Public Relations Journal,* February 1980.

Hunter, Bill. "Where Does a Company's Communication Style Originate?" *Communication World,* January 1985.

Lewis, Carl B. "How to Make Internal Communication Work." *Public Relations Journal,* February 1980.

McCallister, Linda. "The Interpersonal Side of Internal Communications." *Public Relations Journal,* February 1981.

Matthews, Downs. "Write for Results, Not Style." *Communication World* 2(1985):9, 26-27.

Orman, Dave. "Atlantic Richfield's 'Typos-to-Go' Program." *Communication World,* May 1985.

Reuss, Carol, and Donn Silvis, eds. *Inside Organizational Communication.* 2d ed. New York: Longman, Inc., 1984.

Rosenberg, Karen. "What Employees Think of Communication: 1984 Update." *Communication World,* May 1985.

Zuegner, Charles W. "The Communications Program: What Is It, What Does It Do?" *Journal of Organizational Communication* 9(1980):4.

7 External publics

Knowing those publics "out there"

Did it occur to you while reading the previous chapter that classifying a public as "internal" rather than "external" is a judgment call? A valid example would be alumni of a university or college, spread out as they are all over the country and into foreign lands. Are they an external public? Or, because of close ties with the institution long after leaving the campus, are they an internal public? How about the medical practitioners affiliated with a hospital? They bring patients there and are listed on the staff, but they probably conduct the bulk of their practice outside the hospital.

Internal or external? Such labeling is a mere convenience for the public relations specialist. Far more important is the careful identification of all publics, knowing they exist and the influence they exert on success of the mission of the employer or client of the public relations staff. As we will see, communicating with all publics, internal and external, is essential. The type of programs public relations people undertake to foster good relations with a public will depend more on the special interests and needs of that public than on whether it is internal or external.

If, as suggested in Chapter 6, internal publics are "family," external publics are not just everybody else. They are people the family contacts regularly and who are therefore important to the family. They are the family's neighbors and friends, even in a sense the family's employers and co-workers, the family's helpers and protectors.

At Christmas card–writing time or when blessings are counted at Thanksgiving, a real-life family may list these special people. On this smaller scale, it is not necessary to do more; relationships are more spontaneous and less formal.

However, because of the larger scale on which public relations typically operates, practitioners cannot be casual about identifying their publics. If they are inaugurating a new program, they must carefully and

138

thoroughly consider which groups they will deal with most frequently and which groups can exert the most influence on the success or failure of their efforts.

Fortunately, even the new public relations program need not start from scratch. Through the years, important external publics have been identified as common to many PR endeavors. Public relations activity and public relations people are real and must be located somewhere; the people who live in and around that somewhere, residents of the local community, are therefore an important public. They can make life pleasant or miserable, just like friendly or hostile neighbors can make domestic life pleasant or miserable for a family.

Just as it is a basic need for a family, income is important to the employers and clients of public relations practitioners. So, customers and clients by whatever name (patients, students, donors, lessees, visitors, etc.) are an important public. Colleagues, fellow employees, and friends are important to working family members employed outside the home; so, it is not surprising that business, professional, and trade associations are important to corporations, agencies, and institutions. The analogy could be continued with all the other people important to a family, from the police who patrol the city to friendly sales clerks who point out the bargains or advise on product quality. Good relations with all of them will make life happier and smoother. The parallels with public relations and its publics should be clear.

Failure to identify a significant external public is like forgetting a good friend's birthday. The forgotten birthday hurts in public relations, too. For example, the college or university that fails to see its students as an important internal public will find its alumni support eroding in a few years. The clinic that concentrates on cultivating major donors but lets relations languish with another external public, its patients, will find occupancy in its impressive new facilities well below capacity, perhaps suggesting second thoughts to some donors. The business that permits memberships in major industrial organizations to lapse may find few allies when it suddenly is in a major confrontation with a regulatory agency or large union. The ambitious politician who concentrates on enlarging his influence among fellow legislators to the neglect of his constituents may end up a not-too-influential, ordinary citizen.

Identifying key publics is never a one-time-only task for public relations practitioners. Times change. New groups form. Today businesses and government agencies seriously consider their relations with environmentalists and consumer groups, organizations that did not exist or were much less influential years ago. Educators who once had to respond to vociferous demands for bigger and better schools now must deal with taxpayer groups insisting on budget limitations.

In the periodic program review that is part of a practitioner's function, identification of publics must be reexamined. Not only should practitioners ask themselves whether there are new or neglected publics they should be dealing with or serving more effectively, they also must ask if the publics they have identified are too broad or too narrow. For example, are there reasons for a major retailer to deal differently with major appliance customers (also potential repair and maintenance customers) than it deals with clothing customers (whose interest may be style trends and the arrival of new items)? With the opening of its new downtown center, should the community college work more closely with the main branch of the public library nearby (interaction beyond merely mailing brochures and announcements to the library) so the two institutions can cooperate rather than compete and duplicate activities?

As with internal publics, leaders and decision makers among the external publics, and those who are not leaders and decision makers, must be clearly identified.

Identifying and serving key publics

Obviously, the important external publics for the American Cancer Society differ from those of General Motors or General Electric. Yet, there will be some duplication of names on their lists of publics. Government, for example, would be a significant public for all three. We point this out to illustrate why it is impractical to discuss every external public that practitioners will identify and attempt to serve, and why we can nonetheless deal with some external publics that will be common to enterprises ranging from major business corporations to small private associations and agencies.

Before discussing these major external publics separately, it is important to underline the need for each public relations staff, no matter what type of client or employer it is serving, to identify its particular publics. Practitioners can consider lists others have developed, but they must take a fresh look at their own situation. They should ask questions such as, "Whom is our organization/business attempting to serve?" "Who finances our operations?" "Who are the 'outside' people our employees contact most frequently?" "Where do we operate and who are the 'neighbors'?" "Who could hamper our operations by ignoring or actively opposing us?" "Who makes decisions that affect our success?"

The list that the public relations practitioner develops must be reviewed periodically. Perhaps a public was forgotten or neglected. Perhaps a new activity means involvement with a new public or publics. Perhaps a group that was treated as a single public is acting now like several publics.

If a new plant or division office is opened, for example, residents of the new community are now a special public. Recent national studies reveal that high school counselors play an increasing role in serious selection of colleges and universities, but there may be no program at your institution aimed at these counselors. Because of fluctuations in interest rates, the concerns of bondholders are quite different from those of owners of common stock in your corporation, but you may be sending the two groups the same mailings with the same copy, year after year. In each case, a reevaluation is due. The list of external publics needs updating.

That is an initial step. The importance of the new public must be assessed, its current attitudes discovered, and effective yet practical and economical means of communicating with it must be found. To examine this process more thoroughly, let us turn to some of the publics that are common to most public relations practitioners' employers and clients.

THE LOCAL COMMUNITY

As individuals, we know that our enjoyment of our homes, even our motivation to maintain them and make improvements, depends upon our relations with our neighbors. If our neighbors are among our best friends, if we have grown up with them in an atmosphere of warmth and cordiality, we would move away reluctantly. On the other hand, if their pets constantly run loose in our yard and their children always litter our property, if they let their home deteriorate, or if they throw frequent and raucous parties, the old "For Sale" sign may be put out eagerly, and our move cannot come too soon.

There are many similarities in the relations between a business, agency, or institution and its neighbors, the local community. How effectively the business, agency, or institution operates depends at least in part on how it gets along with its neighbors. And because it is more than an individual neighbor, the business, agency, or institution can play a larger role in deciding the character of those relationships. In many small and medium size cities, a large corporation or institution may be the biggest employer and the largest single taxpayer. A government installation may give the agency that operates it similar status.

In this and earlier eras, poor relationships with the neighbors has contributed to businesses and organizations moving. In some cases, the relationships have been the sole cause. To say that the community rather than the departed business or agency is the big loser may often be true, but just in part. Invariably, moving is costly in both dollars and productivity. Those costs may be recouped in a new location, but it is tragic when they could have been avoided entirely by patching up differences before the move became inevitable. Public relations practitioners will find that just as with individuals, not every business or organization *can* move. The long-established educational institution cannot pick up its campus, classrooms, laboratories, and dormitories and head elsewhere. The governmental agency concerned with agriculture, flood control, or forestry cannot move all its operations into an urban skyscraper.

But this is a negative perspective. With the support and acceptance of the local community, with a reciprocal, neighborly spirit, businesses, organizations, and institutions find it easier to achieve their goals. A meat packer that has earned a reputation as a good corporate citizen is more likely to find city officials ready to talk things over and cooperate in solving air and water pollution problems, rather than summarily attacking the company and angrily enacting severe restrictions on its disposal operations. A major truck line that has been generous in supporting civic projects may find government leaders pointing out low-cost financing programs available for relocating a central terminal within the community. With a reputation as a good employer, an insurance company may attract a high caliber staff that improves its efficiency and, in the long run, its standing within the industry nationwide.

BEING A GOOD CITIZEN. One mark of a good individual citizen is thoughtful participation in the electoral process. Others are active involvement in local issues, volunteer service in the community, and willingness to pay a fair share of taxes and contribute to nongovernmental social assistance agencies. A business or institution may not be able to vote, although it can encourage employees to do so. But it can, directly or through its staff, perform all the other citizenship roles. To earn a reputation as a good citizen, it will see that every opportunity is grasped, and it will not wait to be asked.

For instance, currently many large employers invite officials to conduct voter registrations on their premises. This is not only evidence of good citizenship, but a service to employees, a key internal public. Others open their employee publications and offer their bulletin boards to voter registration campaigns.

The Community Chest or United Fund solicitation in most communities depends on strong, active employer support for most of its funds. Businesses, organizations, and institutions lend their corporation leadership to campaign committees. They cooperate in setting up organizations within their plants and offices so that each employee can be contacted, and they facilitate giving by absorbing the cost of payroll deductions. In addition, they routinely make corporate gifts. The broad response to such efforts is much greater today than when the Community Chest concept was born more than a half century ago. At that time, organizers relied almost exclusively on house-to-house and mail canvassing.

A word of caution: some employers lay themselves open to charges that they use too much vigor in supporting solicitations, even for worthy causes. An alert public relations practitioner will counsel against employer action that puts undue pressure on employees to contribute. It can happen in a well-intentioned effort that attempts to show solid support for the welfare of the community, but it alienates employees.

A balance is necessary, too, in making executives available to serve on civic betterment committees or government advisory bodies. Obviously, a business will not only show it is a good citizen by encouraging this participation, it also contributes to more effective local government, which means tax savings for the business and its employees. But if those executives spend a disproportionate amount of time on civic projects, their employer's needs may be neglected or, as we have observed, the executives will be worn out long before retirement age.

Taxes, bond issues, urban redevelopment, and growth restrictions increasingly call for citizens to take sides. A public relations practitioner's employer or client often may wonder if it would not be wiser to "sit this one out" when questions like this stir local passions. Taking a side is guaranteed to win enemies. Our feeling is that most issues such as these are complex and without clear-cut answers, especially considering their political setting. For example, when were voters ever faced with a choice between the "perfect candidate" and the "perfectly awful candidate"? And there may be reasonable, ethically justifiable grounds for deciding not to swing total corporate or organizational support behind either side in a local controversy. But when this is the situation, the business or association known to take sides in other controversies should be frank and open about its reasons for reserve. It still may be accused of self-serving interests, of course, but an honest, forthright statement explaining the decision at least can blunt such charges.

Consider also the example of a church leader we know who faced similar circumstances. He declined to join the forces against a proposed legal limit on public school district spending. He said the issue was not one of principle but a practical one for taxpayers to decide for themselves. This brought a charge of sell out. However, he pointed out the consistent and well-published support he had given bond issues for new facilities when the school district faced burgeoning student populations, hardly the situation now. Personal attacks faded quickly.

Businesses should be as free as any other taxpayer to contest their tax assessments, of course. Yet, they must also be conscious of the fact that their taxpayer role usually is more newsworthy than that of a homeowner seeking a $100 reduction in real estate tax. If a firm wants to be known as a good citizen, it must be on solid ground before protesting and laying itself open to criticism that it is unwilling to pay its fair share of support to local government. From a pragmatic viewpoint, it makes little sense to spend time and effort to save tax dollars that cannot offset community goodwill lost because of the effort. Many businesses unhesitatingly take losses on purchases returned by good customers even if the returns would not have to be accepted. Why? The continued goodwill of these customers is more important. A similar principle applies in community relations, and public relations practitioners may have to point this out.

TELLING ABOUT IT. Word-of-mouth communication tells people in the community much about a business or organization. Employees talk to their families and friends. In addition, there are the real neighbors, those who live or work nearby and observe first-hand what is going on. This person-to-person communication is effective in delivering messages because it is, consciously or unconsciously, tailored to the individual receiver. But frequently it is weakened and sometimes distorted by the retelling. By the time it is third- and fourth-hand information, it can change dramatically.

Local news media are more likely to generate their own coverage of a business or agency that is a major employer or social force in the community. And that can be a definite advantage. However, all too often the more visible news is bad news, accidents, disasters, personal injuries, and violent crime. Frequently, good news is less obvious, and reporters (not just public relations people) will make this point. The need for a formal communications program aimed at telling the community about the "good deeds well done" should be obvious. Such a program must use the local media to reach everyone in the community, use company or organizational media to keep in contact with influential leaders within the community, and use internal communication to provide employees with the facts and figures needed to reinforce media communication when they talk to other local residents.

Professional news staffs in most communities of less than 50,000 are small. The media may depend heavily, even exclusively, on news releases to cover businesses, organizations, and institutions, knowing that most of the reporting will be handled by the various public relations staffs. In such a setting, the importance of the formal community communications program is even greater.

Another general observation is that broadcast stations, especially in smaller markets, may not have anyone assigned full-time to news. Such outlets provide little independent news coverage; yet, they are an excellent means for contacting large segments of the community. A report of interest to young people, for example, may be communicated effectively by a radio outlet whose music programming is currently "in" with the particular age group.

Surveys show that people can be divided into media users and nonusers, and that people who read newspapers and magazines tend also to be television and radio users. Nonusers, on the other hand, often are really light users, frequently restricting their media use to a contemporary music station or to television soap operas. To reach the nonusers or light users, news releases must go to all available media.

Sometimes a good bet is missed by organizations whose communications programs are community-oriented only when it is to their advantage. For example, a large manufacturer of pens and pencils may introduce a new line, a product that could revolutionize the market the way the ballpoint pen did following World War II. Naturally, the manufacturer will recognize this as a national story and aim at the national media: the trade press, wire services, television networks, the *Wall Street Journal* and the news magazines. Forgetting the local media that regularly printed and broadcast the manufacturer's local news releases will be an affront, bringing the reaction, "When you have something really big, you ignore us. Now we know where we stand!"

The local media must be in on the big national stories as well as the local news.

News releases and public relations photographs can never be the sole vehicles for a community communications program. Feature ideas can be passed along to newspapers and television stations. Subjects for special programming or mini-documentaries should be suggested. Program sponsorship and assistance in producing public service programs must be considered also. Smaller broadcasting stations often are eager to air any public service material. Why should they resort to nationally supplied material when they would rather have local copy that would enhance their community service programming?

SHOW AS WELL AS TELL. Most people have neighbors they have greeted for a long time but feel they really do not know. One day those neighbors invite them in, perhaps on the spur of the moment, to see new carpeting or a recently completed recreation room. That invitation is a significant step in a neighborhood relationship. People are less a mystery when we get a look at how they live, as told by the interior of their homes.

This is equally true of organizations and agencies that practice sound public relations. The level of their acquaintanceship with the community may be restricted by the fact that local people have never been invited to "come in." Not only are local residents curious about a new plant or office building, they feel their curiosity deserves to be satisfied.

Some years ago, a new facility was opened in Janesville, Wisconsin, by the Parker Pen Company, one of the nation's first manufacturing plants to feature pastel walls and piped music. Some comments by visitors during an open house were almost possessive, comments like, "I'm glad our plant did it first."

Large daily newspapers, because of their size and the nature of a print medium, often are seen as depersonalized, faceless giants. They have learned that a continuous open house in the form of daily tours is an excellent way to combat that stereotype.

However, an open house when a new building is completed or a tour program that is not promoted constantly will not do the whole job. A public relations program must outline steps to deal with the constant renewal or turnover in its community. Like speakers bureaus, tours must be publicized regularly. Potential visitor groups must be targeted, school children, fraternal organizations, civic and social groups, etc. Otherwise, a significant potential for humanizing the business or agency will be wasted.

Special attractions encourage visitors. The Union Pacific Railroad features a noted museum of railroad history and western Americana, a collection that is updated regularly. In 1985, for example, the railroad completely rebuilt the museum, again acknowledging its significance in Union Pacific's campaign to attract visitors.

The famed Boys Town has a visitors center strategically located astride its main entrance where visitors obtain souvenirs, study historic artifacts, and receive maps for self-guided tours of the campus and many of the buildings. Another sign of the Boys Town awareness of visitors is the design of the industrial arts building, which resembles an indoor shopping mall. Large expanses of glass along the main corridor permit visitors to watch activity in the bakery, carpentry shop, auto mechanics laboratory, and all the rest without disturbing activities in any of the teaching areas.

The Army Corps of Engineers includes beautiful visitors centers adjacent to many of its major flood control projects throughout the country. These centers not only provide vantage points for viewing the man-made lakes but feature exhibitry and audiovisual programs and films developed around the archeology and history of the region and the particular project.

Beyond this, public relations practitioners play the role of "sergeant of the guard." They must understand the points at which their employer or client makes a first impression on both the business caller and the casual visitor. Receptionists and switchboard operators are stationed at most of these points. Nevertheless, despite the fact that everyone supposedly is aware of this, we are appalled at how frequently scant attention is paid to the harm these person can do by assuring that the visitor's first impression is bad.

Groundskeepers, building maintenance personnel, and employees whose work areas are near entrances often are asked directions by the first-time visitor. Certainly, we do not advocate an official greeter's uniform and a canned speech for these employees; we do recommend a comprehensive community communications program that gives special attention to these "outer guards." Brief them when they are employed and periodically review the special contribution they can make to the overall success of the company or organization.

SPECIAL PROGRAMS TOO. Every corporation, association, or agency has landmark dates such as anniversaries or other commemorations. Their observance can contribute to good community as well as good internal relations and serve as reminders of the long-standing contribution the community has received from the celebrant.

A university or college marks its centennial. It is an excellent opportunity to remind neighbors in the local community, as well as people in the state and region, of how its leading citizens have been educated there. Businesses can be informed once again of the contribution made by the university or college to the local economy and reminded of student and faculty buying power.

Or, a hospital admits its 100,000th patient. The number in itself says much about the tremendous amount of care the institution has provided its neighbors. In addition, the efforts made by the hospital to update and expand its services can be reviewed appropriately on this occasion, perhaps comparing how it was with patient number one.

The distinctive competencies or functions of the business or organization can be the basis for special service programs that contribute to sound community relations. Continental Can operates recycling centers for entire communities. An antique dealer may authenticate or appraise items at a state or county fair booth. An affiliate of the American Heart Association offers blood pressure readings in public buildings during Heart Month. Such programs must be publicized effectively, however, if they are to serve as many people as possible. Practitioners must be wary of the naive optimism that can overtake them, making them believe, "This is such a neat service, people will flock to it." They will not if they do not know about it.

Indirectly, we have suggested that management as well as rank-and-file employees can be encouraged to be civically active as a contribution to solid community relations. The motivation, however, must be genuine. The phoney "joiners" are spotted easily, and if it appears that they have been "sent by the company," their participation, even in a volunteer project, can do more harm than good. Public relations counsel must point out to employers that such employee participation is good in itself and, by indirect consequence, beneficial to the employer; therefore, the employer should make clear that it is a great idea for employees to involve themselves in the community. One way of accomplishing this is by citing such activity in employee publications.

Another way for top management to encourage community participation is often totally disregarded. That is by insuring reasonable staff stability. Some corporations earn a reputation of being standoffish in their communities because their management and employees seldom accept positions on the boards of civic groups or become leaders in their churches. They do not join neighborhood councils, the Kiwanis or Rotary, or accept Girl Scout and Little League assignments. Often the reason is that the corporation transfers staff frequently with little choice or warning, and those staff members have learned the frustration of building community ties. In determining transfers, the effect on community relations should be a factor in making those decisions and in setting policies.

CUSTOMERS, CLIENTS, AND SUPPLIERS

All of us as consumers probably have said at some time, "I'll never buy anything there again!" If we have been lucky, we may also have had occasion to say, "Even though they didn't have what I needed this time, I'm coming back here to look again." Analyzing those statements, we find they relate to our treatment as customers. Quality, price, and availability of products and services may be the primary determinants of a customer's attitude toward a business, institution, or professional practitioner. But the way we are treated also is a strong influence, even offsetting price and availability at times. If an automobile dealer's mechanics give you excellent service on your present car, you will probably head in that dealer's direction when you shop for a new car. Conversely, if service and treatment are poor, you will probably check out the competition next time.

Within the legal profession, various bar associations have analyzed situations that led clients to complain against some attorney members. Again and again, studies turn up clients who report they felt neglected before they became dissatisfied with the service. "He never tells me what he is doing" and "She never returns my calls" are common reproaches. Frequently, studies indicate the lawyer actually did a creditable job with the client's legal problems, but the client sensed haughtiness in this failure to keep in touch and report on progress. So, the client objects to the treatment rather than the service. It is but a short step then to complain about the service as well. Contrast this with the experience of a lawyer friend who continued practicing well into his eighties. He gets new clients, many who tell him, "I know you don't remember me, but I recalled your thoughtfulness to my mother when you handled my dad's estate years ago."

A complaint to a bar association is a serious problem for any attorney, and it is becoming more common for the filing of complaints to be made public. Even if the complaint is unwarranted, it can injure the attorney's reputation and cause the loss of clients. If the complaint is sustained, it can bring the ultimate discipline—disbarment. Do not think that retail or wholesale customer complaints against a business are always a less serious matter. Consider consumer lawsuits that have been filed and won in our courts by individuals who once were considered merely dissatisfied customers. Good customer relations, therefore, are not only desirable, they are absolutely necessary. They can also be a great deterrent to serious problems.

IS THE CUSTOMER ALWAYS RIGHT? The serve-yourself or supermarket approach to retailing has reduced direct customer-seller contacts over the last two generations. It has given rise to one of life's small frustrations. Remember wandering through the maze of the discount store on your rapidly expiring lunch hour? You need help and, at last, find a clerk only to be told, "That's not my department." Brief though it was, that customer-seller contact was distinctly negative. The trend toward self-service retailing has seemingly been accompanied by reduced courtesy and consideration shown the customer. If the customer is not always right, at least that customer should receive the benefit of the doubt, and be treated like a person the seller is happy to have as a visitor.

Customers are treated shabbily not only in low-overhead retail outlets. In fact, many such operations are striving to overcome the problem. Several national fast-food chains, for example, have outstanding programs for training employees with the emphasis on courtesy, the front line in good customer relations. Public relations practitioners in all areas of business could learn from the programs vigorously pursued by McDonald's, Godfather's, and other fast-food chains. Strictly speaking, the situation is the direct concern of sales management, but we contend it is also an area where public relations should be involved, because it is a performance area, and public relations' first function is to assure acceptable performance. Before boasting, "We treat our customers like royalty," you must treat your customers like royalty.

Americans' experience with inflation in the 1970s and 1980s makes them discerning, critical customers. They have limited their spending for nonessentials and moreover, they have been exposed to the consumer movement. They are more aware of warranties, their right to rescind sales contracts, and the impact of product liability decisions by the courts. It seems to make sense then to expend every effort to satisfy customers.

In addition to quality and fair price, serious and courteous treatment before, during, and after the sale is vital. This last phase is a key for public relations today. The unsatisfactory way customers' questions are answered or complaints are handled leads to many serious problems in customer relations. And that is a public relations problem.

A landmark defamation case involving customer treatment was decided by the Supreme Court in 1971. The case went all the way to the Supreme Court and thoroughly muddled constitutional law for several years. In fact, American media still felt the backlash in the mid-1980s. From the facts outlining the situation as contained in a lower court opinion, it appears that the lawsuit might never have been filed if the staff of the defendant radio station had listened to the plaintiff at the outset. Instead, the court opinion suggests that the plaintiff visited the station to ask for a correction in its account of his activities, and he was rebuffed by a part-time disk jockey. So, the plaintiff visited a lawyer.

Public relations practitioners should take the initiative in working with sales departments to establish procedures for dealing with customer complaints. The procedures should be as uncomplicated as possible for the customer, enabling that unhappy individual to obtain an exchange, a refund, or an adjustment without carrying the problem to a stockholders meeting. The process should be quick and simple. When the customer is asked the cause of dissatisfaction, the question must not be a challenge but a legitimate attempt to improve customer service.

Chronically or unreasonably dissatisfied customers may have to be referred to a higher level. At that point, a tactful staff member with clearly defined guidelines outlining the level of firmness acceptable in dealing with unscrupulous purchasers should be available. That staff member must be given considerable discretion in dealing with problem customers.

Billing is another critical after-the-sale phase of customer relations. Too many customers can tell war stories about battles with computers or computerlike people when attempting to settle their accounts. Businesses may ignore potential problems in billing or insist that computers never make mistakes, but they do so at the risk of turning a significant number of customers into former customers. The public relations practitioner has a legitimate role in examining complaint procedures here, too, and in urging that personnel be trained to deal with non-routine accounts payable issues. Incidentally, that includes collections;

delinquent accounts should be handled promptly and considerately, without any hint of the heavy-handedness of the loan shark's enforcer.

REMEMBER NONRETAIL CUSTOMERS. Wholesale and long-term contract customer-seller relationships may be more prolonged and involved than those in retail business and professional practice, or they can be more distant and impersonal, closely related to prices and availability of merchandise. But the human factor inevitably will work its way into the relationship. If buyers visit a wholesaler's displays or if wholesaler representatives visit purchasing agents, there is direct personal contact. Yet, even if the buyer makes a large purchase on the basis of catalog descriptions and prices, the buyer will be dealing with someone at the other end of the telephone or mail service line. Public relations practitioners' contributions in such encounters may come in seeing that buyers and potential buyers know about the wholesaler's good performance in producing wares or providing services. The importance of individual sales, because of the larger financial stakes, ordinarily promote courtesy and tact on the part of seller representatives. Problems can arise in other areas (processing orders or deliveries) to undermine the salesperson's effort at finding and keeping satisfied customers.

In both large-volume and one-time contracts, customer relations can be damaged by the attitude that "We've got your signature on the dotted line now; so, we don't have to be nice guys any more." If two large businesses or organizations are involved, new people may replace those who negotiated the transactions, and the new players may not share the excitement of their predecessors who landed the contract. The casualness or heedlessness can easily mean no renewal of the contract in the days ahead.

Even if big customers in major deals are unlikely to be repeat customers, they can spread the word to potential customers about the lack of attention and service encountered from the seller. That type of publicity severely damages any firm.

SUPPLIERS ARE IMPORTANT TOO. The glove is on the other hand when the practitioner's client or employer is the customer. Then it is the supplier's problem to be kind, courteous, upright, and true. Or, is it?

Are you ever the customer who, because of your attitude and conduct, receives special assistance or advice from a salesperson? Instances we remember occurred in hardware and auto parts stores. Frequently we received invaluable tips about items we purchased. This may have been an expression of pity for an obviously inept handyman. Nonetheless, it is apparent that curt or overbearing customers seldom elicit helpful advice in such situations, even if they need expert guidance.

We are not advocating the currying of special favors. Rather, we urge an understanding of the importance of having a cooperative, supportive supplier and showing appreciation for that supplier's motivation, which plays a key role in helping you, the customer, get what you need when you need it. It is applying the Golden Rule in all relationships with the publics, including those in which it appears that others need your approval for a change.

Put another way, public relations people can never be dog kickers. They must never emulate the frustrated employee who grins and bears it all day when he feels abused by superiors and co-workers, then comes home to pick on the family pet because he finally is the superior. A business or institution seeking integrity in its public relations can never expend so much of its energy and resources on performing for external publics, clients and customers, that it excuses itself from maintaining good relations with those who provide it with goods and services.

We know a retailer who gave the impression for years that he was sincere and enthusiastic in dealing with customers. As a result, that retailer could really sell. You just knew he had your best interests at heart. We witnessed an encounter when an advertising account executive tried selling the retailer a space contract. The retailer treated him like a leper. The facade of sincerity crumbled. No more business from us, or from others who observed the incident.

The implications for public relations persons are that suppliers are a public that cannot be ignored or treated like servants. Include suppliers in informational and promotional mailings, particularly if there is a long-term or continuing relationship. In addition, the public relations staff must be alert to dog kicking in the personal relationships between buyers within the organization and suppliers from the other side. Thoughtlessness and discourtesy in this relationship is most revealing. It says that you practice good public relations only when it suits you, that you are a manipulator.

BUSINESS AND PROFESSIONAL GROUPS

Organizations formed by various types of businesses, institutions, agencies, and occupational groups can be divided into two categories for public relations purposes: (1) those with which public relations professionals identify personally (e.g., Public Relations Society of America and International Association of Business Communicators) or through the employer or client (industry, educational and social welfare organizations, etc.), and (2) those "outside" groups whose members have a special interest or concern in the performance of the PR staff's employer or client (e.g., a county or state medical association).

A public relations person need not be a professional joiner to sense the advantages of membership in public relations organizations, the stimulating exchange of ideas and the value of sharing experiences in problem solving and many other areas. Employers of public relations people occasionally must be persuaded of these advantages, especially if the employers are asked to pay dues and meeting expenses.

However, employees who look upon meetings and conventions of their professional organizations as unscheduled, paid vacations sometimes make it difficult for dedicated professionals to persuade employers of their need for continuing encounters with their peers.

Institutional or corporate membership in industrial, social, or civic groups may not be as clearly advantageous to the employers. And we will not suggest that all organizational memberships are of equal value, or that the point of belonging to too many organizations cannot be reached. But public relations practitioners owe it to their employers to detail the value of plugging into the information exchange that takes place among members in every well-run organization. They should be ready also to note the potential for extending influence to other important external publics that active membership in such associations provides.

A further advantage has become increasingly clear in recent years. An entire business, professional, or institutional group suffers from unacceptable performance by just a few. Consider the impact of the Watergate scandals of the 1970s on the image of the legal profession, or the Medicaid fraud scandals on the reputation of the medical profession, or callbacks on American automobile manufacturers fighting for their lives against foreign imports. In each case, very few in each group were guilty of misconduct or misjudgment, but in a sense all suffered.

Can a single business, professional practitioner, or institution police every other member of the field? Or by joining together with others in that field can they exert substantial influence for acceptable performance? Broadcasting and advertising in America are not perfect, but they are vastly better today because of efforts of organizations like the National Association of Broadcasters and the American Association of Advertising Agencies, which have detailed codes setting forth acceptable performance and monitor that performance extensively.

GOVERNMENT

In an earlier day, the prevailing American political philosophy was, as essayist Ralph Waldo Emerson expressed it, "The less government, the better." But for better or worse, various levels of government touch many activities today. Consequently, it is not just the highly regulated public utility, tax-supported school, or welfare agency that must be aware of government as one of its most powerful and, therefore, important publics.

The impact of government regulation and government funding is evident all around us. Frequently, the two go hand in hand as with federal highway funds and a federally mandated speed limit; a state implements the federal policy or loses funds to maintain its highway system.

Private institutions and agencies have become dependent on government funds, in some instances to the degree that it is almost a misnomer to call them private. These range from colleges and universities that seek federal loans and grants for buildings, equipment, research projects, and a multitude of special programs, to small retailers and machine shop–size manufacturers who get started with government-sponsored small business loans.

Units of government themselves must recognize the importance of other units and levels of government. Cities have full-time lobbyists or legislative representatives working with state legislatures. States regularly send emissaries to Congress and to federal agencies. At each level of government, officials recognize that what they do and how successfully they accomplish their goals may depend upon the action, reaction, or interaction of some other level of government.

As a result, government relations is a rapidly expanding specialty within public relations. This development parallels the growing realization that institutions, businesses, and even government programs themselves depend on government acceptance of their performance for their existence. Colleges as well as other types of schools, hospitals, nursing homes, and day-care centers are sensitive to government acceptance. Businesses? Remember some of the grand old names in railroading? The Rock Island? The Pennsylvania Railroad? The Milwaukee Road? Consider government agencies, even at the federal level, that have become mere footnotes in history: NRA and CCC disappeared before World War II, river commissions died in 1980, and the Job Corps and Small Business Administration came under fire in 1985.

With its growth and importance government relations is a key area for public relations practice today.

1. Government is not an amorphous gibbosity that exists along the banks of the Potomac. Government is the local Department of Public Works or Office of Sanitation as well as the Environmental Protection Agency when we uncover the special publics concerned with a manufacturer's waste disposal problems.

2. Communication with government agencies, preferably with key individuals within the agencies, cannot be on a crisis-only basis. These officials should be on the mailing list for publications that report on activities of the public relations person's business or organization. Maintain personal contacts.

3. Be aware of actions and policies governmental bodies are considering. This is a by-product of two-way communication. By law, many federal agencies publish proposed rules and regulations and invite comment before implementation. Monitor *The Federal Register* that publishes them. Ordinarily, proposed legislation is discussed at public meetings before being put to a vote. But in other situations and at other levels, government will not be as accommodating in signaling its intentions. Those in government relations must keep informed through constant inquiry and observation. If you would stop the city planning board in its efforts to rezone as residential the site your firm chose for a new office building, will you begin your effort a year before the vote, or the night before?

4. Discard the "devil" or "bad guy" theory of government. A government relations program based on the biased assumption that government is "a coterie of faceless bureaucrats out to get us" immediately cancels itself. Government officials are responsive men and women with all the virtues and vices that come with the territory. Like everyone else, their very real power may affect how they deal with others, but they are not alone in their ability to direct others' lives and in the temptation to flaunt power. Perhaps more than other major publics, government officials may assume an adversary relationship with a public relations practitioner's client or employer. Ruling out a "devil" theory does not mean public relations people are precluded from opposing

and criticizing government, vigorously if need be. It means dealing with government reasonably and realistically, unhampered by stereotypes.

5. If they seem capricious or arbitrary, question government policies or actions. Even though it has created expansive, far-reaching government, the American political system still honors the First Amendment freedoms of speech and press. The First Amendment right to petition not only protects attempts to persuade government officials to take a certain course of action but encourages such activity. Nonetheless, there are ethical and legal guidelines for lobbying and other attempts to influence policy making. Be aware that many other publics disapprove of attempts at persuasion or influence that go too far. You can win a majority of the legislative vote and lose the support of thousands of citizens who will have the final say at the next election.

6. Recognize that many clients and employers view government as an important source of income and assistance rather than as an adversary. This turns the emphasis in government relations programs to those public relations basics: acceptable performance and effective communication. If government is not a stereotype "bad guy," it also is not an all-knowing, all-wise super being. Like everyone else, government representatives need information, and they need help solving problems. They appreciate accurate information and assistance. When your enterprise seeks government help, it is a real plus to have grateful officials in the funding agency.

MEDIA PERSONNEL

Elsewhere we discuss media relations in detail (see Chapters 10–12). At this point, we remind you that it is important to consider media personnel (reporters, editors, photographers, news directors, and producers) as a distinct public in themselves. We have lamented that the messenger particularly in so-called mass communications, often is blamed for the content of the message. Unjustly so. But the messenger can help determine (1) whether the message is told; (2) how the message is told; and (3) how much of the message is told. This is why we discussed reward programs for in-house news gatherers who work for internal publications.

Rather than wining and dining the press corps in an effort to improve communications with external publics, emphasize services and availabilities that make the job easier for its members: timely briefings, carefully prepared information packets, quality graphics, audio material for media that require them, and ready access to knowledgeable leaders who can speak for the corporation or organization.

Professional organizations such as the Society of Professional Journalists, Sigma Delta Chi, the American Newspaper Publishers Association and the Public Relations Society of America in recent years have questioned the propriety of wining and dining reporters. Even if this were not the case, a good reporter always is more grateful for practical assistance in obtaining a significant story than for a free lunch or drink. The sound professional is even wary of the free lunch.

Summary

Identifying and being aware of special publics is more important than classifying a public as "internal" or "external." Some publics are a little of both, after all. And that identifying has got to be a continuing process like the updating of a Christmas card list.

Within publics, particularly external publics, the formation of group attitudes is a process that must concern the public relations practitioner. Particular attention has to be paid to the views of influential individuals within a public, since the social sciences teach us that attitude formation, like learning, is a product of personal communication and relationships.

Among the most frequently identified external publics are (1) the local community; (2) customers, clients, and suppliers; (3) business and professional groups; (4) government; and (5) media personnel. Each has special interests and needs. Practitioners must constantly strive to keep informed about these ever changing interests and needs.

Finally, in dealing with particular external publics, practitioners must be aware of actions those publics consider appropriate. Media guidelines on the acceptability of free entertainment and other gifts for news reporters are just one important example.

Exercises

1. Identify the external publics that are important to the success of a business, institution, or organization with which you are familiar. You might choose some place you have been employed or some organization or institution with which you have been associated. Are there any publics that seem to be difficult to classify as strictly external?

2. Recall the last time you took a tour of a business or institutional facility. Recall how you learned about the availability of the tour (news story, mailing, word-of-mouth, etc.) and evaluate the effectiveness of this communication. If it were not for the tour, would it be difficult or easy for an outsider to become acquainted with the enterprise or organization operating the facility? What improvements could you suggest for the tour?

3. What lines of communication does your college or university maintain with the local community? Do the local news media carry news releases from your institution regularly? Are there any special events sponsored by the college or university for residents of the local community?

4. Ask a local automobile dealer if the dealer keeps in touch with people who buy new automobiles and trucks. Find out whether a regular mailing list of recent purchasers is kept and whether the dealer keeps track of the best customers, those who come back for a second or third purchase.

5. Does your state require lobbyists who appear before the legislature to register with the state? If so, must the lobbyists indicate which organizations they represent? Try to obtain a list of registered lobbyists (it probably is a public record) and identify the types of businesses and agencies that employ people in this area of government relations.

Case study

Fountain Manufacturing Corporation, which makes plumbing fixtures for residential and industrial use, is building a new plant in Roaring Forks, Wyoming. This community of 4500 is near major mines that produce the coal Fountain will use in its manufacturing process.

Fountain expects initially to employ 250 persons at the plant. Within five years, the level of employment is expected to reach 750. Even when it opens, the plant will be the community's largest employer. At present, Roaring Forks is principally a trading and tourist center, with a small dairy and two small foundries as its only industry.

Some members of the Chamber of Commerce have opposed Fountain's new plant. They are afraid the plant will change the character of the city and destroy its attraction for tourists. Some civic leaders are also wary of the changes a major industry will bring. They have seen some examples in other boom towns, particularly two mining communities less than 100 miles away.

To run its plant, Fountain is bringing in people from its facilities in Tacoma, Washington, and Trenton, New Jersey.

What are the external publics Fountain must identify and work with in its new location?

From the little we know about Fountain's situation in Roaring Forks, what are some of the obvious problems it faces with some of these publics? What preliminary suggestions can you make for dealing with these problems?

Suggested readings

Anshen, Melvin, ed. *Managing the Socially Responsible Corporation.* New York: Macmillan, 1974.

Chickering, A. Lawrence. "Warming Up the Corporate Image." *Public Opinion,* October/November 1982.

Cicero, Arthur. "Consumer Complaints: How 155 Letters Were Handled." *Public Relations Journal,* April 1980.

Corbett, William J. "International Consumerism." *Public Relations Journal,* August 1984.

DeLozier, M. *Marketing Communications Process.* New York: McGraw-Hill, 1976.

Eifler, Thomas. "How to Do a Product Application Story." *Public Relations Journal,* April 1980.

Kelly, Donald C. "Decentralized Community Relations." *Public Relations Journal,* February 1984.

Lesly, Philip. *Public Relations Handbook.* Englewood Cliffs, N.J.: Prentice-Hall, 1971.

Makrianes, James K., Jr. "External Relations and the Chief Executive." *Public Relations Journal,* March 1980.

Moran, Dennis J. "Corporate ID Is Your Major Resource." *Communicator's Journal,* May/June 1983.

Putnam, Bryan. "How to Build a Community Relations Program." *Public Relations Journal,* February 1980.

Roalman, Arthur P. *Investor Relations Handbook.* New York: American Management Association, 1974.

8 Businesses, education, and health support organizations

Our definitions and descriptions of public relations, along with the discussion of how practitioners deal with their publics, make it clear that public relations is involved in hundreds of social functions. The extent of public relations efforts ranges widely too. It is as vast as the programs undertaken by PR-conscious corporate conglomerates and as modest as the efforts of a single-owner retail store or a club's volunteer public relations chairman.

To provide a clearer understanding of the components in this wide variety, this chapter deals with three major areas public relations practitioners are engaged in today.

Business corporations

In reviewing the history of public relations, we saw that the field developed in the United States in response to the need of business to gain popular acceptance. As early as World War I, major corporations and their leaders along with the federal government began employing press agents, promoters, and bad-image repairers who, broadly speaking, were the forerunners of today's public relations practitioners.

Today hundreds of large businesses have joined the ranks of those recognizing the need for public acceptance. As a result, business corporations employ the largest contingent of the estimated 100,000 public relations practitioners in the United States. Some of the largest and most comprehensive public relations staffs and programs are those in the service of such business corporations.

SPECIAL OBJECTIVES

Business corporations are organized to conduct profit-making activities. They obtain the means to make money (capital) by persuading people to invest, to let them use their money to make more money. The objectives of corporate public relations are therefore connected with the financial success of the business.

But leaving the matter there is an oversimplification. Important conditions and qualifications must be tied to profit making, especially if this objective is to be reached with the help of professional, ethical public relations activity.

The profits must be merited profits; they must be return on investment that comes from providing a thoroughly satisfactory product or service. The end of the line must be an acceptable manufactured item or an acceptable service. The way the item is made or the service is provided cannot disregard or mistreat human beings, the people in all those internal and external publics previously discussed.

Financial success must be a long-term goal. A fly-by-night operation has financial success as its goal, too, but it wants to make the money fast and it does not worry about leaving dissatisfied and maybe defrauded customers behind. Such make-it-quick-and-run operators do not worry about good public relations because the only acceptance they seek is so short-lived. For the ethical, truly successful business corporation, the profit objective has to be founded on continuous, consistent good performance. Corporate public relations then is the management function that, first and foremost, tries to assure this kind of on-going performance. Then it works at winning the acceptance or support of interested publics on the basis of that good performance.

When we consider what it takes to achieve the acceptability that leads to financial success, it becomes clear that the corporation itself, as an organization or group of people working together, has to be acceptable. The recent history of manufacturing in the United States offers a number of examples of products rated as superior by consumer groups but unsold because their manufacturer's reputation was under a cloud.

The Chrysler Corporation, for instance, marketed a number of highly rated fuel-efficient automobiles at about the same time (before Lee Iacocca came on board) it was in serious financial straits, seeking government assistance. Analysts agreed that sales were hurt by consumer doubts over whether the company would survive.

During the 1960s, major boycotts of products (ranging from foods and beverages to clothing and fuels) were aimed not at the quality of the products shunned but at the corporate policies or the behavior of the producers. The boycott of California head lettuce and J. P. Stevens garments was targeted at the producers, not the products.

A corporation's reputation, after all, is at least as complex as that of a person. We react to people not only on the basis of what they do but on the basis of how they do it, what they say, how they treat others, and how they treat us. Practitioners in corporate public relations must recognize this is related to the profit goal or they will serve their employer or client poorly.

RELATION TO MANAGEMENT

Public relations practitioners often describe their function in a business corporation as that of a conscience. People who say this have usually been through the PR wars. They know that a corporate conscience, like an individual conscience, is often in the middle of struggle and controversy.

Being a conscience is being a control. It is being one who has to say, "No, we really shouldn't do that." It is being accused of constant negativism, or of being unrealistic or moralistic. Even on the affirmative side, it is sometimes being a nag, the voice that keeps saying, "What are you going to do about it? You have to do something; you can't let things continue the way they are. You have to get out of the easy chair and get the job done!"

Another way to look at the practitioner in corporate public relations is as a highly valued adviser, one who is respected and listened to, whose guidance is constantly sought and whose advice will get a careful hearing even when it is not asked for but is volunteered, even when it is critical and disturbing.

The idea is for a corporation's chief executive officer to be sensitive to public relations considerations and knowledgeable about the true role of public relations. This type of executive will not gratuitously offend key publics, then desperately call on the PR staff to smooth things over. This type of person will seek counsel from the public relations staff, not disregard it until the company finds itself hopelessly floundering in hot water with customers or community.

A key to the success of corporate public relations is access to top management, to the ultimate decision makers. A number of public relations fiascos over the years occurred because management either went ahead and acted without any consultation with its public relations people, in-house or agency, or just disregarded what its public relations people were saying.

Why will such corporations even bother having public relations staffs or public relations agencies? In some cases it may be a matter of window dressing, a matter of prestige or status, a form of keeping up with the corporate Joneses. In some cases it is a matter of keeping an emergency fire-fighting team on the payroll. Just in case management gets enmeshed in a media relations or government relations problem, it will have some skilled help to extricate it.

Balancing this reality, however, is the clearly discernible trend toward the ideal: acceptance of public relations as a true concern and function of management at the highest echelons, along with a realization that public relations is basically acceptable performance.

THE PR STAFF POSITION. A good way to get some idea of how a corporation looks at the importance of its public relations, and even to get an idea of the corporation's public relations philosophy, is to examine where a public relations staff is located in the structure of the corporation. The critical point may not be the level at which public relations is fitted into that structure (although that is very important), but the access that the public relations staff has to top management.

For instance, even if a public relations director is not at the top of the organizational chart with the corporation president, the public relations director may be able to communicate with the president directly on a regular basis. The president may likewise consult with the public relations staff. That is a more ideal situation than one in which a vice-president immediately below the president is in charge of public relations but is crowded out of management's inner circle by a dozen or more other vice-presidents.

As you would imagine, there are many similarities in corporate structures. Every business corporation has shareholders or stockholders who elect a board of directors. While that board has ultimate decision-making and broad policy-making authority, the day-to-day operation of the corporation is in the hands of the CEO, commonly a president, with the assistance of vice-presidents and other officers. The number of these officers and the complexity of their relationships with the rest of the corporation's staff depend on the size and diversity of the corporation's operations.

OPERATION. To give an example of corporate structure and the place of public relations, we will use Phillips Petroleum, an energy firm widely recognized for its good public relations in an era when the energy industry has experienced serious problems in public acceptance.

Figure 8.1 will give you some idea of where Phillips has put its public relations staff and how it has parceled out various public relations activities.

Note that the person designated as public relations director ("Manager, Public and Media Communications") reports to the vice-president for public affairs, who in turn reports to the CEO. Note also that many of the functions of public relations as described in previous chapters are not performed by the public relations office in this organizational setup. Instead, they are separate divisions under the vice-president for public affairs.

The regional public relations offices do not report to the public relations director in the home office in Bartlesville, Oklahoma, but coordinate with the corporate public relations director. The charting indicates the interaction that is obviously necessary in this arrangement.

The public relations director has a staff of eight. Their primary function is media relations, communicating with the corporation's external publics through the news media. They not only gather information and prepare news releases for the general media (national news services like the Associated Press and United Press International, major newspapers, broadcast networks and local stations, news magazines, etc.); they also serve specialized media that devote themselves to covering the economy or the petroleum and energy industries in particular.

The public relations staff also follows media coverage carefully to see how its activities and the activities of the industry are being reported, criticized, or praised. A member of the staff also devotes a good percentage of time to consumer relations.

Coordination with the regional offices is particularly important in media relations. The corporation tries to speak with one voice to be consistent in the information it gives the news media and in the responses it gives to questions or criticisms. The public relations director finds it extremely important to know what the people in the regional offices (especially the offices in Europe) are saying, because the American media will know this very quickly through their own transmissions, and they may be asking for explanation and comment soon afterward.

The Corporate Advertising and Contributions division is involved with the sponsorship of activities carrying the corporation's name, with the distribution of education materials that carry that name as sponsor,

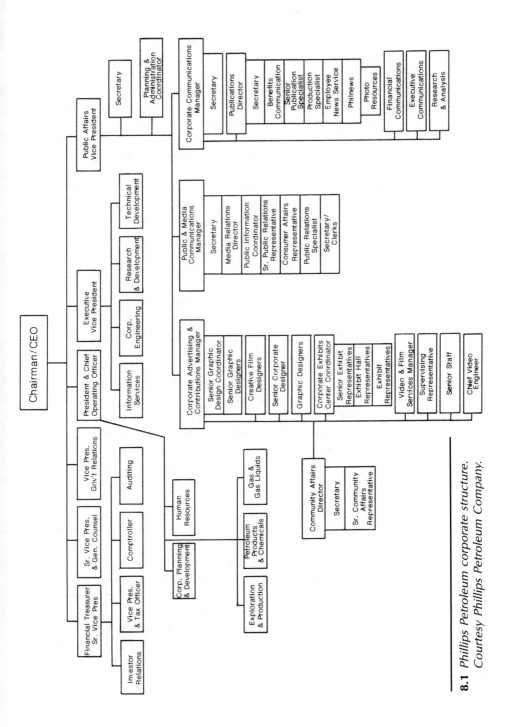

8.1 *Phillips Petroleum corporate structure. Courtesy Phillips Petroleum Company.*

and with the production of commercials and print advertisements that promote the company itself rather than the sale of its products. The need to work with the public relations division in all these activities is clear. In addition, Corporate Advertising and Contributions has access to a graphics staff (artists and photographers) whose services are regularly used by the public relations staff too. Corporate Advertising also has access to a television studio, which public relations shares in training corporate executives to communicate effectively when they make television appearances.

The Corporate Communications division has the assignment of preparing speeches for corporate executives, publishing various company publications (including the employee publication), preparing quarterly and annual reports, and conducting research. The research includes obtaining information from dozens of publications through the use of computer technology. This research service is used regularly by the Public Relations division.

The Financial Communications and Research and Analysis divisions' major concern is the analysis and reporting of financial information of interest to current and prospective shareholders. Government Relations, with a direct line to the CEO, devotes itself to a great extent to monitoring and reporting to management on political developments that affect or have potential for affecting the corporation. In actual approaches to government officials and agencies, Government Relations works closely with Public Relations. Government Relations also must check frequently with the corporation's legal counsel in appraising the possible effects of government actions.

Community Affairs concentrates on involvement by its staff in community organizations and activities. For Phillips this especially involves activities for youth.

If you have been keeping track of this organization in terms of publics and public relations functions discussed earlier, you may have noticed that at least one major public has received only passing mention. That is employees. This public is hardly forgotten, however, especially since the takeover attempts the company has seen. A division that is not under the vice-president for public affairs has the responsibility for employee relations. Although the employee publication is produced by the Corporate Communications division, coordination of public relations in the broad, general sense is a somewhat more difficult assignment for the public affairs people with regard to this public because of the organizational setup.

QUALIFICATIONS. Since Phillips is a large corporation with worldwide interests, and it recognizes the importance of public relations, it recruits proven professionals in its public affairs divisions. The public relations director, for instance, wants people with experience, men and women who have perhaps worked for smaller businesses or who have had experience in the news media.

The preparation of the public relations director, William C. Adams, began with journalism study at the University of Wisconsin. He first went to work for Standard Oil of Indiana (now known as Amoco) at its Chicago headquarters. Eventually moving to Washington, D.C., he became known as virtually the only oil company representative who was willing to talk, and talk candidly, to news reporters during a period when oil shortages, sharply increasing prices, and the long-range energy crisis were major stories and oil companies were the target of widespread criticism.

Today he and his staff at Phillips are known for their willingness to answer questions too. But they have also initiated programs that invite the news media and other key publics to learn more about their company and its industry. When they began around 1980, these efforts were a mixed success. Attendance at some in-depth seminars designed for news reporters who cover the energy field or the oil companies' role in energy was disappointing at times. This may be due to a longstanding tendency of the news media to react rather than act, to wait for an event to occur or an emergency to arise before they pay attention. When the most critical moment has passed, they seem to lose interest, lament public relations practitioners and media critics everywhere.

In addition to experience, the Public Relations division looks at communication competence, the ability to write and report, of prospective staffers. In many ways, Adams says, his people must function like investigative reporters within the corporation, digging out answers to questions their publics are constantly asking.

Knowledge of business generally, including basic economic principles, is important on Adams' list too. Familiarity with the oil industry is obviously a plus, but an eagerness and ability to learn about it quickly are often accepted instead.

While the corporate public relations organization described is by no means the largest among American businesses, it is sizable. Most corporate programs are smaller.

And when we turn to the nonprofit sector, the public relations staff and its operations will usually be much smaller. Just as many publics may be served, and the public relations activities may be just as varied, but fewer people will be doing more different things, with less specializing and less elaborate development of particular programs.

Educational public relations

Like business during the period public relations was first developing, the field of education has come to realize the necessity of winning and holding the support of its publics through the unsettling experiences encountered when those publics have become disaffected. For public school districts and tax-supported colleges and universities, those unsettling experiences have often been tax and appropriation cuts. For independent non-tax-supported school systems and institutions, the experiences have also been tied to financial crises, often complicated by concurrent decreases in enrollment.

While the initial awakening to the need for good public relations has often come as a result of sharp economic nudges, educators have generally had their eyes opened to other compelling reasons for maintaining good relations with their publics. After many years of working with and in education, we would say that teachers and administrators are sincere, for instance, when they say that education cannot be accomplished most effectively without the active cooperation of the families of their students. So much has been discovered in recent years about the importance of parental interest in preparing very young children for their formal learning experience in schools. The roots of so many discipline problems have been traced to family influences. All these developments have pointed clearly to the need for comprehensive public relations programs for school systems and individual institutions so they can involve their key publics in their educational mission.

THE SCHOOL DISTRICT

OBJECTIVES. At first glance, identifying the ultimate goal for a school system would seem easy. It is providing a good education for the children of the district. But how good that education should be, especially in terms of programs and facilities, is often an issue of continuing controversy. The reasons are costs versus the special needs perceived by the public, particularly parents. The ultimate objective then is probably best expressed as "good education at a reasonable cost."

One of the strong points of public education in the United States is that it remains based in the local community, in spite of state standards and supervision and federal aid, programs, and mandates. But this very advantage can turn into a nightmare for the school district's public relations person. Because the public schools are community based, every taxpayer in the community may take a proprietary interest in the schools that can quickly transform itself into the feeling that "since they're my schools, I know what's wrong with them." The public relations director is often faced by citizens who are convinced they know what ought to be taught and how, and how much it ought to cost. Just look at all the criticism that has been aimed at tax-supported school systems in very recent times and you will see this thoroughly documented, everything from the imposition of competency testing and lawsuits against districts because they graduated students who were virtually illiterate to legally imposed spending lids that have forced some large systems to end their school year early when funds ran out.

Faced with a host of kibitzers and critics who consider themselves experts, school public relations practitioners can easily be overwhelmed. They have to see the situation as one that offers fantastic challenge. The key is to steer the widespread desire for good schools in the direction of on-going support for local education.

The goals of public relations in this setting will be (1) to make the schools' management (the board of education and the superintendent) receptive and responsive to legitimate criticism; and (2) to let the all-important community/taxpayer public know what is being accomplished in the schools, both in terms of effective education and careful use of tax funds.

These observations have led us right into identifying key publics in education. Within the community, parents of school children form an extremely important subgroup, one that can often exert tremendous influence within the larger community. Local business and industry are highly influential. As major taxpayers, their example of support for educational improvement, which also seems to be costly, can set the pattern for a communitywide attitude.

Businesses should know, and be reminded frequently, that they have a major stake in local education. A good school system means a pool of well-educated potential employees, and a good school system is an attractive item for employees the businesses may want to bring to the community.

ORGANIZATIONAL RELATIONSHIPS. Full-time public relations prac-titioners are found in larger school systems, especially in metropolitan areas. In smaller districts, public relations may be the function of an assistant superintendent or an administrator near that level, or even of the superintendent. PR functions may well be divided among several people too. In terms of authority and responsibility, of course, public relations is a function of the superintendent's office, whether per-formed by a full-time staff, by an individual, or by the superintendent.

Some students of educational administration also say that public relations is a function of the school board. Their comments, however, suggest that what they mean is that board members have a civic duty to promote the cause of the school district among the citizens of the district.

But, as you have been reminded many times, that function is but a small part of a comprehensive public relations program. More-over, a public relations staff is appointed by the superintendent and works under the superintendent; it does not answer directly to the board of education.

This is significant from several points of view. First, it means that if there is friction between the superintendent and the school board, a PR staff may find itself in a very awkward position. The staff's duty is to help provide good education in the school system and to encourage support for the board's general policies, which are aimed at achieving that goal. At the same time, the staff is hired and fired by the superintendent, who may disagree with the board on some aspects of its policies.

Second, the superintendent may get caught in the cross fire between school board or staff factions. Especially when the factions are almost equally divided, this sort of conflict may make it difficult to pro-vide information about the schools without having it challenged or contradicted by one side or the other.

For example, in one school district several years ago the amount of vandalism at a junior high school raised the ire of several school board members who were already critical of the administration. The junior high principal instituted a peer pressure system in which students were encouraged to deal with the alleged vandals themselves, persuading them their actions were unacceptable among their fellow students. Publicity was given to the success claimed for this program. The princi-pal told the news media the number of broken windows was half of what it had been.

Not so, a teacher retorted. There were just as many broken win-dows as ever and vandalism had not abated a bit.

The upshot seems to have been a loss of PR credibility for the whole district and even deeper factionalism on the school board. Some members supported the principal, some opposed him.

Unlike the board of directors of a business corporation, a board of education in most American school districts is chosen in a nonpartisan general election. The campaign and voting may be nonpartisan, but the elections are still political and often bitter. The alliances or factions that may form among board members may also represent highly politicized alliances and factions within the district. One group, for instance, may be allied with the teachers and their chapter of the National Education Association; another group may be tied to an extremely cost-conscious taxpayer organization. The feuding that occurs is often highly visible, popping up at public meetings and in statements to the news media. It is a special burden the PR staff must bear.

That public relations staff or director, incidentally, most probably will not have a title that uses "public relations," because most government agencies find it almost impossible to get tax funds appropriated for activities described as "public relations." As a result, school public relations people will hold the title of public information officer, public affairs director, or simply assistant to the superintendent. Some even are named board secretaries or assistant secretaries, further muddying their relationship to the board of education and the superintendent.

SERVING THE DISTRICT'S PUBLICS. The internal discord mentioned can make both internal and external public relations difficult for the staff of a school district. Before the staff can tell external publics about the good deeds performed by the schools, the problem of the sharp division among the people who must be encouraged to do the good deeds must be resolved.

A common issue before school boards in recent years has been student discipline. The controversy covers everything from whether corporal punishment is to be condoned to whether disciplinary procedures provide the basic fairness of "due process." If a district is suffering disapproval from its very important community public because of its discipline procedures, the job of the public relations person is to persuade management to remedy the situation.

Discipline often becomes a political issue in which the school board demands a policy-making role. Often a board will have members who want to return to the eighteenth or nineteenth century style of discipline at one end of the opinion spectrum. On the other end are members who want a complex system of courtlike due process guarantees in all rules violations cases. Because they have outspoken constituencies in the community, board members at both extremes may be much less willing to compromise than the decision makers in a business corporation setting.

The division between the superintendent's office and the board of education has, in fact, led many in educational public relations to think in terms of the board as a special public, one of those internal/external publics. As long as the public relations practitioner remembers the legal realities of the typical public school district's organizational structure, treating the board as a special public can be a very practical approach.

In one setting, however, a public relations person will find it difficult to think of the school board as a public—at board meetings. Here the board itself can improve or seriously damage relations with the district's key publics. This can occur when unthinking statements are made, uninformed criticisms are exchanged, or ill-advised actions are taken.

Board meetings pose another public relations problem. Of all the forms of local government in the United States, in the minds of many local news reporters the school district is the most notorious for its reluctance to conduct business in public. In many states, "open meetings" laws have been passed because of the inclination of school boards to bar reporters and other interested citizens from their regular sessions or, more frequently, to go into executive sessions.

Anyone who has dealt with laws requiring open meetings knows that games can be played with the wording of the requirements for public sessions. The most popular game is "When Is a Meeting Not a Meeting?" Any number of board of education members can play. They just get together for a "social gathering," and just happen to discuss school district business, maybe even reaching some consensus on how they will deal with certain issues. They do not have to give notice of this gathering because it is social rather than official.

It is a sticky enough situation for public relations practitioners when corporate management will not be open and candid with the news media. When you are a public relations director for a school district whose meetings must, by law, be open, it is an impossible situation. The board is flouting a requirement that may well have been made law as a result of media effort.

Internal publics for school systems include students (who are easily overlooked, especially at the elementary and secondary level), teachers, staff, and volunteers. Parents and parent-teacher groups may be internal/external types. We have also cited the significance of business and industry as a key segment of the community public. Civic, religious, and service groups are also segments of the community that can give effective support to education.

Because a school district is a unit of local government with its own taxing power, it is possible to overlook other levels of government as special publics. These other levels can have a great impact on local curriculum and financial resources. We are thinking here of state legislators, state departments of public instruction, members of Congress, and even the President. In the late 1970s, it was President Carter who led the effort to establish a cabinet-level Department of Education and President Reagan who indicated he would change this status for education. Health and social welfare agencies of the state and federal governments must also be considered special publics.

THE COLLEGE OR UNIVERSITY

State colleges, vocational and technical institutes, and universities face many of the public relations challenges described for public school districts, particularly if these institutions are governed by elected boards. While popular election of such governing boards is designed to keep higher education close to its constituency, it does permit politicizing of education, or at least of educational policy.

In some states, members of state boards of regents use their position as a stepping-stone to other political positions. This usually involves stirring up controversy, doing something to attract attention, invariably involving unwanted headaches for the public relations people affected.

Technical institutes and junior colleges in most parts of the United States serve a community or region within a state, although some are operated directly by the state. In the case of the community institution, the setting, publics, and public relations challenges may differ only slightly from those of the public school district. The state-supported institution, on the other hand, will have a statewide public as well as a community or local public, and its communications programs will have to be more extensive to reach that broader public.

Because of the age and maturity of students at the post-secondary level, they become a more important public. Parents may not be as active or directly involved in education at this level but they cannot be neglected as a public. In many cases, it is the parent who decides whether a child's college choice is affordable.

Like a public relations person in a school district, the practitioner employed by a tax-supported college or university is frequently appointed by the chief executive officer of the institution (the president or chancellor) and often reports to that CEO.

Los Angeles City College, one of California's many two-year, tuition-free community colleges, may serve as an example of how public relations is handled by institutions in this category.

The college has a full-time public information officer, located in the administrative office area and assisted by a full-time clerk-stenographer and a half-time student assistant. The PIO is accountable directly to the college president, who supervises and evaluates the PIO's work. The budget for the public information office covers salaries and some printing and supplies.

The public information officer spends about 35 percent of the time in media relations, researching, writing, editing, and distributing news releases and public service announcements. Outlets include metropolitan, ethnic, community, and student newspapers; radio and television stations; local chambers of commerce; selected high schools; and college and district administrators.

In addition, the PIO responds to news media inquiries regarding college activities and individual students. Often such media inquiries lead to the issuing of news releases. Because of its location near many major broadcast outlets, the institution and its students often get covered for a "typical college" reaction to a national news event.

About 15 percent of the PIO's time is spent producing publications, occupational brochures, flyers, catalogs, class schedules, handbooks, etc. The PIO writes and edits copy, takes or commissions photographs, consults with graphic artists at the college, and works with other college personnel in planning and developing the various publications.

An equal share of the PIO's effort is devoted to supervising off-campus distribution of class schedules and catalogs. Catalogs, for instance, are sent to 3000 libraries, military installations, and other facilities around the world, and several thousand more are sent in response to inquiries from other California colleges and universities, high schools, employment offices, and businesses.

The public information officer also handles telephone and mail requests for information about the college. That includes mailing brochures, general information letters, and personal letters in response to specific requests.

About 10 percent of the PIO's time is spent supervising, compiling, and editing a weekly campus bulletin that goes to 1250 administrators, teachers, and staff members at the institution, and providing news items and photographs concerning people and events at the college to a bimonthly newsletter circulated to employees of the 10 Los Angeles community colleges. Related activities include assistance in the preparation of a monthly newsletter for the college's nonfaculty staff, and maintenance of three college bulletin boards that carry announcements, job listings, and various information of interest to students and employees.

A little less than 10 percent of the PIO's time is spent working directly with the college president, preparing speeches and remarks for both college and external audiences, drafting responses to letters and surveys, and recommending policies and courses of action on sensitive issues involving students, college employees, or the general public.

About an equal amount of time is devoted to directing the organization, planning, and publicity connected with special events such as inaugurations, dedications, and anniversaries; providing help with recurring major events such as commencements; and assisting with continuing programs such as student recruitment.

The public information officer spends slightly less time advising college committees, such as those on campus beautification, lectures, student recruitment, and commencement; supervising tours of the college's 40-acre campus for visitors, who may range from local elementary and high school students to foreign dignitaries; and helping arrange visits by college representatives with outside publics.

In addition to this, the public information officer fields telephone calls the college switchboard does not know how to handle, provides advice on the college's annual report, works on budgets, and deals with walk-in requests from the general public.

Independent schools, colleges, and universities often have more extensive public relations operations. It is a matter of necessity. The non-tax-supported school or college does not have the general long-term tax-funding commitment that state and community educational institutions have. As a result, potential students, because they may become actual tuition payers, are a more important public. Also important are potential corporate and individual contributors whose gifts substitute, at least in part, for the tax funds the state or community institution receives. The public institution may go to its legislature with outstretched hand every year or every biennium; the independent college or university has its hand outstretched every day and in every direction.

Fund raising is necessary not only to sustain the independent institution but to keep it financially competitive. If it did not engage in fund raising, the independent college or university would have to set tuition so high that its financial disadvantage would turn into no contest with other institutions in the competition for students. Tuition and fees cover only a fraction of the cost of educating students at tax-supported institutions. But tuition covers much more of the cost at independent colleges and universities. As a result, tax-supported institutions, in public relations terms, may win favor from their potential-student public because of their relatively low cost; the independent institutions thus start off at a disadvantage in striving for the acceptance of this same public.

In many instances, the importance of fund raising has shaped the organizational position of public relations in independent colleges and universities. Emphasizing this, the title "university relations" started becoming popular in the 1960s. It is an attempt to get across the idea that such educational institutions recognized the importance of activity much broader than that taken by the public relations or public information offices in neighboring tax-supported institutions.

As the simplified organizational chart in Figure 8.2 indicates, most of the subdivisions of university relations may be oriented toward fund raising. Alumni are important because of their special interest, affection, and loyalty. As a group, they will constitute the most supportive individual donors to the college or university, but to maintain their support, the college or university must maintain close ties with them. This includes the tedious, never-ending task of keeping track of where alumni locate after graduation. It includes providing alumni with publications designed to keep them abreast of events at their old college; organizing alumni clubs in communities where there are sizable numbers of them; and sending representatives of the college or university to meet with them, particularly at gatherings of those alumni clubs.

The federal government, especially through its agencies involved in supporting education, research, and the arts, has become a major source of funding for independent colleges and universities. So a government relations office is a typical division of what is now known as university relations. To a great extent, federal money comes in the form of grants for projects undertaken at the college or university. The government relations office tries to keep informed on all government grant programs, encourages faculty researchers to initiate grant applications, and assists them in writing and processing grant proposals. The staff of

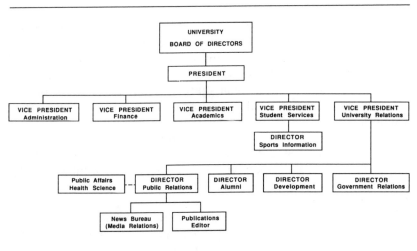

8.2 *Organizational chart for a typical university.*

this office will also visit granting agencies to personalize relations and improve communication.

"Development" is the widely used euphemistic title for more general fund raising. The development office is concerned with obtaining donations from nonalumni as well as alumni, especially from business and industry, affluent individuals, and private foundations. Members of the staff spend most of their effort preparing proposals for such potential donors. The proposals will, of course, be based upon thorough research into the types of gifts or special interests of the businesses, foundations, and individuals contacted.

Like public relations in the business corporation, public relations in the framework represented by Figure 8.2 has media relations as one of its primary concerns. Special events and observances, because they are designed to attract media coverage, will also fall under the jurisdiction of the public relations department. Since special events often call for the preparation of promotional materials, public relations staffers may also produce audio-visual materials as well as print pieces such as directories, brochures, and pamphlets.

The public relations office or department of an independent college or university will usually deal with community relations. The office often organizes a speakers' bureau, encouraging members of the staff to speak to civic and professional groups. The public relations office may also help the news media contact faculty members who are specialists in the arts, sciences, and professions when the media need background or reaction to non-college-connected new developments (e.g., a sociologist to comment on a national study of family living patterns, or a physicist to comment on the work done by this year's Nobel Prize winner).

The staff in the area of university relations will also contribute directly to good community relations by participation in major community projects, becoming members of civic organizations, and encouraging college or university administrators and faculty members to involve themselves in community service.

After referring to Figure 8.2 and reading this description of duties and functions, you might notice some significant publics apparently missing. Perhaps because they are young, perhaps because they are around only a few years, students often get too little attention as a public. And perhaps because historically faculty members have considered themselves professionals and sharers in decision making within a college or university, the faculty is often neglected as a critical internal public. The results of such oversight have too often been friction, resentment, opposition, and distrust, all quite avoidable.

For example, not too long ago an independent college announced a sharp increase in tuition through a news release to the news media. It was the first word students, tuition-paying parents, and faculty members had of the decision.

A large protest meeting was convened by the student government. Student body leaders urged seniors not to pledge any donation to the annual program the college had lovingly nurtured for several years. Reams of negative publicity were produced by the situation.

But a lesson was learned. The college instituted a procedure that calls for its president to discuss tuition projections with the student government before any announcements are made regarding the coming academic year. The procedure calls for the president to provide student leaders with a financial justification for increased costs for room and board as well as tuition, similar to the justification the president must give to the board of regents. The college's faculty and staff are also given word on tuition levels before a general news release is issued, so they will be prepared to respond to questions or negative reactions.

If students often justifiably sense that they are ignored and bypassed, faculty members frequently feel they are taken too much for granted; that decisions, even if they benefit the faculty, are too often made without consulting or informing them, and that their requests are many times left to gather dust on some administrator's desk.

There is an academic fable that could be set just as appropriately in the business world. It tells of a distinguished professor, overworked and underpaid, who asks for a raise or a reduction in teaching load. The dean pays no attention, so the professor finally leaves and has to be replaced by two people who demand higher salaries than the dean was willing to pay the veteran professor. In his new post, the professor, it turns out, replaces another distinguished professor who had been overworked and underpaid. . . .

The story suggests several morals. The most important is like the conclusion Peters and Waterman came to in developing their profile of America's best-run businesses: a key ingredient for success is management's respect and concern for its own people. And faculty members are a critical internal public.

In practical terms, if special publications and programs are designed for alumni and community leaders because they are identified as important publics, at least the same consideration should be given to students and faculty. To accomplish this, a university relations division will have to work with the academic administration. In effect, it will have to counsel management in areas where public relations considerations have too long been ignored. This is fully consistent with the broad role described earlier for public relations in corporate business.

Health support organizations

Like colleges and universities, independent health support organizations must devote a great portion of their public relations effort toward fund raising. They need donations to achieve their goals. They have some important special publics, but they must also reach the general public directly and continually.

OBJECTIVES

An organization concerned with a specific illness or physical condition has the eradication of that illness or the correcting of that condition as its ultimate objective. The American Cancer Society, for example, works for the eventual cure and prevention of the many forms of cancer. But the present state of human knowledge makes it apparent that achieving the ultimate goal of the Cancer Society, and similar goals of other health support organizations, is far in the future. As a result, efforts are directed at more immediate goals: research, education, and the highest level of prevention that medical science can support today.

Health support or health care institutions, on the other hand, have individual healing as their principal objective, but they too must frequently concentrate on intermediate goals. These include relieving pain and stabilizing or reversing the deteriorated physical condition of someone who is ill or injured.

Many dramatic breakthroughs have occurred in promoting and protecting human health in recent decades. We have seen everything from major organ transplants to the development of powerful immunization serums. But many cures, like one for the common cold, continue to elude medical science. There are even reverses from time to time (e.g., the discovery that certain strains of bacteria and viruses become resistant to wonder drugs that were prematurely labeled cures).

The failure of research to produce frequent breakthroughs, especially as research costs keep going up, and the failure of hospitals and clinics to effect cures for so many terminally ill patients can be deeply discouraging for people in health support organizations and institutions. They can get apologetic and even defensive about their work. Or they can begin to isolate themselves from those they serve, and other important publics too, as a kind of protective measure. The impact on public relations, however, is negative.

A situation like this suggests that (1) in health-related public relations, a periodic review of goals and objectives should be considered especially important to aid the administration and staff of the organization or institution maintain a balanced view of their work; and (2) public relations practitioners in this field must be alert to the apparent callousness that people can easily develop and communicate to their publics when they face sickness and death daily.

For example, for many years medical laboratories across the country experienced a shortage of human cadavers for research and instruction. Many people shrink from the thought of having their bodies dissected after death. To offset this reluctance, laboratories and medical schools have tried to emphasize the truly noble contribution people can make by giving their bodies for research and instruction, to lighten the burden of sickness and disability for future generations. Scientists and teachers stress the respect and care exercised in handling donated bodies.

Soon after a very enlightened program like this was launched by one laboratory, with wide publicity throughout the community, several employees did their best to torpedo the program. They were in charge of transporting unclaimed bodies from the county morgue to the laboratory. In a hurry one day, they failed to fasten the tarpaulin on their truck, loaded with a shipment of bodies. As they took a sharp turn onto a major thoroughfare, the tarp blew up and several bodies rolled off the truck into the street. Passersby were aghast when the two men unabashedly picked up the cadavers and flung them back on the truck as if they were firewood.

The pair undoubtedly had psyched themselves into considering the bodies as mere commodities to protect their own emotional stability, but their actions came across as a shocking display of insensitivity, totally contrary to the care and respect pledged by their superiors.

Again, acceptable performance is the essence of good public relations!

SPECIAL PUBLICS

Health support organizations that conduct fund-raising activities among the general population must devote much of their effort to serving and communicating with this broad public. Their public relations people will undoubtedly consider media personnel an important public because the media are so essential in reaching that general population.

But individual volunteers, volunteer organizations, and civic and social groups that may adopt the health support organization as their special philanthropy are also important intermediate publics. They will provide the hours and hours of organizational activity that precede any communitywide fund-raising effort and carry on the person-to-person and door-to-door solicitations.

Members of these three publics are also invaluable ambassadors within the community throughout the year. They cannot be ignored for months, then be expected to turn on their enthusiasm suddenly for "the cause" when the annual fund-raising period comes around again.

Health support organizations also recognize the health professions as special publics since their primary goals are tied so closely to those of health practitioners and researchers. But the health field is broad, so public relations practitioners must always remember to include all its identifiable groups, not just physicians, but dentists, nurses, medical technologists, physical therapists, dietitians, and nutritionists as well.

The customers of health care institutions, their patients, are a key public. Public relations people have to remind staffs of this. Too often patients, who are intelligent, responsible, sensitive human beings who just happen to be sick at the moment, are still treated condescendingly. They are often heedlessly given the "Doctor (or nurse or whoever) knows best" treatment, and they resent it. From top to bottom, staff members have to be diplomatically but pointedly reminded of this truth: just as students grow up and become wealthy alumni, patients get well and become potential donors to the hospital's building fund.

The tax-supported institution is not immune from the need for good patient relations. Even indigent patients can vote for or against bond issues to finance remodeling or expanding the hospital.

A patient also has a family and friends. Often their experiences with the hospital will be spread, for better or worse, through their circle of acquaintances and influence the community long after the patient they visited has been discharged.

Summary

For a practical, hands-on look at the field, public relations can be divided into business and nonprofit spheres such as education and health support organizations. A consideration of the differences between these broad fields can provide an informative perspective on the great variety of activity to be found in public relations practice.

Business remains the largest employer of public relations practitioners. The most elaborate PR programs and the greatest specialization is found in corporate PR.

While the "bottom line" in business is literally the bottom line of the profit-and-loss statement, corporate public relations today is helping American business take a more realistic, long-term view of profit as its sole ultimate objective. This contemporary approach insists that people—employees, customers, neighbors in the community—must be truly served in the process.

To promote this insight, however, public relations practitioners must be in a position to influence policy. The organizational slot for public relations executives and staffs in the corporate chain of command can mean the difference between effectiveness and frustration.

In the nonprofit sphere, the same principle holds. To have an impact on policy, public relations people must have direct access to leadership. This is true in all the major nonbusiness areas: education, health maintenance, and the various professions associated with each.

In looking at special areas, students and practitioners will see that they can adapt the action-as-priority approach to all of them. This, however, must come after they have thoroughly acquainted themselves with the goals, problems, resources, and key publics that characterize each area.

Exercises

1. Examine the administration of school districts in your area to find out (a) who on the staff is in charge of media relations (preparing news releases, answering reporters' questions, and responding to requests for background or statistical information from the news media); (b) what title or job description that person has; and (c) to whom that person reports.

2. Take on the role of critic. Keep your eyes and ears open for public service announcements on radio and television and for public service advertisements in your local newspaper. Note what causes or organizations they support. Then make some judgments about their comparative effectiveness. Do they catch the attention of the people at whom they are aimed? Do they really convey a message? Are they persuasive enough to motivate their target audiences?

3. If there is a sizable business or institution in your community that offers tours of its facilities, schedule a visit and evaluate the community relations effectiveness of the tour. What was your attitude toward the business or institution before you took the tour? Did it change in any way? Why?

4. What type of educational background, beyond public relations and communications, would be most helpful to a practitioner planning a career in corporate public relations? In what areas should such a person take supporting courses? Why?

5. Some business corporations buy out small stockholders because they consider it uneconomical to communicate with them and worry about their attitudes. Does the professional perspective or outlook of a public relations practitioner provide any good reasons for not doing this?

Case study

Sunnyvale, a city of 25,000 about 40 miles from a large metropolitan area, has prided itself for years on the attractiveness of its public facilities. Its city hall was designed by a local architect who donated his services. In its downtown mall is a fountain modeled after a famous original in Italy. Streets and sidewalks have always been maintained in good condition, and public buildings are clean and serviceable.

Sunnyvale's greatest pride has been its park system—four large parks with many forms of recreational facilities, two extended parkways along major thoroughfares, and almost a dozen neighborhood "squares" with trees, picnic tables, benches, and swings for children, etc. In recent years, however, many nonresidents from the metropolitan area have crowded the parks during the summer, and the city budget has had less money for park maintenance. The result is that these once lovely parks have a seedy, run-down look. At the same time, vandalism has hit a number of the neighborhood squares; several have become eyesores.

The Chamber of Commerce in Sunnyvale is seriously concerned that one of the community's greatest assets is being eroded. The directors have turned to members of their public relations committee for suggestions on how the situation can be turned around.

• How does this public relations challenge fit into the various areas of public relations described in this chapter?

• What public relations resources can a mere voluntary Chamber of Commerce committee mobilize to deal with so serious a problem?

• To solve this problem, is there any way in which you can find a role for each of the specialized areas of public relations dealt with in this chapter?

Suggested readings

Botwinick, Pat. "The Image of Corporate Image." *Public Relations Journal,* November 1984.

Budd, John F., Jr. *An Executive's Primer on Public Relations.* Philadelphia: Chilton Book Co., 1969.

Burton, Paul. *Corporate Public Relations.* New York: Reinhold Publ. Corp., 1966.

Cunningham, Lynne. "Not-For-Profit Budgeting." *Public Relations Journal,* May 1983.

Dunn, S. Watson, Martin F. Cahill, and Jean J. Boddewyn. *How Fifteen Transnational Corporations Manage Public Affairs.* Chicago: Crain Books, 1979.

Harrington, Michael. *The Twilight of Capitalism.* New York: Simon and Schuster, 1976.

Hauser, L. J. "Curing Hospitals' Financial Ills." *Public Relations Journal,* May 1983.

Higgins, John. "University Public Relations." *Public Relations Journal,* May 1983.

Kobre, Sidney. *Successful Public Relations for Colleges and Universities.* New York: Hastings House, 1974.

Kreps, Gary L., and Barbara C. Thornton. *Health Communication.* New York: Longman, Inc., 1984.

Lichter, Linda, S. Robert Lichter, and Stanley Rothman. "How Show Business Shows Business." *Public Opinion,* October/November 1982.

O'Hara, Thomas E., and Donald P. Durocher, "The Decade of the Investor." *Public Relations Journal,* April 1980.

Pinsdorf, Marion K. "The Corporate City Room: How One PR Staff Handled a Major News Break." *Public Relations Journal,* April 1980.

Rick, W. Emerson. *The Changing World of College Relations.* Washington, D.C.: Case, 1976.

Rose, Merrill. "Striking a Balance Between Company Goals and Consumer Demands." *Public Relations Journal,* February 1984.

Ruth, Carol A., and Robert C. Hubbell. "Communicating in the New-Issue-Market." *Public Relations Journal,* April 1984.

Shupack, Leslie A. "A New Role for Investor Relations?" *Public Relations Journal,* April 1980.

9 Political and government public relations

Politics, especially American-style politics, appears to have adopted public relations more enthusiastically than almost any other area of contemporary life. Even candidates for local office have campaign managers in charge of public relations strategy and committees with the job of executing all the public relations right moves.

Public relations theorists and practitioners alike may be gratified at this recognition for their field. But they are also aware that in the political setting, PR is too often considered essentially image-building and image-projecting sleight of hand. Joe McGinniss's *The Selling of the President* may have been published in 1968, but it still describes, at many levels, what goes on during political campaigns in the name of public relations. Political candidates and their staffs, to a great extent, have yet to learn that public relations is acceptable performance and two-way communication.

Correctly understood, public relations does have a major role in the political life of a democratic nation. Political candidates need the support and approval of voters to win office. Their campaigns are in great part communication programs aimed at mobilizing support and approval. But the successful campaign requires a "good deeds" element: a record a candidate can cite and run on, saying in effect, "Elect me because of what I have done."

The elected candidate and government officials generally must also communicate their performance to their publics. The political figure who attains office employs a press secretary or media aides who coordinate media relations, and government agencies at many levels have their public information officers and specialists who help with this function.

In examining political public relations, we may find politicians who argue that politics has taught public relations more than it has learned from it. Long before public relations emerged as a profession, political campaigns had developed some of the communications practices that public relations uses widely today, practices like the use of attention-catching slogans and personal "imaging." As discussed earlier, "Tippecanoe and Tyler Too" caught the fancy of voters way back in 1840, and Andrew Jackson was "Old Hickory," exploiting his log cabin birth 40 years before the Lincoln legend was born. But that is only a very small part of public relations.

Political campaigns

In the political arena, the practice of public relations is probably most visible during campaigns in the weeks and months immediately preceding an election.

But any close observer of politics knows that the elected candidate who wants to remain in office never stops campaigning. When legislators get up to speak in the state or national capitol, they are campaigning. When they vote on an issue, they are campaigning. When they meet constituents, answer mail, deal with requests, perform ceremonial functions, they are always, in a very real sense, campaigning. It is their performance in all these functions that will decide the success of their overall public relations effort. Only with the fundamental reality constantly in mind—that acceptable day-to-day performance is the essential element—can we properly discuss some of the special aspects of political public relations.

PLANNING AND FUNDING

Almost the first thing a public relations counselor must do in working with a political candidate is assess financial resources. A quick look at the cost of campaigning in America tells us why.

According to reports filed with the Federal Election Commission, almost $26 million was spent by the two candidates for the U.S. Senate in North Carolina in 1984. That surpassed the previous record of $20 million set in the California election for U.S. Senate in 1982. Even in Iowa, a much less populous state, the Senate candidates spent more than $5 million in 1984. All told, candidates for Congress spent $374 million in their 1984 campaigns.

Herbert Alexander, a leading authority on campaign finance, estimates that it cost $275 million to elect the president in the 1980 campaign. And Howard R. Penniman, an American Enterprise Institute scholar, estimates that two-thirds of the campaign expenditures go for television, newspaper, and radio messages, an area where public relations plays a crucial role.

Spending vast amounts of money will not guarantee winning an election. Just ask former Governor James Hunt, who lost to Senator Jesse Helms in that North Carolina campaign that set a spending record. But this may be true: not spending vast amounts of money may guarantee losing an election.

Professionals can assess campaign costs with remarkable accuracy. This comes from experience with campaigns for the same or similar offices and from knowing the cost of media exposure. People who have worked in political campaigns also learn how to stretch campaign dollars and where to spend limited funds most effectively. They can also tell from experience how much more a relatively unknown candidate will have to spend just to overcome the "familiarity factor" that consistently seems to be an advantage for incumbents.

One of the first bits of advice a public relations consultant may have to give a potential candidate is, "Forget it. You don't have the money to be a serious contender." That is blunt and will come as a blow to the would-be candidate, but it may avoid wasted effort and deeper disappointment in the weeks and months ahead.

Candidates who run for local or small district offices may be able to operate a campaign effectively with several thousand dollars. That may be the cost for a candidate running for school board, city council, or village or county commission where the constituency is no more than 20,000. A well-established, popular incumbent may spend even less to get reelected in such circumstances. Then again, that incumbent may find on election night that she relied too heavily on recognition and popularity and underspent in the face of a vigorous, well-financed campaign by the opposition.

Costs rise as the size of the constituency increases, all the way to the hundreds of millions of dollars spent in the campaigns for the presidency. In between, experience and an appraisal of voter recognition and the strength of the competition must determine the precise dollar amount needed.

Incidentally, it is possible to overspend in a campaign. A few years ago a candidate for mayor of Omaha began his campaign early, using strategic outdoor advertising and employing television heavily. In the primary, the candidate was narrowly defeated by a last-minute but well-known write-in candidate. Even though he had pointed to his budgetary conservatism as a county commissioner, his campaign expenditures seemed to belie the message, surveys of voters after the primary election indicated.

When large amounts of money are needed for a political campaign, public relations counselors know major donors are essential. If a person is going to run for Congress, for instance, at least $150,000 to $200,000 may be necessary just to get through the primary election. This is not the kind of money raised by passing the hat at a rally or even by throwing $100-a-plate dinners. It requires solid prospects for gifts of $10,000 or more from organizations and wealthy individuals who will be willing to be tapped again once the candidate wins the primary.

Identifying those donors, realistically determining how much they can be expected to give, and getting commitments from them are the first steps in campaign public relations. Without the money in hand, a campaign is not just doomed to flounder; it cannot even start.

Fund-raising events and modest contributions from nonwealthy donors are not to be scorned, of course; they must be fitted into any successful campaign. Fund-raising events are included in the activities discussed in Chapter 12.

Planning is inseparable from funding. Fund needs are based not only on what has been spent in previous campaigns for a particular office, but on an estimate of what the competition will spend and the cost of the campaign activities planners determine are necessary or important for the candidate.

Planners list the reasons a candidate is running for office and identify those groups that are most in sympathy with these goals. Then activities are planned to win and keep the support of those groups (e.g., make personal contacts at plants and offices, arrange speaking opportunities, prepare and place media messages, etc.). Once those activities are determined, the campaign plan can be priced. Changes in the plan may have to be made to stay within the budget or to counter moves by the opposition.

MEDIA USE

In campaign public relations, acceptable performance is to a great extent past performance. Candidates, whether they want to or not, run on their records. Nonetheless, their performance as campaigners is also important. In judging people, we learn by seeing them in action, especially when we can observe how they react to challenges, stress, and opposition.

For this reason, candidates must be counseled and prepared for live or "uncontrolled" media appearances, situations in which they are interviewed by news people or photographed and videotaped in action. The same preparation advised for business and organization leaders who deal directly with the media applies to political and governmental figures.

The news conference is used heavily during campaigns for important, large-constituency offices. Candidates are expected to perform smoothly and effectively at the news conferences. Voters feel that someone who must make many public appearances during a campaign should handle a live-television news conference with self-possession and style. They may even consider how the candidate would handle such situations if elected to public office.

While public relations counsel can sponsor, and thus to an extent control, a news conference, news interviews are different. For these, candidates have to be coached to deal with a situation where they may unexpectedly or with little warning have a microphone thrust at their faces, often with a camera rolling. "Coached" does not imply that public relations counsel is supposed to supply stock dodges for hard questions or cutesy responses that avoid issues. Rather, candidates have to be reminded to think before speaking, to be aware that an off-the-cuff remark can easily be misinterpreted, and that a flat assertion made without checking the facts can haunt a would-be officeholder right through election day.

On the other hand, while media advertising is expensive, media news coverage is free newspaper space and air time. Public relations practitioners will want to use every opportunity to get their candidates into the news, often by pointing out ways the candidates can make news.

The most common way for the candidate to make news is to speak out on a campaign issue. Some counselors even operate in the political arena on the premise: "A news release a day keeps voter disinterest away." But this can be easily overdone. We have seen many a wastebasket lined with unused campaign news releases that really were newsless, just a dribbling out of the candidate's comments on too many insubstantial matters. A regular schedule of more selective statements and reactions by the candidate will be more likely to attract news coverage helpful to the campaign.

The amount of money spent on controlled or paid media use indicates the importance political candidates place on this effort. *The Selling of the President* discusses how one successful presidential campaign put almost all of its media use eggs in this basket. Critics of President Ronald Reagan accused him of relying heavily on controlled media use in his successful 1984 campaign also.

But whatever the mix of free and paid use, controlled media use is essential in many campaigns. The news conference and news interview simply do not provide enough exposure for a candidate. The exception may be the campaign for a local, limited-constituency office in which personal appearances and door-to-door canvassing can still be relied upon. In larger campaigns, there simply is no other effective way for candidates to get known, and candidate recognition and familiarity are musts.

In one congressional campaign in which we were involved, our candidate had given hundreds of talks and speeches to groups within his district in the 15 years before he decided to run. He estimated that he had met and shaken hands with thousands of voters during that time. Unfortunately, his opponent in the primary had been a television news commentator on a local station for several years. Preelection polls and the primary election itself confirmed that the opponent's nightly television exposure outdistanced our candidate's personal contacts in achieving the familiarity factor.

In selecting an agency to handle controlled media use, the public relations practitioner should base advice on previous performance. Which agencies have handled successful political campaigns? Does their style suit this particular campaign and candidate? The consultant should also ask whom the agency will have working on the campaign. You do not want the second or third string, and you do not want people who will be over-involved with other accounts, since you want to be able to call for help on short notice. A campaign is unpredictable, and quick action may be necessary to offset the opposition's moves.

ORGANIZATION

Political campaigns frequently misfire for lack of sound organization. The success of the candidate's efforts depends on certain jobs being done fully and promptly. If someone fails to perform, or is late or half-hearted in performing assigned tasks, the campaign may lag or break down.

The slippage may range from precinct canvassing that is spotty (some areas are covered but voters in others are totally neglected) to tardy or haphazard media time and space purchases, depriving the candidate of important access to voters at critical moments.

In a close local election, spotty canvassing can spell disaster. In a national election, lack of candidate visibility at a point when substantial numbers of voters are making up their minds can spell disaster in capital letters.

In the first of his *The Making of the President* books, Theodore S. White tells of Richard Nixon's spending the last days before the 1960 election campaigning in states with a negligible number of electoral votes. Meanwhile John Kennedy was concentrating his efforts in the big population areas. Many considered this lack of last-minute exposure to large numbers of voters a serious wound for the Nixon campaign.

Twenty years later, Ronald Reagan agreed to a one-on-one debate with President Jimmy Carter late in the campaign. Reagan had previously declined, insisting that third party candidate John Anderson appear with Carter and him. This reluctant last-minute exposure, opinion researchers reported, was highly effective in Reagan's winning the support of previously undecided voters.

The management principles a public relations consultant has learned will be important in providing counsel regarding campaign organization. Lines of authority and responsibility must be clearly set forth. All, particularly those in supervisory positions, should know their job.

Any unaccomplished or uncompleted assignments must be discovered promptly and followed up quickly. If major mailings have been planned according to a precise schedule, they must go out on that schedule. If the candidate is to make a dozen appearances in a single day, transportation from one place to another must be available on the dot. The candidate must have in hand the background material and outlines for remarks appropriate to each appearance in time to review them before stepping to the front of the platform at each appearance.

Because political campaigns are so costly, they cannot operate without volunteers, and managing volunteers effectively is one of the major challenges of campaign organization. Volunteers cannot be threatened with the loss of their jobs if they do not perform. Their motivation must be completely positive, and in the thick of a political campaign's exhausting activities and relentless pressures, it is difficult to keep being upbeat with nondiligent volunteers.

Balancing this, however, is the fact that highly motivated volunteers will often provide more invaluable service for free if they believe in a candidate or cause than paid personnel would provide if they were assigned similar tasks. Political campaign experts emphasize the need to (1) make sure volunteers are always given something to do; and (2) give volunteers prompt and continued recognition for their efforts.

Experienced consultants point out that the fastest way to lose volunteers is to give them the notion that their services are really unnecessary or unimportant in winning the election. They also note that volunteers can feel unwanted and unneeded if their work is not praised as really helpful. Even skilled, well-educated people will gladly labor at such menial tasks as stuffing envelopes, making telephone calls, and handing out flyers if they think they are truly helping the cause.

Holding office

Public relations practitioners may tend to emphasize the importance of service to individual constituents as a key to a politician's remaining in office once elected. While it is true that such service is significant, service to the entire constituency public should not be downplayed. Legislators are going to have to run for reelection on their voting record. Administrators are going to have to show the success of programs and the wisdom of decisions they have been responsible for since the last election.

PERFORMANCE

Just as in all the other areas of public relations, good overall performance is the best way for the political officeholder to win and maintain public approval. Therefore, the public relations practitioner can offer the most valuable assistance to the political employer or client by (1) providing as much relevant and carefully organized information as possible to the officeholder to assist in making the right decisions and taking the right actions on behalf of the general constituency; (2) serving as listener and evaluator when individuals and organizations provide feedback on the officeholder's public performance; (3) passing along to the officeholder a realistic appraisal of this feedback; and (4) guiding the officeholder toward an intelligent, effective division of effort between service to the general public in the legislative body or executive office and service to individual constituents and organizations with special needs or interests.

For example, an administrative assistant or aide has to keep abreast of what is happening back in the district while the member of Congress is attending sessions of the House of Representatives and of the committees and subcommittees to which the member has been appointed. This will involve reading as many newspapers published in the district as possible and getting reports on broadcast news coverage of important issues back home. The national news media must be monitored as well.

There may be a danger of removing the politician from direct contact with "the folks back home" by predigesting the news this way. Critics said Presidents Eisenhower and Carter, for instance, became divorced from some of the realities beyond the White House gates because they relied too heavily on their staff briefings. John Kennedy, on the other hand, was widely praised for poring over newspapers each day so that he knew more directly what others in the country were reading and saying.

With a member of Congress, state legislature, or city council heavily involved in lawmaking, it is obvious that someone else must answer the letters and telephone calls from constituents. The effective staff will answer the questions and solve the problems of these writers and callers as independently and as quickly as possible, permitting the employer to concentrate on working for the general public. But again, a wise staffer will be sure to give the officeholder an idea of the kinds of communications that are coming into the office and the feelings of those who are getting in touch. Passing along feedback from the voters will be critical when that feedback is directed at the position taken or statements made by the officeholder. A loyal public relations consultant will not hesitate to tell the politician it is time to mend political fences.

SERVICE TO CONSTITUENTS

In our discussion of attitude formation in Chapter 4, we indicated that efforts at persuasion may succeed in relation to how deeply a pre-existing opinion or conviction is held. Voters who have had a member of Congress, an alderman, or a county supervisor solve a problem for them are generally going to be sincerely grateful, even if the solving was actually done by someone on the officeholder's staff. That gratitude will nurture a favorable attitude quite a bit deeper than one formed simply by listening to a political speech or recorded media message. A vote won by this method is really won. It will not be easily enticed away by an opponent at election time.

Just how deep that gratitude can go was illustrated in connection with the FBI's "Abscam" cases in the early 1980s, investigations in which a number of elected officials were charged with soliciting bribes from undercover agents who played the roles of wealthy influence seekers.

CBS News carried interviews with a number of constituents of a congressman caught up in this web. These voters said they still intended to back their congressman despite his conviction because, as one man said, "he always takes care of his own here in the district."

Voters nailed down this way tend to multiply too. It is not just the individual who has his pension problem ironed out by the legislator's staff but the members of that person's family, many of his close friends, and perhaps some of his neighbors. When they learn of the kindness shown, they are won over too, and solidly, rather than by campaign rhetoric that may be offset by more campaign rhetoric from the other side.

The amount of service a politician can provide to constituents relates to the staff and funding available to the politician's office. Our examples have used members of Congress, because such officeholders are extensively involved in this type of problem solving. In addition, in their offices in Washington and back in the district, they have employees devoting full time to aiding constituents. These people are on the telephone constantly, seeking information and trying to resolve difficulties. Their work is hardly what the founding fathers thought of as the role of the legislative branch, but it is highly rewarding and invaluable public relations. (It can also be quite depressing for an idealistic public relations practitioner, because many of the calls are to government agencies that are the cause of the problems in the first place, often because of insensitivity and inactivity.)

This aspect of political public relations has to be scaled down when we leave the congressional level. State legislators, unless they hold important committee posts, usually have little staff support. On the other hand, state lawmakers spend less time in session than members of Congress, so they may be free to assist voters personally.

County and municipal lawmakers are most often like state legislators. They have little if any staff assistance, but they do have contacts and influence. In large communities where such officials may serve on a full-time basis, they must rely on these resources, since they will not have time to follow up personally on the questions and problems addressed to them.

What is important to remember from a public relations standpoint is that this legislator assistance has become an American tradition, and voters expect it. Failure to provide this service is a severe, sometimes fatal, political detriment and terrible political public relations.

COMMUNICATIONS

Most constituents, except in small communities and districts, have little or no direct contact with an officeholder. They do not write to members of Congress or call the county commissioner. They do not attend the political rallies at which speeches are given and hands are shaken. They may not even be home when the door-to-door canvass is made. Yet this group has the votes a politician needs, and both the candidate for office and the officeholder must try to establish lines of communication with it.

DIRECT MAIL. Members of Congress again have an advantage with their franking (free postage) privilege, but unless they stress that they are using this privilege to inform their constituents and to give an account of their stewardship, they may lay themselves open to criticism for wasting taxpayers' money or misusing the privilege. Mailings often take the form of reports or newsletters, to emphasize this function and to disassociate this form of communication from mere campaigning or politicking. Mailing lists of voters by precinct are available from county or city clerks or election commissioners for a modest fee.

Sometimes an officeholder will use the mails to send a questionnaire or survey to constituents. It asks how the constituents feel on certain issues. Often the survey suggests that the results will guide the officeholder when those issues are voted on. The responses such surveys achieve are seriously unrepresentative of all the voters concerned, however, as we saw in Chapter 4. Well-informed voters will be aware of this flaw, so their reaction to this type of survey tactic may be quite negative.

NEWSPAPER COLUMNS AND BROADCAST TAPES. Weekly newspapers in small cities and rural communities frequently publish "From the Statehouse" or "Congressman Smith Reports" columns. This material has been written by the staff of the local legislator and made available to newspapers. Radio stations and even television stations in small markets may accept similar report tapes and air them as a regular feature. Though under the Communications Act an equal opportunities ("equal time") situation is triggered by such tapes during an election campaign, the tapes are an invaluable means of keeping in touch at other periods.

PUBLIC APPEARANCES. A major job of the political consultant or staffer is to make sure the candidate or officeholder gets exposure by giving speeches to organizations in the district, city, or ward or by participating in civic events and ceremonies. During a campaign particularly, staffers will calendar all sorts of social gatherings (picnics, church bazaars, festivals, dances, parades, etc.) where the candidate can mingle with those in attendance, meet them individually, shake their hands, hand out cards or brochures, and make a bid for support at the polls.

NEWS COVERAGE. In addition to the talks the candidate or officeholder may be invited to give, news coverage can be generated through action, even if the action is a statement of position on an issue or a criticism of an opponent. These can be publicized by news releases or through news conferences. One of the duties of people in political public relations is to keep alert for such news-making opportunities. They should also advise against the overuse of the news conference. Their client or employer should have something substantial to say before a conference is called; otherwise attendance at the next news conference may be nil.

CORRESPONDENCE. Voters will call or write to a public official not only to ask help or a favor but to urge the official to support or oppose a policy or bill. A person's willingness to make this effort is an indication of more than ordinary interest and involvement, so such a person is likely to influence other voters. The opportunity to respond to the call or letter is important, and it should not be muffed by sending back a generalized form letter if at all possible. The response should address the question or issue the constituent is concerned about. A reply that says simply, "Thank you for your recent communication. I am always happy to hear from concerned citizens . . . and I pledge to continue my conscientious service to the people of our district . . ." can be perceived as an insulting lack of attention. Times may arise, of course, when the volume of mail and calls is so great that better targeted responses cannot be sent out. A good practice under those circumstances is a generalized response that mentions the volume and promises a more particularized reply later.

PERSONAL CONTACTS. Because they invariably meet new and influential people during and after a campaign, political figures sometimes are tempted to neglect old friends, most critically, those who were the foundation of their early support. A key element in political public relations is maintenance of those contacts with long-time supporters. Like everyone else, they will find their ardor cooling if they feel they are being taken for granted or jilted.

Politicians and their public relations counsel might well study the role given personal contact by Senator Tom Harkin in his effort to maintain effective, on-going, two-way communication with his constituents. In 1980, with the Republicans winning big on the national and state scene, this Iowa Democrat produced a counter-landslide in his own district with his reelection. Four years later, with his state again going Republican, he defeated an incumbent to win a Senate seat.

Harkin has said the critical factor in his campaign success has been keeping in touch with voters. "I grew up in a community with a population of 180," he recalled. "I never saw a congressman until I was in college." Harkin determined that he would be sure to make contact and keep in touch with the people he represented. In addition to the means of communication already mentioned, Harkin makes frequent weekend trips back to Iowa and inaugurated what he called his "mobile office." While serving in the House, he took a group of staffers with him on regular, previously announced visits to communities throughout his constituency (including hamlets of 180). If he met people with problems, a member of his accompanying staff was assigned on the spot to start trying to resolve the difficulties.

Governmental public relations

As mentioned, government agencies have been reluctant to use the term "public relations" to label the multitude of public relations functions they perform. Instead of public relations people, in government we find public information and public affairs officers at all levels, all of them looking and acting just like public relations people outside government.

SPECIAL STATUS

This says that government agencies tend to be highly circumspect about public relations activity. They tend to be extremely sensitive to the possibility of criticism from the taxpaying public. They do not want to be accused of involvement in something that sounds as commercial (that is, nongovernmental) as public relations.

Nonetheless, some of the earliest public relations was practiced by government. This is where we found presidential press secretaries and war-time information agencies. Recently, we have seen government public relations people exercising tremendous influence on government policies.

Examples are positive and negative. They could include the White House staff's stonewalling to keep the Watergate situation from being revealed, the calculated leaking of news about the antiradar Stealth defense system during the 1980 presidential campaign, or even the undoubtedly regretted decision to have a president honor the dead in a German cemetery that included the graves of SS members.

BUDGETING. The reluctance of elected officials to face criticism for spending tax funds on public relations is reflected in much more than job titles of government employees. It can be seen more starkly in budgets.

Legislators will scrutinize the money requests of administrators and their agencies for any hints of spending on activities that might be considered self-promoting. A persistent, narrow view of an area like media relations often leads to cuts or denials of funds openly requested for that purpose.

Recently a suburban school district had grown so large that its superintendent felt he needed a public relations assistant. But when he went to the board, he asked for a community activities coordinator. When an urban school district wanted to enlarge its community relations staff by hiring an experienced newspaper editor, it created the position of assistant secretary to the board. Money was found for both these positions. The superintendents obviously thought it would not have been found for public relations personnel.

Even when a manufactured title thinly cloaks the status of a public relations person in government, legislators have shown reluctance to fund their activities. Some of this is due to the rivalry and tension between branches of government. A city council at odds with the mayor is not eager to finance the public relations functions of the mayor's office; the mayor's public relations power may some day be used against the council. The situation is duplicated in the relationship of a state legislature with a governor and of Congress with the president.

Legislative bodies exercise another constraint on administrative agencies. They define the functions of those agencies, and those legal definitions of functions may very well preclude many of the activities we consider integral to public relations.

RELATIONS AND STRUCTURES. Beyond this, the organizational structure of government, because it is the product of detailed legislation, cannot be modified easily. Where community relations, public information, and public affairs offices have been established, they almost always occupy an auxiliary rather than a policy-making position.

This is not to say that government public relations people do not influence policy. They obviously do. But they exert this influence despite, rather than because of, where they are situated in the organizational table.

For example, in a municipality, public relations for the executive branch is typically handled by an aide to the mayor. This aide does not have the same status as department heads. The public relations person is an aide, not the director of public works, finance, or public safety. While a strong, talented person may surmount this lack of status, the obstacles to instituting good public relations throughout city government are clear.

Often it is not only structure but formal procedure that places further constraints on public relations practitioners in government. Perhaps a comparison will emphasize the point.

In planning a special event, a nongovernment public relations practitioner may feel free to innovate and strive for informality. If a head table has to be set up for a dinner, the practitioner, after placing the principal speaker and emcee, can seat others for congeniality and better acquaintance.

Not so at many levels of government; not with civil service grades that resemble military ranks and the interdepartmental rivalries that a government of three branches often engenders. If indeed military personnel are involved, or if foreign dignitaries or clergy are to be included, there are precise rules to be followed. Protocol intervenes.

SERVING "THE" PUBLIC

Throughout our discussion of public relations, we have been referring to publics, pointing out the importance of identifying these groups with special influence on the success of the employer or client of the public relations person. Government public relations has its special publics, too, but our experience has shown that its most distinctive mark is its responsibility to the general public. A government public relations practitioner's principal public is everyone. The practitioner, as a government employee, has every citizen as an employer and is answerable to hundreds, thousands, or millions of employers.

It is true that there are special publics as well: the employees of the government department or agency, the community in which the agency's office or installation is located, the heaviest users of the department or agency's services, etc. But the stockholders, so to speak, are all the citizens who support the unit or level of government in which the public relations practitioner's agency is located.

The implications of this are that citizens take a proprietary interest in the activity and services of a governmental agency, and that citizens often feel they have a duty to be critical of such activity and services. There is a significant difference between this relationship and that between a customer and a private business, for example.

The U.S. Army Corps of Engineers, for instance, develops and maintains recreation areas in conjunction with many of its flood control projects. A camper who stops at a commercial campsite may be disappointed in the condition and maintenance of the facilities, and perhaps with the service and manners of the employees too. The camper can retaliate by never coming back and by spending money at a competitor's place the next time. But a camper who is disappointed at a Corps campground or a state or national recreational area may feel, and express, keener resentment. Remember, the site belongs to the camper. The camper's tax money helped purchase it and the camper's tax money helps maintain it.

In addition to being compelled to serve many bosses, government public relations people often have special constraints on the type of activity in which they can engage. Frequently they cannot campaign for changes and improvements they strongly believe in because the law says they cannot.

Congressmen, farmers, environmentalists, and their various organizations can argue publicly and vigorously about the relative importance of flood control versus the importance of navigation on inland waterways. But the public relations people in agencies involved in flood control, food production, outdoor recreation, waterways shipping, and natural conservation cannot make direct appeals for public support for their own or their leaders' point of view. They may be limited to answering questions as objectively as possible, just hoping that the right questions will be asked of them. Unlike the public relations people in the automobile or textile industries who may campaign openly for limitations on foreign imports, they must remember they have many bosses on all sides of the issue, and those bosses have decided public relations people are to be, like old-fashioned children, "seen but not heard."

Summary

Politics and government provide a contrast of public relations activity. Politics appears to have embraced public relations enthusiastically, while government is generally much more restrained and often restricted in its use of public relations.

Successful election campaign managers today are highly conscious of certain aspects of public relations, particularly the need for widespread acceptance and the role of the mass media to communicate messages that contribute to acceptance. The best decision makers in the political arena also recognize the basic need for acceptable performance as well, of course. But there is still much lingering "image-making" thinking in the minds of others who run for office or help others run.

The essential public relations planning for politics today focuses, of necessity, on fund raising. Achieving political office costs a great deal of money. This is particularly true because media use is essential and expensive.

Political public relations does not end with election day. The person elected to office in a very real sense begins running for reelection immediately after taking office. How constituents are served and communicated with will be key factors in that next election, even though it may be two, four, or six years down the road.

Government public relations is often seen as somewhat more discreet or subtle in practice than public relations efforts in other settings because of a longstanding reluctance to spend tax funds on something as "commercial" or potentially self-serving as "PR." That is why the term "public relations" is avoided and euphemistic terms are substituted.

Nonetheless, if it is true that successful public relations is essential for every enterprise that depends on others to achieve its objectives, government, just like businesses, institutions, and interest groups, needs to practice public relations. The special challenge to practitioners serving government is the proprietary interest the general public often feel toward government. After all, it is their money that built the parks, highways, public buildings, and installations.

Exercises

1. Visit the office of your congressional representative or state senator to find out how constituents' requests for assistance are handled by the office staff. How many people are involved in this work and how much time do they spend at it? Check with a city council member or county commissioner if visiting the other two locations is impractical.

2. If your state has a campaign expenditures law, check the reports filed by the candidates for Congress, state legislature, and major county offices. Note the differences in the levels of spending for the various offices and check the purposes for which the largest expenditures were made. What observations about political public relations can you make from these data?

3. How would the fund raising in political public relations differ from the fund raising conducted by practitioners employed by a nonprofit health organization like the American Heart Association? Do you think political fund raising would be more difficult? Why?

4. List half a dozen means other than media appearances that political candidates use to get voter exposure. Of those you list, which do you think are the most effective? Why?

5. Are public relations practitioners in government hampered in any way by being restricted to titles like public affairs officers, director of community relations, information specialist, etc.? Are those titles in any way advantageous? Why?

Case study

Richard T. is the incumbent mayor of Hartwood, an industrial city of 40,000 in the northeast. He served three terms on the city council before winning election as mayor. Now in his late fifties, he has been in government long enough to be widely considered part of the "old guard" at city hall.

Richard's opponent in the general election is Kevin D., a handsome, personable man in his early thirties whose previous government experience consists of four years as deputy county clerk. However, in that appointive position, Kevin really ran the office, since the county clerk was near retirement and in poor health. Kevin achieved a reputation as an efficient administrator. He was well-liked by news reporters, particularly for the way he assisted them in covering county elections administered by the county clerk's office.

The local chapter of the League of Women Voters has invited Richard and Kevin to participate in a presidential campaign style debate in a local high school auditorium. A local television station is to televise the joint appearance by the candidates and two radio stations may also carry it.

- If you were Richard's public relations adviser, would you counsel him to participate in the debate? Why?
- If you were Kevin's public relations adviser, would you tell him to participate? Why?
- Are there any other facts you would want to know before deciding on how to advise your candidate? If so, what are they and how would they figure in your advice?

Suggesting readings

Borden, Edward B. "Somebody Cares." *Public Relations Journal,* December 1979.

Brandenburg, Robert. "Another Way to Lobby." *Public Relations Journal,* October 1980.

Christenson, Reo M., and Robert O. McWilliams, eds. *Voice of the People.* 2d ed. New York: McGraw-Hill, 1967.

Gaby, Daniel M. "Politics and PR." *Public Relations Journal*, October 1980.

Greenfield, Jeff. "A Charm Book for Candidates." *Columbia Journalism Review*, July/August 1980.

Haskell, Anne. "Live from Capitol Hill—Where Politicians Use High Tech to Bypass the Press." *Washington Journalism Review*, November 1982.

Helm, Lewis M., Ray E. Hiebert, Michael R. Naver, and Kenneth Rabin, eds. *Informing the People: A Public Affairs Handbook*. New York: Longman, Inc., 1981.

Jorgensen, Barbara. "Credibility and the President's TMI Commission." *Public Relations Journal*, March 1980.

Lehrman, Robert. "Lessons from Campaign '84." *Public Relations Journal*, December 1984.

Lipset, Seymour Martin. "No Room for the Ins: Elections around the World." *Public Opinion*, October/November 1982.

McGinniss, Joe. *The Selling of the President*. New York: Trident Press, 1969.

Rabin, Kenneth H. "The Government PIO in the '80s." *Public Relations Journal*, December 1979.

Rundell, Richard. "Dade County's Tax-Slash Battle." *Public Relations Journal*, December 1979.

Sethi, S. Prakash. "Corporate Political Activism." *Public Relations Journal*, November 1980.

10 Writing for the media

The PR practitioner is the most visible link between an organization and the news media, and a solid working relationship between the two is vital if the organization is to fulfill its mission in a manner acceptable to its many publics. So, the organization's staff looks to the practitioner for professional advice and guidance in relations with the media, and the media representatives expect PR people to provide them accurate, complete information concerning the organization, both on a day-to-day basis and during breaking news stories. The organization's and the practitioner's future depend upon fulfilling this unwritten contract.

Of course, success presupposes a thorough understanding of the product with which the practitioner will be dealing—news. Basically, anything is considered news that interests, informs, or entertains the reader or listener, and the most important news story is the one that is of the greatest interest to the greatest number. As the *Armed Forces Newspaper Guide* defines it, "News, generally, is new information not previously published or broadcast about something that has happened or is scheduled to happen and about which people need or want to know."

"Straight" news coverage is telling what happened accurately and factually without embellishment. It contains no conclusions, no speculations, no opinions (without attribution), and no distortions or misrepresentations. It contains no implications.

As an extension of straight coverage, interpretive reporting places the news story in its proper context and explains the background of the story. To be handled properly, the interpretive story must be complete, presenting the several sides of the story without bias. Whether straight coverage or interpretive coverage, news reporting attempts to provide only the facts. Editorial writing presents value judgments about the news. The two are not combined. Furthermore, editorializing is a privilege of the media, not a function that can be assumed by the PR practitioner.

The public relations professional services an organization by trans-

208

mitting an accurate picture of its operation to the public. This goal is accomplished by offering a service to the media consisting of more complete organizational news coverage than the media can accomplish with their limited staffs.

If the public relations practitioner provides biased copy containing editorial comments, editors and news directors view that product as unreliable and the PR practitioner as untrustworthy. The public relations effort is wasted, and newsroom doors will close.

Elements of news

Although the basic elements of news are universal, as a public relations writer you will serve a wide variety of media, and you must remember to be versatile in your interpretation. What is newsworthy in a small town may be of no interest to a big city editor.

For example, the *Cascade Pioneer-Advertiser* reports the full story of the man who broke his arm in a combine accident. By contrast, fewer than half of all know homicides are covered by the New York City news media. The *Pioneer-Advertiser* reports individual automobile sales; the *New York Times* editors consider that reporting industry trends is "all the news that's fit to print." Similar determinations are made by broadcast stations in smaller communities, contrasted to those broadcasting in the larger population centers.

Furthermore, news values vary from day to day, even from hour to hour. Competition for news space or time is spirited, regardless of the medium. Thus, the good PR professional remains current, keeping in mind the guidelines in use today by each medium.

Media space and time are severely limited. You are in competition with everything else going on in the world today. Using a large metro daily as an example, a single edition will carry 50 to 60 major stories, more than 100 shorter items, 60 photographs plus syndicated features, columns, puzzles, comics, etc. And approximately half the total news space is given over to departmentalized copy: sports, social and homemaking news, financial coverage, editorials, and other areas. Competition for space is indeed spirited.

If your story is to have a chance in this competition, it must include most of the basic elements:

1. *Timeliness.* News is the most perishable commodity on the market. Readers and viewers expect to be told what is happening or what is

about to happen. From the PR practitioner's viewpoint, delaying release of information can be a critical mistake. The late General Creighton Abrams, as chairman of the Joint Chiefs of Staff, said "I don't know of any bad news that improves with age." Delaying release, for whatever reason, will probably be construed as an attempted cover-up.

2. *Significance.* Names are news. If a person or that person's position is well known, the story probably will be printed or broadcast.

The only coverage the average person receives after chasing fire engines is in the police report for "interfering with an emergency vehicle." However, one man had a lifelong love affair with sirens, the big rigs, and firefighters, yet never risked a ticket. He was welcome in every fire station in the nation and was an honorary member of many departments. Countless newspapers, radio and television stations carried stories about him riding the rigs. He was good copy and brought excellent publicity to any fire company with which he was associated because of his significance. He was Arthur Fiedler, famed conductor of the Boston Pops Orchestra.

3. *Proximity.* Readers and viewers are deeply concerned with events in which they are involved or happenings "right down the block." Three inches of rain and localized flooding knocked the historic eruption of Mount St. Helens out of the lead story position in the upper New York media.

4. *Magnitude.* OPEC nations changing oil prices, legislation reinstituting the military draft, or a threatened invasion by a new strain of corn borers—all have a major impact on the readers and viewers because of the magnitude of the event in their lives, the consequence of the event to them. A story may or may not have national or international implications, but if that story directly affects the individual reader or viewer, that person's pocketbook, life-style, or other relationships, it is of extreme importance to that individual and, therefore, is of great magnitude or significance. It is an important news story for that person.

News story building blocks, most of which fit into one or more of the above elements, include:

Action	Numbers and size	Combat or struggle
Property	Mystery and suspense	Bizarre
Overcoming odds	Humor or pathos	Sex and romance
Children	Scandal	Beauty
Adventure	Prominent places	Unusual numbers
Unusual size	Animals	

Spreading the word

As noted, information can be communicated in many ways once we determine what information we wish to disseminate. Methods range from person-to-person communication (the basic means and still one of the most effective), to the most sophisticated techniques known in the twentieth century. The more significant ones are the several print media, radio, television, audiovisual presentations, speeches, and special (or media) events. This chapter deals almost exclusively with the mass media: newspaper, commercial radio and television, the news services, syndicates, news magazines, and trade publications.

To succeed as a public relations practitioner, you must know the media with which you will deal on a regular basis. You must understand their audiences, goals, deadlines, styles, staffs, and methods of disseminating information. If you expect the media to consider using information you provide, they in turn have every right to expect you to understand how they operate, what they publish or broadcast, and their deadlines. Anything less marks you as casual, uncaring, or at least, unprofessional.

Arrange your schedule, busy as it will be, so that you become acquainted personally with individuals with whom you will deal at the various media. For example, if you work for an educational system or institution, at the very least you owe it to your employer and yourself to become acquainted with reporters covering the school or the education beat, the city editors, and news directors who make the news assignments. Explain who you are, whom you represent, and services you can provide. Emphasize that you can and will be the medium's contact within your organization. You will have the answers, can get the answers, or on rare occasions, provide rationale for answers being unavailable.

Suggest that your organization is open to the reporter. Invite news media representatives to visit your organization at their convenience. Arrange a tour of your facility for them if they are interested. The emphasis must be on openness and a free exchange of information.

The public relations practitioner can augment and expand the personal relationship by assuming an active role in professional societies whenever possible, journalism societies, news photographers organizations, the local press club, and others.

With these suggestions go several cautions:

1. Schedule visits to the various newsrooms so that they do not occur at a time when reporters are fighting deadlines.

2. Never expect that your acquaintance with a reporter or editor will buy good coverage. If it does, the reporter is not worth your friendship anyway. The best you can expect is a fair hearing.

3. You made the contact to establish your credibility. Your professional reputation depends upon maintaining that credibility. Never trade on your contacts in a way that might denigrate the relationships. Whether explicit or implied, the reporter, editor and news director expect you to be candid, forthright, and accurate in all dealings with them.

An editorial in the April 19, 1980, issue of *Editor & Publisher* concluded: "Everything is changed in the newspaper business, yet everything remains the same. Accuracy, accuracy, accuracy still is the dominant theme of responsible journalists just as it has been for decades." Willfully or unwittingly, if you deviate from this theme, you and your organization can become anathema in newsrooms.

By establishing and maintaining credibility, you establish access to various methods of disseminating information through the mass media. As the occasion arises, you can provide information to your newsroom contacts in person, by telephone, or through written copy. You can submit the complete story or merely leads to these contacts. However, on those occasions when a story or a lead is phoned to a reporter or editor, read the information from prepared copy. By doing so, you are assured that you transmitted the complete and accurate story to each phone contact. This procedure guarantees the PR practitioner that no vital facts have been inadvertently omitted and that the telephoned information was transmitted accurately, regardless of the pressures involved.

Newswriting

As the intermediary between the organization and its various publics, the public relations practitioner must analyze each situation as it arises. Whether it is a routine release of information or a sensitive news story, the PR representative must understand the facts, determine the person who must be reached with the message, and decide the proper media for accomplishing that goal. This is equally true whether the medium is a person-to-person conversation or a mass media effort. But for maximum impact, the information must be released while it is still news in a way suitable for use by the media selected, and the message must contain the information needed by those the practitioner intends to reach.

Mass circulation is not always the complete answer. As a case in point, the Missouri River Division of the U.S. Army Corps of Engineers annually announces the dates for commercial navigation to open on the river (i.e., the dates when enough water will be released from the large main stem dams to provide adequate depths in the navigation channel for deep draft barges. The news release (or at least the pertinent facts) normally is picked up by some broadcast stations and general circulation newspapers, ranging from small weeklies to metro dailies with a half-million circulation.

From a practical standpoint, however, the most important medium has a circulation of less than 5000. The *Waterways Journal*, a St. Louis-based magazine, aims at the river shipping and navigation interests. Almost without exception, these persons read the *Journal* carefully, and the navigation dates are vitally important to almost every reader. If the Corps of Engineers' public affairs officer hit the major media in the major Missouri River cities and missed the *Waterways Journal*, the effort would have been in vain. Knowing the media and understanding the target audiences is vital to successful public relations.

In no way does this negate the maxim that the practitioner must not favor one medium over another. The professional will take advantage of the potential and understand the limitations of each in terms of the medium's particular audience, its circulation, and requirements such as acceptable material, preferred form, and adherence to publication or broadcast deadlines.

As a minimum, the practitioner will become familiar with all media in the organization's geographic area, plus the specialized media that aim at the specific audience the organization must reach.

The media that deliver the message

NEWSPAPERS

According to the noted British publisher, Lord Northcliffe, only two reasons exist for buying newspapers, curiosity and habit. Each is powerful in itself, but according to some students of the subject, we should add a third reason, fear. Some persons read the newspaper because they are afraid not to. Perhaps they fear that a war, depression, drought, or half-price sale might occur and they would never hear about it.

Of course, no one reads everything. The average American spends 20 to 30 minutes with the daily newspaper and a total of no more than an hour a day acquiring knowledge of world, national, and local happenings. Included in this total is time spent with newspapers, television, radio, news magazines, and other sources. Nevertheless, most people still feel that reading a newspaper, however quickly, is a duty of the good citizen.

The daily newspaper provides greater depth of coverage than any other news medium, and it offers more permanence than broadcasting. The story that is difficult to understand or that includes detailed information the reader wants to remember can be reread or clipped and saved indefinitely. Depending on tastes, most families have treasured and yellowing newspaper clippings announcing the end of prohibition, VJ Day, the death of a president, or details of the alma mater winning the conference title.

In summary, newspapers permit the reader to explore a story to the depth desired. For the 20-minute reader, that depth means scanning headlines only on some stories, reading the lead on others, and studying the entire coverage on selected stories, including sidebars and follow-ups.

TELEVISION

The newcomer on the block packs a real wallop. A credibility study commissioned by the American Society of Newspaper Editors (1985) revealed that both the general public and frequent readers prefer television over newspapers as their primary source of news. Andrew Radolf, reporting in *Editor & Publisher* (April 13, 1985) said that 57 percent of those surveyed prefer television for state news, 72 percent for national and international news.

Television combines the immediacy and aural intimacy of radio with the impact of visual information. However, television is handicapped because its total information package is limited. As noted, an average half-hour telecast contains fewer words than a single column of type on the front page of a metro-size daily newspaper. Television cannot go into depth on any of the 20 to 25 stories in its newscasts. Nevertheless, the recall factor is high among viewers, the result of communicating with both the ears and eyes of the audience.

RADIO

Since the mid-1920s, radio has been an integral part of American life. Many persons reveal their ages by radio programs they recall: "I remember Gunsmoke and Johnny Dollar on radio. Good shows. And John Cameron Swayze—now, there was a newscaster!"

Programming has changed drastically since those days, but radio is still very much a part of the American scene. We have more radios than telephones, more radios than we have cats and dogs. Radio's obituary following the advent of television was premature to say the least.

Radio is a personal medium, informal, timely, and intimate. Fast-breaking news will be on radio first. Like television, however, radio is limited in the detailed coverage it can provide. The most popular format today is the hourly five-minute newscast, which means only the most important stories are covered, and those in scant detail. The major story is covered in 15 to 30 seconds, 35 to 75 words.

The obvious conclusion drawn by the thinking public relations practitioner is that the various media, when best served, will be provided different packages. Their requirements and their products differ.

Fingers on the keys

If you plan a public relations career, understand that the order of the alphabet is Q-W-E-R-T-Y-U-I-O-P. You will use a typewriter or a computer terminal. And the mechanics of typing are not enough; flawless grammar, spelling, and punctuation are as vital to you as breathing is to a championship swimmer. You must understand sentence structure and the parts of speech so thoroughly they become instinctive. Then, and only then, can you worry about constructing your lead, building a story in the inverted pyramid style, and using the proper format for sending the story to the various media with which you will cooperate.

THE LEAD

The first part of a news story, the lead, plays the same role as the chorus in Grecian drama, the overture in opera, or the master of cere-monies in an after-dinner presentation—gaining attention and provid-ing an idea of things to come. It tells what happened, arouses curiosity, and leads readers, listeners, or viewers into the story. Properly written, it lets them know whether the story is worth their time. The lead helps readers or listeners decide that this is information they need to know, this may be worth a chuckle, this will evoke sympathy, this story will arouse emotions, this will satisfy curiosity.

Some leads that worked:

"In the beginning God created the heavens and the earth; the earth was waste and void; darkness covered the abyss, and the spirit of God was stirring above the waters." The Book of Genesis opens by arousing curiosity and wonder and answers four of the five Ws. An exceptional lead.

"The President is dead." Wire service story on the death of Franklin D. Roosevelt shocked and intrigued readers even though the event was expected.

"These are times that try men's souls." Tom Paine drew the reader into his main thesis by playing on emotions. A successful attempt to incite insurrection.

"Two men in a hurry visited Omaha today." The *Omaha World-Herald* story on a refueling stop by entrants in the Bendix Air Race aroused curiosity and invited the reader to continue the story.

"'Holmes,' said I as I stood one morning in our bow-window looking down the street, 'here is a madman coming along.'" Opening sentence of *The Adventure of the Beryl Coronet* by Sir Arthur Conan Doyle certainly draws the reader into what follows.

Each evidences an economy of words, an irresistible invitation to continue reading, and a thinly veiled hint as to what will follow. Each is a good lead.

Writing is like dancing: you will be much more successful with a good start. The introductory paragraph, the lead, either tells the reader what happened or arouses the reader's curiosity to read beyond the lead. Like music, leads come in many styles and tempos. Their variety is limitless, but some frequently used may be categorized:

1. *Straight news lead.* This is the most useful and most used of the many variations. Imagine that you, the reporter, want to tell a close friend of the events you witnessed. Your only medium is a telegram.

Thus, you must summarize the story in 15 words or less, yet transmit the significance, impact, and excitement of the event in an accurate and undistorted telegram. This type of lead is also called a "summary lead." However, a summary lead occasionally runs longer and lists all major points in the story. An example of a straight news lead: "Fleetwood Dan captured the Maiwand Cup in near record time Saturday at Belmont Park."

   2. *Punch or cartridge lead.* This type uses a terse sentence to induce the reader to continue. Such a brief, compelling statement would be, "Golden Gate bridge collapsed today."

   3. *Astonisher lead.* This features a statement that startles the reader, but it must do so without resorting to the exclamation point, an admission of weakness. Example: "A hydrogen tank will replace your gasoline tank by the end of the decade."

   4. *Question lead.* This device arouses curiosity or challenges the reader but must be used in moderation to avoid boring the reader or raising the question, "Who cares?" An example: "Can you throw the discus 20 meters without moving your feet?"

   5. *Quotation lead.* Such a lead can be effective, again if used in moderation. At times its use becomes epidemic, and it is ineffective. Example: "'I can balance the budget in three years,' said John Doe, independent candidate for president."

   6. *First and second person leads.* This is an affected type of lead most commonly used on by-lined stories, a you-are-there approach. Examples: "You are at the controls of a 747 over the Pacific, and the power fails." And, "I have been confined to a wheelchair for 10 years. Today I walked."

   7. *Suspense lead.* Use of this device is limited. However, it may be used occasionally with a feature story where the punch is saved until the last paragraph (e.g., O. Henry). As an example, we can steal the famous line from Snoopy, "It was a dark and stormy night."

   8. *Comic lead.* Such leads are confined to humorous features or brightener news stories. They are as effective as the writer is creative. Example: "Residents at Parkridge Rest Home cheered as the Easter Bunny was loaded into a squad car today."

   9. *How-to lead.* Simply enough, these are used occasionally on features that explain a difficult procedure or "how to" do something. Examples: "Completing the census form is simple if you follow these hints." And, "Here is a quick way of unclogging that stubborn kitchen drain."

   10. *Advocacy lead.* This device is useful for the writer making a

point. Unless carefully used, however, it can lead the writer into editorializing in the news or feature story, a surefire way to lead your release into the editor's round file. Example: "Interstate traffic is moving at an average speed in excess of 65 miles an hour in only three states. This state is one of them."

Types of leads that appear on news stories are as varied as the individuals who write them, and as successful as the skills of the writer make them. In general, the best leads will be simple, brief, and direct, although they should vary in style. They must match the story because nothing is as inappropriate as a comic lead on a story of tragedy, an astonisher lead on copy that has nothing to be excited about.

Again, the writer must avoid editorializing in news copy. If opinion, criticism, or advocacy appear in the copy, the lead or a paragraph near the lead must reveal the authority behind the statements: "The suggestion was made by John Doe, president of ABC Department Stores"; "according to Chancellor Mary Smith of State College"; or, "the charge was in a report submitted by Mayor J. J. Roe."

THE INVERTED PYRAMID

The bridge between the lead and the main body of the story may be a single sentence or a paragraph of several sentences. Its purpose is to explain the facts that were in the lead and to provide an introduction to the body of the story.

The body, of course, must follow logically from the lead. The most conventional and most frequently used construction to assure achieving this end is the inverted pyramid style of newswriting.

As noted, this style of writing is accomplished by presenting the story elements in order of descending importance. The most important facts are presented first, followed by supporting details. After all important questions that may be raised by the story are answered, the story is complete. From the public relations practitioner's viewpoint, unless the information presented is of earthshaking importance, the news release frequently will be completed in a single page, seldom more than two. Be brief.

The inverted pyramid is used for four reasons:

1. The reader or editor can determine quickly whether the story merits continued attention.

2. Headlines can be written quickly because the important facts (those that should be in a good headline) appear early in the story, thus saving precious newsroom time.

3. The newspaper editor and the broadcast station's news director, always fighting the battle for space and time, can edit quickly by scissoring the proper amount of copy from the end of the story.

4. It is the method used by staff reporters working under the editor and news director. That alone is sufficient reason for the public relations practitioner to use the inverted pyramid.

Write simply. Remember, you are writing for people in a hurry. Your first audience is the editor and news director. They must read rapidly, wading through many times more words than will be printed or broadcast on a given day. If the public relations news release passes them it faces the "typical American" we described earlier, the individual who spends about a half hour with the daily paper, less than an hour acquiring a personal update on the daily news.

Keep sentences simple. Average sentence length should be 15 to 20 words. Paragraphs, too, must be relatively brief, with few longer than 50 words. Thus, we have a short lead, short sentences, and short paragraphs. And, we have readers and listeners.

Use familiar, readily understood words. We are not implying that readers and listeners would not understand a more complex vocabulary, but they are in a hurry, and if they must pause even slightly to recall the meaning of a relatively obscure word, they may decide the story is not worth the time and effort.

Avoid special terminology. If you must use words or phrases not found in a typical vocabulary, explain or define them. Once explained or defined, they may be repeated. This is a problem that cannot be avoided; occasions arise where scientific, medical, engineering, or other special terminology may be necessary to achieve accuracy.

Adjectives, adverbs, and modifying phrases should not be overused. Specific rather than vague or general nouns and verbs bring a sparkle to the copy and to the eyes of editors. Mezzosoprano, knuckleballer, P-51 Mustang, and pharmacy dean are more specific than singer, pitcher, antique aircraft, and college administrator. Use specific terms; they eliminate the need for excess adjectives and adverbs. "Croon," "sprint," and "shout" can avoid modifiers that might be needed with "sing," "run," and "speak."

Writing for the ear

Work as carefully and closely with broadcast reporters as you do with representatives from newspapers and magazines. Unfortunately, some public relations operations tend to treat radio and television as an after-thought or at least in a manner that leads the radio or television reporter to feel that way. One reason the problem arises is a monster of the public relations profession's own creation, the historic tool for measuring success in public relations—the clipping file. Obviously, the file can represent only those victories attained in the print media; it cannot show accomplishments on radio or television. "If we can't show the boss, why bother?" is the attitude of some PR practitioners.

The problem has been partially resolved in some metropolitan areas with the evolution of independent services that monitor the area radio and television outlets, transcribing material from the many news-casts. Printed transcripts of stories affecting the service's subscribers are mailed to them for a fee.

To provide the material that broadcast media require, PR practitioners must make certain adaptations of their material.

GUIDELINES FOR BROADCASTING

As a minimum, the public relations practitioner should provide specially written versions of important stories for radio and television.

As the individual who developed the original story, the PR practitioner is in a better position than anyone else to rewrite the story in a style adapted to radio and television. The public relations professional works for the concerned organization, understands the relative importance of facts in the story, and can determine which should be selected for an abbreviated version suitable for the electronic media.

Because of severe time restrictions, a story that may warrant up to two pages in a regular release may translate into a 30-second story for radio and television. This is 60 to 75 words of copy. Time spent in rewriting the story will be a solid investment. The practice will improve your organization's batting average with the electronic media. (As insurance, include the story as originally written to serve as background information for the radio and television editors.)

All good writing practices apply when developing copy for radio and television. Frequently, however, the tone is slightly less formal than the same story would be for print media. But excess words will be self-defeating. An extra 25 words cheats your organization of 10 seconds air time.

Because the copy must be read aloud by the newscaster, other taboos to observe when writing for radio and television include:

1. Avoid long, complex sentences at all costs.
2. Avoid equal length sentences that will sound choppy.
3. Avoid an excess of "Ps" in copy to be read aloud. Even the most experienced newscaster can become a "p-popper" with phrases such as "Pencil pushers picked Paul as most popular." Repeated explosions of air into the microphone can cause the listener to fear that those expensive speakers may have to be replaced.
4. Eliminate tongue twisters. Included here are most polysyllabic words, other words difficult to pronounce, obscure words and phrases, and foreign words and phrases.
5. Provide attribution preceding a quotation, never following. Although a common practice when writing for print media, the following is anathema on a microphone: "World war is just around the corner, according to Senator John Doe." The newscaster must have it, "According to Senator John Doe, world war is just around the corner."

PRONUNCIATION GUIDES

Difficult or obscure words and names occasionally must be included in copy for newscasters. In such cases, a pronunciation guide must be included. A convenient method is to provide the guide in parentheses following the first appearance of the word. For example: "Dean James B. Clough (CLUE) of State University will visit Iloilo (EE-loe-EE-loe) on the island of Panay (rhymes with Man-EYE)."

VISUALS

Television is a visual medium, and all news producers strive to keep "talking heads" to a minimum on newscasts. They work to replace the newscaster on camera with visuals (slides, tape, film, or other graphics). Or in some cases, visuals are used in conjunction with the newscaster. Therefore, the public relations practitioner will improve the organization's chances of airing a story if visuals accompany the copy.

Whenever possible, provide 35mm color transparencies with the copy. If you can provide quality work, 16mm motion picture film or videotape is even better.

Unless identification of the visuals is readily apparent, cutlines or a rough script must accompany visuals when sent to a television outlet. The preferred method of transmitting the material to the station is in person. However, if the package must be mailed because of the logistics of the situation, include a cover letter explaining the accompanying visuals.

Going electronic

Where budget and staffing permit, some organizations use playback recording equipment or provide tape recordings in addition to typed copy.

Playback units attached to a telephone and employing a voice coil (installed by the telephone company) provide broadcast quality recordings for radio and television stations. The units can be equipped with endless tapes, which range in playing time from 40 seconds to 15 minutes.

Some government agencies and private organizations dealing in services find the units useful in transmitting updated information to organizations and individuals with whom they deal on a regular basis, in addition to providing news copy to the media. The National Weather Service has employed equipment of this type for a number of years.

The public relations department or office contacts area radio stations and other news media, providing news staffs with a so-called hotline number, the telephone number that activates the automatic playback unit. The notice, usually a postcard, is mailed on a two-week frequency as a reminder of the service and suggests that the hotline number be posted in the newsroom.

The tape recording normally opens by identifying individuals speaking on the tape, the occasion for the tape, and why these particular individuals are the spokespersons. Instructions on the tape also should indicate when the message was placed on the machine and when it will be changed.

The reporter will then be told the exact length of the recording in seconds and be given an "outcue," the final three or four words of the message or news story. The actual story is preceded by a 10-second countdown to enable the reporter recording the message in the studio to start the recording machine on the proper cue.

If the recording is a public service announcement rather than a news story, that point must also be made in the preliminary instructions on the tape. And if no message is currently on the tape, that fact must also be noted in the instructions.

"Actualities" are recordings or live broadcasts obtained telephonically by the electronic journalist. When called for an actuality, the PR practitioner will seek the most authoritative person in the organization to talk with the reporter and record or broadcast the message.

Style and form

The appearance of material sent to a news outlet has an impact on its fate at the hands of the editor or news director. If the news release is carelessly packaged, the PR practitioner risks self-destruction.

STYLEBOOK

Style is an area that can confuse the novice practitioner assigned to develop a news release. It is the media's method of bringing consistency into the gray area where any of several interpretations may be technically correct. Even from a purist's standpoint, three and 3, Dr. and Doctor, 3 Nov. 1986 and November 3rd, 1986, are all correct. However, the particular news medium will prefer one over the other.

The average newspaper will lean toward either an "up style" or a "down style." "Up" will favor capitalizing words and avoiding abbreviations while, broadly speaking, "down style" favors the reverse, but there is a wide area between.

If your media list is limited, select the most prominent medium and follow its style. When you are well-acquainted with editors or reporters, you may be able to obtain a copy of their stylebook. Meanwhile, study the medium carefully and determine the rules followed in the particular newsroom.

If you provide news releases to a large media list, purchase the stylebook developed by the Associated Press or United Press International. The book is inexpensive and may be obtained by contacting one of the news services or a university bookstore.

FORMAT

It is quite apparent that public relations can mean many things when a study is made of the various news release formats that come across newsroom desks. Releases are developed by a wide range of individuals, from teachers, accountants, housewives, traffic managers, and secretaries working as volunteers at kitchen tables for the Little League, church, or community theater to the full-time professionals who are part of a public relations team for a major organization. In each case, the news release competes with other news releases and with wire copy, staff stories, syndicated material, and graphics for precious space and time in the newspaper and on the electronic media.

Stay within your budget, but make your release professional and attractive. Develop a letterhead that is an attention-getter but not too flamboyant. Use a one-color masthead that attracts attention but does not waste space that could be better used for copy. A mast that requires more than an inch and a half is wasting space.

The masthead should announce that this is a news release and include information important to the reporter, such as the name, address, and telephone number of the originating office, or name of the contact who can provide additional information.

If not printed on the masthead, the author's name, title, address, and telephone number should be typed in the upper left-hand corner of the first page as shown in Figure 10.1. Thus, the editor or reporter knows whom to contact if additional details or clarification are needed.

The news release should be printed on standard letter-size paper (8½ × 11 inches) for the letterhead and succeeding pages (the succeeding pages do not include the masthead).

The date is typed in the upper right-hand corner of the first page. A slug line (a simple three- or four-word identification of the story) is typed beneath the author identification.

Approximately a third of the way down the page, in all capitals, type instructions to the media—FOR IMMEDIATE RELEASE or HOLD FOR RELEASE AFTER (type date and time). However, unless there is an obvious reason for asking that a story be held for a specific release date, do not place such a hold on the story. Valid reasons might be the official beginning of Armageddon, the programmed sinking of the Titanic, or the imminent loss of your job. Beyond that, few logical reasons are apparent for playing with the deadlines of the various media with which you must work on a daily basis. The first thought that strikes the average reporter is that the hold is on the story to favor a rival news medium.

Begin the story four to six spaces beneath the release instructions. Indent to begin each paragraph. Allow at least an inch on each side and at the bottom of each page for margins. The extra space can be used by the editor or news director to write instructions for printers or newscasters, or to write the headline or placement instructions.

News Release

**US Army Corps
of Engineers**
Missouri River Division
Public Affairs Office

P.O. Box 103 Downtown Sta.
Omaha, NE 68101

Phone: (402) 221-7208/7209

Contact: John Doe

Date: Today's date

Slugline to identify story

FOR IMMEDIATE RELEASE

    Select the most important fact for the lead sentence of the news story. Answer all questions that might arise, including who, what, when, where, why, and how.

    Leave approximately the top third of the page blank. Type the story double-spaced, and use only one side of the paper. However, in unusual circumstances, news media prefer hand-written copy to no story at all.

    Stick to facts. Eliminate personal opinions from the story. Inform news media promptly, but do it accurately.

    Treat all news media within your region impartially, but remember to protect the story if a reporter has an exclusive.

    Note that the fact that this is a news release is printed as part of the letterhead, and the letterhead includes the organization's name, address, telephone number, and the name of the public relations contact.

    If such a printed letterhead were unavailable, the information would be typed at the top of the page would include as a minimum the author's name, address, office telephone number and today's date.

-- 30 --

10.1 *Sample news release.*

225

One page is sufficient length for the average public relations news release. However, if it exceeds that length, type "MORE" at the bottom of the page, number succeeding pages (upper left) and type "30," "The End" or "###" below the last line of the completed story to avoid confusion if the pages become separated in the newsroom.

Summary

An old cliche says that "man shoots rabbit" is not news, but if "rabbit shoots man," it makes the papers and the evening newscasts. Thus, news is current information never before published about something that people need to know, want to know, or will be surprised by knowing.

By reporting news accurately, completely, and professionally, public relations practitioners will aid their organizations. The major elements of news can be expressed as: if it happens now (timeliness) to an important person, place, or object (significance) in this vicinity (proximity) and has either a direct or emotional effect on the audience (magnitude), the story is news.

Practitioners work through the mass media to transmit information (news) about their organizations to their target publics. Therefore, constant study of the mass media is vital for those in the public relations field. In addition to understanding news values, successful practitioners must be able to translate that knowledge into professionally developed news stories, and they must have a keen appreciation of the specific requirements of the media with which they deal.

Successful public relations practitioners write crisp, accurate leads and employ the inverted pyramid style of newswriting. They use short sentences, brief paragraphs, and a vocabulary readily understood by the average reader, one without jargon. Few events covered in news releases from public relations practitioners require more than one or two pages. They use the direct approach as the most effective means of communicating with the public through the mass media; have something to say; say it briefly but completely in an appealing format devoid of opinion; and stop when the message has been transmitted.

Practitioners strive to adjust their resources so they can provide releases specifically tailored for the electronic media in addition to the more comprehensive stories developed for print media. Among significant differences between newspaper stories and those developed for radio and television are that the latter are shorter and avoid not only complex sentence structure but also words and phrases difficult to pronounce or unfamiliar to the newscasters. Pronunciation guides written into radio and television copy are helpful, and if budgets permit, visuals are made available to television outlets so stations need not devote excessive time on newscasts to "talking heads."

Public relations writers employ the style most widely used by the media with which they deal on a regular basis and develop a recognizable letterhead for releases, one which includes organizational information needed by editors or reporters who may be seeking to authenticate a story or obtain additional information.

Competition for media space and time is spirited and unrelenting; so, PR practitioners must be professional journalists who adapt the message to the medium whether it is written or aural. They will do so accurately, completely, and fairly.

Exercises

1. From today's newspaper, clip a news story that features the four major elements of news. Underline statements in the story illustrating each of the four elements.

2. In current publications, find examples that feature the following building blocks: combat or struggle, success against odds, humor or pathos, sex and romance, and animals.

3. Write six leads, each illustrating a different type, for the lead story in today's newspaper.

4. Adapt the lead story in today's newspaper to the 60-second limit of the electronic media.

Case study

Welcome to Sioux Falls, South Dakota, location of the entire Brute Engine Company operation. You have been hired as Brute's first and only public relations director. The company supplies all the engines for Garden-Eze, Inc., manufacturers of garden tractors, and Garden-Eze is Brute's only customer.

Brute has done well until recently. Now, however, because of an industrywide recession and competition from foreign manufacturers, the domestic garden tractor business is in trouble. Yearly profits for each of the past five years have been $1.3 million, $1.1 million, $1.0 million, and $1.4 million. Most of the net was poured back into research and development.

The company employs 250 in Sioux Falls and, although publicly owned, a majority of the company's stockholders also live in the Sioux Falls area.

Bobbie R. Riely, Brute president, tells you that there is good news and bad news. The good news is that Brute is completing tests on a stratified charge engine that will make most other units in the industry obsolete. Tests are extremely encouraging. The engine can replace units used in almost any small tractor and, in addition, the engine can be adapted to light aircraft. However, before the new product comes on line, approximately half the work force must be furloughed for an indefinite period. Not only that, but for the first time in 23 years, Brute will report a loss. And the loss is formidable—$9.7 million.

Riely is confident that the company will survive, thanks to employees' voting to accept a wage freeze for the coming year and executives' volunteering to accept a 15 percent across the board salary reduction.

• Develop a release for general circulation newspapers in the area, explaining the Brute Engine Company situation.

• Prepare a similar story for circulation to radio and television outlets.

• Modify the general release for circulation to trade publications.

• Describe the types of photographs and film or videotape that could accompany the stories.

• Using available media directories, develop a mailing list of commercial newspapers, radio and television outlets within a 100-mile radius of Sioux Falls.

Suggested readings

Associated Press. *The Associated Press Stylebook and Libel Manual.* New York: The Associated Press, 1987.

Caruba, Alan. "International Media Contacts." *Public Relations Journal,* August 1984.

Frazier, Richard S., and Kenneth H. Rabin. "S & T Information: How Editors Want It." *Public Relations Journal,* January 1980.

Gold, Vic. "We Need a New Form of Adversary PR to Meet Adversary Journalism." *Media Institute Forum,* November/December 1984.

Howard, Carole, and Wilma Mathews. *On Deadline: Managing Media Relations.* New York: Longman, Inc., 1985.

Kohlmeier, Louis M., Jr., John G. Udell, and Laurie B. Anderson. *Reporting on Business and the Economy.* Englewood Cliffs, N.J.: Prentice-Hall, 1981.

Kowal, John Paul. "Ten Commandments for Public Service Announcements." *Public Relations Journal,* January 1980.

Metz, William. *Newswriting: From Lead to "30."* 2d ed. Englewood Cliffs, N.J.: Prentice-Hall, 1985.

Plumb, James W. "Hostile Journalists Aren't the Issue; Need Ongoing PR Before Crises Hit." *Media Institute Forum,* November/December 1984.

Stahr, John. *Write to the Point: The Byoir Style Book for Press Material.* New York: Macmillan, 1968.

Strunk, William Jr., and E. B. White. *The Elements of Style* 3d ed. New York: Macmillan, 1979.

"Why New-Product Releases Don't Get Published." *Public Relations Journal,* January 1980.

Without Bias: A Guidebook for Nondiscriminatory Communication. San Francisco: Int. Assoc. Bus. Communicators, 1977.

Young, Robert B. "Fabricote, Duraquote and Clonequote." *Public Relations Journal,* September 1979.

11 The news conference

Going beyond the news release

Although written news releases are the most frequently used method of providing information to the mass media, as noted, they may not be the most reliable, least expensive, or most readily acceptable. Some reporters, editors, and news directors look upon the news release as a "puff" or an attempt to gain free advertising.

When time and circumstances permit, editors prefer assigning their own reporters to cover the story. They believe by having their own staff members seek out the information and write the story, they get the "whole" story, "uncolored" by the possible self-interest of the public relations practitioner. After all, the public relations writer is paid by the organization or the individuals about whom the story will be written.

In most cases where the story is controversial or sufficiently important, the media will find a way to cover it with their own staff. They prefer it that way. Aware of this, the public relations professional will schedule a news conference, an efficient method of getting the organization's representatives and the reporters together.

News conferences are not an everyday event in public relations by any definition. They are scheduled only when the organization has something really important to say, a story of probable major news interest. Consequently, some large organizations operate for months without the need to schedule a news conference. But when one is scheduled, every effort is expended to assure that the event is conducted for maximum benefit to the organization and to the reporters covering the conference.

No inflexible rules determine when to call a news conference; the merits of each occasion are studied separately. News conferences have been used to introduce a new chief executive, a political candidate, a significant scientific discovery, a program that will have a marked effect on the local economy, social patterns, or life-styles. The event may be the announcement of a large construction project, a significant change in the regional work force, or a change in organizational ownership. Frequently, large fund-raising campaigns are introduced through a news conference. In short, the event must be newsworthy.

Whether or not a formal news conference is scheduled, able media professionals will arrange for individual coverage on an important story, seldom relying exclusively on a public relations news release. Reporters will call or visit the organization, seeking knowledgeable individuals to confirm details in the release, provide different angles, fill in the holes that the editors or news directors may consider vital in the complete story. Furthermore, some editors have had unfortunate experiences with unscrupulous or less-than-professional "press agents," so they tend to search out any skeletons that may be hidden in corporate closets.

Therefore, in the overview and in those situations warranting the added emphasis, the public relations practitioner may save time and resources by opting for a news conference from the beginning.

If the organization has egg on its face, the facts probably will surface in a news conference. However, without such a conference, the facts still would become known. By having organizational representatives discuss the situation openly with reporters in a news conference, the organization is assured of a hearing.

Furthermore, more extensive coverage is guaranteed when the news conference is the basic information device. Human nature (organizational nature, if you will) explains why the average news outlet invariably runs a longer, more comprehensive story when it was developed from a new conference. The story and pictorial coverage were developed by staff members from that news outlet rather than from a release written and distributed by a public relations professional. The editor made the assignment and the reporter wrote the story. Each has a personal interest in the ultimate disposition of the story, and each is on the medium's payroll.

Frequently the public relations practitioner employs the news release in conjunction with a news conference. Basic information to be covered in the news conference may be developed as a news release and distributed to reporters in attendance. Or the PR professional may serve as a reporter at the new conference and develop a story following the event. Either or both stories thus written are delivered to media that were unable to staff the conference because of economics or logistics. So, even organizing and staffing a news conference does not preclude the need to develop and distribute a news release.

(Note that we have used "news conference" rather than "press conference" for a specific reason. Either term is understood, and frequently they are used interchangeably, but "press conference" does ruffle an occasional feather among representatives of the electronic media. "We don't do any printing at our television station, you know." So, announce the event as a "news conference.")

Facing reporters

Among the most influential and sensitive contacts affected by an improved internal relations program are those with representatives of the news media. The media play a major role in the total community's understanding of the organization. Most people who are considered external publics will accept or reject the organization, understand or actively distrust it, based on their comprehension of the organization. Unless it is a small neighborhood enterprise, today's complex organization will have an external public that is far too large, with members spread over too wide an area for each to have a personal relationship with it. By and large, the public's opinions are formed and most of its knowledge of the organization is obtained from the media. So the public relations practitioner looks toward the news media to tell the organization's story. As Abraham Lincoln said, "With public sentiment, nothing can fail; without it, nothing can succeed. He who molds public opinion goes deeper than he who enacts statutes or pronounces decisions."

Lincoln was referring directly to the newspapers of his day when literacy was not high. Nevertheless, he understood the power of the public media. In all probability, were he alive today, Lincoln would be even more positive in his attitude because of the far greater impact of modern news media, newspapers, television and radio outlets, news magazines, wire services, and networks.

Unprecedented advances in communications techniques have resulted in an information explosion. One result is that the individual expects to be in on the action. If an organization in any way impacts on the public, because of products placed on the market or services rendered, the citizen views that organization's business as public business. The day that the entrepreneur could believe and say, "The public be damned," is long since past.

The reporter, therefore, pursuing the goal of informing the public, may be found anywhere from the board room to the assembly line, the Pentagon to the battlefield. In today's climate, any member of our internal publics, executive to part-time student helper, may be involved in circumstances that bring out the reporter's pad, tape recorder, microphone, and camera. For most neophytes and many experienced executives, it can be an unnerving experience.

People fear or mistrust that which they do not understand. Fear and mistrust frequently are the emotions experienced by employees in an organization (assembly line or executive suite) when they must face a news reporter. Their understanding of how a reporter operates and why is hazy at best. "I don't know what makes them tick. I just know those reporters are always out to sensationalize a story." As professionals in media relations, public relations staff members can remove some mystery and uneasiness from such encounters for those fellow employees who must face reporters one-on-one or in new conferences.

The news business

Like most enterprises in this nation, the news business is founded on the profit motive. But beyond that base, few other parallels can be drawn between news gathering organizations and other profit-oriented enterprises. And one of the most difficult aspects for most persons to grasp (interview subjects included) is that the reporter remains fiercely independent of the advertising and circulation side (the revenue generating segments) of the news medium. The reporter is not impressed by the fact that the subject of the story is a fourth generation subscriber, a constant viewer of the channel, or a heavy advertiser. This is not to say that the publisher or station manager does not take a proprietary interest in what happens in the newsroom, but on a major outlet, occasions when the business manager or advertising manager interjects opinions on the news side or attempts to sway coverage are almost nonexistent.

Similarly, attempts at economic or political pressure usually are doomed to failure or worse. The attempt to pressure an editor or a reporter can result in an adversary relationship that will be unnecessarily harmful to the organization or individual attempting to exert the pressure. Or, if pressure through a friend within the news organization should be successful this time, it may be a case of winning the battle and losing the war. Remembering the lost battle is an all-too-human failing. The reporter or editor will be doubly diligent in pursuing and researching subsequent stories. Justified or not, deliberately provoking an argument with an adversary who buys ink by the barrel or sends messages from a 700-foot tower is foolhardy.

NEWS BUDGETS

To the uninitiated interview subject, the reporter *is* the newspaper, radio, or television station. Few average citizens realize the limits placed on the reporter. You may safely assume that those few exceptions are not on your staff. So explain the news gathering procedure to members of your organization, either before or after they have been interviewed. It can lessen disappointment or misunderstanding.

Frequently a lengthy interview can result in a story only six inches long buried deep in a newspaper or encompassed in a 20-second news brief just before the commercial, or perhaps no story at all. To a busy executive who devoted an hour to the interview, this can be a puzzling turn of events.

News space is determined by advertising departments in all media. The managing editor or makeup editor receives a "dummy," a rough layout scheme, from the advertising department of the newspaper early in the work day. This dummy shows how many pages will be in the newspaper and the space on each page that will be devoted to advertising. Unless a cataclysmic news event occurs, this dummy is followed scrupulously. Similarly, in the electronic news media, the advertising department informs the news department as to how many seconds of each newscast will be commercial time. Thus, space or time allocated to news is not necessarily tied to the amount or significance of the news available.

Upon receipt of their news budgets, editors subdivide the space or time into several departments: financial, social, sports, entertainment, homemaking, etc. Within each department, regular features must have space allocated and their locations determined. These, of course, include regular columnists, comics, weather, crossword puzzle, horoscope, market listings, recipes, daily record, schedules of events, etc.

The battle is on throughout the work day for the remaining space. At the time the reporter was assigned to interview the representative from the organization, undoubtedly the story was regarded as worthy of extensive coverage. Remember, however, that competition is fierce for that space or time.

During an average day, a metropolitan newspaper will receive news stories from all sources totaling more than a million words, the equivalent of approximately a dozen novels. Material comes from the paper's own news staff, wire services, syndicates, public relations practitioners, and private citizens. The public relations news release competes with the world. Rebellion in the Middle East, tragedy in the

Andes, tax legislation in Congress, curriculum changes in the local schools, a downtown fire, blizzard on the plains, world records, crime, dog shows, and the World Series—each competes for space with the PR practitioner's story. Consequently, a good story may be shoved off the front page, severely cut, or held for a later edition; it may become part of another story, or it may be dropped entirely.

Deadlines are another factor that can determine the ultimate fate of the story. In the news business, the clock is an indisputable fact of life. A metropolitan newspaper that publishes morning and evening may have eight different editions. The first (or "bulldog") hits the streets the evening before the publication date; the second is printed for morning distribution outside the metropolitan area; the third (or "sunrise") is for home delivery in the city. The fourth edition goes to residents of neighboring states; the fifth places heavy emphasis on state news outside the metro area; the sixth covers the suburban areas; the seventh is for home delivery within the city; and the final ("Wall Street") edition features closing prices from the major commodity and stock exchanges.

Thus, such a newspaper has at least eight deadlines each day for late-breaking news. Some papers have more. In addition, separate deadlines are imposed for special sections (local, sports, social, etc.). If a story coming from a news conference misses the scheduled deadline by seconds, it misses a key audience for today, regardless of circumstances. The reporter may have had difficulty with specific details, the organization's public relations staff may have failed to answer a request for information before deadline, or the reporter may have been assigned a late-breaking spot news story that was determined to be more important than the interview.

Meanwhile, the radio reporter might consider today a holiday if only eight deadlines are to be met. Many outlets feature hourly newscasts, each different. In addition, the radio news director may have the option of breaking into regularly scheduled programming with a sufficiently newsworthy story. So when dealing with electronic media, the next deadline is *now.*

Speed in responding to requests for information from the news media cannot be stressed too strongly, whether they are primary requests to be handled by the public relations practitioner or requests that must be relayed by the PR practitioner to someone else within the organization. If you must relay the request, make certain the person who will respond has an appreciation of the speed required.

FROM BEAT SHEET TO YOUR FRONT PORCH

A further buttress against misunderstanding can result if the interview subject knows the path a story follows from the time the reporter learns of the assignment from the "beat sheet," the assignment book maintained by the city editor or news director. Occasionally a reporter "enterprises" a story (develops an idea and follows through without receiving a specific assignment); however, the more common practice is to have the reporter assigned to a particular beat or given a specific assignment.

The reporter will try to gather as much background on a person, organization, or event as time permits prior to an interview, obtaining as much comprehensive information as possible from the public relations staff.

The practicing journalist is a self-assured, thorough professional, and the average interview subject may believe the reporter is solely responsible for everything published or broadcast. Therefore, in addition to explaining what the reporter does, the public relations practitioner can spare the interview subject additional confusion by providing an explanation of what the reporter does not do as well.

The reporter does not edit the final copy, write the headline for the story, determine the length of the final story, nor dictate placement of the story in the publication or the newscast. Once these points are understood, it is much easier for the interview subject to accept some of the strange fates that may befall the story for which he was interviewed.

After the reporter writes the story from notes or tapes obtained during the interview, one of the editors on the city desk (in the case of a newspaper) punches up the story for the first review. The editor in the slot (center spot on a copy desk) or, in some cases, the city editor checks the story briefly and assigns it to one of several persons charged with rim duty: rewriting and editing. At this point, facts are double-checked; spelling and grammar reviewed; the story revised to conform with the publication's style; all extraneous matter is deleted; and changes are incorporated, if necessary, to make the copy more readable.

The editor in the slot grades the story for relative news value compared with other stories scheduled for the current edition, and a headline size is assigned. One of the most challenging feats of mental gymnastics on a newspaper is writing a headline that reflects accurately the sense of a news story, because the head may range from as few as 15 characters to two or three lines of 30 or more characters each.

To your organization's chief executive, there may be a subtle but important difference between "fired" and "relieved." To the headline writer, the only significant difference is that the former is five counts, the later seven and a half. The engineer may prefer "subsidence" because of its precise meaning. The headline writer prefers "settling" because the score is ten to seven, depending upon the headline style used. The point is that the interview subject may have asked the reporter to avoid "fired" and "settling," but the reporter does not write the headline for the story.

Now that the headline has been mated to the story, the makeup editor determines where the story will appear in the publication, or if it is to be combined with yet another story written by a different reporter. In a careful evaluation of copy available for the current edition, the editor may decide the story merits no more than the middle of page 36 next to advertisements for steel-belted radial tires or disposable diapers. Again, the reporter had no part in the decision.

After the copy is in type, the editor may find the story is too long for the space allotted. Because the story was written in the inverted pyramid style, however, the editor can drop the required amount from the end of the copy and still have the most important facts in readable form.

All these decisions were made without input from the reporter, the one person who met and dealt with the interview subject.

SOLVING THE MYSTERY OF RADIO AND TV

The credibility gap is exacerbated when the person has been interviewed by a radio or television reporter because the electronic journalist has even more acute problems with copy length.

A story warranting a column in a daily newspaper may be given a minute (150 words or less) in a 30-minute newscast. If it is carried at all, it could be a 20-second story in an on-the-hour five-minute radio newscast. The radio version, therefore, would be 40 to 50 words, two or three sentences. The result can be disconcerting for the inexperienced interview subject. The public relations staff owes that individual an explanation of the electronic news business and the reasons behind this unexpected turn of events.

Again, in the case of the broadcast reporter, ultimate control of what is aired how and when it will be broadcast is in the hands of other people. The news director and various editors may rewrite the reporter's copy, edit the audio tapes, videotapes, and film. Radio and television offer immediacy and an intimate "you are there" feel for the listener and viewer, but frequently they must sacrifice detail.

Despite obvious difficulties with which the news profession deals on a routine basis, the men and women who work for the media do a remarkable job. Current communication technology directs an increasing amount of information at today's citizens. The type and quality of the information is determined in large measure by the professional journalists. Public relations practitioners find an important part of their duties is assisting these professionals.

An equally important role is helping the individuals from the organization that pays the practitioner's salary, the internal publics. They will be more effective in accurately relaying the organization's story if they understand the news business. Their increased knowledge will go far in relieving the uncertainty, fear, and distrust that may surface in interactions with reporters. Employees and staff members will represent the organization more accurately in communicating with the public through the media. They will be more positive and more self-assured, and that confidence will be apparent to the public through the media.

When the interview subject understands the interviewer's objectives and problems, the two can assist each other, and human frailties such as impatience, contentiousness, and belligerence are less likely to surface. The two participants in the interview meet on a more stable foundation. And even in cases where the result is less than the stirring victory the interview subject expected, the organization may have received a fair hearing, and complete disaster may have been averted.

The interview

All too frequently, executives and other potential spokesmen tend to believe, "All those reporters are out to get us." The company, agency, or institutional executive reasons that journalists are antibusiness, antigovernment, or antieverything. Scientific polls and samples as well as bridge table small talk and barbershop bull sessions show the disease is not confined to reporters. However, journalists reflect attitudes and opinions held by a sizable percentage of their fellow citizens. They reflect prevailing sentiment. Thus, it is the public relations professional's responsibility to keep any paranoia from becoming epidemic among members of the organization's internal publics.

Many executives, aware of the pitfalls in dealing with journalists, may opt for an easy way out by telling the reporter, "Sorry, just no way my schedule will permit us to get together, but our PR folks will be happy to fill you in." The unspoken reason is, "After all, why should I take the heat? That's what those PR types get paid for."

Not good enough! For starters, the reporter seeks the individuals who made the decision, developed the new process, or have their names printed on the letterhead. Furthermore, the reporter may suspect a runaround and conclude that the public relations representative either will not be as knowledgeable or will have instructions to gloss over important aspects of the story.

Conversely, the interview subject too often fears the reporter will be an adversary. Certainly there are occasions when this may be true, but real professional journalists regard getting the complete and correct story as their major duty. Television news commentator David Brinkley once said, "When a reporter asks as question, he is not working for the person being questioned, whether businessman, politician, or bureaucrat, but he is working for the readers and listeners." So, interview subjects cannot expect their views to be accepted without question, but they can enhance their chances of a fair hearing.

Accepting interviews or even actively seeking interview opportunities is in the best interest of an organization or business. It offers the interview subject a rare occasion to make points that need to be made. The interview subject must be reminded, however, that any bias exhibited against the organization by the reporter may well be a reflection of today's world. Business, government, education, and the professions come under the frequent and close scrutiny of a skeptical world.

If an organization's representatives, the people with first-hand knowledge, refuse to talk with the media, be assured that some good reporter will dig until other, secondary sources come to light. Then, it will be their version of the organization's story that will be told by the media.

OVERCOMING FEAR OF THE UNKNOWN

Interview subjects frequently are wary of confrontation with a journalist because of the novelty of the situation. Their complaint: "I don't know how to deal with them!" These same people feel no qualms facing a stockholders meeting, labor negotiations, a faculty meeting, or a variety of other stressful situations, but they reach for antacid tablets before facing a reporter. Their uneasiness has nothing to do with comparative intelligence, but the two individuals, executive and reporter, operate in different theaters. The executive's name is on the door because of finely honed talents as a manager, negotiator, scientist, or whatever. And the reporter, equally skilled, is a trained interviewer capable of unearthing a newsworthy story by framing disarming, penetrating questions and completing painstaking research. So the problem for the executive is one of being totally unfamiliar with the reporter's arena.

The public relations professional can allay some of the organizational spokesman's anxiety by reassuring the executive that the reporter's first responsibility is writing an accurate story. Credibility is the major product sold by news media. No news outlet likes to run corrections or defend itself in a libel suit; so, the reporter is determined to be right because too many mistakes invariably lead a journalist to seek other employment.

To further guarantee accuracy, many journalists use tape recorders or film in conducting interviews. The technique frees them from extensive notetaking so they can concentrate more fully on their questioning. Because the equipment promotes accuracy, rather than being wary of the recorders, the interview subject should welcome them. However, they do destroy claims that "I was misquoted."

The executive should be aware that the reporter probably will not accept the information gleaned in the interview as the entire story, particularly in controversial situations. But by granting the interview, the executive can be assured the organization's points will receive a hearing.

MEET THE PRESS

The executive has listened to your assurances. The interview is imminent. Now what?

The practitioner's job is just beginning. You will advise, assist, and prepare your organization's representative in every possible way. Ten general guidelines, as a minimum, must be covered before and during the interview:

1. *Prepare carefully.* Work closely with the person to be interviewed. Determine all possible subjects to be covered in the forthcoming visit with the reporter. If the interview subject is not fully conversant with these topics, call on persons who are to assist in preparing a written briefing and to develop probable questions and complete answers.

The person to be interviewed must study the material thoroughly; however, it should be learned and understood, not memorized verbatim. Unless the material is extremely technical or highly detailed, notes should not be used as a crutch during the interview. If circumstances warrant, a condensed version of the briefing material can be given to the reporter as background information. In all cases, advise your executive against "winging it" or "playing it by ear."

An incident involving an ill-prepared university athletic director underscores the point. He appeared at a hastily called news conference in advance of an NCAA regional tournament game. In extolling the basketball team, he dwelled on the talents of the point guard. "Keep your eyes on him," he said. "He's the soul of our offense." The reporters were puzzled. Most of them knew the player had been declared ineligible that same morning.

2. *Create an informal atmosphere.* If you control physical arrangements, avoid a "king and peasant" atmosphere. Your spokesman should not use an imposing executive desk as a barrier to hold the reporter at bay. Provide comfortable chairs, perhaps a low table and, if possible, coffee or other light refreshments.

3. *Remember the reader or viewer.* The organization's representative should think and speak with the reader or viewer uppermost in mind. General Bullmoose, the tycoon in the old "Li'l Abner" comic strip, used to say. "What's good for General Bullmoose is good for the country." That philosophy sinks organizations in this day of aware citizens. The interview subject should be able to translate points to be made into what they will mean for the average person. Compare these two statements:

"Those stack scrubbers cost $3 million. That's half our total profit margin for the fiscal year, but we're in compliance with EPA regulations."

"We've installed those $3 million stack scrubbers to bring our pollution level lower than that of any comparable plant in the state. That's about $35 for each of our customers, but we think the investment in clean air is worth it."

In the first statement, the executive is talking for the company management. In the second, he is speaking for the reader and viewer.

4. *Make important points first.* As in writing a news story, the most important points should be mentioned early in an interview, and for many of the same reasons. People remember the first thing said and tend to forget later points. Furthermore, without being facetious, it makes sense to state important points before the reporter uses all her available tape, film, or patience. Finally, under deadline pressure, the

interviewer or editor may complete an acceptable story before reaching your well-calculated climactic point on the tape.

5. *Relax and think.* Whatever the game, each successful player has an individual style; the same is true with competent interviewers. They all use techniques that have been effective for them, ranging from finesse to aggression. Whatever the reporter's style, the interview subject must remember the interview begins with the first exchange with the reporter, so the interview subject should never say anything not intended for publication or airing.

Loaded questions can be used effectively by a reporter, so the interview subject must be alert. Examples:

"Is it true that your car is unsafe at any speed?" (A paraphrase of consumer advocate Ralph Nader).

"What's your reaction to the claim in a national magazine that you have the lowest admission standards in the Southwest?"

"What's your reaction to the County Consumers Guild charge that your rates are almost criminal?"

The words and phrases are provocative and offensive. The well-prepared interview subject will avoid repeating them at all costs. To do so is to fall into a well-laid trap. Remember that the question usually will not be printed and is seldom broadcast. Thus, if the interview subject is goaded into speaking the words or phrases, the story may carry a headline or be given a lead-in like these:

"Spokesman says car not unsafe at any speed."

"Dean claims standards not Southwest's lowest."

"Manager denies rates almost criminal."

The reporter played "Gotcha!" and the company or agency lost. Rather than repeat the offending phrases for publication or broadcast, rework the statements into a positive approach. Thus, we might have:

"Car termed one of industry's safest."

"Admissions standards climbing, Dean says."

"Utility rates below average for services rendered."

6. *Do not argue with reporters.* The skilled interview subject avoids verbal battles with reporters and keeps temper under control, despite provocation. One public relations director said, "I tell my folks to avoid these battles of wits. I don't want them to act as though they're unarmed. They're up against the pros." Rather, with the deliberately rude reporter, the PR director suggested that the executive grab audience sympathy with a knowing smile or tolerant shrug. Remember, the media will have the last word.

7. *Do not demand to check the story.* Warn your interview subject against even suggesting that the story be submitted before publication or broadcast. The practice is against the policy of most media, and such a request insults any reporter or editor.

However, if the reporter asks the interview subject to check technical data or statistics, fine. Even then, caution against the temptation to become a censor by going beyond the request.

8. *Avoid technical terminology whenever possible.* In-house jargon and organizational acronyms lessen understanding and raise reporters' blood pressure. An "aerodynamic decelerator" is still a parachute. The highway department's "impact attenuation device" is still an empty oil drum placed in the median. "Contusions and abrasions" are still cuts and bruises. Regardless of technical advances, there is no communication if the message is gobbledygook. The public relations professional must translate technical jargon into understandable English.

Eliminating gobbledygook does not restrict the interview subject to one-word answers. Rather, the organization's spokesman frequently can expand on an important point by going beyond simple "yes" or "no" answers. "Yes, the strike is settled and in a way we feel is fair to our employees, our many customers, and the company. The union joins us in calling this the only solution that would permit us to hold our price increase below the inflation rate, and they feel the scholarship provision is a real breakthrough in labor relations."

9. *Be impartial with the media.* News is one of the most intensely competitive businesses in our society. Be aware of the many deadlines for media with which you deal routinely and honor them. In cases where you can control release time on newsworthy items, schedule releases on a rotating basis so that you do not consistently favor a single medium or several to the exclusion of others.

Unless you are prepared to write off important news outlets, be sparing in granting exclusive stories to favored media or to favored friends among reporters. However, if a reporter develops an idea and comes to you for information and assistance, treat that story as an exclusive. The reporter enterprised it, so the story is private property. Do not violate the confidence.

10. *Tell the truth.* The final and most important point is to insist that your organizational representatives follow your lead. Even when it hurts, the answer must be truthful. Avoid half-truths. Half-truths equal half-lies. Personal integrity aside for the moment, a sound reason for avoiding lies or half-lies in dealing with reporters is that invariably the culprit is caught. The public will forgive errors in judgment, mistakes of almost any kind, but the public will remember who lied to it. The public was willing to forgive the break-in, records theft, and many other facets of the Watergate incident in the early 1970s, but it never forgave the officials who lied. A major national crisis resulted.

Avoid exaggeration as a vital part of telling the truth. And do not fake it. If you or your interview subject do not have the correct answer, admit it. Be willing to say, "I don't know." But in the same breath, add, "I'll find out and call you right away," or "I will put you in touch with the person who has the handle on that." Then follow up. See that the answer is provided before the reporter's deadline. Do not pass the buck.

While on the subject of truth in interviews, strike two lines from your corporate or organizational lexicon: "This is off the record" and "No comment."

"Off the record" means many things to many people and nothing to others. Some interpret it to mean only that the speaker does not want to be credited with the remark, but the statement in question may be attributed to an anonymous source, "a government spokesman" or "a company official." Another group ignores the phrase. Still others go to the extreme of leaving the room if an interview subject insists on speaking off the record.

When a question elicits "no comment," many knowledgeable reporters deduce that the speaker is in fact saying, "You bet I know, but the answer would hang me." It equates with the judicial plea, "I refuse to answer on the grounds that the information might tend to incriminate me."

Avoid both phrases, and remember to inform your executive that the interview begins when the reporter walks in the door. Anything said may become part of the final story.

The conference itself

HOW DO I LOOK?

The television camera's unwinking eye adds further to the uneasiness of the inexperienced interview subject. Recognizing this, some large organizations send selected executives to seminars that place special emphasis on performance before the lights and camera. The practice has much to recommend it for those who can pay up to five thousand dollars for a four-day program.

MANNERISMS. As tension increases, some individuals tend to breathe shallowly. The result is answers that sound flat and shrill because their voices are originating in their throats rather than deeper in the diaphragm where the chest serves as a resonator. Practice and remembering a few simple techniques can minimize voice problems.

Obviously a complete course in microphone techniques is impractical for many busy executives. However, the public relations practitioner can reduce the level of apprehension for the particularly nervous spokesman. Minor therapy in the form of tongue twisters and speech exercises can be prescribed for the stumblers and the hesitant. Individuals can learn to relax by breathing more deeply, adjusting body position occasionally, and pausing before answering complex questions.

Urge the person who may be interviewed to be natural on camera rather than an imitation network oracle or an amateur comic. A poorly told, hackneyed joke is a disastrous introduction to a detailed explanation of the reasons for closing the local assembly plant. A pompous, posturing executive doing a parlor imitation of Roger Mudd or Barbara Walters can cause an epidemic of dial twisting while explaining the organization's expansion plans. The camera magnifies mannerisms.

Normal emphasis adds interest to filmed interviews, but excessive gesturing and constant head movements kill the message the interview subject is delivering. Suggest that the executive relate to the cameras as though they were individual people.

If the interview subject is to be seated during the news conference, provide a straight-backed chair and instructions to sit well back in the chair. When the conference begins, the interview subject should lean slightly forward, head raised to facilitate looking directly at the interviewer and the camera. The interview subject should not be located between or among the reporters who will ask the questions, because in reacting to flanking reporters the interview subject will appear on camera to be watching a tennis match, eyes darting from side to side.

Unfortunately, the average viewer distrusts a person who appears to be nervous. After a lifelong diet of cops-and-robbers movies, the viewer looks upon the fidgeter as a person with something to hide. Advise executives to avoid tugging at collars and twisting buttons. A clicking ballpoint pen or glasses that constantly need adjusting are distractions. Remind the executives to maintain good eye contact with the interviewer and to remember that downcast eyes are associated with guilt.

USING NOTES. If your representative proposes to use notes during the news conference because of the technical nature of the subject or the need for precise figures, urge against any attempt to hide them. Cameras catch each furtive glance, each evidence of tension. No one is fooled. Keep the notes in view.

Caution against memorizing a script or following a prepared text during an opening statement. Either way, the person will seem like an automaton, dull, devoid of personality, and frightened. Where notes will be needed, the interview subject should highlight or underline key figures, ideas, and words so that the script can serve as a guide for answering questions or delivering a prepared statement.

GOOD GROOMING IS A MUST. The interview subject represents the entire organization, so the public relations practitioner should emphasize the importance of looking good. As a minimum, men should have a fresh shave and women must refresh their makeup before appearing on camera.

Flamboyance in dress disturbs viewers and frustrates cameramen and engineers. Wild patterns and high contrast stripes and color combinations must be avoided. Select shirts and blouses in pastels because television cameras have difficulty compensating for the high contrast presented by white shirts and blouses with dark jackets. Medium gray, blue, or brown suits flatter men on camera. Women should select medium-tone solid color street-length dresses or suits. Whether it is a dress, suit, or pantsuit, the choice should be conservative.

Bow ties ride the Adam's apple as the interview subject talks, so they should be avoided. If jewelry is worn, it must be kept simple. Bright stones and metals produce disconcerting light reflections and refractions.

Women seated before a camera must be aware of their hemlines. The camera is. In fact, even men have problems with long shots. When a man sits before the camera and trousers hike to reveal white socks or white skin, the viewer may concentrate on the wrong subject. Wear calf-length, dark socks. Any distraction reduces effectiveness and threatens credibility.

Remove eyeglasses if the interview subject is comfortable without them, although reflections from glasses do not present as great a problem as they once did. However, sunglasses or tinted prescription glasses, indoors or outside, should be removed because they hide the eyes. The audience views with suspicion anyone whose eyes are hidden.

PHYSICAL ARRANGEMENTS

Now that the organization has a properly prepared spokesman, the public relations practitioner can arrange for the news conference. Advance preparation in arranging facilities is as important as it was in tutoring the company or agency representative. Thorough planning goes far toward eliminating unexpected problems. Remember that many of the following preparations are required whether the invitation list is confined to local media or is expanded to include national news media.

THE SITE. Site selection is a primary concern. If reporters are being invited to the unveiling of a new product, process, or structure and the major elements are suitable, the conference should be held in a location where the product, process, or structure can serve as the background.

Normally, however, this is not the case, so the site will be chosen that is best suited to the needs of media representatives. Simple is best. The room must be easily accessible and located in an area free of traffic noises and other distractions. It should be well ventilated to compensate for heat buildup caused by a large crowd and television lights.

Use a standing lectern or a table set before an uncluttered background. Provide namecards if several persons will be seated at the table. The best background is a light-colored wall. Avoid mirrored walls and draperies or wall coverings which feature large, colorful, and distracting patterns. Provide straight-backed chairs for the individual or individuals to be interviewed and for the media representatives. Allow approximately 20 square feet of free floor space for each television crew that will attend.

If resources permit, install adequate television lights in advance of the news conference to avoid the confusion created by a number of television crews setting up their own lighting. If a large attendance by broadcast media representatives is expected, prior installation of a multiple outlet box for audio feed will eliminate the need for a forest of microphones in front of the people being interviewed.

The following is an example of what could have been a public relations embarrassment resulting from inadequate advance planning.

A news conference was scheduled for Jefferson City, Missouri, to unveil recent developments in commercial river navigation. The evening conference was held aboard a riverboat to emphasize the subject and to provide suitable video background. A television crew boarded the vessel and began searching for an electrical outlet for its quartz lights. The boat had a 24-volt DC system, and the crew's lights, of course, were 110-volt AC. The problem arose because of inadequate planning by both the public relations staff and the camera crew.

A recently hired public relations assistant improvised a solution. He had the boat's captain focus the vessels powerful searchlight on the interview subject, providing almost theatrical lighting for the film crew. The audio was perfunctory, but the video was dramatic.

PRESS ROOM. When many out-of-town reporters will attend a news conference, providing a press room in conjunction with the news conference can further reduce confusion and delays. Telephones and typewriters are made available in this room for use by reporters. If a press room is not provided, telephones must still be readily available for reporters.

SECURITY. Where the organization involved operates a large, closed installation or plant, and where there is an internal security force, the public relations staff must clear arrangements with the security force. The security staff should receive a schedule, a list of probable media representation (complete with names of individuals, if possible), and clear directions to the site of the news conference.

INVITATIONS. Two weeks in advance of the conference date, mail announcements to individual radio and television stations, networks, newspapers, trade publications, and wire services that cover the region or the particular field of interest involved. Announce the date, time, specific location, probable spokesmen, the organization, and the general subject matter to be covered. Include a self-addressed, stamped card to be returned by the media, thus providing an attendance estimate.

A day or two before the conference, the public relations staff will telephone editors, news directors, and bureau chiefs with a reminder of the event. Ask Associated Press, United Press International, and the city news bureau if one operates in the vicinity about the possibility of announcing the news conference on their wires. Included in each announcement or reminder of the news conference will be the name and telephone number of the public relations contact who can provide additional information.

An experienced public relations professional for a major land developer once forgot the basics or decided the importance of the occasion was so obvious that thorough preparation for a news conference was unnecessary. Announcements of the news conference were mailed to principal news media in the Denver metropolitan area. The invitation hinted vaguely that "recent findings of interest to area residents" would be discussed.

The organization's chief executive was prepared; a well-appointed room was leased; and suitable press kits were set on the chairs. Only one problem surfaced: nobody attended the news conference, not a single media representative. Super Bowl kickoff and the receiving team failed to take the field.

Subsequent news conferences set up by this organization are models of efficiency. Invitations are specific as to subject matter. Return cards are a must. Follow-up telephone calls are made. And when practical, the public relations representative personally visits the invited media.

FORMAT. A workable structure for the news conference is to have the public relations director open the event by welcoming media representatives and briefly introducing the individual(s) featured in the conference. Generally, the ranking executive also makes brief opening remarks before answering questions. With few exceptions, successful news conferences are those during which the organization's representatives answer all questions that arise. Or if they do not know the answer to a specific question, they provide the facts as soon as possible after the conference.

In those instances where a tight schedule must be maintained, a frequently used method of closing a news conference is for the public relations director or the organization's chief spokesman to announce, "We have time for just one or two more questions."

Whether the main thrust of the news conference is detailing an industry breakthrough or an organizational disaster, competent advance planning will assure a well-reported story. That is why the public relations practitioner is on the payroll.

CHECKLIST. For many events handled by the public relations practitioner, a checklist is indispensable. The news conference is one of these, and an example of a news conference checklist is shown in Figure 11.1. Use of a list minimizes the chance of overlooking one of the many details vital for a successful news conference.

Summary

Preparing employees and staff members to meet reporters is an important duty of the modern public relations practitioner. A first step in this process is helping the possible interview subjects feel comfortable with media representatives by explaining how the news media operate, reducing much of the tension and misunderstanding that come between today's executives and reporters. Your executives will be more comfortable if they understand that dissemination of news is a profit-motivated business, a fiercely competitive one, but unlike most that the organizational executive knows.

Interview subjects should have a basic understanding of the significant differences in coverage provided by the various media, the roles of the reporters and editors or news director, the probable reasons behind the length and placement of the final story, or the reason the story failed to appear.

Commodities of the news business are information and time. All journalists fight the clock in their struggle to obtain a complete and accurate story, and being complete means exploring all sides of the story. Thus, if we sponsor a news conference, our interview subjects can expect good reporters to go beyond the information provided by the organization. If the event, process, or product

NEWS CONFERENCE CHECKLIST

   I. Analyze event to determine if a news conference is warranted

      A. Develop statement summarizing event _____

      B. List advantages and disadvantages of feasible methods of disseminating story. If news conference is best method:

          1. List news media with possible interest _____

          2. Attendance estimate _____

          3. Organizational spokesmen selected _____

          4. Date and time based on availability of spokesmen and media deadlines _____

  II. Invitations: Responsible PR staffer _____

      A. Comprehensive media list prepared _____

      B. Mailing prepared to include:

          1. Background and statement of conference purpose _____

          2. Location with locator map, if needed _____

          3. Notice of date and time _____

          4. Identification of organization _____

          5. Identification of organizational representatives _____

          6. Credentials for media reps, if needed _____

          7. Postage paid response card _____

          8. Name, identification, and telephone number of PR contact for additional information _____

      C. Announcements to media 10 days in advance of event _____

      D. Follow-up calls, in person or by telephone, within 48 hours of news conference _____

 III. Organizational reps: Responsible PR staffer _____

      A. Involved in story and can speak for organization _____

11.1 *News conference checklist.*

B. All speakers:

    1. Briefed on subject _____

    2. Supplied with comprehensive Q & A list _____

    3. Briefed on working with reporters _____

C. Opening statements provided _____

D. PR staffer to make introductions _____

IV. Site: Responsible PR staffer _____

A. Convenient for news media _____

B. If practical, site convenient for plant tour, demonstration of product, service or facility _____

C. Accessible to TV crews carrying heavy gear _____

D. No distracting noise _____

E. Ventilation, heating and air conditioning suitable _____

V. Conference facilities: Responsible PR staffer _____

A. Photo background (mirrors? distracting wall patterns?) _____

B. Standing lectern or table _____

C. Visual aids _____

D. Acoustical check to determine sound system needs _____

    1. Install and check at least an hour before event _____

E. Provide name cards legible throughout room _____

F. Straight-backed chairs for everyone _____

G. Adequate electrical outlets for electronic media _____

H. 20 square feet minimum for each expected TV crew _____

I. If practical, install TV lights, check in advance _____

J. Multiple outlet box needed _____ Checked _____

252

VI. Press room _____: Responsible PR staffer _____

    A. Telephones installed based on estimated attendance _____

    B. Typewriters available _____

    C. If available and requested, terminals with modems _____

    D. Copy paper and other supplies available _____

VII. Security (if applicable): Responsible PR staffer _____

    A. Security chief briefed _____

    B. Security chief assists with credentials, if needed _____

    C. Guard force alerted on time, location, attendees _____

    D. Security force provided printed directions to site _____

    E. Parking arrangements _____

VIII. Media kits: Responsible PR staffer _____

    A. Story on subject of news conference _____

    B. Background information on organization _____

    C. Biographies of organization's representatives _____

    D. Photographic subjects:

        1. Portraits of speakers _____

        2. Subject(s) of news conference _____

    E. Photography:

        1. 8 x 10 in. B/W for newspapers _____

        2. 35mm transparencies, film clips, or VTR for TV _____

        3. Other coverage as requested _____

    F. Kits distributed _____

central to the news conference is controversial, our executives should expect the better reporters to contact those who have differing views as part of obtaining the complete story. Further, the good reporter will get the story whether the organization cooperates or not.

If the affected organization erects a stone wall, the reporter will seek out secondary sources and still produce a story. So the organization is better served if that reporter is provided with information and interview subjects of the organization's choosing; thus, its viewpoint will have a far better chance of becoming part of the record. The representatives of the PR practitioner's organization must also be made aware that reporters, editors, and news directors are seldom subject to economic or political pressure. Use of pressure tactics is always counter productive.

For improved media relations, PR practitioners must work closely with their internal publics. Most especially, they must assist any organizational representatives who will be interviewed or be principals in a news conference.

Chances of favorable interviews are enhanced if the interview subjects are prepared carefully, meet the reporters in an informal atmosphere, remember the reader or viewer, make important points first, relax and think, never argue with reporters, never expect to see the story in advance of publication, avoid jargon, remain impartial with reporters, and tell the truth.

Practitioners can assist interview subjects in overcoming some of their natural nervousness by providing basic hints on using microphones and facing cameras, on the proper dress, and in providing suitable physical arrangements for the interview or news conference.

By assisting members of the organization's internal publics in meeting with representatives of the news media, public relations practitioners perform a vital role in the preservation or enhancement of their organization's public image.

Exercises

1. Your employer will announce as a candidate for the United States House of Representatives from Michigan's Seventh District. List the advantages and disadvantages of the several methods of making the announcement and make your recommendations as to the method to use.

2. A scientist is moving from a relatively isolated research post to chief executive. Although a brilliant chemist and administrator, the new chief executive has little experience with reporters. How will you prepare the new boss for the news conference announcing the promotion?

3. Your company will unveil a solar cell no larger than a 40-gallon water heater, but it can supply all energy needs for a family and works at 75 percent efficiency even on overcast days. Write an invitation to the news conference and describe other enclosures that will accompany the letter.

4. Use various media directories to develop a mailing list for the news conference in number 3. The site is La Jolla, California.

5. The conference will be in a local hotel. Describe the room needed, how the room is to be arranged, and equipment to be installed.

6. What are the news deadlines for the local daily newspapers and commercial television stations?

Case study

The Evansville (Indiana) Triplets of the AAA American Association finished dead last in their division last season. Attendance was down. Jackie Johnson replaced the manager. Rumors in the "hot stove league" say that the franchise is in trouble, and the parent club may pull out of Evansville.

As business manager, one of your duties is handling public relations for the Triplets. The club will break training and head north for the season in 10 days, and you learn from the general manager that a new man will be signed by the team after your arrival in Evansville. The new player is Emory Smythe, known to fans as "Bucky." He will sign at a news conference in Evansville no later than three days after your return. You arrange for him to make the two-day auto trip with you.

Bucky gained fame as the Heisman Trophy winner two years ago. As running back, he was the main reason Rutgers University had a 9–3 record. He led them to a conference title and victory in the Liberty Bowl.

The nuclear physics graduate also averaged .427 in four seasons as Rutgers' shortstop. Team records were 24–21, 33–13, 35–9, and 39–11. In his senior year, Rutgers went to the College World Series but lost the first two games. He spent the period between the CWS and signing the baseball contract with the Peace Corps in Mindanao.

Plan a news conference, including the following:
- Points to be emphasized, how and by whom
- Mailing list for the conference
- Physical arrangements
- The announcement mailing
- The press kit

Suggested readings

Abbate, Fred J. "Training for the Interview." *Public Relations Journal,* May 1980.

Bachrach, Hank, "The 72-Hour Countdown at General Electric." *Communication World* 2(1985):9, 29–31.

Borschee, Jerr. "Anatomy of an Interview." *Communication World,* April 1985.

Burke, Thomas E. "Advice for PR Folks Facing Reporters: Expect Foul-Ups, and Don't Be Afraid to Fight Back." *ASNE Bulletin,* September 1984.

Detwiler, Richard M. "When Will CBS Be Calling? Typical Questions That Trigger a Fight or Flight Response." *Public Relations Journal,* July 1980.

Goodman, Ronald, and Richard S. Ruch. "In the Image of the CEO." *Public Relations Journal,* February 1981.

Hattal, Alvin M. "Checklist: Setting Up a News Conference." *Public Relations Journal,* May 1985.

Jones, Clarence. *How to Speak TV: A Self-Defense Manual When You're the News.* Marathon, Fla.: Video Consultants, Inc., 1983.

Metz, William. *Newswriting: From Lead to "30."* 2d ed. Englewood Cliffs, N.J.: Prentice-Hall, 1985.

Miller, Susan E. "Surviving a Media Blitz." *Communication World* 2(1985): 9, 17–19.

Schenker, Jonathan. "Training to Give Viewers the Business." *Communicator's Journal,* March/April 1984.

Simon, Howard, and Joseph A. Califano, Jr. *The Media and Business.* New York: Vintage Books, 1979.

Williams, Paul N. *Investigative Reporting and Editing.* Englewood Cliffs, N.J.: Prentice-Hall, 1978.

Wydro, Kenneth. *Thinking on Your Feet: The Art of Thinking and Speaking Under Pressure.* Englewood Cliffs, N.J.: Prentice-Hall, 1985.

12 Special events

A more apt chapter title might be "Cockroaches, Short Circuits, and Ptomaine." As anyone who ever planned or directed a special event can attest, Murphy's Law exists: if anything can go wrong, it will. Success depends on careful planning, meticulous attention to detail, and understanding cooperation by everyone involved.

In the broadest sense, a special event is one created and staged to enhance understanding of the organization by dramatizing a message for a public or publics. In most cases, the special event is news; therefore, a special event may be considered a media event.

A wide spectrum of activities falls within the definition of special events, ranging from parents days and athletic banquets to convocations and commencements on the academic scene; unveiling new models and dedication of facilities to stockholders meetings and company picnics. A Boy Scout Court of Honor is a special event. So is a national political convention.

Public relations practitioners are deeply involved in planning, organizing, and conducting the special events sponsored by most organizations. Frequently, the public relations staff has the lead. So, public relations plays a major role in special events and, conversely, special events are a major part of most public relations programs.

Determining objectives

The special event is proposed to solve a problem, spotlight a milestone, or draw attention to a particular organizational strength. A well-planned special event can either enhance an organization's reputation or, if that is its purpose, emphasize change in the character of the organization. Such a change in character was reinforced in the following examples:

> The medium-size private university lacked appeal for prospective students from outside the immediate geographic area. The school was perceived as a stodgy member of its community, com-

258

fortable, conservative, apparently uninterested in either physical or academic expansion. Eventually the school got into a position requiring a dramatic change in image if it were to survive in the face of declining enrollment and waning financial support. Special events would be part of the answer.

Although accustomed to conservative budgeting, the regents agreed to a sizable investment in a series of special events commemorating the university's diamond jubilee. The concerts, seminars, and banquets featured a parade of theatrical stars; nationally prominent figures from industry, education, and government; sports heroes; and noted men and women from the arts. For the climactic event, a black-tie civic dinner, the university cited alumni who had gained national and international prominence. So much for local orientation, stodgy and conservative. The university's character had changed, now the special events were needed to bring its reputation in line with its new character.

A large food processing plant, owned and operated by a national firm, is the dominant industry in a midwestern city. Recent technical advances resulted in loss of some jobs and considerable labor unrest. The corporation became the target of severe criticism from city government, the local newspaper, and its own employees. Prevailing sentiment in the city was that the corporate giant, headquartered several hundred miles away, was interested only in profits and played no role in civic affairs. In short, the corporation did not understand or care about local problems.

To counter public perception of the corporation as an unfeeling and uncaring absentee landlord, the corporation sponsored a civic dinner. A number of long-time employees were guests, and a top corporate executive was the featured speaker. He recounted the history of his corporation's involvement in the city and region. As proof of continued interest in the area, he announced that a large real estate tract would be given to the city, and that the corporation would match any funds raised locally to build an athletic complex on the land.

Two principles can be learned from these examples. The first, of course, is to determine the objectives to be attained by conducting a special event. Second, determine the public or publics that must be reached to realize the goals or objectives. In the examples cited, both internal and external publics were involved. Frequently in cases where the organization is concerned with its posture as an employer who cares about employee attitudes and well-being, the internal publics are the targeted audience of a special event. Promotion and awards ceremonies, employee dinners, company picnics, and receptions for employees' families are examples.

Even more effective, however, are the growing number of cases where the organization invites feedback from internal audiences, listens, and acts on that feedback. Examples range from employee suggestion programs to unit brainstorming sessions conducted in a shirtsleeve atmosphere. Specific organizational problems are discussed openly by all members of a department or division. Meanwhile, at a higher level, these have been extended into executive retreats with spouses at locations distant from organizational headquarters. Frank discussions are the norm in both cases with management seeking ideas and acting upon them.

Major overhauls of corporate structures have resulted. Modification of product lines is not unusual. A personal letter from a plant janitor to the chief executive of GMC's Pontiac Division resulted in changing the name of that division's popular two-seater before it was introduced in 1984 as the Fiero. Soldiers in the field sparked development of the freeze-dried rations introduced in 1986.

If a problem is determined to be communitywide or with a specific external group such as environmental interests, the financial community, educators, ministerial groups, etc., a special event may be tailored for that specific audience. The event can be as simple as a public meeting to which the target group is invited for an exchange of ideas or as complex as a multisession seminar complete with displays, open house, tours, and social get-togethers.

The Army Corps of Engineers' Missouri River Division was the frequent target of dedicated environmental organizations. The division engineer recognized that the problem was both internal and external. Many but not all of the environmentalists' complaints were justified. Externally, many of the most vocal critics were unfamiliar with the inner workings of the Corps and frequently based their comments and writings on hearsay, the justifiably suspect "conventional wisdom."

The agency executive determined that his first priority was to get the Corps' house in order. Regional universities were contacted, and experts in the natural sciences conducted a series of lectures and seminars for the agency's key employees. The hour-long sessions were scheduled each Thursday afternoon for 12 weeks.

"Nobody became an expert," one division head commented, "but at least we learned the need for safeguarding our environment. And we learned that those folks are just as dedicated and sincere as we are."

The series concluded with a visit by Corps' staff members to a regional nature center. But it did not end there. The division engineer revised his annual budget to permit employment of environmentalists in key positions within the agency.

On the other side of the coin, in relating to external audiences, the Corps' public affairs staff developed a plan of action that involved (1) conducting a series of open houses in the division offices and idea exchanges with environmental groups, both in the division headquarters and at various field locations; (2) sponsoring a series of public meetings for open discussion of real and perceived problems; and (3) actively seeking speaking engagements for key staff members before science societies, environmental organizations, and school science classes. "We didn't expect to resolve all our differences," the division engineer admitted. "Today, however, we're talking. And both sides can discuss problems from a solid base of knowledge and understanding."

Selecting the event

After determining the objectives and the target audience, the third point is selection of the most appropriate special event for reaching that audience and attaining those objectives. The selection is demonstrated by the approach used by the Corps of Engineers in the example. An awards banquet, even if a federal agency were permitted to devote funds to such an activity, or a slick public relations-type briefing would have been merely cosmetic and, in fact, such an approach might have polarized the groups the division engineer wanted to reach. But a sincere, comprehensive educational program made reasoned conversation possible.

A decision must be made as to the scope and nature of the event. At this point, the answer will be determined by analyzing available resources and a justifiable budget that considers all costs involved. In addition to the printed budget line, planners must consider the costs involved in use of existing resources and manpower that will be diverted to the special event.

Planning meetings require that important and expensive executives be borrowed from other organization business. Many hours of secretarial and clerical staff work will go into the event. Security, technical, and housekeeping employees also are involved in the project.

Costs of reproduction, art talent, postage, telephone charges, and other significant items too frequently are hidden, but they must be figured into the total cost. Vehicles, facilities, and support equipment are taken from other areas for use during the special event. These too are chargeable costs.

During open houses and special ceremonies conducted within the organization's facilities, normal production is interrupted for long periods. Occasionally it is halted completely, requiring special start-up procedures. All are costs of the special event, and must be considered. Thus, the event must be tailored to a size that is justified in view of the objectives. Do not hunt rabbits with a howitzer.

Budgetary considerations are important, of course, but they are not the sole determinant of the type of event the organization will sponsor. The occasion itself may make that decision. The event may be a groundbreaking or a dedication, a grand opening or an honors convocation. In each case, the occasion has a large bearing on the type of event sponsored.

Of course, externals may vary. A groundbreaking can be the usual ceremony with a dignitary or group of dignitaries with goldplated shovels, or it can be a variation.

On one such occasion, the venerable longtime principal of a private high school teamed with his board chairman to break ground for a new building. In caps and gowns they mounted a large bulldozer, slipped it into gear, and began the excavation. Because they were prominent members of the community and the action was far out of character, the particular groundbreaking gained exceptional media coverage.

One public relations practitioner routinely visits the site of each groundbreaking for a final check several hours before the event. After ascertaining that he has no witnesses, his last chore before leaving the site is to perform his own groundbreaking with a spade brought along for the purpose. He loosens the earth where the ceremony will take place, then smooths it back in place. "Some of our dignitaries aren't all that virile, and some of our building sites are in clay the consistency of concrete."

The conclusion: every special event involves a multitude of details, any of which can result in overall disaster if it is ignored or improperly handled.

Among the most important considerations in planning the special event is to make certain that the guests, the ceremony, even any proposed entertainment is appropriate for the sponsoring organization. The targeted publics will associate the programs with the sponsor, and such an association must reflect favorably on the organization or institution. Promising public relations careers have been jeopardized by lack of foresight, ignoring taste, or forgetting public mores.

One well-meaning organizer opened a social event at a dignified private school with professional entertainers—a scantily-clad chorus line in a precision performance. Another engaged a keynote speaker whose political and social views were diametrically opposed to those held by the chief executive officer of the sponsoring organization. In another instance, the chairman of the event suggested, quite seriously, that the evening open with a wine-tasting party. The guest of honor was a member of Alcoholics Anonymous.

Planning the event

Success of the special event depends heavily on answers to several important questions:

1. Are you planning far enough in advance?
2. Has an effective committee been selected?
3. Has an adequate budget been provided?
4. Have the best dates, free of crippling conflicts, been selected?

ENOUGH TIME

Planning begins as soon as the sponsor decides to hold a special event. Arranging for people, places, and services must be completed well in advance.

Whether requiring hotel/motel space, public facilities, or an area controlled by the sponsoring organization, reservations must be made early. As general rules, the more space required, the more services needed, the more significant the date, the further in advance reservations must be made. Thus, in most locations, a dinner dance for a thousand persons to welcome in the new year must be arranged at least two years in advance. Normally, six months is enough lead time when making reservations for fewer than a hundred persons who will need food service and facilities for a two- or three-day meeting. Even then, the sponsoring organization must remain flexible in selection of exact dates until reservations are confirmed.

Planners must learn as much as possible about competing activities because some events are incompatible. A religious convocation, for example, presents problems if coexisting with a national sales meeting. A formal banquet and a square dance competition would be incompatible in a divided ballroom.

Special guests, keynote speakers, the toastmaster, and popular entertainers must be booked early. If they are talented or important enough to warrant inclusion in the program, they are busy individuals. Their schedules are completed well in advance. Many entertainers, for example, book appearances in advance for an entire nine-month season. And the prominent individual, anyone for that matter, is less reluctant to accept an invitation for next spring than for next week.

By planning six to eight months in advance, a competent committee can act and an adequate budget can be arranged before competing events and activities enter the field.

A PRODUCING COMMITTEE

No individual has enough time or sufficient knowledge in all areas to single-handedly plan, organize, and operate a special event. So, a representative, active committee is vital for a successful special event.

The greatest contribution will be made by a respected leader who can delegate tasks. Specific areas will be assigned to members of the committee who have demonstrated competence in arrangement of facilities, selection of guests and handling invitations, protocol and hospitality, budgeting, publicity, decorations, entertainment, etc.

SOUND BUDGETING

Availability of funds determines in large measure the type of special event or, more particularly, the scale of any special event. Once provided, an adequate budget is broken into categories: facilities rental, honoraria for speakers and/or performers, entertainment, hospitality, printing, promotion, decorations and flowers, special equipment purchase or rental (sound systems, lighting, special construction, etc.). In each case, a contingency fund is established to provide for the inevitable, last-minute emergency items.

THE RIGHT DAY

Dates of some special events are predetermined (commencements, holidays, anniversary observances); neither the committee nor the organization's executives control them. However, scheduling of many events can be controlled. Availability of facilities, weather, and competing events are considered in the selection.

The first order of business is a check of all local calendars. In addition to the organization's schedule, other calendars to check are those maintained by the Chamber of Commerce; major civic, social, business, church, and educational organizations; and sponsors of sports and entertainment events. Avoid conflicts with major events. The kickoff for an institutional fund-raising campaign, for example, must not compete with major events in the annual United Fund campaign or with fund-raising efforts scheduled by other institutions within the organization's target region.

Such conflicts can result in disaster or, occasionally, in shared disaster when neither the special event nor its competitor succeed. In a particular instance, organizers of a special event at a university made a cursory check with the local Chamber of Commerce and several other institutions in the area, then selected a date. Unfortunately, they apparently failed to check their own campus calendar. After publicly announcing the event, reserving facilities, and contacting the caterer, the arrangements committee learned to its chagrin that the date selected was also the date of the opening game of the university's football season. Several influential members of their target audience were long-time boosters of the football team who zealously attended every home game.

In a less obvious but equally disastrous situation, the sponsoring organization considered prominent local political figures as the primary target audience for a special event. Again, all local leads were followed to avoid conflicts, but the obvious was overlooked. The selected date coincided with the national convention of a major political party, and the organization's mailbox overflowed with formal regrets.

Consider the probable work schedules of the majority of participants. If the event is scheduled during daylight hours (a groundbreaking or dedication, for example), selecting a Saturday, Sunday, or holiday will enhance attendance. If daylight and travel are not considerations, a dinner or evening event may be held on a week night, but attendance may still be affected.

Long-range weather forecasting is an inexact science at best.

However, in colder climates, you need not be an expert to realize that scheduling an outdoor event during the winter is foolhardy, and all too often sadistic, unless the event is a winter sports festival. Conversely, cruel and unusual punishment often has been inflicted upon outdoor audiences forced to endure an unrelenting sun through an overlong program. So, study weather patterns in the area.

Prepare for the worst possible weather. If an outdoor event is scheduled, develop an alternate plan. That is, if inclement weather strikes on the selected date, the event either will be moved to a pre-selected (and reserved) sheltered location or will be rescheduled on a specific, publicized date. However, on almost all occasions, rescheduling is an unpalatable solution. Special guests, invited speakers, and large segments of the audience may be unable to adjust to an alternate date.

Every organizer of a special event would sacrifice full retirement for an infallible meteorologist, a guaranteed *Farmer's Almanac*, or an understanding with the Almighty. In lieu of such improbabilities, always prepare an alternate plan that takes into account the worst possible conditions.

Promotion and printing

Each organization develops special mailing lists of individuals and groups whose opinions and activities are important to or impact on the organization. Normally lists of this type are the nucleus of the master list for invitations to special events. In addition, media lists are essential for use in advance publicity because, as noted, most special events are also media events.

Invitations take one of several forms depending on the type of event being sponsored. Formal social or diplomatic events will require handwritten invitations. Guests at less formal special events may receive personally typed (computer-printed or mag-taped) letters. Formal printed invitations are appropriate for some events. However, addresses are handwritten for the latter.

Most special events require a significant budget for publications. Included are invitations, return cards or postage paid envelopes, and promotional literature including brochures, posters, programs, and miscellaneous publications. The impact of a special event is enhanced by quality printing. No single item makes a greater impression or has a longer life than a quality printed program. Thus, careful attention is given to copy quality, layout, typography, paper stock, and delivery dates. Capabilities of commercial printers vary, but an order for quality printing should be placed at least three weeks before your deadline. Then there is ample time to correct a mistake, even if it requires discarding an entire press run.

Where advance distribution of printing is involved, allow for various time-consuming tasks. Depending on complexity and personal schedules, developing copy and laying out the work may require a week. Refining a mailing list of a thousand names, then hand addressing and mailing that list will require a work week as a minimum. Invitations to special events should be received by guests at least three weeks in advance.

Dealing with VIPs

Successful public relations practitioners consider each person with whom they deal to be a VIP (Very Important Person) and treat that individual accordingly. But in all candor, some are "VIPer" than others and require special treatment.

Many events involve appearances by VIPs as speakers or honorees, presiding at particular ceremonies. The appearance of such individuals creates challenges for the host organization. While it is imperative that the individuals be made comfortable and enjoy time spent as guests of the organization, the organization hopes to profit from their appearance.

Average VIPs expect the organization to seek extensive media coverage based on their appearance, but the coverage should be planned to avoid having the media monopolize guests' free time. The VIPs should be queried in advance as to their policy on granting interviews and participating in news conferences.

The most efficient method of obtaining media coverage is through a news conference followed by an invitation to media representatives to cover the event (speech, honors convocation, groundbreaking) in which the VIP is involved. For maximum coverage, the host public relations unit will obtain a resumé, publicity photographs, and a copy of the VIP's speech (if that is the occasion) well in advance of the special event.

The host organization must resist the temptation to schedule the guest's free time to the last second. Meetings with the organization's top executives, receptions for key officials and community leaders, and other engagements are good news copy. But they are secondary to the special event to which the VIP was invited. If organizers fall prey to the many temptations, the VIP may be too hoarse to speak or may have said everything that needs saying, all before the special occasion. Thus, an itinerary should be agreed upon between the host organization and the visiting dignitary well in advance.

VIP CHECKLIST

As with most facets of a special event, a checklist should be prepared for care and feeding of VIPs. If a working committee has been established for the event, the person responsible for hospitality or protocol should anticipate most needs of the visiting dignitary. Items to be covered include:

1. *Travel arrangements.* Will the VIPs make their own travel arrangements or is the organization assuming responsibility for this? In any event, a competent committee member will apprise them of possible arrangements and make recommendations. Obviously included are arrangements to meet the VIPs upon arrival, with a welcoming group if appropriate.

2. *Housing.* Do VIPs expect the organization to arrange accommodations or prefer to handle that themselves? Again, regardless of who handles this important matter, the host group must make last-minute checks to assure facilities are adequate and no snag has developed.

In one case, the guest was a foreign ambassador to the United States. Everything was in readiness, but a final check revealed that the room adjacent to the ambassador's suite had been let to a honeymooning couple. Specific instructions were to reserve the room for the chargé d'affaires traveling with the ambassador. Deft diplomacy by the guilty hotel staff and amused tolerance by the young couple avoided an international incident. But the responsible public relations practitioner edged ever closer to ulcers. The incident leads to another point.

3. *Traveling party.* Who will accompany the VIPs? Spouses? Other family members? Business associates? And what arrangements should the host organization make for them? In many instances, while the visiting dignitaries are involved with the host organization, a special social event or tour is provided for the spouses.

4. *Local ties.* Do the VIPs have friends, relatives, or associates in the area they would like to visit while on this trip? The host organization must investigate local ties with the VIPs, and time should be allotted for

such meetings in the prepared agenda. Arrangements may be made to have the local persons join the VIPs during the formal occasion.

5. *Media relations.* As noted, contact the VIPs well before the event to determine the preferred method of dealing with media. Also well in advance, obtain biographies and suitable publicity photographs. Normally, the visiting dignitaries' organizational public relations departments or secretaries will furnish these items.

It is professional courtesy to provide details of the coming event and publicity plans involving VIPs to their public relations representatives. Their PR departments can apprise the host public relations unit of special requirements or unusual demands that may be associated with the VIPs. For example, one executive who makes frequent public appearances expects to find a deck of cards and two chilled bottles of ale in the hotel room. The last hour before leaving for an engagement, the executive plays solitaire, drinks the ale, and will tolerate no interruptions.

Arrange for copies of speeches as far in advance as possible. Then check the speaker's preference for distribution. The experienced public relations professional also determines if the speaker has any special individuals, organizations, or media that should receive copies of the speech and other news coverage of the event.

6. *Honoraria and expenses.* Many prominent individuals (and some not so prominent) expect a fee for appearing at special events. Size of the honorarium can range from payment of expenses to thousands of dollars. For some, demanding a large sum is a method of limiting the number of appearances they are asked to make, for many it is a significant portion of their income. Considering the time and talent they invest in their task, many are well worth the honoraria they demand.

Remember, in each case it is absolutely essential to have a clear understanding of the financial arrangements before the special event goes beyond the early planning stages.

7. *Miscellaneous information.* Provide VIPs with a detailed outline of events, complete with an accurate timetable, and the names and identifications of all other important persons in attendance.

Detailed information on dress must be provided long before the event. The VIPs must know if the particular events require formal or informal attire. If academic garb is required, will it be provided by the host institution? Expected dress is particularly important when military dignitaries are involved.

Protocol

Protocol is an important consideration in the organizing and planning of every special event. It dictates who belongs where in a variety of social occasions. Avoid guessing when it is time to arrange the receiving line or to seat the VIPs at the head table. A mistake here can have a lasting impression throughout the community and beyond.

No definitive authority is available to cover all cases, but a number of dependable guides can be consulted. That includes knowledgeable individuals and/or resource volumes in libraries. The protocol officer at a military installation is one of the best-informed sources if the protocol problems involve foreign or domestic government dignitaries. Others knowledgeable in this area include maîtres d'hôtel, managers and secretaries of social organizations, and society editors and columnists.

The checklist

Each event is unique and presents its own set of problems. But in each case, an advance brainstorming session must be devoted to developing a comprehensive checklist.

A study of the checklist in Figure 12.1 will demonstrate the minutiae that must be considered to minimize the number of unpleasant surprises. This checklist, with minor variations, has been used for many years by the Creighton University Public Relations Department. It is designed for use in the university's dining facilities.

MENU

Avoid generalities in working with the caterer. Know precisely the type of food to be served and how it will be prepared. Know whether the caterer proposes to use your kitchen facilities or his own. Obtain the caterer's best estimate of the time required to complete service. And right at the top, have a written contract that details the exact cost per plate, including any tax and gratuities.

Note any dietary restrictions or eccentricities of your organization's top executives and special guests.

Because they were cheap, cabbage and cucumbers were a frequent part of his diet when one chief executive grew up in near poverty. Now that he heads a major corporation, he is convinced that serving coleslaw and cucumbers will lead guests to believe that his corporation is niggardly. So individuals responsible for banquet arrangements within his corporation veto any menu containing these items.

An otherwise normal executive has a morbid fear of trichinosis, so all meats served at dinners sponsored by that organization are well done. Dry and tasteless maybe, but there is no chance of trichinosis. The executive is satisfied, and his public relations staff can relax insofar as menus are concerned.

Heavily spiced foods and exotic dishes are seldom served at large banquets. In most cases, the caterer is asked to stick to widely accepted favorites such as roast beef or fowl. The average guest at special events is not an adventurer at the dining table.

In addition to an agreement on the exact per plate price of any meals, the person in charge of arrangements must have an understanding, preferably written, of the acceptable deadline for reservations and the tolerance permitted by the caterer in the number of reservations. Costs of food and preparation being what they are, no caterer can afford to overprepare. No host can tolerate underpreparation.

For large banquets many caterers demand a firm reservation figure at least three days in advance of the event and permit a variation of no more than 2 percent. Thus, if the individual in charge makes reservations Thursday for 300 persons at a Sunday banquet, the caterer will be prepared to serve from 294 to 306 dinners. If more guests attend, some may not be fed. If fewer attend, the host organization must still pay full price for at least 294 dinners.

BAR

Social hours, a euphemism for cocktail parties, precede a large percentage of today's banquets. Again, close attention to the smallest details is imperative.

As a rule of thumb, approximately half as large an area is required for a successful social hour as for the same number of guests at a dinner. And during a social hour, an area that is slightly too small provides for a more successful event that an area that is too large. The idea is to create togetherness.

You need to provide seating for only two-thirds of the expected number of guests because a social hour crowd is mobile. However, available seating should be arranged around small tables rather than along walls. Covered tables with decorations will create a more favorable impression. Provide ashtrays.

Exact planning is almost impossible because there are so many

BANQUET CHECKLIST

1. <u>Menu</u>

    Entree _____   Relish trays _____

    Potatoes _____   Butter & rolls _____

    Vegetables _____   Dessert _____

    Salad _____   Other _____

    Beverage _____   Price/plate _____ Total _____

2. <u>Bar</u>

    No. of tables _____   No. of bars _____

        Chairs/table _____   Staff in place _____

        Ashtrays _____   Glassware _____

        Cloths _____   Ice _____

    Tickets & sellers _____   Mix, soft drinks _____

    Beer stocked _____   Liquor in place (a) ____

    Wine stocked _____   (b) ____ (c) ____

3. <u>Facilities & Staffing</u>

    Parking lots clear _____   Head table personnel:

    Parking guides _____   Guides & hosts _____

    Parking security _____   Secure waiting room ____

    Checkroom ready _____   Checkroom attendant ____

        Attendants _____   Refreshments _____

    Crowd controls _____   Head table leader _____

    Crowd facilities _____   Ticket takers _____

12.1 *Sample banquet checklist.*

Restrooms ready _____

Ticket sales:

    Tables ready _____

    Sellers ready _____

    Tickets ready _____

    Change ready _____

All VIPs present _____

Hosts w/guest badges ____

Nametags available _____

    Pens/typewriters ___

All facilities clean ____

Route clear _____

4. Dining Room

Platforms placed _____

Banners placed _____

Lectern placed _____

Lectern light OK _____

PA checked _____

A/V checked _____

No. of plates _____

Places/table _____

Reserved signs _____

Other graphics OK _____

Programs ea place _____

Head table seating _____

Place cards placed _____

Final check, A/V _____

Final check, lights _____

Programs, etc., head table ___

Awards in place _____

Drapes closed _____

Overhead lights _____

Special lighting _____

Decorations checked _____

Flowers in place _____

Flowers to be saved _____

Extra programs ready _____

Seating charts ready _____

Head table route cleared _____

Final predinner cleanup _____

Final check, toastmaster _____

Final check, entertainers ____

variables in preparing for a social hour. For example, regardless of the affluence of the guests, per capita consumption is markedly higher if the sponsoring organization hosts the bar rather than operating a cash bar. However, with a cash bar, the prices charged have little bearing on the per capita consumption.

However, that is just one factor in the equation. Per capita consumption increases if the event is stag or an in-house affair. And an in-house group that is mixed (management and labor) will consume less than either group meeting alone. An informally dressed crowd will consume more than the same persons at a formal function. The variations are almost endless. Even the region of the country affects the quantity consumed.

The average cash bar operates more smoothly if drink tickets are sold at tables separated from the bars. Thus, bartenders can care for approximately 75 guests each if they are not responsible for handling sales. The average portable bar can be worked most effectively by no more than two bartenders, and one ticket seller for two portable bars is an efficient ratio.

Costs aside, the staff should be advised that they are expected to provide a reasonable drink, but they are not doing anyone a favor by pushing heavy drinks. Sociability, not drunkenness, is the goal of a social hour. In fact, bartenders frequently are instructed to provide relatively heavy drinks during the first round and then reduce the quantity of liquor per drink as the social hour progresses.

Liquor preferences vary from section to section of the country, even from season to season within the same area. Again in providing for a social period, be aware of possible pitfalls and seemingly unimportant details.

As an example, a relative newcomer to the public relations department was given responsibility for a large special event. The newcomer shopped for price when purchasing liquor. It was not until the evening of the banquet that the newcomer discovered that a prominent and vocal member of the board of directors was also the chief executive officer of a major distillery. The lowest price had been obtained on the products of an arch rival. Antacid tablets were a staple in the public relations practitioner's diet that evening.

Alert public relations professionals frequently charged with organizing and managing social hours will develop pocket notebooks for personal use. Available bartenders are listed complete with their phone numbers and hourly rates. After a series of such events, the public relations practitioners can develop rough formulas indicating fairly close estimates of relative consumption rates by the several different audiences with which they must deal.

The notebooks also will list the various sources of competitively priced merchandise. Among the acquaintances cultivated and listed in the notebook will be local authorities who can offer sound guidance as to types and brands. By prior arrangement, most retailers will refund the purchase price on returned, unopened merchandise. So, make the necessary prior arrangements.

FACILITIES AND STAFFING

Hospitality and cleanliness are indispensable for a successful special event. Guests must feel welcome in an ordered, well-manicured facility. So, the organization's security forces and engineering or maintenance staffs are an integral part of every special event.

Guests received advance information as to available parking, but they must find the parking areas clear of other vehicles, debris, or snow. When the host organization is an educational institution, student groups (sororities, fraternities, service clubs) frequently are involved as guides, hosts and hostesses, checkroom attendants, etc. Occasionally students are hired to augment security forces.

A final check of each small detail is vital to the success of a special event. For some inexplicable reason, designated cloakrooms have been known to lock themselves just before the first guest arrives, crowd control devices set themselves in the traffic pattern, and paper towels vanish mysteriously from the restrooms.

SPECIAL ATTENTION FOR SPECIAL GUESTS

Specially instructed hosts are designated to meet important guests. These hosts also are responsible for security of the VIPs' personal effects during the special event, and they arrange for refreshments as the VIPs wait for the beginning of the function.

After other guests are seated in the dining room, special guests who have mingled with the head table personnel are ushered to their reserved places at the front of the dining room.

A staff or committee member known to most of the VIPs is designated as leader for the head table. Following the seating chart provided, the leader of the head table aligns the VIPs in the order in which they will be seated and leads them to the dining room. This individual does not enter the dining room at this time but directs the line of guests to the proper point from which they will make their entrance.

DINING ROOM

When the guest list is large (200 or more), the head table may be elevated. The tables are placed on platforms up to 18 inches higher than the dining room floor. Testing platform sections is an important part of the responsible individual's final check. The units have an unfortunate tendency to unlock and shift, thus opening a space between sections just wide enough to trap a spike heel.

The toastmaster and featured speaker should be contacted when the final check is made of the sound system. Frequently these persons prefer to check the system themselves. At the very least, a sound system check is a two-person task, one on the microphone and the second stationed in the most distant corner of the dining room. The sound level should be set slightly too loud for the empty room because the addition of several hundred people will absorb some sound, and the conversational buzz will further compete with the electronic sound.

A last-minute check of visual aids, projectors, and recorders is imperative. This is an area where Murphy's Law works overtime.

The top public relations practitioner in a large southeastern organization was delighted to reserve an exclusive dining room in a hotel that a major national chain had just completed. His was the first organization to use the facility with a motor driven projection screen built into the ceiling.

Half an hour before the first guests arrived, the relaxed and confident PR practitioner made a final check of facilities. The projectors were in place. The automated screen worked perfectly, except through a construction oversight, the screen descended directly behind a beautiful, low-hanging crystal chandelier. A frantic call to an equipment rental firm, and a portable screen was installed minutes before the first course was served. The final check averted disaster.

FINAL CHECK WITH THE TOASTMASTER

At the last opportunity, the public relations practitioner alerts the toastmaster to the location of persons in the audience who should be recognized, reviews pronunciation of unusual names, and advises of any special guests who failed to appear. Finally, the toastmaster must be informed that every detail has been checked: place cards properly located, sound system operating, lectern lights working, and especially, any awards are in place and in the order of presentation. The toastmaster has a difficult job. Any help or encouragement is appreciated.

Obviously the checklist, Figure 12.1, is for a banquet in a controlled situation. Other events in other locations mean other checklists. Depending upon the event, it may be advisable to provide emergency medical service or first aid, an ambulance on standby, baby-sitting services, tours, drinking water, portable toilets, limousine or chartered bus service, uniformed escorts, or closed circuit television for overflow crowds. In short, a special event properly conducted may require anything from umbrellas to fireworks, check cashing services to hard hats.

Media coverage

Because media attention is an integral part of almost every special event, various facets of the coverage have been discussed in this chapter. A well-organized, carefully considered media program is a must if maximum benefit is to be realized from a special event. After all, a primary reason for organizing the event is to convey information, reinforce or change an image, or raise public consciousness concerning the sponsoring organization. The media are indispensable partners in attaining each of these goals.

ADVANCE PREPARATION

The newsworthiness, size, and complexity of the special event determine the advance public information work necessary. A single news release announcing the pertinent information suffices for a simple event, but a large, complex event can justify a series of advance stories or teasers. These include separate stories announcing the event, naming the various committees, revealing VIPs who will participate, outlining the program, etc.

Do not ignore advance photo coverage possibilities. Committee members or organizational executives can be photographed preparing for the event, distinguished visitors can be shown, and, in groundbreakings and dedications, architectural drawings or construction photos should be provided the media.

As noted, biographic sketches and photographs of special guests should be obtained well in advance. Obtain advance copies of speeches to be delivered by the various principals. When these are unavailable in advance, the best alternative is to have copies for distribution to media representatives during the event if the speeches merit news coverage.

Seek advance cooperation from VIPs whom media representatives will want to interview. If they agree to news conferences and their participation is newsworthy, make advance arrangements and provide at least 10 days notice to media representatives. Then, follow up with personal reminders a day or two in advance of the conferences.

Contact the various VIPs, their secretaries, or their public relations representatives to determine hometown outlets and any other special outlets that should be included in the media list for the special event.

ON-THE-SPOT

Arrange for on-the-spot coverage well in advance. Provide detailed itineraries, advance stories, accurate directions for reporters and photographers attending the special event or news conference, and include tickets for those who will provide live coverage of any events that include food.

If anticipated attendance and/or probable media interest indicate the need, reserved tables or special reserved seating can be provided the media. In cases where adequate telephone service is not routinely available, special lines should be arranged. Provide electrical power if conditions and budget permit.

Build elevated photographers' platforms when truly unusual media interest is shown, such as probable participation by the Washington press corps. Build the units to the same height or slightly higher than the level of the speakers' platform. Place the photographers' platforms toward the front and approximately 45 degrees off the audience line of sight. Thus constructed, the platforms provide an unobstructed view for photographers and camera crews, and confusion is lessened because crews with bulky equipment are not competing with spectators for space.

Platform size is determined by the expected attendance. Ideally, 15 to 20 square feet is allotted to each recording or remote feed television crew, with smaller space allotments for individual photographers. Unfortunately but realistically, the ideal is seldom realized.

If the complexity of the event warrants, media kits are prepared and distributed to reporters and photographers when they arrive for on-the-spot coverage of the event. Kits include background information on the organization, the event, and the principals involved. Glossy black-and-white photos are distributed to print media; 35mm color transparencies are given to television crews as back up for their own photographers.

Publications not normally interested in the organization may consider certain aspects of the event or especially relevant remarks by a featured speaker as newsworthy. The story or speech manuscript and accompanying graphics should be provided to the publication's local correspondent or sent directly to the editor by the most expeditious means.

Wrap-up stories are sent immediately following the event by the public relations unit. Even media that staffed the event are included on the distribution list for the follow-up. When possible, this copy is delivered personally by a member of the public relations staff to preserve the timeliness of the news coverage.

Following up on the event

Never overlook those who made it happen. It is not only good manners, it is good politics to acknowledge everyone who helped. After all, the whole thing may happen again, and the public relations practitioner again will need all the available help.

Letters of appreciation for everyone from parking guides to featured speaker, honorary chairman to carpenter, should be sent within a week following the event, signed by the chief executive officer or the individual directly responsible for conducting the event.

Many special events such as convocations, tours, and seminars return greater benefits to the organization if participants are contacted by mail within the first two weeks following the event. They receive the results of their deliberations, a digest of the proceedings, or a review of what they learned during the event. And the added attention draws them closer to the organization, one of the original goals of the special event.

HOW DID WE DO?

A postmortem is imperative. Persons who played significant roles in the special event must review everything that happened while the important points are still fresh.

Study the attendance. What percentage of the overall invitation list actually participated in the event? Were those who attended an accurate cross section of the invited guests? Does the attendance show trends? What techniques could be used to improve future response? Did those who participated receive the message the organization intended them to receive?

Complete a detailed and comprehensive study of costs. Include all financial and budgetary data to determine whether the event was cost effective. Did the sponsoring organization get its money's worth? Study each budgetary entry separately to determine the possibility of accomplishing the particular function in an alternative, more cost effective manner. Was each item or function on the balance sheet necessary to the overall success of the special event?

A follow-up study of news coverage will reveal the winning ideas and the also-rans. If coverage was marginal or disappointing, determine areas where future coverage can be strengthened. Would more face-to-face contact with reporters and editors have improved coverage sufficiently to warrant the added expenditure of personnel? Was the event worth the investment from the standpoint of media attention? What residual benefits, if any, will be realized in media relations?

The complete follow-up report is a record of the mechanics behind the organization and production of the special event. It must be sufficiently detailed to enable the organization to repeat those actions that were successful and to avoid mistakes that surfaced in this special event. And while the operation is fresh, methods must be devised to avoid repeating these same mistakes in future events.

Everything that had an impact must be detailed. Include a description of the weather, the news climate during the period, all schedules, menus, correspondence, news releases and clippings, photographs, speech manuscripts, and tape recordings, even drawings and photos of special construction used during the event.

Summary

Basically, a special event is created to improve the understanding or acceptance of the sponsoring organization. Clearly stated objectives must be determined to justify the expenditure of funds and personnel. Furthermore, specific audiences the organization hopes to reach must be clearly identified before the type of event is selected.

Several ingredients are essential for the success of any special event: provide ample lead time, develop a working committee, secure an adequate budget, and select the date carefully.

The relationship with VIPs is hospitality elevated to the highest plane. Although the organization must be a good host, remember that the special guests were invited because their participation will benefit the organization. As with most details in conducting special events, checklists are important tools in dealing with VIPs. The lists minimize the chance for error in arranging travel, housing, local activities, and media coverage.

Because of the type of individual involved, most special events require close adherence to proper protocol. Again, prior planning and checklists are necessary.

So, planning for special events means making checklists. The small details can fall through the cracks if the checklist does not call attention to the mechanics of arranging transportation, crowd control, menus, facilities, program, and staffing.

In the broad view, media coverage is a major reason for sponsoring the special event. So, an organized professional public information effort is a vital part of the total special events package.

Exercises

1. Interview an official from an organization of your choice who had responsibility for a recent special event that drew an attendance of at least 50 persons. Determine the organization's objectives, factors considered in selecting the audience, the percentage of invitations accepted, and why this type of event was selected.

2. As committee chair for a groundbreaking ceremony sponsored by one of the area's largest manufacturing firms, select the most appropriate date for the event, select members of your committee by functional assignments, and draw up an estimated budget. Justify each decision.

3. Develop a checklist for the groundbreaking.

4. Outline a media plan for the event.

5. Select a VIP from outside the state as guest speaker at a local Chamber of Commerce function. What procedure would you follow to determine whether the VIP can participate? Write a letter of invitation for signature by the president of the Chamber of Commerce.

6. Develop a checklist for handling the VIP and describe necessary advance arrangements.

Case study

Bentwood General is one of three major hospitals in River Bend, a city of 50,000. Bentwood, established 100 years ago, is the oldest. It gained a reputation as a forward-looking health facility by being the regional pioneer in the use of whole blood in chemotherapy and in bypass surgery. However, each of River Bend's other two hospitals moved into new buildings within the past 10 years, and Bentwood General Hospital's facilities were built 40 years ago.

Although the facilities are older, Bentwood General has a deserved reputation for the excellence of its burn treatment facilities and as a center for autistic children. Nevertheless, patient count has fallen since the other two hospitals opened their new facilities, and younger practitioners are turning to the other hospitals. The situation is not critical yet, but board members of Bentwood General are concerned by the trend.

You head a committee to organize a special event or series of events to signal a change in Bentwood General's operation, "Our move forward into the new century."
• Describe the event or events you will sponsor, the objectives to be gained, and the dates selected.
• Develop a timetable.
• Develop needed checklists.
• Develop a comprehensive media plan, including news releases, news conferences, and a list of necessary invitations.

Suggested readings

Bonnem, Shirley. "How to Plan a Special Event." *Public Relations Journal,* April 1980.

Carnes, William T. *Effective Meetings for Successful People.* New York: McGraw-Hill, 1980.

Caruba, Alan. "A Boom in Meetings—A Bust for PR." *Public Relations Journal,* April 1980.

Manilla, James. "The Meeting Room of the Future." *Public Relations Journal,* September 1980.

Marsh, W. W. "PR and the Big Blow Up." *Public Relations Journal,* October 1980.

_____. "PR and the Big Blow Up: Part II." *Public Relations Journal,* November 1980.

Schermerhorn, Derick D. "How to Celebrate an Anniversary." *Public Relations Journal,* October 1979.

13 The eyes of public relations

Primary emphasis has been on words in previous chapters. But never underestimate the power of illustration. Photographs, line drawings, cartoons, maps, artist's concepts, and all other forms of illustration are methods of communication that have enormous impact.

Photography is an integral part of public relations communications today. The public relations practitioner must develop a professional understanding of the various forms of photography and the techniques for using them in communicating with many audiences.

No magic is involved. Photographers and those who edit their product are not sorcerers. As with other fields in communication, photographic practitioners are skilled individuals who have learned well the tools and techniques of their profession. The good ones use a practiced artist's eye.

No formal rules exist as to posing, editing, or selecting good photography, but good photography is a must in the modern newspaper, magazine, and book. It is a requirement for every television outlet in the world. Exhibits, displays, and advertising layouts are dependent on photography. Many speakers today expect their presentations to be illustrated with quality photography; audiovisual presentations are extremely popular. So, know photography and know photographers.

The interest and tastes of readers or viewers determine the artwork to be used by the average medium. If the public relations photograph that comes across the editor's desk captures those interests and tastes, that public relations photo stands an excellent chance of being published.

The reader and editor will react to a good photograph. It will be a stopper because it evokes an emotion. The viewer experiences sympathy for the subject, anger or curiosity because of the action or because of the subjects. The reader is impressed by the beauty or tranquillity, is

284

stimulated by the action. The reader may get a chuckle from the photo or feel nostalgia. The good photograph has impact.

Either because of the subject matter or the way it is used, most photographs can be divided into two types: (1) record or historic illustrations and (2) action photographs. Of course in many instances the line between the two types is obscure. Basically, maps, standard mug shots, and aerial views of cities or areas can be considered record or historic shots. Many times, however, the record shot can be converted into an action photo through the photographer's ingenuity.

A recently unveiled fighter aircraft can be shown in a static pose on the ground or it may be shot in a vertical climb away from the field or peeling off into a steep dive. The first example is a record shot, the latter two are action.

An aerial view of a finished lake and dam is a record or historic photograph. A close-up of a fisherman with the project in the background or of water rushing over the spillway transform the shot into action photographs. The aerial may satisfy the engineer's need for overall detail, but the action shots attract readers.

The standard mug shot of the school's star low post is fine for the athletic brochure, and it is a good historic record of how Lefty appeared as a senior. But a close-up of the star grimacing at the free throw line or fighting for a rebound may be just as identifiable, and the record shot has become an action photo. Obviously, the average editor is more inclined to use the action shot, even though it may not be the favorite of Lefty's mother.

The purpose of a public relations photograph or illustration is to promote an idea, product, or service; an editor understands this motivation. Therefore, for an editor to accept such a photograph, it must be of exceptionally high quality. It is competing with photos from the editor's own staff photographers, syndicate representatives and photo agencies, free-lance photographers, and other PR practitioners and publications. The public relations photographer must have something to say and say it better than all the competition.

Of course many standard public relations shots have a ready market. Americans still love the automobile. So, each time a new model is introduced, a number of publications print record photographs. Photo records of major local construction usually find a market in local media. Specialized publications will show new or revolutionary products or processes.

The alert public relations practitioner will also turn to television and motion pictures as avenues for showcasing products or promoting geographic regions. A study of the credits accompanying dramatic programs or movies will show that the automobiles, wardrobes, and settings were furnished by specific manufacturers or the film was shot on location "through the cooperation of" a specific state, national government, or federal agency. Occasionally, campuses, vacation resorts, and other institutions get into the act.

Mug shots frequently are provided to editors when executive appointments or retirements are announced. However, some form of action posing would increase the chance that a photograph will accompany the promotion story. That action could be added to the photograph if the new executive were examining a product on the assembly line or were seated in the cockpit of the firm's latest aircraft.

As with every aspect of public relations, thorough planning and attention to detail are vital in PR photography. In a recent example, the chief executive of an auto firm was to be photographed driving a completed automobile off the assembly line. The executive smiled for the cameras and inserted the keys, but the auto refused to start. The firm received more publicity than it really wanted or could handle comfortably. Thorough planning might have prevented the problem.

News media depend upon public relations practitioners for much of their photographic coverage just as they do for much of the editorial copy they use. Without organizational and agency public relations practitioners, the various media would be required to enlarge their staffs significantly.

It is common practice for newspaper, magazine, and book editors as well as television and motion picture directors to turn to the public relations practitioner. They frequently request scenic photos, pictures of processes, products, or specific subjects to illustrate stories being developed. These may be record shots from the organization's files; or on occasion, the requests may be covered as special assignments by public relations photographers. Either way, the public relations department fulfills such requests. Generally, the overall public relations goals of the organization are advanced, and media relations are enhanced.

The most subtle form of public relations photography is promotion of an idea. Included here are offbeat photographs which are not tied directly to the public relations practitioner's client, such as the beautiful shots of Hawaii, Rome, or Latin America provided by airlines to promote the idea of vacationing in those scenic lands. Safe boating, fire prevention, and fuel conservation are ideas promoted by outboard motor manufacturers, the insurance industry, and major oil companies. Frequently, the sponsoring organization is not mentioned in the copy, and many times the organization's products are not shown or are only incidental in the photographs.

In each case where illustrations are used by public relations practitioners, the PR professional will know the subject well and fully understand the medium being used, be it still or motion photography, cartography, line drawings, architectural sketches, or a wide variety of other techniques. If photography is the medium, the public relations practitioner must be an exceptional photographer or have access to one.

Then, the public relations practitioner must determine the best method of telling the story visually. And finally, the successful practitioner knows the various media and what their editors need and expect.

The public relations professional and photography

Photographic equipment is as vital to a successful public relations program as typewriters and telephones. Through proper use of camera gear, the practitioner will show the various publics what the organization wants them to see rather than simply telling them about it. In public relations, a picture *is* worth a thousand words.

Depending upon the budget, staff size, and staff assignments, the entering public relations practitioner may be required to handle camera gear in competition with experts. As in most cases, the requisite skills are learned by doing, and the public relations hopeful can acquire a basic understanding of what can be produced by observing a professional public relations photographer and the artistry that can be the end product when good equipment is placed in the hands of a creative, knowledgeable individual. If beginners in public relations are not assigned cameras and expected to produce quality photos, they would be well advised to quickly establish a sound working relationship with the organization's photographers, who can help immeasurably as the beginners struggle to become accepted professionals.

Many larger organizations include professional photographers as staff members in their public relations operations, but the practice is not universal. Photographers in some organizations operate independently of public relations, receiving public relations assignments just as they receive assignments from personnel, advertising, marketing, research, or any of the many other divisions within the organization. The Army

Corps of Engineers photo unit is part of the reproduction branch that also includes a printing plant and a commercial art unit. Although handling many assignments for public relations, the unit completes jobs on a reimbursable basis (i.e., salaries, travel, per diem, and overhead for photographers are paid through interoffice funds transfer). The system is not applauded by the public relations staff, but it is a fact with which they live.

Organizational structures are as varied as the number of public relations operations. They range from large photo staffs working directly within public relations to those public relations departments hiring outside photographers to handle assignments. Many one- or two-person operations are organized so that the public relations practitioners are the photo unit.

Where photographers work within the public relations structure, their number and the type of equipment available to them depend on overall staffing and the budget allotted for public relations. Photography may be a secondary talent expected of regular staff members, as noted, or the photographic unit may be sufficiently large to warrant assigning individual professional photographers to portrait, spot news, architectural, scenic photography, and other specialties.

Many larger organizations have in-house photographic laboratories while other public relations practitioners depend on commercial laboratories for all their work. In fact, some organizations are so cost conscious that they must contract with the low bidder regardless of quality. The result is that contracts are awarded frequently to automated laboratories geared to serve all photographers with the emphasis on amateurs. Obviously, where cost is the paramount factor, quality and adherence to tight deadlines become variables.

Wide variation is also the rule in those organizations with their own laboratories. These range from small darkrooms staffed by the photographers themselves to elaborate facilities employing specialized laboratory technicians and the latest electronic units for correcting color temperatures and providing precise exposures.

Public relations photographic units

Upon occasion, public relations directors have been allowed or assigned to establish photographic units within their organization. In such cases, the prudent PR practitioner will begin equipping the unit modestly, expanding as the work demands and the budget permits.

EQUIPPING THE PHOTOGRAPHER

CAMERA. The obvious first acquisition will be a camera. But it is not that simple. Before the purchase, a decision must be reached as to what will be expected of the camera. Only then can the choice be made between 35-millimeter (35mm) or a larger format. (The larger format can range up to a 4"×5" or 8"×10" studio view camera.)

In photography as in almost everything, the individual gets what is paid for. In cameras this means that a 35mm (either single lens reflex or viewfinder model) will provide versatility, excellent portability, and a wide assortment of attachments and accessories. However, the user forsakes the extreme sharpness provided by the larger negative size and the extreme perspective control offered by the view camera's swings and tilts, both on the lens board and at the film plane. Nevertheless, a practiced professional, both behind the camera and in the darkroom, working with modern high-resolution lenses and today's quality films can produce acceptable image sharpness with the 35mm format. And limited perspective control is possible with some special lenses available on the higher quality small format cameras. Conversely, covering a fast-changing scene and working rapidly with models are extremely difficult with large format cameras.

Thus, because of its versatility and portability, the 35mm camera is an acceptable compromise if handled carefully by competent people. It does a number of things well.

But, for the finely detailed, sharply defined photograph that lends itself to outstanding enlargements (calendar art or large murals) and can be cropped severely, the answer is the large format. And, there are many compromise solutions between these two extremes (cameras that produce negatives in the 2¼"×2¼" format, 2¼"×3½", and others).

Subminiature cameras (16mm and smaller) have minimum usefulness in public relations

Whatever the solution, the camera will be expensive. No quality camera can be obtained at a bargain-basement price.

METER. An accurate exposure meter is an absolute must. Lunchroom talk to the contrary, the photographer who can estimate exposures accurately without a meter is rare. The claimant may obtain a usable print or transparency, but the quality would be infinitely better if the exposure were absolutely correct. Modern laboratory techniques will compensate for exposures that are slightly inaccurate, but the best quality comes from the best exposure.

So, obtain a good meter before purchasing the first film. Fortunately for portability and convenience, many of today's fine cameras have accurate built-in meters.

TRIPOD. Another accessory to be obtained early is a quality tripod. When shooting at speeds slower than 1/60 second, the most careful photographer has difficulty avoiding camera motion. Many solutions are available: tabletop tripods, monopods, chest pods, C-clamp pods, etc. But the first tripod should be a quality-built standard model sturdy enough to handle the equipment being used.

LIGHTS. Quality photographs require proper lighting. As a minimum, the public relations photographer must obtain a lightweight, camera-mounted stroboscopic light. Most modern units designed to be mounted on cameras have a built-in electric eye. This device regulates the amount of light or the duration of the flash to provide an accurate exposure.

As the photographer becomes more proficient and the budget more liberal, additional lights are a sound investment. Great flexibility with a modest investment can be realized by adding a second strobe light with a slave device mounted in its base. This second unit can supplement the basic unit or be set up to one side of the subject, serving as a modeling light and adding a three-dimensional effect to the resulting photograph. The slave unit is a photoelectric cell that triggers the second light as it senses the flash of the first strobe. Thus, long connecting cords are unnecessary.

Further, as situations warrant and budget permits, the public relations photographer can install a set of studio strobe lights or, on a lesser budget, floodlights. Either solution greatly enhances lighting possibilities for in-house photography: portraits, tabletop product displays, group poses, interiors, etc.

In essence, the photographer uses light the way a painter uses brush strokes. Proper lighting can separate the subject from the background, emphasize salient features of the subject, establish a mood, alter color saturation, etc. The good photographer is as exacting in placement of lights as in the selection of aperture and shutter settings.

Eye-catching photographs sell a story to editors and readers. Good lighting makes them eye-catching.

The thinking photographer uses a wide variety of other tools, including an assortment of filters for both color and black-and-white photography, special effects attachments, close-up devices, various lenses, sunshades, hoods, extra camera bodies or replaceable backs, cases, gadget bags, and many other devices. Most photographers eventually become well equipped, either through the organization's budget or through expenditure of personal funds.

TRAINING THE PHOTOGRAPHER

Photographic techniques, once mastered, are logical and relatively simple. The photographer and the person who makes photo assignments must first remember that there is nothing free in photography. For each point gained, the photographer pays a price. However, there are variables in the equation with which the photographer works.

An analogy demonstrating the interaction of photographic variables uses a container that must be filled with liquid (proper exposure). The liquid can be watery thin or a heavy viscous oil (film speed). The tap can be adjusted to permit a small stream for a long period (small aperture, slow shutter speed) or a large stream for a short period (large aperture, fast shutter speed). By adjusting the variables, an almost infinite variety of combinations can be used to fill the container, but for an acceptable exposure, the container must be filled.

LIGHTING. To a certain extent, the photographer can control light, augmenting natural light or reducing it, dependent upon the situation. To obtain additional light, the photographer pays a price in the weight of the equipment carried. The very bulkiness of the added equipment frequently eliminates the chance for informality. Some subjects are visibly disturbed by frequent use of flash equipment, thus affecting their facial expressions and the mood of the resultant photograph. And in certain situations photographers are prohibited from using flashguns (e.g., during certain athletic contests such as tournament basketball games or in cases where the concentration of individuals or solemnity of an event would be affected).

FILM SPEED. Film speeds (ASA or ISO ratings) run the gamut from a rating of less than ASA or ISO 24 to films measured at ASA or ISO 800 on the commercial market. In addition, the higher speed films (both color and black-and-white) can be pushed to double their rated speeds and more. But again, the photographer pays a price.

As a dangerous oversimplification, film can be described as similar to a layer cake. The carrier, or middle layer, is a plastic sheet. The layer that rests on the cake pan (or against the film plane in the camera) has a thin undercoating of antihalation substance designed to absorb ambient light and minimize the objectionable reflection or halo effect that would otherwise result. The top layer (the layer facing the lens) is the emulsion, an inactive substance that carries crystals of silver bromides, halides, or a substitute. These tiny crystals are affected by light and, in an involved chemical process, produce the photographic image. Slower films (lower ASA or ISO ratings) have extremely small crystals. Faster films have larger crystals and thinner layers of emulsion.

Here is the trade-off. A fast film permits short exposures at reasonably small aperture settings with a minimum of light level. But under the enlarger lens or through the projector, these larger crystals become visible, sometimes annoyingly so. In the trade, the result is referred to as "grain." To minimize grain, the photographer switches to a slow film. Problem solved. Except now the proper exposure requires more light, slower shutter speed, a larger aperture, or a combination of the three. So, eliminate graininess, lose speed. The same basic trade-off exists in both color and black-and-white films.

SHUTTER SPEED. The simplest photographic variable to understand is shutter speed. Speeds are expressed in seconds or fractions of seconds. Starting from the top of the speed range (1/1000 second with the average 35mm camera), each shutter speed moving down the scale doubles the amount of light permitted to strike the film. The scale usually is: 1/1000, 1/500, 1/250, 1/125, 1/60, 1/30, 1/15, 1/8, 1/4, 1/2, and 1 second. By using the "B" or "T" setting (bulb and time) the photographer can extend exposure almost indefinitely. Beyond this, for special effects, photographic exposures can be adjusted to durations measured in millionths of a second.

The trade-off here is in the parallel adjustment that must be made in the size of the lens aperture.

DIAPHRAGM. The f-stop or aperture number is actually a fractional expression of the lens diameter or diaphragm opening. An aperture setting of 1 or f/1 means that the diameter of the lens opening is exactly equal (1/1) to the distance from the lens to the film plane when the camera is focused on infinity. Thus, if the focal length of the lens being used is 50mm (normal focal length of the lens in the average 35mm camera), an f/2 lens on the same camera would have a diameter of 25mm. If that camera is set on f/8, the effective aperture has been closed so that its diameter has been reduced to 6.25mm or an eighth of the focal length of the lens.

As with the shutter speed settings, by starting at the maximum lens opening, each alternate lens setting halves the amount of light that can strike the film. With f/1.4, f/2, f/2.8, f/4, f/5.6, f/8, f/11, f/16, and f/22, each alternate setting effectively halves the amount of light permitted to strike the film during a specific time.

So, the photographic industry presents photographers with a tidy arrangement. If settings of 1/125 and f/11 provide perfect exposure, the same amount of light strikes the film at 1/250 and f/8 or 1/60 and f/16.

An exact amount of light must strike the film for the proper exposure. Practically speaking, it does not matter whether light comes from a wide opening during a brief period or through a small opening over a longer period of time. But to stop action and minimize problems with camera motion, a fast shutter speed is desirable. So, the fast shutter speed is coupled with a wide aperture setting. Except that a wide aperture setting reduces the acceptable depth of field. Depth of field is that zone in which objects are in acceptable focus, from the subject nearest the camera to that object furthest from the camera.

Short exposure, large aperture may be ideal for catching the corner man on a jump shot, but the player guarding against that shot may be out of focus. So, slower shutter, smaller aperture? The action blurs. Fine grain pattern, good depth of field and blurred action versus grainy prints, shallow depth of focus, stopped action. Photographers pay for what they get.

FOCUS. Many aspiring photographers have lost once-in-a-lifetime shots because they were struggling to focus on the action. The professional overcomes the problem by using a technique called *zone focusing*.

Using a basketball game as an example, the photographer sets up shop before the game starts. He will get in position out of bounds, approximately 10 feet either side of the backboard.

Metering available light, the photographer determines that the camera should be set at f/5.6 and 1/500 sec. Now, the photographer prefocuses the camera at 11 ft, studies the scene (using the preview button) and finds that the camera is in acceptable focus on objects as close as 8 ft from the camera and as far away as 17 ft. The photographer draws an imaginary band that is a semicircle 9 ft wide beginning 8 ft in front of the lens. Even the once-in-a-lifetime shot is ignored if it occurs outside the zone. No time to focus. But a satisfying percentage of game action will transpire within the zone. The system has worked for years.

Because proper focus is critical and controllable, many professionals use it to their advantage. They achieve *selective focus* by adjusting aperture setting. By opting for a shallow depth of field (large aperture), the photographer highlights specific subjects or areas in the photo while throwing distracting background and foreground out of focus. Conversely, by using a small aperture, the photographer can increase dramatically the depth of field, bringing objects close to the lens and those in the distance into acceptably sharp focus.

PROVIDING DARKROOM SUPPORT

Much of the professional photographer's success is the result of competent laboratory techniques. In a public relations operation, the best of all worlds is a darkroom operated by the in-house photographic unit.

However, even the simplest photographic laboratory can cost more than $2500, not including the costs of space and operating personnel, and those skilled technicians are expensive. Quality processing is time consuming because the lab is where various remedial actions are taken, such as proper cropping, dodging, vignetting, correcting for exposure errors, adjusting contrast, and many others. Some actions are to correct problems photographers could not avoid, while some make good photographers better.

If budget or personnel limitations make an in-house laboratory impractical, the public relations photographer enhances her value to the organization by discovering and contracting with good professional laboratories, ones that follow instructions and produce quality work on rigid deadlines. Whatever the cost, film and processing are the cheapest, and the indispensable, parts of photography.

EXERCISING CARE IN PUBLIC RELATIONS PHOTOGRAPHY

Photographic equipment and the products it provides play vital roles in a successful public relations operation; so, special precautions must be observed when dealing with the equipment and the photo products.

1. Keep photographic equipment clean and dry. If it becomes wet, dry immediately with a soft cloth. Maintain camera gear properly, and have it professionally serviced periodically.

2. Store equipment in a cool, dry location. Never keep equipment for prolonged periods in an automobile. Glove boxes, rear window shelves, and trunks become hot enough to melt lens cement, ruin film emulsion, and shorten battery life.

3. Never store cameras with shutters cocked for a prolonged period because the springs will lose tension.

4. Remove batteries from stored equipment to prevent leakage that will severely damage equipment.

5. Store excess film in a cool, dry place such as a refrigerator.

6. Check the expiration date to assure that new film stocks are fresh, and process film soon after exposure.

7. For best color reproduction, both in publications and in projected images, use first generation slides. Second and third generation transparencies (duplicates and duplicates of duplicates) are markedly inferior.

8. Do not type or write with hard lead pencils or ballpoint pens on the backs of photo prints, and do not use paper clips with photographs. The resulting impressions on the face of the photograph will be picked up in the engraving process.

9. Cutlines or photo identifications should be typed on separate sheets and fastened to the backs or the bottom edges of the photographs with transparent tape.

10. Protect all photographs, negatives, and transparencies when shipping. Place them between sheets of corrugated paper or heavy card stock cut slightly larger than the items being protected.

Public relations photographs cannot be snapshots

Some of the finest technical photographers never get beyond the snap-shot stage, never produce outstanding photographs. Their exposures are always on the button; they avoid other bugaboos like improper focus and camera motion; they always select the proper film, the right camera and lens combination. A computer-directed automaton could do no better. And no worse. Their pictures have no soul, show no imagi-nation. They fail to recognize that good photography is an art form.

A successful public relations photograph must tell a story just as does a successful news release or special publication. Composition and posing are major parts of that story.

COMPOSITION

A well-composed photograph, just as a well-composed painting, forces the reader to study the photo as the photographer intended it to be studied. The eyes follow a pattern. The classic patterns are those which lead the viewer's eyes in the lines of a **C**, **S**, **X**, or a variation.

With few exceptions, viewers of Joe Rosenthal's immortal photo of the Marine flag-raising on Iwo Jima follow the same eye pattern climax-ing with the flag itself. The pattern is the reverse of the eye travel experienced by a viewer of the old American classic, "Washington Crossing the Delaware."

We can set forth general guidelines for composition, but in truth good composition frequently is a product of the photographer's sub-conscious. The ability to recognize good composition is what sets outstanding photographers apart from their counterparts. But knowing some of the general guidelines can help the good photographer become better.

The memorable photograph has a focal point, a single subject to draw the reader's attention, and all other elements are subordi-nate to that focal point. The point may be an individual, a group, a building, a flower, or a mountain, but unmistakably it will dominate the good photograph.

Whatever the background, it must be selected only to set off the focal point, never to compete with it or distract from it. The main subject can be emphasized by its location within the photograph, by contrast-ing light values, or by lines in the photo that lead to the subject.

Unnecessary blending of tones must be avoided. Melding the focal point into another object or the background because of equal tonal values ruins definition. The background or foreground should contrast with the focal point. The greater the contrast, the greater the emphasis given to the focal point.

Formal balance results in dull photographs. Whether portrait or scenic, the focal point should not be in the exact center of the print, nor should items of equal value be placed equidistant from the center of the frame. A common type of formal balance is evidenced in those instances where the horizon splits the photograph into equal halves, creating formal balance and dull composition.

Important subjects should be grouped together or overlapped so that their relationship as the focal point is obvious. Avoid the appearance of disorganization or haphazard shooting.

Of course this does not mean cramming all elements to one side, or the top, or the bottom of the finished print. It is seldom good photography to leave a large empty space in the center of the photo, unless that empty space is the focal point.

Be acutely aware of backgrounds. A power pole growing out of a woman's coiffure or a branch stabbing into the chief executive's ear can be disconcerting. In many ways, good composition is the application of common sense.

Lighting as a part of good composition is a tool used by master photographers. Portraits by Yousuf Karsh of Ottawa evidence the technique. Subtle lighting, through sound application of established techniques, forces the viewer to study the magnificent scowl in the oft-printed portrait of Winston Churchill; the brooding, intelligent eyes in his photograph of Albert Einstein; and Jimmy Carter's strong hands.

In almost every memorable photograph, either by genius or design, the audience's attention is directed to those elements the person behind the camera wanted them to see. Each masterpiece has a story to tell, and that story is told in the composition.

CROPPING

Proper cropping makes a good public relations photograph a better one. Extraneous matter is eliminated. Of course, the best place to eliminate the unwanted area is in the camera itself, especially if that is a 35mm camera.

The 35mm negative provides a working area that is only 1″×1½″. So, the photographer cannot afford waste. Even with a full 35mm

13.1 *A public relations staple, the architectural photograph can be improved by framing the structure with trees, as in this example. Some construction details may be obscured, but the foliage adds perspective and warmth. The photograph was taken with a Rolleiflex and Plus-X film Wratten F (dark red) filter, f/11 at 1/125 second.*

negative, the resulting 8"×10" print represents an eight-diameter enlargement; whereas, enlarging a 4"×5" negative to the same size requires only a two-diameter blowup. Additional enlargement required to crop the small negative will make any grain, fuzziness, or other imperfections more evident.

However, occasions arise where cropping is the answer, regardless of negative size. The photographer was unable to get close enough to obtain a tight portrait shot; an unwanted desk corner, automobile fender, or power pole is in the foreground or background. The photo can be improved by changing the position of the horizon, eliminating excess foreground or sky. Perhaps the camera was inadvertently tilted during the exposure or the photograph could be improved by intentionally tilting.

The final print might be saved by changing emphasis completely or even changing format from horizontal to vertical. It may be possible to bring the final print alive through extreme cropping (i.e., moving from the standard 4″×5″ format to 1″×5″, 4″×4″ or some other unusual shape).

Most photographer and picture editors work with a pair of cropping devices cut from cardboard or stiff paper. They place these L-shaped cards on their prints and move them around until they achieve the best possible composition. They then mark the print with a grease pencil to indicate the way they want the final cropped photograph to appear.

The print that includes the cropping marks is sent with the negative to the laboratory technicians. Cropping is accomplished through judicious use of the enlarger. The photographer cannot afford waste, but cropping can improve a good photo. At times, it can even save a poor photograph.

THE PHOTOGRAPHER AND THE SUBJECT

Many persons are self-conscious before a lens. Their hands are monsters beyond their control; so they assume the "fig leaf" pose, which is neither flattering nor meaningful. A thinking photographer will provide props or directions to help the subject avoid the problem of hands.

Too many photos have been taken just as the subject was beginning to speak, was breaking into an inane grin, or at the precise moment the subject was blinking. The latter problem is an inescapable coincidence. It is one reason most photographers insist on taking "just one more."

The photographer or the public relations professional accompanying the photographer should be acutely aware of facial expressions, body position, arrangement of clothing, grooming of the subject, background, and other details.

On one occasion, lack of coaching or inattention to detail by the photographer from a major organization created a problem that has lived with that organization for years. A rising executive posed for a series of portraits. The prints returned, and the executive considered them the most flattering ever taken, except for one thing: his necktie was crooked. It was very crooked.

During the ensuing nine years, the photographer's subject rose from regional director to chief executive of the national organization. A photograph was needed with each promotion and major appearance. Each time the top executive referred to the regional office for one of the prints with the crooked necktie. Each time the print was retouched to straighten the tie, at no little cost in labor and time. If only the photographer had noticed that small detail.

When possible, the subject should be posed naturally in a familiar setting. Otherwise the uneasiness of the subject will distract from the reason for the photograph. The photo must look natural whether the scene has been planned or is a candid shot.

Routine photographs come alive through use of filters and special effects attachments. In this series, Figure 13.2 is unfiltered; Figure 13.3 was exposed through a red filter; and the final exposure, Figure 13.4, was taken through both a red filter and a star filter. The three successive exposures were f/22 at 1/500 second, f/16 at 1/125 second, and f/16 at 1/125 second, all with a Nikon F and Tri-X film.

13.2

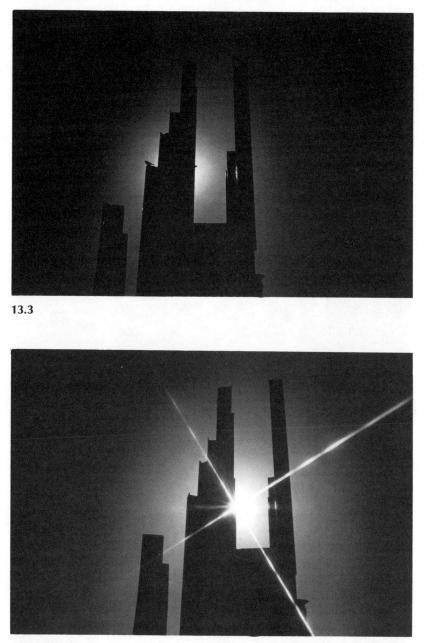

13.3

13.4

Various lens lengths determine emphasis in photographs from setting the scene (a wide shot) to pinpointing the action. This series shows the progressive effect of using 28mm (wide angle), 50mm (normal), 105mm (modified telephoto), and 200mm (telephoto) lenses. The camera was a Nikon F, Tri-X film, and red filter. Each exposure was f/16 at 1/125 second.

13.5

13.6

13.7

13.8

FOOLING MOTHER NATURE

The professional public relations photographer realizes that anything that enhances the final photograph increases the chances it will be printed and published. The pro takes advantage of the many techniques and tools available.

Proper filters build contrast between sky and clouds, sky and subject. These include the several types of red and yellow filters for black-and-white photography, subtle color filters, or polarizing filters for color films. The polarizing filter deepens a blue sky, and it minimizes nonmetallic reflections in all photography.

The professional uses star screens for special lighting effects, soft focus devices to flatter faces, vignetting masks to emphasize subjects, anything to enhance the artistry of the product.

On special occasions, the professional uses special effects such as collages, multiple exposures, bas relief, micro- and macro-photography, or special darkroom techniques. The professional knows the techniques and what they can accomplish to further the public relations message the photograph is intended to convey.

COLOR OR BLACK-AND-WHITE

Color reproduction in general circulation newspapers has been a fact since before the turn of the century. The *Milwaukee Journal, Chicago Tribune*, and several of the New York City newspapers used tinted stock and blocks of colored ink in the 1890s. Of course, widespread use of color in newspapers did not become practical until the latter half of the twentieth century.

Most dailies and many weeklies have ROP (run of the paper) color capability today. So, if the public relations practitioner creates an arresting color photograph, newspapers can reproduce that prize shot.

Public relations use of color photography is not confined to newspapers. The public relations practitioner makes wide use of color in special publications, exhibits, in-house displays, and audiovisual presentations. The latter, increasingly popular with the public relations practitioner, are insatiable in their demand for color transparencies. And when properly handled, the impact of audiovisual presentations is immense.

But the public relations practitioner must not give up on black-and-white photography. In dealing with print media, black-and-white is still in control. Furthermore, black-and-white film is more forgiving than color film. Acceptable results can be obtained from black-and-white

13.9 *The mood projected by an urban skyline is enhanced in this photograph using a 3-P prismatic device, one of many special effects which can be achieved by an imaginative photographer. The camera was a Nikon F, 50mm lens, Tri-X film at f/16, 1/125 second, using a red filter and the 3-P in combination.*

film with less accurate exposures; the film is more flexible and more economical to process and handle. But, a caution: despite assurances to the contrary, black-and-white prints from color negatives are not equal in quality to those produced from black-and-white negatives. So, if both color and black-and-white are required for an assignment, insist that the photographer use both types of film.

The movies and public relations

Verisimilitude reached a new plateau through another tool in the public relations practitioner's kit. Motion picture photography and its younger cousin, videotape recording (VTR), create an unparalleled "you are there" feeling for the audience. Since motion pictures went public at the beginning of the century, generations have been informed and entertained sitting before the silver screen. With the melding of sound, color, and more recently through VTR, immediacy, the impact of sight, sound, and motion has been an unequalled conduit for information. The medium is a storyteller without peer.

The similarities with still photography are many. Here again, there are ASA and ISO numbers, focus, aperture settings, lens selection, and a broad range of attachments and gadgets. Beyond that, however, the relationship with still cameras is tenuous. Knowledge of still cameras and techniques is no guarantee of success with motion pictures and videotape recordings.

Although knowledge of motion picture and VTR equipment and techniques is a valuable asset, cinematography in whatever form is not as basic at this time to the needs of a beginning public relations practitioner as is skill in still photography. Therefore, a detailed exploration of equipment and cinematographic techniques is impractical in this context.

The wise course for the PR practitioner not proficient in cinematography is to call on the experts. A poorly executed motion picture or amateurish videotape is as counterproductive as family album-type still photos or poorly written copy.

Good professionals are expensive, but worth every cent. Most major metropolitan areas have commercial studios capable of delivering anything from record footage and news clips to network quality spots and full-length industrial motion pictures. These studios can provide the entire product, story boards, rough and finished scripts, professional acting talent, direction, and production and distribution facilities.

The finished product has a wide variety of applications in the public relations field. Meetings of marketing personnel and stockholders frequently use motion pictures and/or videotapes to introduce new products, services, processes, or special messages from executives. Corporate histories and product applications have been developed into motion pictures of sufficient general interest to warrant national distribution to schools, civic clubs, and special interest groups.

Depending upon subject matter and the sponsoring organization, industrial films are shown frequently on commercial and public television. If the quality is acceptable, tape or film produced by public relations units may be used by regional television stations in newscasts, because occasions arise where the organization may have tape or film that cannot be duplicated by the television station.

As an example, the Army Corps of Engineers in certain locations uses a small, unmanned submarine to check deep underwater structures. The Corps also uses a television camera-equipped electrical robot to check the huge flood control and power tunnels buried deep in the bowels of some of the nation's largest dams. The units carry powerful light sources in addition to the miniature television cameras. They relay footage to engineers and technicians on the surface. Some of this film has been used in feature coverage by commercial stations. This is a public relations bonus never considered as a possible benefit when the equipment was designed and purchased.

In another area, like many organizations, the Army Corps of Engineers has benefitted from extensive files of motion picture film shot before commercial television entered the American living room. The clips have been woven into historical features developed by commercial studios and television stations, and the Corps of Engineers uses it for in-house productions detailing the history and/or operation of multipurpose structures as they fit into the developmental stories of various sections of the nation.

By combining the visual and aural impact into a single medium, the public relations practitioner has a tool of immense power if it is used well.

The equipment is expensive, and it requires the minds and hands of knowledgeable specialists to produce quality results. Until the public relations practitioner dedicated to this medium has developed the requisite talent, the nod should go to practicing professionals. Substituting anything less is shortchanging the organization that pays the bills.

Photography in public relations

Photography in its various forms is an indispensable tool of the competent public relations practitioner. Suitable graphics that meet the technical and esthetic standards of the target medium exponentially increase the chance of gaining publication for a news story.

Whether photographers and filmmakers are part of the public relations department or operate independently, and whether public relations is handled by a single individual or an entire division, the organization has every right to expect that the photographs and film produced by public relations are technically correct.

However, the public relations practitioner may not assume that the institutional photographers and cameramen understand the requirements of quality public relations. Excellent portrait, architectural, or scientific photographers and competent motion picture camera operators may have limited exposure to public relations, news photography, or film needs. Thus, the public relations practitioner must be capable of explaining what is needed or directing the photographer and camera operator in obtaining the acceptable product. Ultimately the PR practitioner is responsible for producing photographs and film of the proper esthetic and professional quality.

GET OUT OF THE RUT

Most editors cringe when faced with the typical "grip and grin" shot or the all-too-frequent large group pose straight out of the family album. The former, where two participants grip the certificate, trophy, gavel, etc., grasp right hands, and grin vacuously into the lens, is the most obviously posed situation in photography. But there are as many alternatives as there are photographers or public relations practitioners. The photographer can avoid these deadly dull poses by shooting over the shoulder of the presenter toward the recipient; the recipient can be posed leaning over the executive who signs the certificate; the two can hold the trophy over their heads in triumph; they can be caught pouring champagne into the cup. The possibilities are limited only by imagination and good taste. The photographer's technical skills must be augmented by imagination.

The bread-and-butter photograph in public relations is the portrait or mug shot. But do it right. Judicious and severe cropping, use of an occasional prop, augmented lighting, and carefully selected backgrounds can raise the mug shot to the level of a portrait, well out of the time-worn rut.

Interesting framing makes an ordinary photograph stand out from the other ordinary photos. The thinking photographer will use foreground tree branches, architectural features, other people, or dozens of creative ideas to frame the shot. Through attention to lighting and proper filter selection, the photographer can attract the editor's or reader's attention. Filters can dramatize clouds, separate subjects from background, intensify colors. Then, the news release accompanying the photograph will receive a more careful reading.

Most editors of print media, when working with black-and-white photographs, prefer 8"×10" glossy prints, well defined, good contrast, minimum grain, and single theme. And unless the photograph is of unusual interest, the editor avoids photos of large groups of persons, hands clasped in the fig leaf pose, grinning inanely at the reader. In fact, some editors consider any grouping of more than four persons to be a mob scene.

When dealing with still photographs, most television news directors prefer 35mm color transparencies shot on the horizontal axis. Never vertical shots.

All public relations departments provide photographs for print and television use. Most departments also receive frequent requests for graphics to accompany magazine articles and books. The requests normally indicate the type of material desired (black-and-white prints, color prints, negatives or transparencies, line drawings, maps, etc.) plus the preferred size.

In-house demand for photography exceeds external requirements in many public relations situations. Judicious use of illustrative material heightens interest in and enhances readability of internally produced material such as annual and stockholders reports, product brochures, employee publications, etc.

AUGMENTING FILES

Exhibits, displays, bulletin boards, and audiovisual productions consume an increasing number of quality photographs. Not infrequently, demand for specific types of coverage exceeds the capabilities of the organization's photographic staff. In these instances, the public relations department may turn to professional studios, free-lancers, regional media or special photo agencies, and syndicates. Many of the latter have voluminous files and far-flung networks of professional photographers.

The public relations department of a large organization with representatives located in many different states developed yet another approach for supplementing the department's photo files.

The department sponsors periodic photo minicourses for interested employees and conducts annual photo contests open to all employees. All entries become the property of the organization. Winners receive trophies, gift certificates, and organizationwide publicity. Each time a contest entry is printed in an organizational publication, proper individual recognition is given the photographer. The contest's success has spawned similar competitions in several sister organizations throughout the country. Photos acquired through the contest have been used as color covers on various publications, in regional newspapers, and as important elements in displays and audiovisual presentations.

As noted, imagination is a vital ingredient in photography, not only in composing a good photograph but in acquiring a good photographic library.

Summary

Cameras are the eyes that help the public relations practitioner promote ideas, products, and services. The good photographer—part technician, part artist—has no convenient set of guidelines that lead to quality; yet, readers react to good photography. And good photography is a vital element in any successful public relations operation.

No firm rules exist to determine where photographers should be located within the organizational structure. Similarly, the size of photo units varies from organizations where the public relations practitioner is the photographer to those that have photo specialists in a number of different areas.

But wherever those photographers are located, the wise beginner in public relations will cultivate a close working relationship with them. Their cooperation and creative talents can ease the beginner's climb on the professional ladder.

The public relations practitioner charged with equipping a photo unit learns that no universal camera exists. A careful study of the organization's requirements will determine the camera equipment that best satisfies those requirements. Furthermore, the responsible individual remembers that quality begets quality. The most important element in the operation is the talented photographer, and that individual should be equipped with the best technical tools available within the budget.

The public relations practitioner, photographer or not, must understand photographic quality and the parameters within which photographers work. The PR practitioner must understand composition, cropping, working with photo subjects, proper use of the end product, and picture editing.

The competent public relations professional will understand the vital role played by a skilled photographic technician with imagination.

Exercises

1. Provide six examples each of record shots and action photos. Explain how each record shot could have been converted into an action photograph.

2. Provide six examples of photography that promote an idea. Determine a probable sponsor for the public relations photos and explain the idea being promoted.

3. List the equipment, complete with brand name, that you would purchase for the photographer in your public relations unit. Include a modest in-house studio. Justify the types of equipment and the brands selected.

4. Completely equip a modest laboratory. Do not worry about brand names, but develop a floor plan and explain the layout.

5. Provide five examples of published photographs that can be made more effective by cropping and then complete the cropping.

6. Working with a group of six persons competing for a single prize, either photograph the group or stage the proper arrangement in class, demonstrating a pose that avoids the stereotyped group shot.

Case study

Cyclops Electronics is under new management. The most obvious result is that the corporation is expanding its product line into industrial communications and will make a strong pitch for the two-way communications business, including airline, public safety, marine radio, and other areas.

As part of the new direction, a stronger public relations effort will be mounted to attract the new line of customers. You are charged with organizing a photo unit within the public relations department. The only limitations are that the unit can employ only two persons and its annual budget may not exceed $50,000, exclusive of salaries and travel expenses. The new management team expects results. Two ideas that surfaced through channels are that emphasis will be placed on audiovisual presentations and that "it would be nice if we produced an attractive calendar each year."

- Develop a basic equipment list for the unit.
- Determine the experience level expected of the unit's employees and the approximate salary range.
- Describe suggested photographs to be featured in the first calendar.
- Explain and give examples of types of publications you will cultivate in an effort to promote the new product lines.
- Describe other audiovisual presentation you will suggest to promote the lines.

Suggested readings

Fajardo, Fred J. "Super Photos for Super Projects." *Public Relations Journal,* August 1979.

Herwig, Ellis. "Photo Terminology for Non-Photographers." *Public Relations Journal,* August 1979.

Miller, Martin, and Frank Pagani. "How to Cut Four-Color Costs." *Public Relations Journal,* August 1980.

Welch, William F. "How to Plan Those Really Great Photos." *Public Relations Journal,* August 1979.

"The Why and How of Panoramic Photography." *Public Relations Journal,* August 1980.

14 Organizational show and tell

Historic overview

Displays and exhibitry have been part of humankind since the early cave dwellers' paintings and crude art efforts. Many detail the prowess of the artist or the unusual and frightening experiences of a lifetime among mastodons and sabre-toothed tigers. Much of what is known of their lives and times has been gleaned from displays left on the walls of their primitive homes.

Early in recorded history, Egyptians built the pyramids, among the world's most ambitious public works projects. This was exhibitry on a grand scale, proclaiming the greatness and grandeur of the several reigning monarchs along the Nile. Among the first visitor centers? Perhaps.

Parades staged by returning conquerors showed stay-at-home Romans the prowess of the mighty legions with emphasis on the particular commander featured in that day's spectacular. "It's Augustus. See the banners?" And if that public relations ploy did not convince them, circuses should. Again, exhibitry. Fearsome animals brought from afar and reluctant prisoners thrown against each other in deadly combat entertained the locals. Circuses took their minds off the mundane problems of taxation, food shortages, and simple survival. Kind of public relations by misdirection. The naked reverse.

But advertising—and public relations—can be traced more directly to the Anglo-Saxons. The original family unit was self-sustaining with nothing to buy or sell. Eventually, rudimentary tools were developed, making the individual more productive. The farmer grew more crops than his family needed and had produce to barter. Meanwhile, the artisan who fashioned the tools, the smith, was vital to community welfare. The productive community prospered, and the smith was the major contributor.

He was the only specialized tradesman for a long time. So, while others were identified by their place of residence, general appearance, or family relationship (Tom by Water, Dick the Black, or Harry John's son), this artisan was John the Smith.

John was followed by other specialists as they developed—Baker, Wright, Tailor, Weaver, Dyer, and many more. And before family names were widely adopted, industry became more specialized. Smiths developed specialties and those specialties were reflected in their eventual family names—goldsmith, arrowsmith, hammersmith, nailsmith, and variations of the trade such as cooper, arkwright, and millwright.

So, in earlier times, identification was the sole role of this primitive but effective form of public relations or advertising. Villagers knew who was capable of supplying specific needs simply because of the individual's name.

The next evolutionary step was development of signs—exhibits. The sign not only explained graphically what the artisan could do but also where he was located. Furthermore, the first craftsman with a sign had an advantage over the competition. The village could find him.

Early signs were pictorial because most of the artisan's customers and probably the artisan himself were illiterate. Thus, an anvil indicated the smith, a barrel was the cooper's sign, a boot meant the shoemaker, a loaf of bread pinpointed the baker. A red-and-white striped pole was the sign used by barbers because the early barber was also the community physician, and the stripes represented surgical bandages. This is one of the few surviving historic signs.

As competition increased, signs became more distinctive. Frequently a distinguishing mark was placed on the product to identify the individual craftsman or the guild hall to which he belonged; hence, the hallmark. The hallmark or trademark identified the maker and, by inference, was an implied guarantee for the purchaser, protecting him from inferior merchandise.

The slogan was a natural follow-up of the trademark. Then as now, the most successful slogans were the easiest to remember and the ones that positively identified the artisan. "Tom the Shoemaker for boots that fit," "Dick the Miller for finer flour." It is a short transition to "At Ford—Quality is Job 1" and "It's no downstream beer. It's Coors."

Through the years, the most successful trade names and slogans have common traits. They are:

1. Short and simple, easy to recognize and remember.
2. Easy to spell, read, and pronounce.

3. Pleasing to hear or read.
4. Readily adaptable to the product package or label.
5. Suggestive of the product and use.
6. Distinctive, dissimilar from other trade names or slogans.
7. Easily tied to a picture or graphic device (the trademark).
8. Never offensive, obscene, or negative.

No aggressive salesmanship was permitted when guilds controlled industry, but guilds sought to enhance the prestige of their membership. So they turned to exhibitry of a sort. Members wore distinctive clothing, staged pageants, and designed displays and floats to demonstrate their talents, wealth, and relatively high standing in the community. In a sense, this was the Middle Ages' version of a trade fair or modern exhibitry.

At this time the primitive forms of public relations and advertising shifted into a higher gear. Development of movable type and the printing press heralded a gradual increase in literacy. Originally, printing benefitted the clergy and a small percentage of the nobility, the only citizens who could read. Thus, although the printing press became reality in the latter part of the fifteenth century, 75 years passed before the first handbill was developed to promote a specific product.

The pamphlet became increasingly important as literacy spread. And in 1612 pamphlets appeared in England, distributed by the Virginia Company, extolling the virtues of the New World and seeking to entice colonists to America. By the latter part of the seventeenth century, printed media such as posters, handbills, pamphlets, and sign boards were widely used. They identified merchants and their products, built markets for products, and sought goodwill for people and companies.

Public relations and advertising, by whatever names, were an established fact of life. And their precursors were displays, exhibitry, and shows.

Modern exhibitry

PURPOSE

Exhibitry is communication. But it must have a message to communicate. A particular display or exhibit may represent the ultimate in public relations technique. It may be strikingly beautiful, loaded with audience participation gadgetry, and incorporate versatile construction. But if it has no worthwhile message or theme, or fails to tell that message or theme well, it is so much wasted resources and labor.

A second and equally important ingredient that must be incorporated into exhibitry is a clear understanding of the audience to be reached. School children? Young adults? Retirees? Medical practitioners? Hunters? Joggers? Parents? Minority groups? Redheads? Prospective employees? Shoplifters? Clergy?

Successful displays are those that focus on the target audience and transmit the desired message or theme quickly and understandably. The most successful are those that communicate in such a way the message is remembered well after its delivery.

Shannon W. Jones, Jr., president of Shannon and Associates, isolated and identified the problem in the publication *Guidelines for the Planning and Development of Corps of Engineers Visitor Centers.* He wrote: "At that time (when he completed his first exhibit), I thought I had designed the most beautiful creation in the world. It was dazzling . . . it was versatile . . . it was an engineering marvel . . . it was a failure.

"That was the first time I discovered that the theory of what ought to be, which we learned in school, sometimes bears little resemblance to what is as found in the real world.

"Thousands of exhibit designs for hundreds of clients have taught that disillusioned young designer, who is no longer quite as young but a lot more enthusiastic, one very important rule: If a design doesn't communicate, all the beauty, versatility and engineering expertise in the world will not sell a product or present an idea."

RANGE

The designer's imagination is the only practical limit on the scope of this form of communication. A clear idea can be successfully transmitted and received through use of a simple calling card. Whereas, an entire building, a visitor center complete with the latest technology, can fail to transmit the same message or theme if the creative minds behind the center misinterpreted the message, the audience, or the media with which they dealt.

A former chief of the U.S. Army Corps of Engineers, Lieutenant General John W. Morris, recognized that some persons, even some employees, looked upon his organization as an unfeeling bureaucracy. As an important visualization of his campaign to change that image, he distributed small white lapel pins that proclaimed in red letters the

simple message, "The Corps Cares." Worn by both civilian and uniformed employees, the pins induced questions from visitors at Corps
projects. Employees had the opportunity to explain the human side of
their operations and the organization's efforts to preserve, enhance,
and conserve environmental values. Although they chided each other
about their pins, Corps employees experienced a marked improvement
in morale and in attention to their duties. In short, the simple device was
both cause and effect.

The same central theme, "The Corps Cares," was expressed in
speeches delivered by staff members, audiovisual presentations, and
exhibits at projects throughout the country. But the lapel button was the
most persuasive device. The pervasive little pins have turned up on at
least five continents, some worn by persons who never heard of the U.S.
Army Corps of Engineers and, in fact, by individuals who speak no
English and cannot read the pins they wear.

So, exhibitry can mean a lapel button costing a nickel. It can be a
multimedia presentation with a budget in six figures. Exhibitry can
involve a visitor-activated working model of the space shuttle, and it can
be a city-sponsored float in the Parade of Roses. But for the sponsoring
organization to realize value received, each effort must transmit a message or theme to a recognized audience.

SIMPLE DESIGN

Logical but severe restraints are imposed on most exhibit designers. Generally, the first questions to be answered are:

- What is the message or theme?
- Who is the audience?
- What is the budget?
- What are the space limitations?
- What technical limitations are imposed?
- Will the exhibit be fixed or transient?

After deciding upon the message and selecting the audience, size,
design, and complexity of the exhibit may well be determined by the
amount of money budgeted to the project. In determining cost effectiveness, the public relations practitioner must include all costs associated with the particular exhibit. These include fees paid consultants and
fabricators, of course. But if the project is handled in-house, careful
accounting includes such items as construction materials, hardware,

electronic components, photography, finished art, and space rental. An accurate figure also includes pro rata charges for organizational equipment, facilities, and vehicles; personnel time; and shipping and transportation costs. Totals include time devoted by employees to planning, exhibit design, construction, promotion, assembly, and display. Salaries, travel expenses, and per diem costs are computed.

SIZE. Many organizations sharply reduce per showing costs by designing exhibits to be used repeatedly in different settings, either with or without modification.

Public relations practitioners responsible for design and/or placement of exhibits must be acutely aware of size limitations. Many large shows (auto shows; outdoor sports, vacation, and boat shows; home shows; occupational expositions; etc.) provide exhibitor space in eight-foot multiples (i.e., areas that are 8'×8', 8'×16', 16'×24', etc.). The designer must know space limitations before buying the first board foot of lumber. Designing an exhibit to dimensions that do not match industry standards in the area means eventually wasting space leased at a high cost.

Furthermore, if the exhibit will be shown in hotel meeting rooms, office waiting areas, and locations other than auditoriums or exhibition halls, the designer must be aware of ceiling heights, hanging chandeliers, and other obstructions that can limit exhibit heights.

Designing a technical and engineering marvel that requires utility hookups before determining whether the exhibition area has the required utilities is a risky practice. In certain situations, even a basic electrical connection is unavailable, or if it is, it may be a simple household circuit without enough amperage to handle complex electronic gadgetry.

Portability is a prime consideration in design of exhibitry. If the unit will be moved from place to place (e.g., schools, conventions, trade shows, etc.), transporting and assembling the exhibit should be well within the capability of a one- or two-person crew. The public relations practitioner frequently learns this fact the hard way if he is appointed as that one-person crew.

PREFABRICATED UNITS. A wide variety of commercial display units is on the market. Most are durable, attractive, and remarkably flexible. They are sold with carrying cases sized so the components may be carried in a standard station wagon. Artwork, photos, display panels, and signing are affixed before the components are loaded into their cases for the journey to the showing.

Depending upon space available for display, the public relations practitioner may decide to bring a single four-foot panel or a dozen. When assembled, panels may be arranged in a straight line along a wall, in a box configuration, a triangle, or an extended zigzag. When the prefabricated exhibit is freestanding, the practitioner displays material on both sides of each panel.

THE PRINTED MESSAGE. Average viewers are more conditioned to the television set than the classroom. They visit your exhibit hoping to be entertained and, perhaps, educated if no great effort is required. So, even though almost every exhibit requires the viewer to read a message, remember to keep it brief and easily understood.

Write copy for the target audience. Many designers work on the principle that the lead line or title of the exhibit announces the subject matter or name of the exhibit and should be easily read from across any size room.

The second category of written information provides general data or a summary of the message the exhibit is designed to convey. The block or blocks of copy are placed at eye level for the average viewer and seldom exceed one or two short sentences. The information is basic, requiring little or no technical background of the viewer.

The third category of printed information (if more detail is required) includes more comprehensive data such as statistics, scientific names, and references. Many viewers who read this third category have previous knowledge of the subject. The copy in this category is lengthier than that in the second category, and it may include charts or graphs because the visitor who reads this copy is interested enough to spend the additional time with the exhibit. Thus, the material is printed in smaller type and need not be as conveniently located as the copy in category two.

Generally speaking, type faces as well as colors are selected for readability. A standard Roman face is an excellent choice; Cheltenham, Century, and Schoolbook are examples.

The most legible type colors, in the order of their readability, are black, blue, purple, green, and red, when printed on a white background. If the background is in color and a relatively large amount of copy is used, the most comfortable combination for the viewer is type the same color as the background, only in a much darker shade. Thus, if a light green background is selected, dark green is used for the type. Reversed type (light-colored type on a dark background) is more difficult to read than the standard dark on light.

In those instances where a short copy block is used, type may be in a color that is complementary to the background color; e.g., type could be dark maroon on a light green background.

In most cases, simple is best when designing an exhibit, whether it is a single display panel or a multimedia mammoth. Graphics, typography, and other elements are arranged in keeping with the principles of good artistic design. Simplicity, informal balance, careful color selection, and general good taste combine in an effective exhibit.

Audiovisual programs

BASIC COMPOSITION

The need for imagination in creating the good photograph was discussed earlier. Good photography is a must, whether in publications or as part of exhibits. Imagination after taking the photograph is equally important.

The next logical step is using photographs to illustrate the spoken word by entertaining, educating, and informing. It is a technique that dates back to the first lantern slides, but it came of age in the latter third of the twentieth century with the advent of exceptionally fine 35mm cameras, improved color films, and less trouble-prone slide projectors. These better projectors feature rapid slide advance, remote controls, automatic focusing, and a broad range of lenses and accessories.

The audiovisual presentation in its simplest form involves a speaker and a projector. Most commonly used are the 35mm slide projector and the overhead model that projects 8″×10″ transparencies on the screen. Many of the same guidelines apply to both.

The speaker uses either a remote control changer or an assistant who changes slides on command. Even with this basic arrangement, carefully selected slides can clarify and illustrate points made by the speaker. The emphasis is on carefully selected.

Some principles of good photography were discussed earlier. They are equally applicable when those photographs are projected. Audiovisual presentations can be further enhanced by observing common-sense guidelines when projecting graphics.

FORMAT. Always remember the format within which you are working. The ratio is 1:1.5 when working with 35mm transparencies. Thus, if the screen is 6 ft wide, the image will be 4 ft high. Avoid slides shot on the vertical axis, if possible, when using 35mm transparencies. Mixing them with horizontal slides makes the presentation appear amateurish, and it is disconcerting to the audience when the projected image splashes off the screen onto the ceiling or wall.

Most transparencies used with overhead projectors are 8"×10", a 4:5 ratio. Projecting on the same 6 ft wide screen used for the above 35mm slides, would provide a horizontal image 4.8 ft high and a vertical image 7.5 ft high. Because slide placement is not as exact with an overhead projector, the advantages of using single-axis transparencies are not as pronounced as with 35mm projection.

SIMPLICITY. Printing too much copy on a single slide is a common fault in audiovisual presentations. Even viewers with keen eyesight become confused and irritated. Lines should not exceed seven words each, and type must be reduced to a barely legible size if more than six lines are flashed on the screen. If the copy requires a headline or if a separate title slide is used, that line should not exceed four words.

Graphs and charts must be simple and easily understood. Two charts are better than one chart which depicts two relationships. Simple bar charts, line charts, and pie charts are the best graphic devices for their purposes. "Cute" art work can confuse the viewer. For example, if pictures of oil drums rather than a bar graph are used to show that consumption has doubled, the drum twice the height of its neighbor actually has eight times the volume. We are lying to the viewer. And if we depict a drum with twice the capacity, it does not appear on screen to be twice as large. So, keep it simple. In this case, stick with the bar graph.

COLOR. Insist on good color saturation when designing graphics for audiovisual presentations. Brilliant colors are more attractive and they demand the viewer's attention. Work for good contrast and for color harmony.

If for some reason graphics will be superimposed on a photograph or illustration, keep them simple. Select the background with extreme care to prevent having it compete with the graphics for audience attention. The best solution is to avoid the problem in the first place. Stick to unadorned backgrounds.

MESSAGE. As with all communications, the only effective audiovisual presentation is the one with something to say. Identify and clearly state the message or theme to be transmitted and the audience to whom it will be directed. The presentation must concentrate on a single idea or theme. All else supports that. The laundry list approach cataloging and describing all accomplishments may be necessary in technical briefings, but it is confusing, dull, and deadly in another setting.

AN A/V SAMPLER

The person at the lectern supplements the spoken word with slides. The audience sees, hears, and better understands the intended message. An A/V program has been born, but it is a primitive one because the mechanics are distracting. With each slide change, the projector clunks and the screen is momentarily blank, emphasizing the clunk. The program is only a step ahead of your neighbor's boring annual review of vacation slides. A step ahead because the script is professional and the slides have been edited to remove the real losers.

MULTIPROJECTOR. Now it is time to get serious about A/V, and the first step is the elimination of the "clunk-blank-clunk" sequence. A pair of projectors is mated, each focused on the same screen and wired together through a dissolve unit. The person delivering the speech or an assistant changes slides with a remote control unit.

Slides are loaded alternately into the trays of the two projectors; thus, projector A shows odd-numbered slides and projector B shows even-numbered slides in the program. When the speaker signals a slide change, the lamp in projector A fades from full "on" to "off." Concurrently, the lamp in projector B fades from "off" to full "on." The audience sees the new image appear gradually on the screen as the slide they had been watching fades away. Following the two or three seconds required for the change, the "off" projector automatically advances to the next slide in its tray, and the equipment is ready to change to that next slide. The result is a smooth, professional show.

ELEMENTARY MULTIMEDIA. As A/V presentations become more polished and more automated, the simple dissolve is discarded and the
spokesman replaced. A specially designed audiovisual tape player
replaces the organization's speaker. It may not have naturally curly hair
or a winning smile, but the tape machine says what it is programmed to
say without stammering, coughing, or losing its place. And it can do it
with sound effects and music too.

The basic dissolve unit is discarded in favor of a programmer that
handles the dissolve function and more. This unit reads silent signals
transmitted to it by the tape player and automatically changes slides,
precisely on cue and as directed. For example, it can change slides on a
fast cut (i.e., immediately and with no dissolve). The programmer can
provide a rapid dissolve (approximately 2 seconds) or a slow dissolve
(from 4 to 15 seconds). And it will mix these signals in any sequence,
reading the different cues from the tape player. The equipment can
order a pause at a predetermined point in the program to allow comments, questions, or just a change of pace.

With this combination (two projectors, tape player, and programmer) the public relations practitioner has a fully automated A/V
program, albeit a rather rudimentary one. With this equipment, basic
programming can be handled in-house. If adequate talent is available,
the audio tape can be recorded complete with programming cues by
the public relations staff.

Remarkable flexibility is a major advantage of a program of this type
compared with other automated presentations. Tapes can be revised,
slides replaced, or the series augmented, and programming cues can be
altered at any time.

A/V IN THE SPACE AGE. System growth is almost limitless in modern
A/V programming. Solid-state computer technology makes possible
multiimage productions that bring a new level of excitement and artistic
creativity to public relations presentations.

Quality multiimage productions exceed the creative possibilities
of almost any other medium, including motion pictures, because
16mm projectors and videotape players can be incorporated as just
one part of a total multiimage show. The concept opens a new world, a
world of multiscreen and multiprojector, multitrack sound and electronic wizardry.

In addition to programming chores, a modern A/V package can
automatically control houselights. It can notify the receptionist in

another room through a light panel that a specific projector is malfunctioning, and it will reset projector trays to the proper point to begin the next show. Modified projectors automatically replace burned-out lamps.

Equipment is complex, but operation and maintenance is comparatively simple. A person need not be an automotive expert to drive an automobile or to perform simple maintenance on the car. Similarly, those responsible for showing A/V programs need not be electronic technicians. The average system is designed so that troubleshooting involves replacing entire units rather than repair of specific malfunctions.

Nine-screen programs are not unusual in visitor center and museum exhibitry. Trade shows and corporate meetings may combine 15 or more 35mm slide projectors and a 16mm motion picture projector, all programmed on a single tape and shown on five screens. The visuals include color photos, graphics, and animation produced by 35mm transparencies.

This level of sophistication requires equipment and talent well beyond the average public relations budget. Although basic commercial projectors are standard (Kodak Ektagraphic units are most widely used), a complicated program requires special matched lenses and pin-registered slides. Dissolve animators, record-playback machines, and high-technology programmers plus accessory equipment and spares can make any organization's comptroller nervous.

Serious commercial use of this advanced technology began in the mid-1960s. Development has been so rapid that software firms (those producing the programs) that guarantee their customers the latest in animation technology, for example, are on the horns of a dilemma. They may invest heavily in the latest sophisticated equipment, but their volume and price must be at a level that will permit them to amortize that equipment in six months. By that time, their sophisticated gear is obsolescent. They write off the gear and invest in still more advanced technology.

Once the decision is made to use multiimage, multiscreen programs, it is no time for amateur night. Contract with professionals and have the show produced, directed, scripted, and programmed. Get professionals for on-mike work. With the heavy investment in both the software and hardware, anything less than the best is a disservice to the public relations practitioner's employer or client.

Even with the professionals on your side, remember the earlier warning to know the message and know the audience. If the message or theme is ill-defined, the audience becomes so intrigued by the excitement on screen and the technology that is unfolding that it never hears or sees the vague message the corporation or organization hoped the audience would receive. The audience falls in love with R2D2 but cannot understand a word he says.

GUIDELINES FOR A/V PRESENTATIONS

As rules of thumb when presenting an audiovisual program to a group, have the bottom of the screen at least 4.5 ft above the floor; seat the nearest viewer no closer to the screen than twice the height of the screen and the most distant viewer no further from the screen than eight times the height of the screen. Following these guidelines, if we are projecting on a screen 5 ft high, the audience will be in an area ranging from 10 ft to 40 ft from the screen, and the top of the screen will be at least 9.5 ft above the floor. Even if the hotel provides a floor plan, the plan will probably not indicate ceiling height or locations of accordion-fold walls or hanging chandeliers. To minimize problems, the conscientious public relations practitioner visits the site well in advance of the program date.

The simplest of audiovisual programs requires a slide projector, tape recorder, speaker and speaker cable, projection stand, and screen, each with its attendant problems. The greater the sophistication, the greater the opportunity for problems. Technical gremlins lurk everywhere. The list of equipment includes a number of slide projectors, motion picture projectors, dissolver animators, dissolve units, projector controls, recorder-playback units, programmers, etc.

If the program is a complex multimedia presentation, the safest course is to bring in the professionals who produced the program, or a firm they recommend. These specialists can handle program setup and troubleshooting, including the myriad problems that can beset a complicated program. If your organization has made a considerable investment in a high technology multimedia production, proper presentation by trained professionals is money well spent.

SELECTING THE PROGRAM

The use for which the program is intended will determine in large measure the type of program to be produced. If the program is scheduled for permanent installation in a theater setting, a complex, multiimage, multiscreen presentation may be the answer. Equipment can be fixed in place, lenses matched, sound levels adjusted and balanced, so the program will be ready at an instant's notice.

Some organizations choose the complex A/V program for special occasions, even if it means relocating and setting up in hotel ballrooms or exhibition halls and accepting the expenses involved. Normally the contract between the organization and the software firm that produced the program includes transporting, setting up, rolling the show, and tearing down in the various locations. This is expensive, but these software firms understand the equipment, and their personnel are capable of handling the operation successfully. The show will go off without glitches and equipment will be moved with minimum chance of damage.

At least a half working day is standard for a two-person crew to set up the equipment, make proper adjustments, test run the program, and have enough cushion to repair or replace units that may fail.

One national organization developed a 6-screen, 12-projector program that toured the country. Two two-person crews devoted full time to the endeavor. An itinerary was established for each crew and each traveled in a single-axle closed van with hydraulic lift gate. Equipment was built into modules, the heaviest weighing approximately 200 pounds. The program was designed for rear screen projection; so, screens were also built into the modules.

Each truck carried a hundred folding chairs in addition to the program modules. Thus, the two-person crew could set up a little theater wherever their schedules took them (shopping malls, school gymnasiums, civic centers, ballrooms, or outdoor recreation areas).

The trucks also carried replacement projectors, dissolvers, programmers, and tape players. Crew members, although not electronics experts, had sufficient training to replace malfunctioning units and make simple repairs. Units requiring overhaul or major repair were air expressed to the repair facility.

The sponsor was a large organization with representatives in all sections of the country; so, the expense of the operation was justified. The total audience for the season approached a half million. Thus, the cost of the program was well within budget at less than 75 cents per person.

In the case of a smaller sponsoring organization, the effort usually is more modest. The public relations department normally develops an A/V program that emphasizes portability and simplicity if it is scheduled to go on the road. In most instances, a public relations staff member is responsible for transporting and setting up equipment, then presenting the program. A single- or twin-screen presentation with two or three

projectors, programmer-dissolves, and tape player is enough freight to
carry and enough responsibility for any individual.

DEVELOPING THE PROGRAM

SCRIPTING. After the audience has been determined and the
message formulated, the decision on the proper medium must be
made. Developing a rough script is the first step if it is to be an
audiovisual program.

Most public relations practitioners begin with a basic outline of the
presentation and hang the rough script on that framework. The script
must be built as a series of peaks building gradually to the climax. One
successful approach that has been employed frequently is to open with
a brief introduction to orient the audience; develop one or more incidents as historic background; and then lead to the point the program is
emphasizing.

The sponsoring organization, for example, an insurance company, aims to impress stockholders with its service to clients. The
program dramatizes incidents where the company's adjusters are on
the scene assisting policyholders within hours of a natural disaster; an
adjuster leaves home at midnight to assist a policyholder involved in
an auto accident; and a company representative finds a kitten to
replace the pet lost by a little girl in a fire. Now that the audience is well
into the program and interested in the narrative, they hear the message, "Service is our life."

After arriving at this miniclimax, the program changes pace and
highlights the historic development of the concept within the organization. "Our founder, Richard Doe, believed in service because he was a
super guy. He may not have realized it, but our company succeeded
because of that belief. People bought insurance from old Richard
because they knew he was concerned for them and would be there
when they needed him." Again, incidents from the past are incorporated into the script to show that "service has become a way of life for
us." The audience is led to today's operation where the company still
believes in service to the customer, another miniclimax.

The program has now built to the climax, the major selling point in
the A/V presentation. Stockholders learn that providing service has
guaranteed constant growth in the company and increasing profits.
Both benefit stockholders. So, the audience finds that "Service is our

life" because it is the right thing to do, but also it guarantees a prosperous company, and that means a greater return for the stockholders and an excellent outlook for the future. Now figures on growth and profits are shown the audience, proof that service is the answer. The program concludes with a restatement of the message, "Service is our life."

Many variations of this theme exist, but the basic outline is sound.

As the rough script is developed, the author determines how to address the audience. Special care is taken to avoid either talking down to them or over their heads.

Again as always, avoid jargon. Acronyms and verbal shorthand used by in-house specialists are a form of communication that will only confuse and irritate the audience.

When presenting figures in the graphics and the spoken word, avoid cluttering the message with precise numbers. Round off large numbers. "We have more than two million policies in effect" is more impressive and will be remembered longer than "The company has 2,013,768 policies in effect."

Have someone read the script aloud as it approaches final form. Catch the unwieldy and overlong sentences and the tough pronunciation combinations. Do not write a script that encourages a chronic case of "fumblemouth."

The effective A/V presentation is merciful to the audience. It gives listeners a chance to catch their breath and digest what has gone before. The narrator or narrators should be on-mike only about two-thirds of the total program. Thus, an 8-minute script results in a program at least 12 minutes long. If theater seating will be provided, greatest impact is achieved with an audiovisual program approximately 12 to 15 minutes long. If the A/V segment will be viewed by a standing audience, it should not run for more than 3 minutes.

Finally, based on the message and the audience, determine the type of narrator who will be most effective, a child, a senior citizen, a regional or foreign accent, a no-nonsense type, a relaxed actor, character actor, man or woman. Determine whether two or more narrators would be more effective than a single voice.

TAPING AND CASTING. With the script well in hand, the savvy A/V producer begins selection of music and sound effects. Musical style and the type of voices determine mood and pace of the show. Music and sound effects also serve to separate segments of long shows. Because audience attention span is limited, music can provide a brief change of pace, rekindling interest in the program.

However, indiscriminate use of music in audiovisual programming is a legally dangerous game. Using recordings from your private collection is a clear violation of the copyright law. The transgression may go undetected if the program has limited in-house circulation, but extensive public showing is risky. The organization's law and accounting departments will work overtime unless legal permission is obtained from each artist involved in the recording and from the composer and the record company. If currently popular music is used, be aware that permission may be difficult and expensive to obtain.

Initial contact is made with the copyright owner, but in some cases that may be only the beginning. There have been instances in which contracts call for a search by the musicians' union for each musician who participated in the recording. They along with the composer, arranger, and recording firm may have to be compensated, and the union must be paid for its search.

Hiring an artist to compose special music for the production is an alternative. Depending on the availability of quality talent, this could be more practical, less expensive, and certainly less time-consuming. If this route is followed, artists are engaged and a studio obtained for the recording session. Contracts must be negotiated with all involved. The public relations practitioner should get legal advice so that these agreements give full use of the recorded music to the company or institution paying the tab.

Yet another alternative, and the one most commonly used, is to work with a professional music library. The A/V program producer studies descriptions of compositions printed in the music library's catalog. The producer orders the records that seem appropriate from the description, reviews them, and selects those to be purchased. The remaining records are returned to the record library. The producer pays only for those records kept.

However, that is the least expensive part of obtaining music. The major expense is incurred in purchasing rights to that music. Using the records selected, the producer determines which parts of them will be used in the final production. Payment is by the minute, by the "needle drop," by the composition in total, or a flat fee for music rights for a certain length show. This latter course, purchasing rights to unlimited use of music for a specific length of A/V show, offers the producer the greatest flexibility.

Larger music libraries offer wide variety. The same general musical theme may be available as an introduction, a closing, or as background music for use with voice-over. The theme may be available, played by a small group or a full orchestra.

These recordings offered by commercial music libraries are especially composed for sale. The libraries normally offer all rights with the possible exception of the right to use the music on television. This right may be available by payment of an extra fee.

Proper selection of talent often makes or breaks an audiovisual program. The program may be designed so that in-house talent, a top executive or an individual from the assembly line, is the answer. These voices can lend credibility to the message being delivered.

Or outside talent may be hired. Going this route, however, should not lead automatically to contracting with a radio or television personality. They may sound too commercial and set the wrong mood for the show.

Shannon Jones, mentioned earlier, advocates auditioning individuals from theater groups. In many A/V programs, the script calls for acting rather than narrating. If the voice seems right for the message and the mood, rewrite the script if necessary to fit that voice. Whoever the talent, insist on ample rehearsal time. In most instances, talent is paid based on the length of the show, not on time spent in the studio.

If the voice is not precisely correct for the role, a well-equipped recording studio can modify voice quality for an A/V program. Within limits, the studio can alter pitch, speed, and timbre of the voice. The voice can be made to sound older or younger, darker or brighter; highs or lows can be filtered. Talented performers can alter their voices to fit the mood of the program. This, of course, is another reason for insisting on rehearsal of the talent.

SELECTING VISUALS AND PROGRAMMING. Choosing the best available visuals is vital to the success of an audiovisual program. Slides must be of uniformly high quality. A poor slide mixed with good slides is the one the audience remembers. Of course this means working exclusively with first generation slides (originals). Duplicates and duplicates of duplicates drag overall quality down because color saturation and contrast are adversely affected.

Visuals must tie into the script. The statement may seem gratuitous, but all too many A/V programs feature slides because they are "pretty," whether or not they apply to the words being spoken. It is an attractive trap, but avoid it.

The average A/V producer, when determining what slides will be used and where they will appear in the program, uses a light table—a large table with a translucent top illuminated by fluorescent tubes under the glass surface. The producer marks the approximate place in the script where specific slides are to be shown on screen. Slides are arranged in order on the table. Adequate working surface is available so that the slides can be organized for multiscreen productions.

When the show is actually programmed, cues are placed on the tape to coincide with specific words in the narration or at precise points in the musical sound track. The particular action is cued up because it is psychologically correct for the effect the producer seeks, quick cut, dissolve, fade, wash, blackout, animation, etc.

The end product (scripting, music, sound effects, casting, visuals, and programming) is a unified whole. It delivers the idea or message to the target audience. If it is an artistic triumph, so much the better.

MARKETING THE A/V PROGRAM. Many audiovisual programs are produced for one-time use before a particular audience. They may be for a stockholders meeting, a specific trade show, or to mark an anniversary. More often, however, shows are developed for repeated use. They may be a semipermanent feature of a visitor center or a program designed for repeated use before school groups, professional organizations, or civic clubs. They may be available to any interested audience.

When such a general interest A/V show is available, the organization's public relations department publicizes it by sending brochures and letters to persons responsible for arranging programs for special groups. Frequently the public relations staff includes information about A/V shows in circulars distributed to promote the organization's speakers bureau. In many cases, word-of-mouth advertising circulates information about the show. "Interesting program at Rotary today. It would fit in well as part of the seminar we're planning."

A representative from the organization, frequently from the public relations department, sets up and operates the equipment, introduces the show, and leads a discussion or answers questions following the presentation.

Regional offices of some national organizations have the A/V equipment required for presenting programs produced by the national headquarters and sent to these field offices. Promotional material frequently accompanies the A/V shows when they are sent to the field.

Visitor centers—the ultimate in mass display

Each of the many types of exhibitry has its use, but the major test of each is its cost effectiveness. Does it do what it is supposed to do at a reasonable cost per viewer or visitor? If the question cannot be answered affirmatively, the money is wasted, whatever the amount. A display panel costing $25 represents money down the drain if the public at which it is directed does not see the panel or chooses to ignore it. Conversely, the organization has a bargain if it spent $50,000 for a multimedia presentation that does in fact reach the intended audience and that audience receives the intended message.

So, if the organization is large enough and the message is sufficiently important, a million dollar visitor center can be justified, if it transmits the message correctly to a large enough segment of the public the organization wishes to reach, and if that audience interprets the message correctly.

Visitor centers range from a part of the reception area in the main office building set aside for the purpose to separate buildings especially designed for visitors. Exhibitry can be a few simple, inexpensive displays or a broad spectrum of media.

WHY A VISITOR CENTER?

Government agencies and many large private organizations and corporations invest in visitor centers. However, simply keeping up with the organizational or corporate Joneses is a poor reason for investing in a center. But it does happen. Top management is impressed by the facility opened by Organization B; therefore, Organization A must have a visitor center, a better one, of course.

Planning begins with little or no understanding of the basic need to be filled by the center. The organization turns to one of the many excellent professional firms in the design field to "tell us what we should have in our visitor center." The basic problem, of course, is that the organization has determined neither the message to be transmitted nor the audience at which it will be beamed. So, the professional firm is equally unaware of the message and audience.

The design firm conducts an exhaustive search in libraries and in the organization's files to determine information and artifacts to be exhibited. The end product may be an attractive museum, but although similarities exist, a visitor center is not a museum.

Using the National Park Service as an example, visitor centers are erected near some Park Service projects to inform the public about these tax-supported facilities. The centers are not designed to sell NPS but to explain the reasons these projects are maintained, how they are economically justified, and why tax money is spent for them. The centers explain what the NPS is and what it does. But of greater importance, they explain what the Park Service did here and why.

Thus, each visitor center is unique because each Park Service project differs from every other project. Nevertheless, there are similarities because each center provides some localized background information about the NPS, and project purposes can be similar from one location to another.

In those instances where a building will be constructed especially as a visitor center, the exhibit designer can have the best of all possible worlds, but sometimes, unfortunately, does not. A mistake frequently made in these situations is designing and erecting the structure before contracting with the exhibit specialist who will handle the exhibitry. A parallel would be to have an architect design a dirigible hangar without having any idea of the general shape or size of such an aircraft.

The exhibit specialists should be on the team with the architect before development of the first concept if the organization is to have an effective center. To work effectively, the exhibit specialist must exercise some control over design, including:

- All interior lighting, both natural and artificial. Mood is affected by light.
- Utility hookups, their locations and type. Some specialized displays require water, natural gas, or unique electrical service.
- Interior space. Outsize or uniquely shaped exhibit units may require unusual ceiling heights or wall placement.
- Textures, colors, and coverings. The impact of displays is affected by each of these and by drapery fabrics and floor coverings.

In fact, the overall architectural approach must match the general exhibitry design. For example, an ultramodern structure is most inappropriate for exhibitry emphasizing the organization's distant past or ties with the Old World.

Siting of the structure also affects architectural treatment. Many visitor centers incorporate an overlook as a principal feature. Thus, site topography affects architecture because the center is located where the visitors have the best view of the project, plant, or product. Examples include situations such as: a major oil company structure offering an excellent view of rigs working in a busy field; a center built in conjunction with a water resource project, on a high bluff overlooking the river valley; and an unobstructed view of the airfield from which an aircraft manufacturer's latest planes take off on test flights.

So, for greatest cost effectiveness, several decisions are made before bulldozers come on the site: (1) Determine the message; (2) Determine the audience; (3) Select the architect and exhibit firm and insist that they collaborate throughout design and construction; and (4) Select the proper site.

EXISTING BUILDING. Many visitor centers are built in existing structures to save money or preserve a historic building. Again in these situations, architect and exhibit specialist must work together until project completion.

Working with an existing structure, planners are subject to constraints not present when developing a new building. Such factors as location of doors frequently adversely affect visitor flow. Natural light may be difficult to control. Existing features may have to be incorporated into exhibit design. Heating, cooling, electrical service, and other utilities may require major modification. Shape of interior space may be difficult to adapt to exhibitry requirements.

In one such case, a theater was constructed in the only possible area within an existing structure. Designers had to accept the fact that two weight-bearing pillars were located precisely in the center of an otherwise ideal multimedia theater.

Nevertheless, attractive visitor centers have been developed in unlikely structures (e.g., a former assembly plant, a prefabricated aircraft hangar, a school building, and a carpenter shop). Most such successful adaptations require relatively heavy investments in both funds and ingenuity.

VISITOR CENTER FACILITIES. Ample parking and easy access are vital to any visitor center. The well-designed facility includes a lobby/reception area, exhibit areas, and restrooms. Many also include an enclosed or open observation deck, outdoor display areas, and special features such as a theater or multipurpose auditorium. All facilities must be accessible to handicapped persons.

The visitor center will feature a clear definition of the sponsor's objective or purpose. It answers questions about why it was built, who built it, and who needs it.

Resources around which exhibitry is designed include the purpose of the project, plant, or product; the geographic area; the general discipline of which this project, plant, or product is an example; and, in instances where the visitor center or project is named as a memorial, an explanation or recognition of the project namesake.

The visitor leaving a well-conceived center will feel that time spent was well invested. The experience entertained and educated.

THE ORGANIZATION'S ROLE. Even when exhibit specialists are called in, the sponsoring organization or firm alone can best handle certain aspects in development of a visitor center. Normally this means the public relations specialists are the persons involved. They are better equipped to handle the particular types of problems that can arise.

For example, full-time staff members "know where the bodies are hidden"; they are in the best position to know where needed information may be found. They can play a lead role in creating the story line and the story-flow pattern that will be carried throughout the visitor center. And although the outside firm will recommend the proper vehicles for carrying the message, in-house representatives will make the final decisions on media to be used in the facility.

In-house specialists are far more knowledgeable about the organization, purpose, and theme of the center than outside experts. So, the in-house specialists must accept responsibility for outlining scripts and display copy that will go into the center.

The consulting firm, on the other hand, develops the interpretive concepts, complete to architectural renderings of the various areas and separate exhibit units. These specialists determine hardware and software requirements. They frequently advise on selection of the fabricator.

This implies that the consulting firm does not handle final fabrication and installation of exhibitry. Separate contracts are the practice with many organizations, based on the assumption that every firm is not equally proficient at each type of exhibitry. One may be an industry leader in executing static displays while a second may excel in development of audiovisual programs.

A firm hired to develop only the concepts, therefore, is not constrained in its design by its own limitations in designing or working specific media. If necessary, the successful bidder on the fabrication and installation can subcontract in areas where its skills are limited.

MAKING IT WITH THE PUBLIC. The successful visitor center is one in which:

1. Visitors are met and made welcome as soon as they enter.
2. Visitors are never bored.
3. Visitors hear, see, and feel a story related to the project, plant, product, or organizational purpose in some way (by an explanation of its use, history, geology, etc.).
4. The showcase approach and the flat wall display are avoided. Even in simple, low-budget centers, designers can employ three-dimensional displays.
5. Printed copy is at a minimum because visitors will resist reading.
6. Gobbledygook and technical jargon are avoided.
7. The staff has been trained to handle basic equipment maintenance on working models and A/V equipment. The practice is an economy move, but of far greater importance, the training overcomes staff resistance and fear of the unknown. The center also will have fewer program interruptions.

Summary

Exhibitry is a form of communication that has been widely used for centuries. The most successful craftsmen in the Middle Ages used signs to publicize their talents and to help potential customers locate their shops.

Media employed in today's exhibitry may be as simple as the placards at political conventions. At the other extreme, its complexity is limited only by the imaginations of the talented men and women who develop the concepts.

Exhibitry is communication, but it must have direction. To succeed, practitioners using exhibitry must understand clearly the message or theme of the particular display and the audience for whom it is intended.

Complex audiovisual programming is a comparative newcomer in the public relations practitioner's assortment of tools.

Used properly, however, modern A/V is tremendously effective. The successful A/V program develops a major theme, then graphics, photos, film, script, cast, and programming are developed into an integrated whole. The unified program transmits the message or theme to the target audience with impact.

The visitor center is the ultimate in exhibitry. It combines a number of exhibit media into a cohesive whole, an experience. Centers range from a small part of an organization's reception area to entire buildings constructed for this single purpose.

Visitor centers are developed in conjunction with an organization's or government agency's project, testing area, production facility, headquarters, etc. Large fairs and expositions routinely feature entire buildings designed and constructed by an organization or agency as visitor centers.

Fundamental to all successful organization exhibitry is a clear understanding of the message or theme to be transmitted and the audience for whom it is intended. The principle applies whether the exhibitry is a church bulletin board or a multiscreen, multimedia extravaganza.

Exercises

1. List a dozen family names, other than those mentioned in the text, that reflect an ancestral occupation.

2. Select six well-known slogans that can be identified readily with an organization or product, even though that organization's name is not part of the slogan.

3. Develop a new slogan and a trademark for one of the city's leading businesses or organizations. Explain your selection.

4. Design a three-dimensional, static display for use by your hometown in promoting tourism.

5. When could the above display be shown during the next year?

6. Develop a theme for a state-sponsored visitor center to be built on a major highway. Describe exhibitry to be incorporated into the center.

Case study

Riverton, a city of 25,000, deserves its reputation as "a good place to live and grow." Its temperate climate results in temperatures that seldom exceed 85 degrees or drop below 20 degrees. Most outdoor sports are available within a radius of 50 miles because of the proximity of the Tinhorn Mountains and a chain of natural lakes.

Despite its size, the city is served by three major airlines and two railroads. Two interstate highways intersect at Riverton, and the city is on a navigable river.

Trade center for a rich agricultural area, Riverton has manufacturing plants in such diverse fields as electronics, automobile sub-assemblies, and sports equipment. A branch of the state university and a private college are located in the city. Riverton has four banks, two hospitals, a community theater, and an excellent school system.

The community prospered until the largest electronics firm closed. Recent electronics developments made much of their product line obsolete, and they failed to adjust. Consequently, 8.5 percent of the local work force is unemployed, most skilled workers and technicians.

To help solve the problem, the Riverton Industrial Development Corporation was formed by local business interests. You are the only salaried employee of the corporation. As your first effort, the corporation's directors suggest that you develop a 5-minute audiovisual program promoting Riverton as a potential industry site.

- Write the script.
- Describe the graphics to accompany the script.
- Develop a marketing plan for the audiovisual show, including audiences that should be reached and the events or methods to use in establishing the contacts.

Suggested readings

Alten, Stanley R. *Audio in Media.* Belmont, Calif.: Wadsworth Publishing Co., 1981.

Beiswinger, George L. "The A/V Presentation: What They Never Taught You in School." *Public Relations Journal,* September 1980.

Coelln, Ott. "A/V: The Business Side of 'Picture Street.'" *Public Relations Journal,* September 1980.

Griswold, George. "A/V Reaches for the Sky." *Public Relations Journal,* September 1979.

Leech, Thomas. "It's Show Time." *Communicator's Journal,* March/April 1984.

Peck, David. "Tips for Exceptional Exhibits." *Communication World,* March 1985.

Rafe, Stephen C. "Problems and Pitfalls of Using A/V." *Public Relations Journal,* September 1979.

Rimer, Irving. "Cable as a Teach-in Tool." *Public Relations Journal,* September 1980.

Sutherland, Don. "Designing Audiovisuals? Just Think Backward." *Communication World,* January 1985.

———. "Training the Client in Audiovisuals." *Communication World,* March 1985.

Tauber, Caren. "Video Answers the H&R Block Knock." *Communication World,* January 1985.

Wood, Joan H. "How to Arrange Successful Media Tours." *Public Relations Journal,* May 1985.

15 The speech and public relations

The practitioner as ghostwriter

The cathedral clock tolled midnight. An executive hurrying toward an elevator in the deserted building turned a corner and almost collided with a shadowy figure. "Gadfry, you startled me! I thought you were a ghost."

The figure said, "How do you know I'm not?" and disappeared.

The wraith was probably on the executive's public relations staff, not a ghost but a ghostwriter. Most public relations practitioners spend a significant number of working hours as ghostwriters. The profession dates back centuries, and in today's complex society it is a talent in increasing demand. Corporate, organizational, and governmental officials lean heavily upon public relations staffs to produce articles, books, and speeches under executives' by-lines. Top executives are too involved in their primary duties to spend time writing their own material. Or in many cases, the executives do not have the skills to develop articles, books, or speeches, but they are expected to publish and to make speeches nevertheless.

Those who learn to work well with their ghostwriters gain reputations as top speakers and writers. Success for them begins with discovering a talented ghostwriter, then relying on that individual's judgment. The executive's contribution is vital to team success, of course, because he must devote considerable time to the endeavor and be able to insert his own personality into the finished work.

Ghostwriters produce a variety of material, but speeches are their forte. Skilled speechwriters are rare; therefore good ones are well paid. Theirs is an elite job, an honored profession, although its practitioners lead a shadowy existence. The best stay in the background, seldom acknowledged publicly for their skill.

Most widely known are the members of the speechwriting corps

339

employed in the White House. Almost all American presidents rely on professional speechwriters. However, the best speakers in that long, distinguished line indelibly imprinted their own personalities on work produced by their writers.

In one of the most quoted speeches by a president, Franklin D. Roosevelt raised a statement of fact to literature. As originally drafted, the opening sentence read. "Yesterday, December 7, 1941, a date which will live in world history, the United States of America was simultaneously and deliberately attacked by naval and air forces of the Empire of Japan."

Roosevelt retained the basic wording but by judicious editing transformed it to, "Yesterday, December 7, 1941—a date which will live in infamy—the United States of America was suddenly and deliberately attacked by naval and air forces of the Empire of Japan."

In the June 23, 1985, issue of *Parade Magazine*, Lloyd Shearer reported, "It is no secret that the Bergen-Belsen speech (delivered by President Reagan May 5, 1985, at the West German site of the former concentration camp) was written by Ken Khachigian." Shearer noted further that the San Clemente attorney was Reagan's chief speechwriter early in his presidency and that he had performed similar service for Presidents Nixon and Ford.

According to the *New York Times*, a number of major figures in world history depended on ghostwriters. Evidence points to Seneca as author of Emperor Nero's speeches; Alexander Hamilton is thought to have written George Washington's Farewell Address; and Mark Twain was the probable author of *The Autobiography of Ulysses S. Grant*. (From "The Ghostwriters: Who Is Writing for Whom?" by Dudley Clendinen, the *New York Times*, July 7, 1980.)

Ghostwriters lurk in the shadows behind many top-flight comedians. Commenting on the fact that one of his peers employed a large staff of comedy writers, Fred Allen said, "He couldn't ad lib a belch after a Hungarian dinner."

And the practice of subjugating self should be adopted by anyone serving as a ghostwriter, whether developing a full-length book or a speech for delivery before the local Rotary Club. When digging for information within the organization, the able and politically savvy speechwriter will say, "I'm helping the boss write a speech," not, "I'm writing a speech for the boss."

The public relations practitioner is drawn into ghostwriting, especially speeches, because he is on the payroll as a writer, a literate individual. In addition, as a staff member, he is expected to be familiar with the organization and with the executive's approach to subjects that should be introduced into speeches.

The correct approach

KNOW THE TERRITORY

To be effective, the speechwriter must understand the organization, know what it does, how it is organized, its history, its position in the community and nation, its goals and aspirations, and the prevailing attitudes of top executives toward sensitive issues. Almost without exception, audiences look upon speeches as coming from the organization, not just as opinions of the speaker.

The speech will have the effect of organizational policy. In fact, statements made publicly become organizational policy. This is a heavy responsibility for the speechwriter, but on occasion it places that individual in the unique position of making policy for the organization, if the executive does not change the speech. That is a privilege denied all but the top echelon in any organization.

The effect of many public utterances by top executives goes far beyond the audience that heard the original presentation. Significant remarks frequently are reported by the news media. Some speeches are reprinted, and many times word-of-mouth spreads the impact well beyond the original audience. Thus, the speechwriter must be aware of the possible impact of what is written.

A rash political statement, for example, will reflect on the organization, speaker, and certainly on the speechwriter. The impact of even a casual remark was dramatically emphasized by President Jimmy Carter when he referred to "Montezuma's revenge" during a state visit to Mexico.

Speeches by many executives must be apolitical. For example, the top executive from a corporation holding large defense contracts would be ill-advised to speak out on political candidates or issues. Furthermore, it should be noted that the practice is illegal for Civil Service employees.

MEET THE SPEAKER. Researching and writing a speech for delivery by another is never done in an ivory tower; it cannot be accomplished by a recluse. In the ideal relationship, the writer and the speaker work closely together. The speechwriter becomes familiar with the executive's official biography, reads memos and letters written by the executive, studies speeches delivered in the past by the executive.

The person who writes speeches for delivery by another must explore many avenues to learn about the person who will present the message. The executive's secretary is an excellent pipeline. No one in the organization knows the individual as well, from speaking habits to personal life. The secretary knows anecdotes, personality traits, and favorite words and phrases.

THE AUDIENCE. A vital part of preliminary research is obtained through contact with the group sponsoring the executive's appearance. The person in charge of programs or the group's president can help the writer clearly define the type of presentation expected. The writer can learn whether the group heard recently from a speaker on the same or a similar topic or from a person in a position similar to that held by the executive.

The sponsoring group can answer questions concerning the amount of time allotted to the program, whether a question-and-answer session is expected, the type of information the group wants covered, and whether visual aids are needed.

The writer will learn audience composition (men, women, or both), economic level, occupational mix, approximate age of the average member, etc. And of course, the writer will learn the estimated size of the audience, whether any of the executive's business or social acquaintances will attend, and the expected dress (casual, informal, or formal). The writer will learn the purposes, goals, and brief history of the sponsoring group.

At this point, the writer puts everything known on paper, including subject, audience composition, etc. The paper outlines what has gone before, what this speech should accomplish, and how audience questions will be answered.

FACE-TO-FACE. The next step after this exploratory research is a personal visit with the executive for whom the speech will be written. The writer need not have an outline developed prior to the meeting. Rather, the writer and executive discuss the major topic to be developed in the speech and determine jointly what the speech is to accomplish.

If the executive does not object, a tape recorder is used during this conference or interview. However, the writer should take notes in addition to using the recorder. The tape captures the executive's exact words and phrasing, and the ideas are on tape as they flowed in conversation.

Above all, the writer must remember that the executive is in charge. So, let the executive talk. Do not interrupt. The writer is there to ask questions, not to make speeches. The writer will stick to the point and establish the best possible working relationship. The interview continues as long as the executive is willing to talk.

This first interview with the speaker-designate is critical. Coming out of the meeting, the writer must completely understand the assignment or the interview was wasted time. The writer must know why the speaking engagement was accepted and what the organization or the executive will gain from this appearance.

Following the first meeting, the writer researches the subject in library sources and by conducting additional interviews with other authorities within the organization.

During the second visit to discuss the speech with the executive, the writer will lay out the information learned to date, including an in-depth analysis of the audience, and present a suggested outline of the speech.

Now the writer is ready to write.

Focusing the speech

An invitation to speak is not an invitation to deliver a briefing. To repeat an old story, the sponsoring group asked for the time of day not how to build a watch. So, focus on a major point, an idea, or a single thrust. Determine the single element and develop it as vividly as possible. In days past, executives were overexposed. Subjects of speeches were selected for their entertainment value and without regard for any benefit to the organization. Goodwill, they said. Today, however, such an approach is recognized as a waste of valuable time and expensive talent.

Executive talent in today's organization is a resource in short supply. Avoid diluting that talent by overexposure. Determine objectives the organization seeks and accept speaking engagements that hit that objective. Seek top audiences. Public speaking by organization executives is a programmed activity. It is as deliberate and well planned as any other aspect of the organization's public relations program.

Top executives have a specific role to play in an organization's public relations program. Conscientious effort is devoted to having something for them to say that is significant; consequently, in most cases, they speak in specifics, terms related to the purpose and business of their organization. This "something to say" is evident in speeches developed for top executives following the preparation outlined here.

TYPES OF SPEECHES

Every speech is developed to evoke audience response, some action or reaction by them. The action may be as significant as casting a vote or purchasing stock, or it may be as inconsequential as drawing laughter or applause.

Most speeches drafted by ghostwriters for organizational executives will be speeches of persuasion or those designed to transmit information or instructions.

PERSUASION. Demands on their time are such that today's major executives are increasingly selective in accepting speaking engagements. Most invitations accepted must promise return benefits to the individual executive or the organization. The platform is an opportunity to put forth an idea important to the individual or the organization. And the well-crafted, effectively delivered speech will help the audience understand that idea or lead its members to act favorably toward the concept. Thus, the prominent executive normally delivers speeches of persuasion. The persuasive speech is designed to influence the audience, causing them to modify their opinions or take a specific action.

Today's prominent executives deliberately strive to comment on public policy and usually speak in specific terms related to their own organization or industry. Some executives, for example, analyze their organization's policies and public policies that affect their operation in public speeches. In any case, the subject matter is not determined in a haphazard fashion. Objectives of the public speaking program for the organization or industry are established and the basic program planned for a year or more in advance.

In the modern business climate, more executives are speaking out on overregulation by government, international trade policies, environmental issues, and other important topics. This is a marked departure from the practice of earlier days when prominent executives spoke on less controversial subjects and more in glowing generalities.

INFORMATION AND INSTRUCTION. The organizational speechwriter frequently is called upon to deliver presentations to instruct or inform. Audiences may be stockholders, employees, potential employees or customers, and civic or professional groups that the executive seeks to keep well informed on operations of the organization. Classroom lectures are a type of informational or instructional speech, as is the testimony prepared for delivery before a congressional committee by an industry or governmental agency representative.

Frequently these speeches contain complex facts and detailed figures. Therefore, many such presentations are supplemented by visual aids (slides, films, models, flip charts, etc.) to accurately convey the technical details to the audience. Quite often copies of the information are distributed to the audience.

Circumstances vary, of course, but in many such presentations, the speaker reads from a prepared text, minimizing misunderstanding or transmission of inaccurate data. An oft-repeated mistake made by individuals presenting this type of material, however, is their unwillingness to devote sufficient time to practicing the presentation. "After all, the whole speech is written. All I have to do is read it."

This attitude results in a delivery that sounds as though it is being read, and most people read poorly. Unfamiliarity with the script leads the unwary to emphasize the wrong words or phrases, mispronounce words, read through punctuation, and in general, botch the presentation and bore the audience. The speaker must practice, practice, practice. The presentation is important to the organization or it would not be developed in such detail.

ENTERTAINMENT. Executives and other prominent persons frequently are called upon to entertain an audience. For many this can be preprogrammed disaster. Despite weak and mock-modest protests to the contrary, most are convinced that they have a well-developed sense of humor. But as the Gershwin song says, "It Ain't Necessarily So." The problem may not surface until the individual is drafted as master of ceremonies or toastmaster. The newly crowned emcee contacts the public relations speechwriter with a request to "figure out the seating arrangement and give me a few jokes." When the emcee bombs, the stock comment to the speechwriter is, "*Your* jokes didn't go over with that crowd."

Humor is neither demanded nor expected from every master of

ceremonies or toastmaster. If the program is kept on track and rolling, the emcee has performed professionally and competently.

Introducing guests and speakers is a major function of the master of ceremonies or toastmaster. Again, this simple task frequently is handled poorly. It can be a bitter learning process for the public relations practitioner when well-laid plans splinter at the hands of an inept master of ceremonies. Too often a program chairman or emcee obtains a biography of an individual who must be introduced. Then, the guest of honor and the entire audience are embarrassed as the emcee reads it all as an introduction. The audience hears about birthplace, family members, schools attended, home addresses, and childhood diseases.

The best introductions are one or two sentences long and include something other than academic degrees and basic biographic data. An effective technique is sparse biographic data plus anecdotes. Another effective method is to tie the introduction to the guest's hobby or avocation.

Shun the prepared obituary. Keep the introduction brief and to the point.

POTPOURRI. Speeches of welcome or tribute, remarks prepared for retirements or "hails and farewells," presentations of awards, or remarks commemorating special events or holidays should be prepared with the same thoughts as those applying to introductions. Be brief and to the point. Avoid a comprehensive recital of history and look to the anecdotal approach as an interesting way to make the necessary point(s).

Developing the speech

As noted, writing is the simplest part of preparing a speech. Much more taxing are researching the event and the speech topic and, finally, editing the manuscript.

RESEARCH

Initial steps in researching the presentation, as discussed, include learning about the speaker, the event, and the audience, and determining the type of presentation expected and most readily accepted by the audience. At this point, many successful speechwriters think through the topic before obtaining additional information. They determine the main theme of the message and the major points to be made.

The speechwriter canvasses resident experts. If the executive is scheduled to discuss the present and future status of the organization, the speechwriter picks the brains of experts in marketing or sales. If the speech concerns interaction with regulatory agencies, the writer explores the topic with the organization's legal counsel. If the speaker will explore future technology, the ghostwriter meets with research scientists and industrial designers. Whatever the subject, the writer gleans all possible information from in-house experts who understand what is going on and have a firm grasp of the organization's role as it applies to the subject.

For research beyond that easily available from in-house authorities and other individuals, the speechwriter draws on the many invaluable sources available in organization libraries. Exhausting this source, the writer researches in public and nearby college libraries.

In addition to obvious sources such as encyclopedias, texts, and trade publications, the researcher studies *The Reader's Guide to Periodical Literature*, *Vital Speeches*, indices printed by various publications, and other sources.

In this age of knowledge explosion, a dramatic tool available to researchers is the computerized information bank. Nexis, Lexis, Lockheed's Dialog service, and the Information Bank, a subsidiary of the *New York Times*, are among the leaders in this growing field.

The Lockheed service provides instant access to millions of references and abstracts in all fields of study. In addition, Newsearch is a data base exclusive to the Lockheed Dialog service that provides indexing of leading newspapers, popular magazines, and journals. Subscribers type requests on a terminal connected by telephone lines to Lockheed's computers in California. The computers respond with a list of articles on the topic, displayed on a videoscreen or on a print-out.

The *Times'* Information Bank provides detailed abstracts of articles from a number of general circulation newspapers; business, international affairs, and scientific publications; and other leading periodicals. The user specifies the topic, the extent of coverage required plus a single name or a combination of subjects. The abstract retrieved is displayed on the computer terminal together with a bibliographic citation for the original article.

Although an involved process, through computerized data banks, information is available to the speechwriter on almost any subject.

WRITING THE SPEECH

Each part of a typical speech must be a moving part. Nothing is wasted. Thus, the opening, body, and closing must each affect the audience and get a reaction from them. In its simplest form, each speech has three parts.

THE OPENING. The first part of the speech is designed to gain audience attention. An anecdote illustrates or dramatizes the topic. A rhetorical question or shocking declaration may also serve to gain attention. Some speakers employ humor to relax the audience and cause them to listen closely to what follows.

THE BODY. The speaker explains the topic with emphasis on how the audience is affected because of the topic and, frequently, a brief history of the topic, at least that part of its history that ties the audience into the topic. The speaker develops the points to be made about the topic, explains how the proposed developments will work, their cost, how they will impact the audience.

THE CLOSING. The topic is wrapped up in the closing as the speaker reviews points made earlier, draws conclusions, summarizes, and appeals to the audience for the desired action. This can range from simply understanding or even approving recent activities of the speaker's organization to making a substantial investment of time or money.

WRITING TECHNIQUES

While writing, allow the words to flow. Write. Do not edit as you write. If a mental block arises on a particular point, leave a blank to be filled in later. The writing need not be done in a particular order. Writing nonsense? Go ahead. Edit later.

Basically, oral writing is vivid writing. Use vivid verbs, few adjectives, and write in the active voice. If the speaker talks in the idiom, write in the idiom. Use short sentences and simple words. And with most audiences, avoid jargon. If for some obscure reason it must be included in the speech, define the jargon.

Remember that old-fashioned oratory is dead. So in the drive to find an original way of expressing a thought, avoid becoming too flamboyant. Many phrases that read well are impossible to say or sound foolish.

No inflexible rules exist in developing or delivering speeches. However, some techniques or principles may work well for some speakers and not for others.

1. *Avoid the lengthy preamble.* Some speakers go into such an involved windup, they seem never to throw the pitch.

2. *Avoid apologies.* The good speaker does not apologize for presumed shortcomings, either in delivery or content, because the speech must reflect positive thinking from opening to conclusion. Certainly, the speaker avoids any hint of apology for the message being delivered.

3. *Identify with the audience.* "Here's what we are doing. Here's how you are involved."

4. *Do not rely heavily on outside research.* It is valuable and necessary background, but the effective speech comes from the writer and the speaker who draw on personal resources and experiences.

5. *Avoid overly long quotations.* Rework the quotation so that the thought is fresh and in the speaker's own words. Thus, although a long quotation may have triggered the writer's thoughts, the statement becomes original and cogent. An occasional short quotation is quite acceptable, however.

6. *Make complicated information memorable.* Rather than relate facts and statistics, round off numbers or provide comparisons which are easily remembered. "Our total investment was $14,987,811" is far less memorable than the bald assertion that "We spent almost 15 million dollars on the process," or better yet, "This process cost almost as much as an F-16 fighter plane."

7. *Use rhetorical questions.* Routinely, these are used just to produce an effect, not to obtain a reply. But do answer such questions. The device is effective; however, the speaker must be comfortable using rhetorical questions before the writer considers incorporating them into a speech. Some speakers are embarrassed by asking an audience, "Do you believe in miracles?" or "What animal is man's best friend?"

EDITING

Moving from the writing process to editing, the ghostwriter must keep an important fact in mind: this is the executive's speech, not the writer's. If the executive does not accept the first draft, or the second, or the third, that is the executive's prerogative. The object of the exercise is to develop a speech that satisfies the executive, not to produce a masterpiece that pleases the writer.

When editing, once again remember that the speech is for the ear, not the eye. Short sentences. Strong verbs. Few adjectives. A relatively basic vocabulary. Avoid jargon and eliminate acronyms. Be specific.

The final check will help eliminate any parts of the speech that talk down to or over the heads of the audience. The vocabulary is adjusted to the audience because the overall aim of any speech is communication. It must be delivered in language the audience understands readily.

Humor in speeches

Frequently, the executive who accepts a speaking engagement assumes that success in the assignment will be measured on a laugh meter. All too often, the speaker assumes this means telling a series of jokes, and the problems begin. The executive will better serve the organization by demonstrating a ready wit, a keen sense of humor. There is a difference. The comedian amuses by telling jokes, a stand-up routine. The executive with a ready wit will use clever anecdotes or well-turned phrases rather than memorized jokes.

The joke known to the public relations practitioner and the speaker is probably known by some members of the audience, and they may have the talent for telling it far better than the executive. Nothing is so deflating as to have someone say, "That's a good story, but the way I heard it, the salesman says to the farmer . . ."

Unless the speaker rose through the ranks from stand-up comedian to executive, the best advice is to avoid the "funny story." However, if the executive insists on jokes, the public relations practitioner can create the jokes or, failing that, research *old* sources. Dig into copies of *The Reader's Digest*, *Saturday Evening Post*, and other publications that are 20 or 30 years old. Rewrite and update the old stories, and develop humor that is relevant and focuses attention on the subject at hand.

Jokes should not be written into the script but provided as a separate list. Insert a key word in the script indicating where the speaker could use a specific joke. The reason for using the key word approach is that a joke poorly told is not quite as boring as a joke poorly read.

GUIDELINES TO HUMOR

At its best, humor in a serious speech can relieve tension and gain audience attention, making them more receptive to the speaker's ideas. A good opening reassures the audience that their time may be well spent. But remember the purpose of the speech. The writer is not sending the executive on the nightclub circuit as a comedian. Two or three laughs should be the maximum in the opening of a serious speech. More than that and the audience becomes bored with the amateur comic or views the entire speech as a comedy routine.

A wise writer and speaker avoid humor aimed at ethnic, religious, and political groups or at personal afflictions. Supposed humor at the expense of these individuals is cruel, unthinking, and counterproductive. Any speaker fails if a single member of the audience is offended.

Avoid off-color stories. They may be acceptable in nightclubs and at smokers, but in other situations they make the audience uncomfortable and destroy the speaker's rapport with the audience.

The incident may have played only a minor role in the outcome, but even that possibility should be warning enough for any speaker.

The State Adjutant General spoke before an officers call of the National Guard. His address consisted of a few solid points hidden in a long recitation of barnyard humor and bedroom wisecracks. His audience included a major who found the presentation embarrassing and distasteful. Two years later the major was elected governor of the state. Within six months of the election, the general was retired and replaced.

If a single member of the audience is offended, the speaker failed.

INGREDIENTS

No deeply hidden secret can be revealed to make a writer or speaker succeed with humor. The quip, story, or witty remark may involve exaggeration, the unexpected, satire, or a jab at human foibles and pretensions. Distilled to basics, successful humor is a combination of audience conditioning, the personality of the speaker as perceived by the audience, the topic, the method of presentation, and timing.

The practiced speaker is well into the story or anecdote before the audience realizes what is happening. The story is never overbuilt, and it is never telegraphed. Only the amateur will dare the audience to laugh with statements such as, "I got a laugh out of this one," "That reminds me of a story," or "Have you heard the one about . . ."

The experienced writer includes only anecdotes that fit the topic. A

pointless story confuses the audience and causes it to forget momentarily the ideas the speaker is developing.

The writer will develop anecdotes that fit the speaker's personality.
An urbane intellectual must have unusually professional platform talent
to use anecdotes involving the Beverly Hillbillies or Joe McPug, the
punch-drunk boxer. So, developing anecdotes that fit the speaker is
another compelling reason for the writer to learn as much as possible
about the person who will deliver the speech.

Generally, the speaker who hopes to succeed with humor must be
willing to invite the audience to laugh at him. Audiences will laugh at the
speaker's shortcomings because it makes the speaker seem human, a
person with whom they can identify. Conversely, the speaker with a
serious message must be extremely careful in personalizing an anecdote in which another person is the brunt of the joke. Even if they laugh,
the audience may label the speaker insensitive.

When employing humor, successful speakers use quips, witty
expressions, or word plays to illustrate a point. The overly long story
often disappoints the audience. Accomplished speakers seldom relate
a pat joke to a personal experience because, too often, the audience is
familiar with the joke. Good speakers never overstay their welcome.
They always leave the audience wanting more. No speaker was ever
convicted for leaving the platform too soon.

The speaker who intends to use humor will practice, trying the
anecdote on friends, relatives, co-workers—anyone who will listen—
before using it in a speech. Thus the speaker learns whether the story
will succeed and the phrasing and timing that will draw a laugh.

TIMING

Far more important than the quality of the joke or anecdote itself is
the timing. The speaker whose timing is good is the speaker who is in
tune with the audience. Timing is knowing when to deliver the punch
line, the tempo of delivery, and when to pause.

Timing is not a memorized thing. The individual who handles
humor well seldom relates the same anecdote or joke twice in the same
way. The delivery—the timing—is geared to the particular audience
because no two audiences are exactly alike.

The speaker or the person helping another prepare for the platform
will work on timing by practicing to develop familiarity with the material, greater self-confidence, and a feel for proper timing.

Jack Benny drew more and greater laughs from the single word

"Well!" than most comedians realize from an entire routine. His secret was flawless timing.

SOURCES

Good comedy writers find material everywhere. They are unusually keen observers who spot comic potential in the actions of others as well as in their own experiences. And they adapt the material to the situation and to the audience they face.

The successful comedy writer is an avid reader. Much topical humor was born in news stories read or heard by comedy writers. They pore over newspapers and magazines. They adapt cartoon lines to spoken comedy. They revise and rewrite the tens of thousands of anecdotes and jokes printed in hundreds of books each year.

Successful speakers listen to and learn from other speakers. They revise situations and lines from stage productions, motion pictures, and television shows. They are always "on duty," researching material that can be adapted for their use. Many successful speechwriters and speakers maintain extensive card files of material gathered through the years. They learn to twist a phrase and develop the methods of writing a story that work best for their style of delivery. And they write, write, and rewrite until the material suits them and their audiences.

Hints for more effective speaking

One frustration for the public relations practitioner preparing the individual for a platform appearance is that most executives have schedules too cramped to permit adequate preparation, and sometimes they are reluctant to accept advice and criticism from a staff member. Resolution of the dilemma is difficult, perhaps impossible. The successful public relations practitioner relies on tact and diplomacy in dealing with the executive to overcome these frustrating problems.

SWEATY PALMS

Accept the fact that everyone is apprehensive about speaking before an audience. Nervousness or anxiety is natural. Some of the greatest speakers and stage personalities admit to having butterflies before stepping before an audience.

A certain amount of nervousness can help the speaker. The

tension, if properly channeled, results in a more forceful presentation, and the excitement of the moment is transmitted to the audience.

The speaker should be fully briefed on the size, composition, and special interests of the audience. An individual is more relaxed and self-assured speaking before persons he knows and understands.

Encourage the executive to become completely familiar with the speech, practicing the address before a small in-house audience if possible. A bonus gained from adequate practice is that the typewritten text may be put aside and the executive can work from notes. Any speaker comes across better when working from notes than when reading a text. The speaker is more relaxed, establishes the all important eye contact, and can gesture if done naturally and appropriately.

If the text must be read to assure accuracy, the speaker should be familiar enough with the opening and closing paragraphs to leave the text momentarily. The opening and closing are the moments when the speaker establishes rapport and drives home the major points of the presentation.

The speaker working from a prepared text must avoid pitfalls associated with reading to an audience, the most obvious being the tendency to speak in a boring monotone. The monotone delivery can be avoided if the speaker will mark the text. Pencilled slashes (///) can indicate pauses of varying lengths. Underscoring or highlighting words and phrases will pinpoint places for emphasis. Additional stage directions can be noted on the copy to help the individual sound like a speaker rather than a reader, but the copy should be annotated by the speaker, not the writer. Only in this way can the instructions be meaningful and the text adapted to the individual's speaking style.

MANNERISMS

The good speaker selects several audience members located in different parts of the room and establishes eye contact, focusing on each in turn. He is conversing directly with the six or eight different individuals but gives the audience the impression that each of them has established eye contact.

The speaker must not use the lectern as a shield to ward off the audience. Too many assume the lectern is placed before them to be mutually supportive. It is quite unnecessary for the speaker to lean on the lectern for support and equally fruitless for the speaker to clutch the lectern as if it were about to collapse. The lectern is simply a convenient device to hold notes and a microphone.

The person who stands erect, independent of the lectern, projects a positive image. Constant movement is distracting; however, the individual should shift body position occasionally to help overcome nervousness and show animation. Occasionally placing a hand on the lectern is no problem, but the speaker should not lean forward on the lectern. If the movement is natural, even putting one hand in a pocket is acceptable provided the speaker avoids jingling keys and coins. A gesture is appropriate if it emphasizes a point, but only if the movement is natural. A stiff, learned gesture detracts from the impact of the remark.

An effective speaker looks and acts natural by using body language for emphasis, varying volume and tone, changing speed of delivery, and using facial expressions to convey meaning.

DRESSING THE PART

The physical appearance of the executive will have a direct impact on audience acceptance of the message being delivered. So, the public relations practitioner must assume responsibility for guiding the executive who has limited experience before audiences. The practitioner must help the executive appear professional, a credible representative of the organization, both in the method of delivery and in dress. The executive must be well groomed but not ostentatious.

Advise men that a dark suit with a light blue or white shirt is most appropriate. The outfit is complemented with freshly polished shoes, dark socks, and a necktie featuring a small pattern or conservative stripes. The suit jacket is buttoned before the man rises to approach the lectern.

Practitioners with this responsibility normally advise women executives to wear relatively conservative attire, possibly the tailored look, with a minimum of jewelry. Large colorful pieces or dangling earrings distract the audience. And if the speech is filmed, flares produced by highly reflective jewelry can be disastrous.

Advise speakers who need reading glasses to avoid removing and replacing them repeatedly. If the person cannot see the audience with glasses in place, advise the speaker to pretend to see the audience. Leave the glasses alone.

Speakers bureaus

Organizations have used formal speakers bureaus to serve their communities for more than a half century. The range of subjects and the types of speakers have varied widely from organization to organization. However, today most corporations are convinced that the crises in society are too great to have their speakers bureaus operate without a tightly structured series of topics and specific goals. A growing trend exists within these organizations to seek audiences where their speakers can address topics of future social concern as viewed by the organization. The aim is to develop these topics while there is sufficient time to have an impact on whatever is happening, be it social trend or legislative action. Thus, from the original purpose of creating goodwill, many speakers bureaus today concentrate on solving problems.

However, Northwestern Bell Telephone Company has such extensive participation by employees in its speakers program that engagements are still accepted where company speakers discuss topics that have no relationship to the company. Employees speak on such diverse subjects as water safety, hobbies, and office etiquette. Northwestern Bell views corporate speakers as goodwill ambassadors in addition to being a channel for disseminating information about the company.

At the other end of the spectrum, some large organizations hire a cadre whose single responsibility is public speaking. Frequently these individuals have special titles within the organization, such as assistant to the president, regional vice-president, etc. General Motors has used this technique.

In some organizations, the speakers bureau is confined to executives, while a few open their speakers groups to include employees at all levels. In addition to Northwestern Bell, another organization with wide representation in its speakers program is Continental Oil Company.

In 1977, 535 Conoco employees presented 2,976 speeches before a broad range of audiences, and the program is still growing. Each speaker receives a loose-leaf binder divided into two parts, one for prepared speeches to be tailored to individual style, and a section for data on subjects such as energy supply, environment, profits, imports, and decontrol, etc. The binder also includes typical questions that may be asked together with suggested answers. Updated information is sent periodically to the speakers.

Slides and films are available to Conoco speakers. Twenty coordinators are located throughout the country to assist the volunteer speakers and to secure speaking engagements for employees. News coverage is sought and press releases are sent to publicize each appearance. Active volunteer speakers are encouraged through a series of awards from the company.

The successful speakers program is one with an objective, one that is well managed and properly implemented. The overall objective must mesh with the objectives of the organization's public relations program.

A well-run speakers program is complex, and if it is operated for optimum returns, it will be expensive. Although some organizations operate an effective program at a cost roughly equivalent to the salary of one and a half to two public relations executives, many spend far more.

An effective speakers program requires the services of a full-time employee. The program will operate more smoothly if it is in the public relations department but handled by a separate individual or staff.

Speakers are selected; membership in the speakers bureau is not open to every person willing to face an audience. A successful selection method is to contract with an outside consultant for evaluation of individuals who are prospective members. The advantages are that an acknowledged expert is making the judgments, minimizing possibilities of organizational politics influencing selections.

In-house recognition through awards, a luncheon or dinner hosted by the organization's chief executive, and internal publicity are the only incentives for members of the speakers group in most organizations.

TRAINING SPEAKERS

The most successful speakers groups provide concentrated instruction for corporate speakers. Occasionally organizations send selected individuals to local educational institutions for short courses, but more often an instructor or a team is brought to the organization under contract to train prospective speakers. The cost varies but may be from $300 to $600 per student.

Similar training is sponsored for members by some professional organizations and occupational groups. By 1980 the American Dental Association had trained more than 1500 members and was offering a one-day seminar to at least 1500 additional dentists. The program is designed to make members more effective spokesmen for the profession. Special emphasis is placed on preparation for television talk shows.

Twice each year the American Dental Association writes letters to television stations across the country offering speakers on four specified topics. In instances where stations do not respond, an Association representative contacts the program director by telephone to provide additional information about suggested speakers. Following each television appearance by a member, the Association submits a questionnaire to the dentist and another to the television station. Thus, the ADA continually improves training offered its members.

An effective method of securing instructors for in-house training is to contact educational institutions in the area, seeking written proposals from two-person teaching teams. Receipts of at least five such proposals places the organization in a good bargaining position. The top two teams are selected by evaluating the written proposals. These two teams are invited for personal interviews. Selection is based on the written proposals and the personal interviews.

PROMOTING THE SPEAKERS BUREAU

Many national organizations promote their speakers through paid radio and television announcements and advertising in general circulation newspapers and trade publications. Educators are sent letters announcing availability of speakers, and advertisements are placed in educational journals offering speakers to various groups. But this method of promotion is haphazard. Although a larger investment in time and money is required, a more precise method of reaching the right audience is through development of a special mailing list for the speakers group.

These lists are evaluated and refined to determine which include segments of the general population that the organization wants to contact through its speakers program. Analysis will determine that some groups, although large, are not important to the organization. After the refined list has been developed, the organization sends a mailing to specific officers, president, program chairperson, etc. A brochure describing available programs and individuals who will present them is the focal point of the mailing. A cover letter describes the service available and the sponsoring organization. The letter introduces a contact who will assist in obtaining speakers and programs. Frequently, a self-addressed, stamped card is included for easy reply. If no response is received, the addressee is contacted by telephone after two weeks.

The sponsoring group and the speaker's organization agree as to which will handle publicity for the appearance. Then, photos of the speaker and news releases are sent to local media in advance of the event. Depending on the significance of the topic or the stature of the speaker, spot coverage by radio and television is invited. And the speaker is made available for interviews while in the community. If the individual or the topic merits such treatment, the speech is reprinted for distribution. Some organizations convert speeches to brochures with the legend, "Based on a speech by . . ." Audio and videotapes of the presentation are sent occasionally to the organization's field offices.

A MODEL SPEAKERS BUREAU

Based on the foregoing, this model is proposed for an architectural firm with 200 employees. In consultation with the top executives, including the director of public relations, the decision is made to organize a group of 20 speakers.

OBJECTIVES. The stated objectives are to convince the proper audiences that (1) the company provides customers with quality products and services, and (2) the company is a leader in energy conservation and in safeguarding the environment.

The company's major divisions (architecture, engineering, planning, and administration) must be represented in the speakers group. From architecture, volunteers will be sought who specialize in educational, health care, commercial, and religious facilities. Structural, civil, electrical, hydrologic, mechanical, and soils engineers should be represented, as a minimum. Environmentalists, economists, urban planners, and landscape architects can add greatly to the team.

ANNOUNCEMENT. The chief executive officer announces formation of the speakers group in a formal staff meeting and follows with a letter to each involved division or office chief asking for a reply within two weeks. The letter reviews objectives of the program, the type of person most appropriate for the group, and the number of speakers needed from the specific division or office.

ORGANIZATIONAL MEETING. The chief executive chairs the first meeting of the prospective speakers, explaining the needs to be filled by the group and the formal objectives of the program. The individuals learn that they were selected because they are uniquely qualified.

The public relations director explains the operation of the speakers bureau and displays kits to be provided. These include nuts and bolts of several basic speeches, sample fact sheets, and question-and-answer sheets. Attendees are asked for comments.

The director or another public relations staff member describes and demonstrates available aids: slides and/or tapes with equipment; films and projectors; videotapes and other graphics; plus literature for distribution to audiences.

The chief executive officer reiterates the importance of the group to the company and explains benefits to be realized by the individual speakers, also reassuring the speakers that no member will be required to make more than six presentations a year through the bureau.

TRAINING. The two-person teaching team is selected with the understanding that the company furnishes facilities, including hardware (videotape cameras and recorders, audiovisual equipment, etc.) if deemed necessary. The team furnishes instructional materials.

The speakers group is divided into two training sections of ten members each. Two hours training is provided each week for ten consecutive weeks on company time for each section. At the conclusion of training, the teaching team evaluates the various speakers, indicating probable audiences with which each would be most successful.

MERCHANDISING. After evaluation of potential audiences, these audiences are canvassed as part of the formal promotional program for the speakers bureau. As a bonus, the public relations specialist, representing the speakers bureau, can present media contacts with fact sheets on speakers and on their particular fields of expertise. Thus, talk show hosts and reporters attempting to localize stories have a ready source of experts on call.

Biographies and introductions are prepared and photographs are taken for distribution to persons responsible for programs. These mailings also include basic information for advance and follow-up news releases.

Speeches are screened for possible conversion to articles in trade publications. The more significant ones are reprinted by the organization itself.

In addition to publicizing appearances by speakers in-house, outstanding members of the group are cited at an annual dinner hosted by the organization's chief executive.

Summary

Developing and writing speeches for delivery by others is a significant requirement for many public relations jobs, and many practitioners find speechwriting their sole duty. Although theirs is an unheralded role, competent speechwriters are in increasing demand, and they are comparatively well paid for their skills. Topflight corporate writers receive as much as $75,000 or more per year.

Thorough knowledge of the organization and its relationship to the community is vital for speechwriters. Successful writers also become well acquainted with persons who will deliver their speeches, their duties, personal tastes, speaking talents, even their speech mannerisms.

The trend in corporate America is for executives to deliver speeches of persuasion. However, writers also master construction of informative and instructional presentations, entertaining speeches, and a variety of other types. Included are remarks for award presentations, special observances, welcomes, and retirements.

Research, writing, and editing are the three phases in developing a speech. Least important is the actual writing. Thorough research and competent editing make for a memorable presentation.

Humor is used sparingly if at all in a serious speech to be delivered by a spokesperson for the business, institution, or organization. A light approach is acceptable for release of tension and change of pace, but humor should not be overdone.

Organized speakers groups are an important tool in many public relations programs. They succeed if members are selected carefully and trained well. Outside experts can be contracted to screen speakers and provide intensive training.

A sound promotional program is an integral part of success for any speakers bureau. Objectives of the speakers group must be defined clearly, speaking engagements arranged, appearances publicized, and speakers rewarded for their participation. Each aspect depends on a well-developed promotional program.

Whether the chief executive, a middle manager, or a trainee, that individual *is* the organization when appearing before an audience. A well-constructed message clearly articulated before an influential audience can achieve results available through no other public relations tool.

Exercises

Select one of the United Fund agencies in your community for these exercises.

1. Analyze the agency, outlining its goals, organization, and staff. Determine objectives for a speakers bureau that mesh with the objectives of the public relations program.

2. Utilizing both permanent and volunteer workers, select ten persons as tentative members of the speakers bureau. What types of audiences should be targeted for each member to realize the bureau's objective(s)? Explain your selections.

3. Develop two basic ten-minute speeches for agency speakers, one for delivery to service clubs such as Kiwanis or Rotary and the second to be presented to union audiences. Be prepared to deliver one of the speeches in class.

4. Prepare a speakers' kit, including the above speeches, fact sheets, question-and-answer sheet, and anything else that would be valuable to the person facing an audience on behalf of the agency.

5. Develop a media packet to be used in publicizing your appearance as a speakers bureau member.

6. Deliver an anecdote or humorous story before the class. Demonstrate how the story may be enhanced by change of timing.

Case study

The chief executive officer of Ajax National Bank perceives the institution as a regional leader in the financial industry. Consequently, the executive is convinced that Ajax must speak out on subjects affecting the region. Deficit spending, whether by individuals, organizations, or government, is seen as a major problem.

A group of 12 bank officers and employees willing to speak on the subject has been assembled. However, they are inexperienced as speakers and must be trained. The training, funded by the bank, will be conducted in bank facilities each Thursday from 3:15 to 4:30 p.m. for nine weeks. You have contracted to conduct the training.

- Develop a detailed outline for each of the nine sessions.
- Prepare a checklist for individuals appearing for the first time as representatives of the bank.
- Write a form letter, directed to various regional organizations, announcing the Ajax Speakers Bureau.
- Research deficit spending.
- After the research is complete, spend a maximum of 90 minutes writing a sample speech on deficit spending for delivery by bank representatives.

Suggested readings

Cronkhite, Gary. *Communication and Awareness.* Menlo Park, Calif.: Cumings Publishing Co., 1976.

Emmert, Philip, and William C. Donaghy. *Human Communication—Elements and Contexts.* Reading, Mass.: Addison-Wesley Publishing Co., 1981.

Heinz, John F. "Effective Speech Writing: An Overview." *Communication World,* October 1985.

Kranja, Nariman N. "The Nitty-Gritty of Speechwriting." *Public Relations Journal,* May 1980.

Maloney, Stephen R. "The Speechwriter's Desk." *Public Relations Journal,* February 1984.

Tarver, Jerry. "How to Put 'Good' Humor in Your Next Speech." *Public Relations Journal,* February 1975.

Welsh, James J. *The Speech Writing Guide.* New York: John Wiley, 1968.

16 The law and the practitioner

In examining the legal aspects and fundamental ethical considerations of public relations, we ought to be aware that law and ethics are distinct but their concerns often overlap.

The overlapping is perhaps emphasized by a thoughtful analysis of that old argument used in so many debates over public policy: "You can't legislate morality." That probably comes as news to the lawmakers who prohibited murder, robbery, arson, and rape.

As a matter of plain fact, society does set, by law, certain minimum standards of ethical conduct. "Thou shalt not kill" has become, "A person commits murder in the first degree if he kills another person purposely and with deliberate and premeditated malice. Murder in the first degree shall be punished as a Class I or Class IA felony. . . ."

It is fairly obvious, on the other hand, that simply because you are obeying the letter of the law, you are not necessarily acting ethically. The prevailing attitude toward so-called loopholes in the law attests to this. A public relations practitioner may not be breaking a specific law by telling news reporters that a client is not exporting drug products rejected for consumption in the United States when the practitioner knows full well that such "dumping" is actually going on. But the lack of ethics in such a lie is obvious.

Equally important is this: Just because you think you are acting ethically does not mean that you are acting legally. Demonstrators who feel a moral imperative to enter a military base or the grounds of a munitions factory to dramatize their views are still trespassers in the eyes of the civil law. Similarly, with a clear conscience a public relations person may send out news releases on a new product and unwittingly break the law. Unless carefully drafted and properly timed, those apparently innocent news releases may violate the reporting procedures required by federal securities laws designed to protect investors.

Since being an ethical "good guy" alone will not shield a practi-

364

tioner from legal difficulties, public relations people have to know something about the laws that affect their professional activities. They should be aware of the danger areas so that they can seek prompt, competent legal counsel. Preventive law, like preventive medicine, is much preferable to the curative variety. It is also almost always a lot less painful and expensive.

Freedom of speech and press

Because such a large part of public relations involves communication, a knowledge of the laws governing speech and press is critical for practitioners. Such laws stem from or are related to the First Amendment to the Constitution of the United States, which guarantees freedom of speech and press. State constitutions have similar guarantees.

The First Amendment also protects freedom of religion, freedom of assembly, and the right to petition government for redress of grievances. The latter two are also of significance for public relations practice, since they are related to communication.

The text of the First Amendment consists of a prohibition against Congress's enacting laws abridging the freedoms of speech, press, religion, assembly, and petition. But through court interpretation and the adoption of the Fourteenth Amendment, this prohibition has been extended to all three branches of the federal government and to state and local governments as well.

In practice, again through court interpretation, the guarantees of speech and press freedom have come to mean that government can exercise no prior restraint on communication. In other words, government generally cannot prevent someone from speaking, publishing, or broadcasting. Once the message has been spoken, published, or broadcast, the sender of the message can be held responsible for it. But the sender cannot be prevented from sending it.

Even when the Bill of Rights was adopted, however, there were implicit exceptions to that broad guarantee of freedom from prior restraint. At least that seems to be the consensus of constitutional law scholars. A communication calling for the immediate, violent overthrow of the government is one such exception. Obscene communication is another exception.

A number of additional exceptions have developed through the years. For instance, if you would attempt to broadcast a message over the airwaves without obtaining a license from the Federal Communications Commission, you would be breaking the law, even though the license requirement is obviously a prior restraint on communication. Even with a commercial broadcast license, you could not advertise cigarettes over the air. There is a law against that, and no one has successfully challenged its constitutionality, despite the fact that it too is a prior restraint on communication.

Nonetheless, the thrust of American law is to guarantee communication that is as free as possible. Particularly on matters of public concern, the Supreme Court of the United States has many times called for discussion that is "unrestrained, robust and wide open." It is in this environment of communication freedom that public relations operates.

This means that practitioners can participate in and enjoy freedom of speech and press when they communicate on behalf of their employers and clients. This means, for instance, that a Sears Roebuck and Company can, and did, criticize government agencies for their regulatory practices when those agencies accused Sears of not complying with some regulations. It means that a Kaiser Aluminum and Chemical Corporation can circulate a detailed brochure attacking government policies that enable broadcasters to limit access to the airwaves. No matter how loud and how sharp that criticism is, the government cannot silence such corporations nor use its regulatory powers to retaliate against such outspoken critics.

A battle between the railroads and the trucking industry in the 1950s supplies an example of the extent to which freedom of expression can be exercised by public relations practitioners in attacking competitors. That situation arose when the Eastern Railroad Presidents Conference launched a campaign of media attacks on efforts in Pennsylvania to lift restrictions that the trucking industry said kept it from competing effectively for freight-hauling business.

The conflict eventually wound up in the courts. The trucking representative sued the railroad organization and its public relations agency for conspiring to blunt competition through a media campaign against the trucking industry. The Supreme Court, however, protected the railroad group's right to conduct what Justice Hugo Black termed a "no-holds-barred fight" in the media, despite the fact that the court noted that both sides had been guilty of deceptions in their communications. The case is known as *Noerr Motor Freight, Inc., et al. v. Eastern Railroad Presidents Conference et al.* (365 U.S. 127; 1961).

It is different, however, when communication is a significant factor in a genuine conspiracy to stifle the effectiveness of a rival. Then First Amendment protection can be drawn so thin it disappears, and the antitrust laws will take over and impose penalties.

In addition to remembering the exceptions to freedom from prior restraint, the public relations practitioner must be aware that "restraint" means government action. Nongovernment persons and agencies can use their legal and economic power to influence communication if they wish. The owner of a newspaper can order an editor not to publish a news story about his son's arrest and fire the editor if the story is published despite the order. A large retailer can threaten to withdraw its advertising to protest what a broadcast station puts on the air.

In our experience, these private pressures are applied much more rarely than many people believe. For one thing, there are many checks and balances that prevent them. Other news media may report the arrest of the newspaper publisher's son, so why should the publisher make his own newspaper look bad by not printing the story? The large retailer may be one of dozens of large advertisers, so loss of its account will certainly not put the station out of business. Maybe the retailer needs exposure on the station more than the station needs the retailer's commercials.

Nonetheless, the point is that nongovernment persons and organizations can legally exercise prior restraint. The company president can order a news release killed. The officers of a professional association can direct that no publicity be given a major policy decision. The administrator of an institution can reject copy for a brochure. First Amendment rights just do not apply to those situations. The decisions may be shortsighted or even unethical and unreasonable, but they are nonetheless legal. The First Amendment theory underscoring this distinction between private and governmental restraint is spelled out in a 1974 Supreme Court decision, *Miami Herald Publishing Co. v. Tornillo* (418 U.S. 241).

ACCESS TO INFORMATION

Related to the fundamental freedoms of speech and press is the issue of access to the communications media. Media managements decide what those media print and broadcast, with some qualifications regarding broadcasting. Public relations practitioners cannot wave a First Amendment flag in front of a city editor or news director and demand that a news release be printed or aired. Since the media are not part of government, these are not First Amendment situations.

In fact, the courts have ruled that laws, like Florida's former right-of-reply law involved in the *Tornillo* case, cannot give people general access to privately owned print media. Access not only can be legally denied but sometimes is. Editors have arbitrarily rejected news releases and have refused to publish letters. Sometimes news releases are rejected because an editor or news director thinks the releases are timed to give preference to competing media. In retaliation, news from the public relations source is subjected to a blackout.

As long as media management supports an editor or news director in such a policy, there is no legal action available to remedy this unprofessional but constitutional prior restraint. The moral is: If you want access to newspapers, do not cross city editors. (Just change the titles for broadcast stations.)

Turning the situation around, public relations practitioners, along with the management or leadership they serve, should be aware that the news media have no legal right of access to most information about their clients and employers. Now obviously public relations people will want to give the media access to much information of this sort. But when it comes to information the management of a nongovernmental agency or institution does not want to disclose, the general principle is that the news media will have no legal power to extract it.

Government agencies and institutions are in a different situation. They may well be required by the Federal Public Records Law (5 U.S.C. 552 *et seq.*), popularly known as the Freedom of Information Act, and similar public records laws at the state and local level, to disclose information. Not only does the federal act make disclosure a general policy, it requires federal agencies to publish information about how to get information from them.

There are exceptions or exemptions from the federal policy of disclosure. These are designed to protect national security, trade secrets, current law enforcement investigations, and matters of individual privacy (e.g., personal medical records of government employees).

The history of the Freedom of Information Act has been marked by controversy. At first, news media personnel found many agencies ignoring or flouting the law by making it as expensive and time-consuming as possible to obtain information. With prodding from Congress and the courts, the situation improved somewhat for several years. One factor was the *ACCESS Reports* newsletter that monitored the situation. More recently this publication suggested an increase in the roadblocks for those seeking information from government. Concern for national security in light of espionage arrests may also be used as a reason for a general tightening up on the availability of government-held information.

Meanwhile, critics continue to detail the unconscionable delays that requests for nonsensitive information encounter. Lawsuits aimed at forcing agencies to comply with the law are still common. With effective internal public relations counsel, of course, the foot-dragging agencies should not ever have to be taken to court.

Public relations practitioners should be aware of the strong social pressures for disclosure of government information over the past decade. Open records and open meetings laws have been broadened and strengthened at the state level. Legislators try to be sensitive to public opinion, so it seems safe to surmise that the lawmakers are feeling significant public support when they pass such laws. As an example of this sensitivity, a state workmen's compensation judge recently was called to task for opening case files to the news media. Even before he was exonerated, the legislature amended its public information law to make it perfectly clear that such files are open to all segments of the public.

ACCESS TO THE MEDIA

The access issue is a bit more complicated in considering the media themselves. As noted, non-broadcast media have a legal right, in general, to refuse access to their channels of communication. Broadcast media are in a slightly different position.

Radio and television stations are licensed by the Federal Communications Commission under a law requiring every licensee to serve the "public interest, convenience or necessity." The law spells out special access for political candidates in Section 315, the well-known Equal Opportunities provision. ("Equal time" is misleading and not the term used in the law.)

The Equal Opportunities provision applies only to legally qualified candidates for public office. In essence, it says that if a broadcast station permits use of its facilities by any legally qualified candidate for a public office, the station must provide an equal opportunity to use its facilities to every other legally qualified candidate for the same office. Within the last decade Congress required broadcast stations to give access to all candidates for federal office regardless of any competition. Appearances during newscasts, news interviews, news documentaries, and on-the-spot coverage of news events are not considered "use" of the broadcast station's facilities for Equal Opportunities purposes.

For the practitioner involved in political public relations, knowledge of the Equal Opportunities provision is important in making certain the candidate gets what is due in terms of broadcast access. Otherwise, embarrassing and expensive mistakes can be made. Several years ago, two members of a city council appeared on a charity telethon in response to an invitation to give testimonials for the charity. No one alluded to the fact that they were political candidates running for reelection.

Nonetheless, this triggered the Equal Opportunities provision, the attorney for the station carrying the telethon advised. The station's management therefore had to give (literally!) an equal opportunity to appear on the air to each of the other candidates in the primary election for the council.

Section 315 is also cited by some lawyers as the basis for what has become known as the Fairness Doctrine. This has been a policy under which the commission imposed an obligation on broadcasters to afford "reasonable opportunity for the discussion of conflicting views" when issues of public importance were the subject of a broadcast. Without alluding to the language of Section 315, a majority of the FCC commissioners in mid-1987 repudiated the Fairness Doctrine. Even though it had withstood tests before the Supreme Court, the commissioners said the Fairness Doctrine violated the First Amendment. Whether the FCC's discarding of the doctrine is overruled by the courts or Congress remains to be seen.

For the public relations practitioner, the Fairness Doctrine has provided a legal basis for insisting on radio and television access to give their employer or client's side in a controversy. Without it, practitioners will obviously have to be more persuasive in their appeals to broadcasters' sense of equity in airing different points of view.

Fairness requirements are distinct from the Equal Opportunities portion of Section 315. But Equal Opportunities rights must be actively sought. Requests must be made within seven days of the first "use" of a broadcast facility by an opposing candidate. There is no formal procedure for such requests. Ordinarily the candidate, the candidate's organization, or the candidate's advertising agency will simply telephone or visit the station to ask to buy time.

The Personal Attack Rules which the FCC had formulated in connection with the Fairness Doctrine might be nullified too if the doctrine itself is discarded. Those rules also provided media access for persons whose character, honesty, or integrity was attacked during programming devoted to issues of public importance.

The situation with regard to broadcast editorials—expressions of station management's views—is clouded in the wake of the FCC's repudiation of the Fairness Doctrine. Broadcast editorials were first prohibited by the FCC in its earliest days but for the past thirty-five years they have been not only permitted but encouraged. The FCC required that broadcast editorials be accompanied by an invitation to those who would like to respond to make their opinions known. This provided an alert public relations practitioner another legally sanctioned opportunity for media access.

Whenever difficulties are encountered in Equal Opportunities situations, it is apparent requests ought to be documented. If a certified or registered letter is sent to a broadcaster, it may be introduced later as evidence of the substance and timing of the request if the issue has to be carried to an FCC hearing.

A number of major corporations in recent years have been buying space in newspapers and magazines and air time on radio and television to tell their story or their side of a controversial issue. This is one way to make sure they get adequate time and space. But in addition to the expense, there may still be that question of access. A newspaper, a broadcast station, or even a network can refuse to sell space or time in most circumstances. That legal right of refusal might be exercised more vigorously by broadcasters if the FCC's moves toward deregulation, exemplified by the Fairness Doctrine repudiation, are not countered by the courts or Congress.

Legal responsibilities

An ancient bit of legal wisdom is contained in the warning, "He who publishes, publishes at his peril." In modern terms, even though the sender of a message generally may not be subjected to a prior restraint by government, once the message is sent the sender can be held legally responsible for its contents and the impact of those contents.

Think about it this way. Nobody can prevent you from calling someone else a thief, but once you do, you better have a good legal defense. You may be sued for defamation, wrongfully injuring a person's reputation. Historically, the architects of the American legal system have seen no contradiction in this, saying that generally government cannot prevent communication but government can punish wrongful communication.

That is why for 200 years the most common legal problem for the communications media has been defamation, lawsuits filed after publication, charging that a reputation was injured by the publication. The lawsuits seek money damages. They are not aimed at suppressing the defamer's expression, although a large judgment has put more than one medium out of business. While it may not be the most frequent legal problem for public relations people, defamation can be a danger for them, so they should know some of its fundamentals.

LIBEL AND SLANDER

Defamation is divided into libel and slander. Both are known as *torts*, personal wrongs for which damages can be sought in a court of law. Slander, the older of the two, is word-of-mouth defamation. Libel is graphic (printing, writing, pictures, caricatures, even three-dimensional depictions) defamation. Libel came to England, from which so much of the U.S. legal system was inherited, with the development of movable-type printing in the fifteen century.

This technological breakthrough was hardly a giant step forward for humanity in the eyes of the uneasy English kings and queens. They were sitting on a cauldron of political and religious turmoil. To them, printing was a means of spreading treason and dissent more widely than ever before. So libel came into English law as a crime, and graphic defamation for centuries afterward has been treated as more serious than slander.

Because public relations communication is commonly telling "good deeds well done," it does not face the libel danger that the mass media do with their accounts of crimes, conflicts, scandalous behavior, etc. But the danger still exists.

Whenever people are named or otherwise identified in any communication, there may be an impact on their reputation. In external and especially internal communication, individuals must be clearly identified.

The employee publication may announce births, weddings, deaths, and bowling scores. A typographic error that takes 100 pins off the average of the company's top bowler may not be sufficient basis for a libel suit though it may be enough to lose that bowler as a friendly reader. But it is defamatory to print that A was married to B when B is already married to C. And while it is not considered injurious to reputation to report that X died when he did not, it is defamatory to report, erroneously, that Y gave birth to her first child when Y is not married.

Therefore, even the routine and apparently innocuous personal item must be checked to avoid the hazard of libel. Moreover, if news releases and other external communications used in a battle for public support criticize individuals, groups, corporations, or unincorporated associations, the public relations staff should be on a libel alert.

The prevailing rule for centuries was that expressed earlier in "He who publishes, publishes at his peril." In other words, even an honest mistake was inexcusable; it was a risk the publisher assumed. On top of that, the law presumed that mistakes were made with a malicious intent to injure someone's good name.

Today the honest mistake, or, more correctly, a lack of "actual malice" as the Supreme Court has defined it, may be a defense against a libel suit by someone classified as a public official or public figure. But with the private figure, negligence, or "lack of due care," may be all that is necessary to establish liability. State law will determine whether negligence qualifies as the "fault" the Supreme Court requires before damages can be awarded.

Courts still wrestle with the distinction between the public and private person. The Supreme Court, in *Gertz v. Robert Welch, Inc.* (418 U.S. 323; 1974), has given descriptions of three types of public figures as some guidance.

1. Persons who achieve "such pervasive fame or notoriety" or occupy positions "of such persuasive power and influence" that they are public figures in all situations.

2. Persons who "voluntarily inject themselves into a particular public controversy . . . in order to influence the resolution of the issues involved."

3. Persons who do not voluntarily involve themselves in a public controversy but are "drawn into" it.

Since the mid-1970s, the Supreme Court has tended to apply the public figure status more narrowly. That, along with the requirement of mere negligence for liability in many states, is all the more reason for public relations practitioners to establish systems to check factual accuracy in all communications.

If anything, those who produce public relations releases and publications should be more exact with names (of places and organizations as well as of people) than the news media. After all, the public relations staff ordinarily will not be facing the constant and fairly inflexible deadlines of daily newspapers and broadcast stations, and public relations people will be dealing with more specialized information than the general media must handle. Additionally, careless inaccuracy can destroy the defense of truth in defamation situations.

Like the well-run newsroom, public relations staffs should also have a policy that requires prompt, prominent, and gracious correction of errors. Many a libel situation that might have ended in the courts has ended with an obviously sincere apology coupled with a correction. (Those corrections, incidentally, should be triple-checked to avoid compounding the original error.) In a number of states, if a correction does not avoid a libel suit altogether, it may be a partial defense if it is published promptly and with as much prominence as the error.

If public relations practitioners are ever threatened with a libel suit, they should seek legal counsel immediately. Trying to deal with the situation on their own at that stage might result in their doing things that simply make a bad situation worse, despite good intentions. The great majority of legal disputes are settled without litigation, so give the lawyers a chance to patch things up before that is no longer possible.

VIOLATIONS OF PRIVACY

Compared to defamation, some aspects of the law of privacy are relatively new in the United States. That is significant because when an area of the law is new, it tends to be unsettled. That means the guidelines are not as clear and the questions are not as fully answered as you might like if you are to avoid trouble.

Privacy is also a kind of legal thicket because it has developed by bits and pieces and now encompasses at least four quite distinct wrongs or torts:

1. *Intrusion on a person's physical or "territorial" privacy.* This is a form of trespass. It can involve barging into someone's motel room as well as invading a person's private home. It can also involve placing hidden listening or recording devices in someone's private area or tapping someone's telephone without a warrant.

Public relations people customarily are not pursuing information on private premises without permission, but they may be on the other side of such activity. They must know that the law of privacy protects people who may happen to be their employers or clients. Practitioners will be making spokesmen available to the media, but they should also know that there is a legal basis for protecting the privacy of key figures within a business or organization from physically intrusive prying.

2. *Publication of "private matters" relating to a person.* This type of privacy violation is to a large extent the feeding ground of scandalmongers and exposé publications. However, a public relations practitioner, who may see a tremendously moving human interest story in an employee, an executive, a volunteer, or anyone else connected with the enterprise the practitioner is serving, should realize the promotional value of that story cannot force the subject to abandon the right to keep personal matters private.

For instance, the volunteer in a community health program who is a volunteer because of his own experience with mental illness may have, depending on state law, a legal right to keep private the motivation for his service. A highly successful executive who went through the company's program for alcoholism before reaching a management pinnacle may have grounds for a lawsuit if her personal story is told, even though it would be inspiring to other employees and perhaps encourage some to enter the alcoholism program.

In addition, special legislation has established rights of privacy for certain classes of people and certain types of personal information. The laws and regulations range from restrictions on access to arrest and conviction records in criminal proceedings, to personal information in educational settings.

The Family Educational Rights and Privacy Act, commonly referred to as the Buckley Amendment, forbids educational institutions that receive federal funds to make public any personally identifiable records or files of students "or personal information contained therein." This law also gives students and their parents legal access to student records and files.

For practitioners in educational public relations, the law has implications for internal and external communications. Internally, the public relations staff of a school system or institution should see to it that a clear policy is in effect covering both confidentiality of records and access to them by students, parents, and other persons specifically authorized by the law to have access. To avoid problems, the implementation of the policy should be monitored.

Externally, publicizing the activities and achievements of college students, in the local community and in the students' home towns, is standard practice. To avoid problems concerning personal information, the best practice is to have students provide directory-type information (name, address, telephone number, parents' names, educational backgrounds, etc.) on a separate form at registration. The form should include a statement giving permission for use of this information in news releases about the student's achievements and should bear the student's signature. The permission may be revocable if given by a student who is not legally an adult. But it may be relied upon by the public relations office until the unlikely instance in which the student notifies the office of revocation.

3. *Use of a person's name or image for purposes of trade or advertising.* This area may have the greatest danger potential for public relations people. Many employers assume that they can take photographs of employees, especially during working hours, and use those photographs in promotional brochures, new employee orientation pamphlets, or even advertising illustrations. This is done all the time, happily with hardly a ripple of disapproval. After all, it is flattering to have your picture published, especially as a good example of a loyal employee, careful worker, or contented user of the company's product.

In our lawsuit-prone society, however, there is a risk, especially with the disgruntled employee, of a claim that the use of the photograph was not within the scope of the employment contract. There may be claim that the use constitutes an exploitation of the employee and a violation of the right of privacy. It is the type of reaction that could arise in a period of tense labor-management relations, or when charges of discrimination have been filed against the employer.

4. *Placing the person in a "false light."* This is one of the most difficult situations to deal with because it is really more like defamation than the other kinds of privacy violations. A person is put in a false light when something untrue but not necessarily injurious to reputation is said or published about the person, causing the victim mental or emotional distress.

A notable example of false light is offered by the famous case of the Hill family. Their home was taken over by fugitive convicts, providing the inspiration for the plot of a successful play and movie, "The Desperate Hours." The fictional script had one of the convicts making sexually suggestive advances toward a member of the family. The family insisted that nothing like this happened. When a magazine tied the fictional script too closely to the Hills' actual ordeal, the family sued for false light invasion of privacy.

The fictionalized version did not allege any misconduct on the part of a family member, but the family said the untrue-to-life version caused embarrassment. The principle to remember is that it is dangerous to embroider reality.

Perhaps the most elementary and important defense for public relations people in all these areas of privacy law is a preventive one. Get the prior consent of the individuals involved and, whenever possible, get it in writing. Specifically:

1. If you want to photograph something from a striking perspective that can be captured only if the camera is set on private property, do not trespass. Ask permission of the property owner.

2. If you want to do that great story about the volunteer who came back from mental illness and now treats others with unmatchable empathy, get the volunteer's approval.

3. If you want to feel free to use employees' photos and names in your publications and promotional materials, add a consent form to the dozens of other papers employees are asked to read and sign when they join the company or organization.

4. If you want to fictionalize a true incident involving identifiable persons, get their okay ahead of time.

Although consents in these cases need not always be in writing to be operative, they can be much more effective in avoiding, or winning, lawsuits if they are in black and white and signed on the dotted line. They must meet the requirements of a binding contract, so they should be drafted or at least checked by an attorney to make certain they meet your particular requirements.

In addition, newsworthiness is a defense against claims of privacy invasion that involve publication of private matters. Truth—as with defamation, provable truth—is a defense against false light allegations.

Other restrictions

COPYRIGHT

In a sense, copyrighted material constitutes another exception to the First Amendment's protection against prior restraint by government. You can be restrained from using copyrighted material, and you can be punished for using it if you go ahead despite the copyright notice the material carries.

Copyright law is important to public relations people in at least two areas: (1) their desire to use material that may be protected by copyright in their publications and brochures, and (2) their desire to protect the products of their own creativity from use by competitors. In the first area are situations in which public relations writers and designers want to quote from published material, or they would like to incorporate graphics from other publications into their own. The second area involves a commonsense business principle that holds that you ought to protect your valuables, at least not give away what you might be able to sell or get credit for.

In the first area, correct procedure calls for determining whether the material is copyrighted and, if so, whether it is possible to get permission to use it from the copyright owner. In the second area, the steps to take are those that will give copyright protection to the material.

PRESENT LAW. Protection of copyright is a matter within the jurisdiction of the federal government. A copyright is a limited, exclusive property or ownership right in a literary, musical (including dance), dramatic (including pantomime), pictorial, graphic, sculptural, or audiovisual work.

The right is made exclusive so that producers of these works can profit from them, by selling original works, controlling the production of copies, or collecting royalties from users of the works. The reasoning behind copyright laws is simple. With this profit motivation, producers of creative works will keep producing, and society will be enriched as a result. The right is also limited so that eventually everyone will have access, in one form or another, to true masterpieces.

American copyright underwent major changes with the passage of a law that went into effect in 1978. The law was written to update copyright in relation to materials—computer programs and tapes, microfilms, and various forms of sound and video recordings—that were not even imagined when the previous law, passed in 1909 and amended piecemeal thereafter, went into effect. The previous law also had a hard time coping with the use of material by cable television systems and the rampant use of photocopiers.

Beyond dealing with those issues, the present copyright law changed the duration of copyrights and extended statutory protection to unpublished works. Until 1978, though some pre-1978 copyrights were extended to conform more closely to new copyrights, copyrights existed for 28 years but could be renewed for an additional 28 years. Now the standard period is the life of the author or creator plus 50 years. If a copyrighted work is produced "for hire," the copyright period is 75 years from the date of first publication or 100 years from the date of creation, whichever period is shorter.

The concern of public relations practitioners will focus on works produced "for hire," work done for another person, business, agency, or organization under contract (the situation in which the practitioner is serving clients) or work done for an employer as part of the employment agreement or arrangement.

The copyright law provides that an author, composer, choreographer, playwright, poet, photographer, painter, sculptor, etc., is the owner of a copyright in the work produced unless it is a "work for hire." Copyright in these works is owned by the employer of employees who produced the works as part of their employment, or by the person, corporation, or organization that contracted for the production of the work if the author or creator has agreed to this status.

The law defines "work for hire" as: (1) a work prepared by an employee within the scope of employment; or (2) a work specially ordered or commissioned as a contribution, part, or supplement to another work if there is a signed agreement that the work is to be considered a work for hire.

Public relations agency people sometimes found copyright ownership a problem under previous law when the question was not covered in their contract with a client. It was a bone of contention, especially when the work the public relations agency created was outstanding, or when the client paid a lot less for the work than it turned out to be worth, or where the client used the material in other activities in which the agency had no role or compensation.

Now the law puts both the agency and client on notice as to the ownership of "for hire" work, and the issue may be negotiated. In the face of competitors eager to lure a client away, an agency may feel it cannot seek to retain copyright in its work product. But then the agency should be sure to charge what its services and product are worth.

Other "for hire" questions may arise when practitioners engage free-lancers for special writing or photography assignments. The importance of spelling out ownership of the work product should be apparent from the principles outlined. The issue of who owns the photographic negatives is one that frequently arises in such relationships. If prints are ordered and prints are provided, with nothing more said, the photographer owns the negatives. If that is undesirable, it can easily be avoided by a written agreement that provides otherwise.

WHAT CAN BE COPYRIGHTED. The copyright law says "original works of authorship fixed in any tangible medium of expression now known or later developed, from which it can be perceived, reproduced or otherwise communicated" can be copyrighted. The language obviously is intended to include all sorts of subcategories within the literary, musical, graphic, and audiovisual works mentioned.

Literary works, incidentally, are "works other than audiovisual works, expressed in words, numbers or other verbal or numerical symbols or indicia, regardless of the nature of the material objects, such as books, periodicals, manuscripts, phonorecords, film, tape, disks or cards, in which they are embodied," according to Section 101 of the law. The term, in other words, does not mean "works of literature." It can include catalogs and directories.

Articles, features, essays, editorials, columns, photographs and drawings, charts and graphs—just about every bit of material that will be found in the materials published by public relations practitioners—can be copyrighted then. What cannot be copyrighted are the ideas or facts within those forms. Instead, it is the manner of expression or the embodiment of the ideas and facts that can be protected.

Copyrighting an article about a program of employee incentives in a cost-savings project, as an example, does not mean that no one else can write an article on cost-savings projects or even on employee incentives in such projects. It means the original article itself, not its ideas or subject matter, cannot be used to any substantial degree without infringement.

Trends in literature as well as fashion develop because ideas are borrowed but given new twists and applications. Even Shakespeare took his plots where he could find them, and many of his sources are still available today. Anyone could use the plots, but what Shakespeare did with them is what copyright could protect.

Speaking of Shakespeare, a word of caution about using material whose author has long since died. Adaptations and translations can be copyrighted in their own right as "original" works, since the adapting and translating are new. For example, there have been many translations of Dante's *Comedy*, written centuries ago. But some of these translations are fairly recent, and their copyrights will be in effect for many years to come.

To find out whether a work is copyrighted, a person must look for a copyright notice. In most instances, the notice will include the name of the copyright owner and the year the copyright was obtained. If the date of the author's death is known, the "life plus 50 years" calculation can be made easily to determine whether the copyright is in effect. But the new copyright period does make it more difficult to be sure if the copyright is in effect when an author is not well known. As an aid in such situations, the Register of Copyrights official records are open to inspection during business hours. For an hourly fee the staff will conduct a search and provide a report of results.

The copyright law gives five fundamental rights to copyright owners: (1) the right to reproduction (making and selling copies); (2) the right to adaptation (e.g., making a book into a movie); (3) the right to publication; (4) the right to performance; and (5) the right to display. These rights may overlap, and they may also be divided and subdivided by the owner. A writer may sell a magazine "first serial" (first periodical) rights to an article but retain republication rights and sell them to a digest-type magazine later, for example.

From the public relations perspective, the exclusive right of publication and reproduction are probably most relevant. First of all, a right of publication implies that copyright may protect something that has not been published. This had been the case under the states' common law copyright. The 1978 federal law, however, specifically extends its protection to unpublished works. The earlier common law copyright, protected by the states and their courts, continued until publication, which could have been much longer than the period provided now.

The exclusive right of reproduction means that no one can reproduce or make copies of a copyrighted work. If someone violates that exclusive right, the copyright owner can sue for monetary damages and ask the court to prohibit any further infringement or violation of the exclusive right. If the infringement is willful and flagrant, the copyright owner may request that the infringer be prosecuted under the criminal provisions of the law.

If a practitioner wants to use reprints of copyrighted material, the request can be directed to the publication in which the material first appeared. Frequently a publication, particularly a technical or scholarly journal, will have an agreement with the authors whose works it publishes that a specified number of reprints can be supplied without the author's express permission. Or the publication may have obtained all reprint rights from the author. In either case, the practitioner who obtains reprints this way is not violating copyright. But the reproduction of the material, by photocopying or transcription, without permission from the parties who own the copyright is infringement.

Though the law speaks of copyright as an exclusive right, it does permit some very limited and very sensible exceptions. These it labels "fair use," and these exceptions are important to the public relations practitioner.

Copyrighted works used or quoted in reviews, critiques, and news stories or used in research and teaching may be covered by fair use. Section 107 of the copyright law lists four factors that are to be considered in determining whether a situation is one of fair use:

1. The purpose and character of the use, including whether the use is commercial or noncommercial (e.g., for nonprofit educational purposes).

2. The nature of the copyrighted work.

3. The amount and substantiality of the portion used in relation to the copyrighted work as a whole. (A 50-word quotation from a 400,000-word novel would obviously not be substantial, but a two-line quote from a short poem might well be.)

4. The effect the use has on the potential market and value of the copyrighted work.

The practitioner should be able to conclude from these guidelines that fair use permits limited quoting of copyrighted works, particularly if the purpose is not commercial profit. This is important to know when the question of using a quotation comes up at deadline time. It may not be necessary to discard the quotation simply because permission has not been obtained if the use of the quotation will be so insubstantial that it constitutes fair use.

On the other hand, whenever a real question of potential infringement arises, formal permissions should be sought. Even if time is short, a telephone call can be made. It should be carefully logged and followed up by correspondence. Naturally, this informal procedure is appropriate only when mere permission is to be granted, not when a substantial royalty has to be negotiated.

For a work to be protected by copyright, it must carry proper copyright notice. Although regulations provide for variations according to the particular type of work to be protected, the law has a general requirement that the notice include the name of the copyright owner, the year the copyright is first claimed (ordinarily the year of creation or publication) and the word "Copyright," or an abbreviation, or the established symbol ©.

The affixing of notice, rather than the registration of a copyright, is what gives protection. However, before a court will entertain a suit for infringement, a copyright must be registered. Also, no statutory damages or attorney's fees are awarded for infringements that occur before registration unless, with a published work, registration is completed within three months of first publication.

Publication of a work without copyright notice ordinarily makes it public property, available to anyone to use at will. The new copyright law provides protection, however, where the omission of copyright notice is inadvertent and quickly remedied. The sharing of uncopyrighted works with an individual or a very limited number of individuals (e.g., the situation when a writer submits a manuscript to a potential publisher) is not publication, so the author's property right is not surrendered when this occurs.

USING COPYRIGHT. Public relations people should not be victims of false modesty. They produce considerable material (reports, feature articles, photographs, drawings, and designs) as well as audiovisuals that have commercial value. They owe it to their employers and clients to protect the investment in their time and talent. Practitioners' work products can be as worthy of copyright as that of other professional writers and artists.

While there is a possibility of at least recovering some of the expenses incurred in producing material that can be copyrighted through charging royalties, control is a more persuasive reason for securing copyright. Since copyright is generally respected, public relations people who have established copyright will know who is interested in their copyrighted material through the requests they get for use of the material. They will also be able to say no to those, competitors perhaps, whom they are unwilling to assist. All they must do is follow the simple steps required to establish copyright.

Registration of a copyright is not a complex or expensive process. A person can write to the Register of Copyrights (Library of Congress, Washington, D.C. 20559) describing the material for which a copyright application form is needed.

The application form is easily completed. The information sought includes the name and address of the copyright claimant; the nationality or domicile (legal residence) of the author/creator; a statement about the "for hire" or "not for hire" status of the work; a brief statement, if the claimant is not the author, of how the claimant obtained ownership of the copyright; the title of the work; the year in which the work was completed; and the identity of any preexisting work from which the work was derived, along with a brief statement describing the new or additional material.

INVESTMENT INFORMATION

So important did the directors of the Public Relations Society of America consider knowledge of the law in the area of information provided to investors and potential investors that they drafted an official interpretation of the society's Code of Professional Standards which says:

> It is the responsibility of PRSA members who practice financial public relations to be thoroughly familiar with and understand the rules and regulations of the Securities and Exchange Commission and the laws which it administers, as well as other laws, rules and regulations affecting financial public relations, and to act in accordance with their letter and spirit. In carrying out this responsibility, members shall also seek legal counsel, when appropriate, on matters concerning financial public relations.

For its part, the Securities and Exchange Commission has taken the position that the financial and investment information provided by public relations practitioners, especially in news releases, is to be encouraged, in line with the commission's general encouragement of broad, continuing disclosure as a protection for investors.

Problems arise, however, with the timing and content of news releases dealing with businesses in which investors may be interested. Before investments can be offered for sale, the law requires that the investments and their sponsors be described in detail in documents filed with the SEC. After a prescribed period, the investments can be marketed. If the investments are publicized before they are registered or before the required waiting period has expired, the news release providing the information violates the law. If the news release is inaccurate, particularly if it exaggerates or makes claims not included in the material submitted to the SEC, it will also violate the law.

News releases that understate information may violate the law too. The thinking behind this is that investors may sell stock, for instance, if news releases indicate a corporation is not doing well when, in fact, it is doing very well or is about to launch a very promising activity.

In these situations, public relations practitioners will also feel the weight of responsibility that comes with the status they have achieved within their corporation. The SEC has, with some success, attempted to hold individual practitioners liable for false or misleading information contained in their corporate news releases. This means that practitioners who know that claims are premature, exaggerated, or understated can face prosecution. There is even precedent for moving against practitioners who, because of their background and knowledge and because of the special circumstances surrounding the issue of a news release, should have known that their claims in news releases were unsubstantiated.

Because they are typically at the center of corporate activities, public relations personnel may have access to information known principally by highest management. This makes them "insiders" in the language of securities trading. If practitioners use the insider information that comes to them because of their special communication and other roles within a business, they cannot ethically or legally use this information to achieve personal profit to the disadvantage of other investors.

For instance, an automobile manufacturer develops a new lightweight high-efficiency engine. It has passed all tests and will be marketed in models for the coming year. The announcement is timed for greatest impact on sales.

This means there is time for the public relations practitioners who are preparing the publicity to buy stock in the manufacturing company before the new engine becomes public knowledge. Stock in the company will undoubtedly go up in price when the news goes out. Insiders like the public relations people could buy the stock at $18 a share now and expect that they could sell it for at least $25 a share in two months when the new engine is unveiled.

But the law says they must not. They cannot use their insider information to make a quick profit. They must not use an advantage (knowledge of a new product) that the general investing public does not have.

DANGER AREAS. While the specific requirements of investment information regulations may be complex and changing, they can be learned. The guidance of lawyers who specialize in securities law can also be sought. In fact, because of the complexities of the laws regarding securities marketing, practitioners in financial public relations will probably work more closely with lawyers than practitioners in any other aspect of public relations.

In its *Special Study of Securities Markets*, the SEC identified some areas and practices that it considered the source of legal problems. Those areas remain causes for concern today. They include:

1. Upbeat or optimistic reports of sales and earnings, particularly projections or predictions that have little basis in solid fact.

2. Enthusiastic descriptions of technical achievements and product developments, especially when the achievements or products have not yet been thoroughly tested under ordinary use conditions.

3. Reports of the merger of corporations, or the acquisition of one corporation by another, when such actions are barely at the talking stage and no definitive action has been taken.

4. Slanted reports of business activity, exaggerating achievements and minimizing or ignoring unresolved problems.

5. Direct or personal contacts with favored business reporters or market analysts, so that they have information that bears on financial conditions that other reporters, analysts, and the public do not have.

6. "Prefiling" news releases carrying financial information. An example would be sending out a release saying that a corporation will pay a specific amount per share of stock as a dividend before the corporation's board had officially approved or decided on the dividend.

DISCLOSURE AND FRAUD. The rule of full and prompt disclosure of all relevant information clearly implies that false and misleading information can bring prosecution. The SEC regulations also specifically state that it is unlawful to "omit to state a material fact necessary in order to make the statements made, in light of the circumstances under which they were made, not misleading . . ."

Under court interpretation, a statement may be technically true but still misleading. And "any person," not just a member of the board of directors, a corporate officer, or a major stockholder, can be charged under these antifraud provisions.

The law and the SEC regulations require formal filing of many different kinds of information relating to the financial condition of businesses whose securities come under these enactments. Financial public relations will be concerned with sending out news releases about the events and decisions reported to the SEC.

TIMING. Timeliness is important in disseminating such information. Experts in the field advise detailed plans for telephoning, wiring, and hand-carrying releases to the media that will immediately spread the story as widely as possible. Because it is used in making immediate investment decisions, financial information has to be made available as quickly as possible.

In addition, practitioners should have a checklist of the types of financial information requiring immediately release. These would obviously include such items as decisions on dividends, earnings statements, stock splits, mergers, new product developments, new contracts, and government action affecting the business.

In terms of timing, a corporation's annual report is in a different category from material that requires immediacy in distribution. But the annual report too must be governed by the full disclosure rule. The descriptive and narrative material that accompanies the balance sheets must not mislead by overstatement or omission.

New issues of stocks and other securities raise frequent questions about disclosure and timing. If the securities fall under the jurisdiction of the SEC, the general rule is that no publicity can be given the issue until after its registration statement has been filed with the commission. Only after the registration statement is effective can releases safely describe the securities issue. The idea is that the regulatory agency should be told all it must know about the corporation selling the securities before any attempt is made, including by publicity, to sell the securities to the public.

Some questions have arisen with regard to other corporate publicity during such periods. The response of the SEC has been that normal corporate information can continue to be disseminated to the public at this time. The decision on what is normal information and what is promotional information can plainly be a close one, however. Some experts even advise against providing responses to news reporters who independently seek information about a security issue before its registration has become effective. The possibility that someone has tipped a reporter to ask certain questions or that a news story has been planted by an interested party can raise suspicions of wrongdoing.

In the area of product claims, public relations practitioners should also be aware of the jurisdiction and interest of the Federal Trade

Commission. Although this agency concerns itself primarily with anti-competitive practices including false and misleading advertising, the promotional efforts of public relations practitioners may be scrutinized as well.

Recall the earlier discussion of the similarities between advertising and public relations and how thin the line of distinction between them can be drawn. It is the content and character of the claims for products and services that the FTC focuses on, not whether the claims appear in paid advertising or in promotional news releases produced by public relations people and published or broadcast without charge.

To avoid action by the FTC, practitioners should remember these points with regard to product claims:

1. Ambiguous claims will be considered misleading if just one of the possible meanings cannot be supported by fact.

2. Even if a claim is literally true, it will be considered misleading if it gives an impression of offering more than the literal meaning conveys, and that more cannot be substantiated.

3. The understanding of the general public, rather than a narrow meaning based on the precise definitions of the words in a claim, will be the basis for determining whether a claim is misleading or not.

4. Even a tendency to deceive, not just actual deception, can bring FTC action against a claim and the party making it.

5. Knowledge that a claim is false or misleading is not required before the FTC can move against the party making the claim. The reverse is true: the party making the claim must be able to prove the truth of the claim at all times.

6. Lack of intent to mislead will not block FTC action. The effect of a claim, rather than the intent behind it, is the key.

LABOR RELATIONS

In an attempt to put individual employees in a better position to protect their interests, since the 1930s Congress has passed a number of laws relating to unions and collective bargaining. These laws prescribe methods to be followed in winning recognition for a union as the agent of employees in negotiating work contracts with management. The labor laws generally were inspired by sympathy for the unequal bargaining position of individuals in relation to the large businesses that hired them. Practices that allowed businesses to intimidate employees or flout their unions can be designated unfair labor practices and are prohibited under these laws.

It is easy to see that communication could be used to intimidate employees. If communication is used this way, it can be considered an unfair labor practice, and it can be both punished and forbidden, despite the First Amendment and its prohibition against governmental prior restraint of communication.

The major federal labor laws were amended after World War II. Congress addressed this issue then by acknowledging that the mere expression of a view or the presentation of an argument (presumably against unions or union positions) by management could not be considered an unlawful practice without doing violence to the philosophy of the First Amendment.

At the same time, current law prohibits management threats of reprisal if workers vote against a management position. It also forbids promises of special benefits if workers vote for a management position.

A problem of interpretation remains. When does an argument suggesting certain action is bad because of its possible bad effects become a threat that those bad effects will occur? Over the past decade, court decisions have struggled with this problem as they faced the wording of what is now 29 U.S.C. 158(c). Generally they seem to honor the principle of freedom of speech as strongly as they can. In a 1979 case, for instance, even a statement that a plant might be shut down if workers supported the union position was ruled a "prediction" rather than a threat in a widely noted U.S. Court of Appeals decision.

A positive approach to public relations will keep practitioners away from threat rhetoric, even though uninhibited public relations communication is protected by the Constitution. Because of the legal interpretations contained in case law that must be applied to close questions in this area, however, legal counsel should be sought promptly in these situations. That way employee communications programs will not provide the basis for a finding of unfair labor practices.

At the same time, practitioners should not hesitate to remind their legal counsel that the First Amendment has not been repealed. There is a respectable line of court cases supporting management's freedom to tell employees its full views, even regarding union representation and proposed work contract terms.

AGENT REGISTRATION

Public relations practitioners who represent clients before legislative bodies and practitioners who represent foreign governments must be aware of special requirements that the law has established in those areas. Disclosure and registration requirements are the most notable.

Most states direct that persons or firms that represent clients in their relations with the legislature register with the state, disclosing the identity of their clients. Sometimes the requirement, like that in the federal lobbyist registration law, depends on the extent of the representation or lobbying and includes financial disclosure. Like some of the other legislation mentioned, these lobbying control laws run into constitutional principles. The First Amendment protects a citizen's right to petition government, and this is the essence of lobbying. Controls that unreasonably restrict lobbying face a constitutional challenge. Public relations practitioners should be alert to the fact that they can quite legitimately raise this challenge in appropriate circumstances. At the same time, most legal disclosure requirements seem to be in harmony with the ethical requirements discussed in the next chapter.

Although the registration of representatives of foreign governments was required by legislation passed during the decade after World War II, it remains a requirement of federal law. The Foreign Agents Act has an ominous title, making it sound more like an antiespionage measure than something affecting public relations. But it specifically covers such activities, including practitioners and public relations agencies. A few practitioners have run afoul of its requirements. Violations can bring both criminal and civil action by the U.S. Department of Justice.

In the 1960s, Igor Cassini, who was a newspaper columnist but apparently operated through a public relations agency as well, was fined $10,000. He was accused of failing to register as an agent for Rafael Trujillo, ruler of the Dominican Republic. In 1975, several public relations agencies were sued by the Department of Justice for failure to register as foreign agents in connection with promoting the French supersonic Concorde jetliner. In the mid-1980s, another major public relations agency was investigated for possible failure to comply with the law's requirements.

To avoid problems, agencies and individuals who represent such clients should consult an attorney, seek guidance on registration and disclosure requirements, and comply fully and promptly.

Summary

Public relations in a democratic society like that in the United States operates in an open market of ideas, opinions, and information. That is not only a blessing for citizens in general but a great advantage for public relations, which needs free channels of communication to achieve its goals.

But freedom of expression, even in the most democratic society, is not absolute. And exercise of freedom of speech and press carries some legal responsibilities. Public relations practitioners need to know basic First Amendment principles and some of the fundamentals of the laws of defamation and privacy. They should also be familiar with the legal principles governing access, both to information held by government and to communications media, especially those licensed by government.

Like all communicators, public relations practitioners must also be aware of both the protections and the impediments that copyright law creates. This will enable them to avoid giving away valuable property on the one hand and causing embarrassment, perhaps competitive as well as legal, on the other.

In specialized areas like investor public relations and labor relations, practitioners must not only be aware of legal restrictions and requirements; they must recognize the limits of their expertise and know when to call for professional legal guidance.

Exercises

1. Does your state have an open meetings law that applies to public bodies like city councils, village boards, boards of education, and boards of regents? Check your state statutes in your college or local library. Ask the reference librarian for help if necessary. Then try to determine whether these public bodies, or any one of them, welcome or discourage observers at their meetings.

2. Contact a local radio or television station to ask if it has any restrictions on political advertising, especially during primary election periods when there are often dozens of candidates for local office. Ask what the station would do if all its commercial time were sold and a candidate asked to buy time for a political commercial.

3. Try to determine which, if any, local stations broadcast editorials. If you monitor the station, be sure to check the periods right before and right after major newscasts to catch the editorials. If a station does not air any editorials, ask the general manager or program director why. If the station broadcasts editorials, ask how opposing viewpoints are dealt with.

4. What practical problems, as far as determining whether a copyright is still in effect, does the present period for American copyrights pose? How would you go about determining whether a copyright is still in effect?

5. "If the union people get their way, the company will face hard times. We may even have to shut down this plant." That is what the company president really believes and that is what he wants to say in the employee publication during labor contract negotiations. Is his statement an unlawful threat? (Read *National Labor Relations Board v. Intertherm, Inc.* for an answer.)

Case study

Century Brigade, Inc., a manufacturing firm, produced CB (citizen band) radios and accessories for 20 years before the CB craze erupted in the 1970s. In response to the expanded market at that time, it opened plants in three cities in the Midwest to augment production at its original site in the Northeast. Then foreign products entered the market and the craze suddenly ended.

The company almost went bankrupt. Its three Midwest plants were closed, employees were laid off and heavy indebtedness was incurred. Finally, the company hopes to make a comeback. Its research department has developed a new product. It is a solar energy storage unit, or "battery," that can recharge itself from sunlight at the same time it is powering a lightweight vehicle.

However, the labor union that represents most employees at Century Brigade is about to go on strike. The union has been seeking a substantial wage increase to let employees catch up after five years of less-than-inflation pay increases while the company was in financial straits. Because he has heard rumors, the union president issues a statement saying, "Century Brigade is about to hatch a golden egg and we want to share it. After all, we stuck by the company during the lean years and we deserve it."

The company president is furious when he learns of this statement. He calls in Century Brigade's public relations director and says, "I want you to send out a news release based on this statement. I want you to use the exact words too. I'm calling that union president a despicable liar, and I'm going to squelch those rumors at the same time by denying this 'golden egg' nonsense. After all, we have no guarantee we will make as much as we hope to on that energy storage unit."

If you were that public relations director, what legal problems might you point out for Century Brigade's president? What solutions?

Suggested readings

Anderson, Judy. "Off-Air Videotaping: Are You Guilty of Copyright Violations?" *Public Relations Journal,* September 1984.

Brandscomb, Anne W. *The First Amendment as a Shield or a Sword: An Integrated Look at Regulation of Multi-Media Ownership.* Santa Monica, Calif.: The Rand Paper Series, 1975.

Brebbia, John Henry. "First Amendment Rights and the Corporation." *Public Relations Journal,* December 1979.

Cullen, Maurice R., Jr. *Mass Media and the First Amendment.* Dubuque, Iowa: Wm. C. Brown, 1981.

Cutlip, Scott M. "Attendant Responsibility: Public Relations and the SEC." *Public Relations Journal,* January 1985.

Gillmor, Donald M., and Jerome A. Baron, *Mass Communication Law.* 3d ed. St. Paul: West Publishing Co., 1984.

Ginsburg, Douglas H. *Regulation of Broadcasting: Law and Policy Towards Radio, Television and Cable Communications.* St. Paul: West Publishing Co., 1979.

Homet, Roland S., Jr. "The Future of Public Interest Law." In *The Public Interest Media Reform Movement: A Look at the Mandate and a New Agenda.* Washington, D.C.: Aspen Institute for Humanistic Studies, 1976.

Kleber, Louis C. "Playing Poker with the Courts." *Communication World,* May 1985.

Nelson, Harold L., and Dwight L. Teeter, Jr. *Law of Mass Communication.* 4th ed. Mineola, N.Y.: Foundation Press, Inc., 1982.

Simon, Morton J. *Public Relations Law.* New York: Meredith Corporation, 1969.

Taft, Robert W., and Cullen Couch. "Disclosure: An Unsettling Update." *Public Relations Journal,* April 1980.

17 The ethical practice of public relations

Starting with the right approach

"IMAGE" PSYCHOLOGY

At the outset, we noted the flawed view many outsiders have of public relations and the faulty perception even some insiders have of their calling. Too many practitioners are still infected with the idea that public relations is essentially image building. This is reflected in their concern that only positive messages come from their offices, that favorable impressions are to be made at almost any cost, no matter what the reality.

The result of this kind of "image" psychology can be seen in many situations. It has in some cases led to a sort of management paranoia, an unrealistic expectation that "since we've always worked so hard to project a positive image, it's unfair to spoil things for us by telling about the unpleasant things that are happening to us now." Some public relations practitioners react this way themselves. But the paranoia is often more acute among nonpublic relations management people who feel strongly that negative news is "what we pay our PR people to prevent."

Often enough, a bit of "kill the messenger" (because the message is unpleasant) psychology enters in too. The news media are accused of "irresponsibility," "sensationalism," "scandalmongering," "yellow journalism," etc. "After all," this attitude goes, "they didn't have to make such a big thing out of the fact that two employees were killed in that chemical explosion, or that the Labor Department is forcing us to pay 27 employees $130,000 in back pay for overtime we denied them, or that a federal prosecutor has filed charges against us for offering bribes to representatives of foreign governments. Why don't they stick to the *real* news—like our profit picture this year, the increase in orders for our second quarter, the fine safety record we compiled until that unfortunate explosion this morning?"

This image-building and image-protection psychology was never appropriate for sound, ethical public relations. The best practitioners have always been above it, recognizing how it condemns them to the narrow, often demeaning role of mere publicity agents.

Today it is obvious to anyone who will take the time to look around that public relations can no longer accept the straitjacket of an image-oriented psychology. People are unwilling to give their trust, much less their enthusiastic acceptance, to a corporation, institution, organization, or government that will not level with them.

Social scientists and pundits alike report a growing skepticism and lack of public confidence in government, business, the professions, and even in many private nonprofit social welfare agencies. They ascribe this to various causes. These range from the cynicism toward government and public institutions spawned by the Watergate scandal and unpopular war in Vietnam during the 1970s to the disillusionment that has followed revelations by the consumer and environmentalist movements. The business, institution, organization, or governmental agency that tries to portray itself as totally benign and infallible will by that very effort tell its publics it is not to be trusted.

Just think about it for a moment. Someone comes up to you and says, "Hey, I've got something important to tell you, and you can trust me because I absolutely never tell lies and I never make mistakes." Will you be an instant believer or instant skeptic?

On the other hand, someone says, "I've got an important message that I've tried to make as complete and accurate as I can. If I find out that I've forgotten something or failed to get it right, I'll get back to you as soon as possible." Will you be more inclined to listen and trust?

There is something very human about the second approach that cannot help but appeal to people. Those on the frontiers of public relations today realize this and have already made it a cornerstone of their programs and policies.

One of the country's largest insurance companies, Aetna Life and Casualty, has published a two-page advertising spread in magazines leading off with a photograph of a well-tailored manager about to eat a very dead-looking crow. The caption: "New diet for insurance executives!" The accompanying copy says Aetna has come to realize that a lot of people were unhappy with some of the things it had done, so the company realized it had to make changes.

In the United States, the Roman Catholic Church, which has always claimed the mark of infallibility in its doctrinal teaching, has conducted outreach programs aimed at the return of "alienated members." In those outreach programs, the church has proclaimed in its media messages that its leaders and members may well have been the cause of alienation. They ask for forgiveness of those they have offended.

Beyond these examples, of course, there is the principle we have tried to hammer on throughout this book: Public relations is action—good deeds—before anything else. If a business, organization, or institution wants a good image, the best and only way to achieve it is to perform acceptably.

So much, then, for the image-building psychology that says public relations simply creates favorable images regardless of the sometimes awful truth.

Of course, image is not a bad word, and practitioners should not have their mouths washed out with soap every time they use it. In the communication process, the goal of the sender-communicator is to convey a message to the receiver-audience in a form as identical as possible to what is in the mind of that sender. What the receiver gets after the message is encoded, sent, and decoded, however, is really an image or reproduction of the thoughts or feelings of the sender, not the thoughts or feelings themselves.

One of the most wonderful aspects of communication is that humans can succeed in conveying messages that can represent thought and feeling as near to the original as they do, that the images men and women create are as representative as they are. Conversely, one of the most frustrating aspects of human communication is that, try as we may, we are unable to put into the mind of the receiver exactly what was in the mind of the sender. The image a person creates is always just that, an image, a reflection, a reproduction, not the original.

As communicators, public relations people certainly create images in this sense, and that is good. When public relations people take pains to be accurate and understandable in their writing, for instance, so that the images they create in the minds of reader-receivers are as close to the original thought as possible, that is very good. Creating images in this sense is beautiful, and these types of images are great human achievements.

It is when image is used to describe a kind of heavily touched-up photograph, one in which the blemishes are painted out, the unruly hair put into place and the missing tooth drawn in, that we are critical. This type of image is a deliberate distortion of reality, a conscious attempt to make the unpretty original look beautiful. It is twisting the truth, an attempt to mislead, an effort to gain approval for something that is not worthy of approval or that may not even exist. Not only does it corrupt the sender-communicator and misinform the receiver, it also encourages senders, if they get away with false images, to avoid changing the bad conditions they have covered up. "Why should we change?" they ask. "Nobody knows how bad we are. They think we're great."

CANDOR, RECEPTIVITY, DILIGENCE

Instead of negative image psychology, the psychology for public relations today and in the years ahead must be one that is built upon candor, receptivity, and diligence. As it has from the beginning, public relations must continue to require acceptable performance as its foundation.

Practitioners must continue to have as their principal responsibility seeing to it that their employer or client is "doing good deeds." They may actually have an easier task in persuading top decision makers that this is essential for acceptance and credibility, because in the past few years, many business, professional, and government leaders have learned painful, well-publicized lessons.

Beyond this, practitioners will have to spread the word that mistakes in judgment and lapses in performance are inevitable in any human endeavor. To pretend that they are not is unrealistic and immediately "un-credible." The public relations response to such failures must be candor, an unhesitating admission of fault.

That does not mean that a corporation must employ professional mourners who will weep on cue for the cameras. Candor does not imply exhibitionist breast-beating. It implies undramatic straightforwardness. Nor does candor imply that accounts of genuine corrective measures cannot be tied to admissions of fault. Such accounts are as much a part of the real picture as the need for corrective action.

Candor does, however, encompass more than telling the truth and admitting mistakes. It implies telling the whole truth and telling it straight.

There is a tendency among practitioners, and it is understandable and defensible, to approach an unpleasant situation with the attitude, "Okay, we'll put out a news release or make an announcement telling what happened, but we'll make it as positive as possible." Trouble arises at the point where "positive" starts to crowd out candor.

The provost at a state university in the Midwest resigned several years ago. The university's public relations office sent out a news release indicating the provost resigned voluntarily to return to teaching. His superior, the university's new president, was quoted praising the provost for exemplary service. Local news media published the release without question. The university's student newspaper, however, reported that the provost had not resigned voluntarily and quoted him to the effect that he left his post at the president's request.

In classic understatement, the editor of one of the newspapers that had printed the news release unquestioningly later commented, "We're going to be more careful hereafter." Translated into public relations talk, that means, "The credibility of the university's news releases has just suffered a serious blow as far as we're concerned."

Candor by itself it not enough either. A public relations staff or program not only has to be candid but has to be perceived as candid by its publics. The way people on the staff or in the program find out how they are perceived is by listening to their publics, by being receptive.

We have tried in this text to join serious scholars as well as practitioners in emphasizing the need for feedback and two-way communication in successful public relations. Our mention of receptivity here is intended to underline the importance of the attitude it implies.

Practitioners must encourage their employers and clients to be willing to listen to, not just hear, feedback, especially the feedback that comes in the form of complaints, objections, protests, and even lawsuits. A complaint has to be seen not just as "bitching" by some "crank." It must be accepted as a communication that may require serious concern and deserves careful investigation. As soon as you casually label someone a crank, you are saying such a person is to be ignored. But if you admit that complainers are people who take time to communicate their unhappiness, then you will be inclined to heed them and examine the source of their concern promptly.

A steel tank manufacturing plant some years ago had an assembly line in which tanks were tested for leaks. Time-study experts had rated handling time for the various sizes of tanks on the line. But the crews never came near testing the number of tanks the experts figured they should when it came to one variety, a large liquid petroleum gas tank that weighed about 350 pounds when filled with water. The reason was that workers were afraid of the tanks, because legend had it that a man had been killed once when a hoist bearing one had broken, hurtling the heavy tank down on him.

All management ever did about the situation, however, was send time-study experts back to reexamine and rerate the job. No one ever investigated why employees suddenly went home sick when assigned to test these tanks or why they requested transfers to other jobs. Over the months and years, thousands of dollars of productivity were undoubtedly lost through management's tuning out these employees.

More recently a similar management situation went into the courts. It involved workers' refusal to go out onto a platform they considered unsafe. The case went to the Supreme Court where a majority of the justices finally got the attention of an unreceptive management. The justices said the workers had a very good reason for their refusal—fear for their physical safety.

But even a receptive management has to have something to be receptive to. Not every problem is going to be brought in and spelled out for the appropriate manager or supervisor. Foremen may not be told why employees slow down on a particular job or avoid certain tasks. In a sense, management, particularly through its public relations staff, has to be willing to go looking for trouble. The purpose is not to make trouble but to avoid or resolve it. This is where diligence comes in.

The public relations staff must be on constant alert for potential conflict, ready to prescribe ways to deal with it successfully or, better still, to suggest ways to avoid it. Experts tell society they are convinced the most effective way to reduce loss from fire is to conduct vigorous fire prevention programs and the best way to prevent certain epidemics is to immunize. We expect society's leaders to be diligent in acting on this advice. It is reasonable to expect the same kind of diligence in identifying and heading off human relations problems.

Public relations staffs might, in fact, use modern firefighters as a model. Instead of whiling away the hours at checkerboards and card tables or watching daytime TV while they wait for an alarm to go off, today's firefighters are inspecting buildings for hazards and talking to schoolchildren about fire prevention. They are also training, studying, and checking their equipment back at the station.

They do not wait for fires to break out. They look for sources of fires, and they alert others to preventive steps and teach them what to do immediately when fires occur.

Like firefighters, public relations staffs should be out inspecting for public relations hazards and preaching prevention to key management personnel. They should be urging foremen not to wait until the employees under them are so upset they are complaining. The public relations staff should be setting out suggestion boxes, encouraging executives to adopt reasonable open door policies, inviting readers of company or organization publications to write in their reactions, criticisms, and questions.

When the public relations staffs discover potential conflict, they should be ready to move promptly and not panic. They should have at their disposal the equipment, like well-designed and well-read employee publications, well-paved access to the news media, well-informed management or leadership spokesmen, that they can use skillfully and confidently because they too are trained, alert, and ready.

An excellent example of public relations alertness and diligence was provided when the staff of.television's "60 Minutes" came to do a story involving the Illinois Power Company. This was not too long after the release of the popular movie, "China Syndrome," which dealt with a potentially disastrous nuclear power generating accident, and within a year of the highly publicized problems at the Three Mile Island nuclear power plant near Harrisburg, Pennsylvania. The focus of the "60 Minutes" piece, however, was on the cost of a new Illinois Power nuclear energy plant.

An executive of Illinois Power saw to it that the company made its own videotape of all the interviews "60 Minutes" conducted with William Gerstner, the principal company spokesman. When the edited "60 Minutes" interviews were broadcast, Illinois Power management was indignant, claiming the abbreviated material was seriously misleading.

The claims "I was misquoted" and "What I said was taken out of context" are so old and worn that news people almost automatically discount them, and the general public frequently reacts with skepticism too. But Illinois Power had a full videotaped record and proceeded to make it available to interested parties. The National Center for Business and Economic Communication reported that when students were shown the videotape with the "60 Minutes" segments on Illinois Power, their responses indicated that Illinois Power made its point with extreme effectiveness, despite all the prestige connected with one of television's most-watched programs.

TAKING THE OFFENSIVE

While the videotaping of news interviews by Illinois Power was primarily a defensive, precautionary tactic, there is no reason why a sound, ethical public relations program cannot take the offensive in appropriate circumstances. Throughout this book we have talked about internal and external publics as groups whose support and approval are to be won and kept by sound public relations policies, performance, and communication. Yet practitioners must be realistic enough to recognize that their employers and clients are sometimes going to face inherently unreceptive or downright hostile publics too.

To avoid confusion, they should be termed adversaries rather than publics. Adversaries exist in many areas where public relations tries to function, not just in political public relations where they may be most obvious.

They must be dealt with, although obviously not through an "enemies list" or a "dirty tricks" campaign. Instead, common sense calls for public relations people to assess their opposition and deal with it in terms of issues and policies, not personalities. This means gathering evidence and marshaling arguments, not digging up dirt to discredit individuals. Legitimate evidence, however, does include material that reveals personal incompetence or wrongdoing. If well-documented and germane, it may be perfectly ethical to display such evidence.

In any case, it is the candid, receptive, diligent public relations program that is best suited for mounting an offensive against adversaries. Our courts have their "clean hands" doctrine, which holds that unless a party comes to court with a record of fair dealing, the judge may not heed that party's request for relief. In a public relations setting, the general public or key special publics may be the judge. The public relations spokesman without clean hands may not get much of a hearing from this judge either. The public will be skeptical of criticism from a source whose own record is seriously blemished.

Consider that in recent years, more and more businesses have criticized increased regulation by government. As a business person, you might think the Federal Trade Commission has "gone too far this time," so you want to curtail its activity by getting Congress to reduce its authority. Would you be more effective in your effort if your company had been the successful target of FTC false advertising prosecutions or if your company had defeated FTC attacks on its advertising, or if your company had never run afoul of the FTC at all?

In several places (e.g., responses to hostile questions) we have already discussed some of the pitfalls in dealing with adversaries. One that you will always want to avoid is giving the appearance of picking a fight. This may well cause a public relations offensive to boomerang. If an adversary is not active in its opposition, apparently unprovoked criticism of that adversary, especially if it is sharp or harsh, will do more harm than good.

Public relations should mount no "search and destroy" missions. Instead, it should have a willingness to criticize active adversaries, to persuade publics that the adversary is wrong, that the adversary's evidence is weak, that its arguments are unsound. Practitioners should not engage in overkill by calling for the annihilation of adversaries.

Specific ethical standards

THE PRSA AND IABC CODES

In the foregoing, we have tried to lay the groundwork for ethical performance by public relations professionals. Get your client or employer to act justly and honorably and tell the truth about those actions, even when they may not be fully just and honorable. That is something like the basic moral imperative, "Do good and avoid evil." Good advice, but what does it mean in everyday life?

Appended to this chapter are the Code of Professional Standards for the Practice of Public Relations adopted by the Public Relations Society of America and the Code of Ethics of the International Association of Business Communicators. They are excellent statements of principle. Try to read between the lines of the more specific provisions to get an idea of the types of ethical problems that they address. That should give you an awareness of the types of ethical problems many practitioners meet in their everyday professional lives.

The codes are guidelines rather than laws, of course. No one can be compelled to follow them, except by conscience perhaps. The most serious sanction voluntary associations can apply is expulsion from their ranks. With professional organizations, this is an extreme and rare sanction. And many active practitioners in the United States are not members of PRSA and IABC in the first place. Nonetheless, the codes are widely cited and followed, by nonmembers as well as members.

RECOGNIZING AND RESOLVING CONFLICTS. Note that in the PRSA code, the words "truth," "accuracy," and "fairness" are repeated, certainly emphasizing them as primary standards of public relations conduct. Then note the codes' concern over conflicts of interest, a concern that has become much more conspicuous in many areas of public life over the past decade, as reflected in "sunshine" laws, for instance, requiring public officials to disclose their financial interests. Conflicts of interest will be most obvious, and perhaps most frequent, for practitioners who work for independent public relations agencies having many clients. Clearly, the more clients an agency serves, the more likely it is that competing interests may be involved.

In connection with the codes' treatment of conflicts of interest, three points should be added:

1. One of the most difficult aspects of conflicts of interest is recognizing them and admitting they exist.

2. Although the PRSA standards and similar professional codes hold that full disclosure to the affected parties, along with their consent, is required in conflict of interest situations, such disclosure and consent do not necessarily cure a situation. A client can still be hurt.

3. Conflicts of interest occur even when the public relations person works full-time for a single employer.

The practitioner who subscribes to a philosophy of honesty and candor may experience a little self-congratulatory pride. This pride has a way of subtly encouraging self-deception. "Who, me? I work in a truth-however-painful PR program! I would never stand for a conflict of interest."

This state of mind sometimes permits conflicts to sneak up on people, particularly if they have persuaded themselves they are good guys who would never even be tempted to violate ethical guidelines. The unhappy truth is that everyone is tempted, regardless of good intentions. That means you have to be on guard, particularly for relationships that have no conflict of interest to begin with but slowly, imperceptibly develop conflicts as time passes.

Take a comparatively simple situation. A public relations agency has two retailers as clients. One is a chain of pizza restaurants. The other is a discount chain that sells general merchandise. The discount stores add cafeterias at their outlets, initially as a service and convenience to customers.

One day an executive notes that the chef-manager of one cafeteria has done an extravagantly successful business. The executive investigates. It turns out the chef-manager has offered a pizza special that has become unbelievably popular with its "secret recipe" sauce, inimitable crust, etc. The recipe is introduced at other outlets. It is an overnight smash.

Suddenly the discount chain has a successful pizza enterprise it is pushing. The stores are now in direct and substantial competition with the agency's other client.

The conflict may be clearer and more immediate if an advertising agency is serving these two clients. But the public relations agency is supposed to be as dedicated as an in-house staff to achieving each client's corporate goals. Thus the public relations agency has problems here too. In theory, but possibly also in practice, anything the agency does for one client can make it a stronger competitor, and it is clear that stronger competition will threaten the economic standing of any rival.

The possibilities for similar developments are many. Who, a few years ago, would have thought that supermarkets would start renting videotapes and discs?

Even when developing conflicts like these are recognized (and remember they do not come about overnight), there are subtle dangers that an agency may have to avoid even when clients accept the situation. These dangers include unconscious favoritism, possibly based on friendships built up over the years or based on the amount of money spent with the agency. They include unwitting use of confidential information to protect one client from the moves of another.

A public relations program design may also be affected by watered down creativity because the agency's best effort has been provided another client. Even when individuals within an agency can honestly say they have given their best to one or the other client, can the agency say the same? Or will it have to admit that Client A got the best writer the agency has, while Client B was served by its most creative talent in visuals or graphics?

Also subtle are the conflicts that face practitioners as individuals, even when they devote all their regular working hours to a single employer. Part of their employment may involve them with professional, trade, and community organizations. A hospital public relations director, for example, may be active in one or more organizations devoted to raising funds for research and treatment of a particular disease. One of these organizations considers a special fund-raising project.

It turns out, however, that the project is similar to one the hospital auxiliary is planning. Or maybe the organization's project is scheduled when the hospital has a fund raiser on its calendar. In real life, would you be surprised if the hospital public relations director tried to persuade the organization's officers to change the nature of their project or to move the date of their event? Certainly both will benefit from avoiding unnecessary competition. But who will wind up with the best project and date, and will the hospital public relations director be able to play an impartial role in making those decisions?

Another type of individual problem may involve the public relations person who loves to write and who has come across some excellent material for a free-lance article in the course of working for his employer. If the practitioner is working for a client, it may be a simple matter to persuade the client to pay for an article as an additional service. But if the practitioner is an employee, the question is: Can I sell an article based on material I came across while working for my employer? If the article is written at home (i.e., not on company time) does that alone make it ethical for me to accept payment from a magazine? What if, with a little more on-the-job effort, I could have written the piece at work and sent it out as a release, a free promotional piece, compliments of my employer?

If you have harbored any thoughts about free lancing, you will be glad to know that practical common sense can quickly resolve many such problems. Magazines will often reject articles submitted as public relations releases (the problem of credibility again) in favor of articles on the same subject written by a free-lancer. That may be true even though the free-lancer is involved with the article's subject matter because the free-lancer is also a public relations practitioner.

There is always the option of getting the boss's approval. Often employers are pleased to have their public relations people get into free lancing because they realize they will benefit from the results. For one thing, in producing free-lance articles, the practitioners may be improving writing and research skills that are valuable on the full-time job. For another, if free-lancers are identified by employment in the publishing magazine, their employer gets an indirect plug.

More difficult conflict of interest problems for the in-house public relations staff occur in serving different publics with different interests. There may well be conflicts between what appears to be in the interest of employees and what appears to be in the interest of stockholders in a business corporation. There may be conflicts between the interests of administrators and students in a college or university setting. Can a public relations staff serve each of these publics equally well, or can it divide its loyalty exactly in half when two publics are at odds over goals?

The answer is clearly no. To deny this is almost to guarantee losing the confidence of both publics. Public relations people in a corporate setting have to accept the fact that they work for the owners and directors, the leaders that a majority of the owners have selected. Practitioners who work for organizations and agencies must accept that they work for the officers and directors who chart objectives and formulate policy.

This does not ignore the fact that public relations people have the job of persuading their management or leadership to act acceptably toward employees, students, or residents of the local community, etc. But when practical policy decisions rather than social justice decisions are at issue, public relations employees must be forthright about whom they represent. We cannot insist that public relations is one of the most important aspects of management and have it otherwise.

True, practitioners must be advocates for various publics with corporate management or institutional and agency leaders. Practitioners must decide whether they can accept the response of corporate management or of organizational leadership and defend it before the publics affected.

If the controversy is over practical policy rather than moral principle, acceptance should be expected. If the controversy revolves around a matter of justice or honesty, acceptance should be based on the moral judgment of the practitioner. It may come down to a matter of compromising your own principles or getting out.

Getting out is almost always hard for the individual. It is often easier to tell yourself, "I can do more good if I stick around and keep trying to change things."

That may be true. It may also be rationalizing.

Inviting a client to get out is also difficult when conflict of interest is recognized, even if ending the relationship is the only ethical solution. It is difficult for the public relations agency if the client relationship is longstanding and if the client's business has been substantial. It may be difficult for the client, too, and the agency or independent practitioner should realize this.

Any agency that abruptly drops an older, smaller client for a newer, larger client should be challenged as to what kind of public relations it is practicing with its most important public, its clients. At a minimum, the client who must be dropped deserves fair warning, a full explanation of the difficulty that brings the action, and every possible assistance in retaining continuity in its programs and in finding a reputable successor agency.

DISCLOSURE AND CONFIDENTIALITY. The planted news item is one of the old ploys of press agentry. It is one of the tactics that has given public relations a bad name. The idea behind the "plant" is to get a person or cause mentioned in an account that appears to come from a disinterested source. At least the very interested source is not revealed, because identification of the source would suggest the story is self-serving, which it is of course.

A "front" or "front organization" is a group whose backing is concealed. The group gives itself an innocuous name or even a virtuous title, like the Society for the Prevention of Corrupt Government. It campaigns against political incumbents, say, on the apparently unassailable ground that the society is composed of nonpartisan citizens who want to put capable and honest men and women, the best qualified people, or new leaders with a fresh outlook into public office. Actually, however, the society is financed and staffed by the party of the political "outs." If that were known, voters would quickly discount what the society has to say.

Both the plant and the front are condemned as unethical by the PRSA code. They are examples of failure to disclose enough information to the general public, or to specific publics, so that well-informed, balanced judgments can be made. The code says a practitioner should always be ready to identify clients or employers. Some see this as a loophole, since Article 8 of the PRSA code does not say this must actually be carried out. However, read in conjunction with Articles 7 and 9, the intent of this article certainly seems to suggest the requirement of actual disclosure.

The principle is certainly sound. Any public should know the sponsor of the message a public relations person is sending, so that the sponsor's self-interest can be filtered out of the message, or the message can be discounted with an appropriate number of grains of salt. For a public relations program dedicated to candor and honesty, this is a minimal requirement that should pose no difficulty at all.

There are difficulties, however, when you move from what various publics should be told to what those publics should not be told, chiefly because the information was obtained by public relations people only after they promised implicitly or explicitly to keep it confidential.

The PRSA code rightly distinguishes between disclosure of the sponsorship of communications and the nondisclosure or protection of the confidences of those sponsors, both present and former clients and employers. Ethical practice will require much broader disclosures than sponsorship alone. Ethical practice will also require silence about much more than what has carefully been labeled confidential by a client or employer.

Unlike wartime censors, most people in and out of management and leadership positions are not constantly concerned about secrecy. Many people, executives and nonexecutives, are trusting. They will impart information to people who seem sympathetic even though it is unnecessary to do so and probably would be more prudent not to. Some people too are compulsive talkers and revealers. In addition, because public relations people are so much a part of the sender part of communication, they are going to hear and see much behind-the-scenes activity that is not communicated to targeted receivers.

The PRSA code mentions injuring the reputation of other professionals as unethical conduct. But naturally the ethical practitioner will extend this principle to clients and employers, in fact to all with whom the practitioner works. In all these relationships, the practitioner has to act as a professional, recognizing these realities and exercising mature discretion, often with a tight lip.

QUESTIONS OF PRACTICE

In trying to win the support of publics and key individuals in the publics, a practitioner has to make sure that approval is earned. This principle has been repeated throughout our discussion of public relations.

A corollary is that approval cannot be bought, and practitioners are bound not to try to buy it. That is the implication of Article 6 of the PRSA code. The principle extends beyond the channels of communication and the processes of government, however. It is important to read how the society has spelled out the matter of gifts or inducements in its interpretation of this code provision.

Two points should be added:

1. *The ethical codes of journalists have become quite strict and specific regarding the acceptance by reporters and others of gifts and favors from sources.* That should be recognized in connection with the mention of "channels of communication." Even the trips and tours, or junkets as critics dub them, approved by the PRSA code might be considered contrary to the code of the Society of Professional Journalists, Sigma Delta Chi, for instance. That code says, "Gifts, favors, free travel, special treatment or privileges can compromise the integrity of journalists and their employers. Nothing of value should be accepted." The public relations practitioner therefore must be extremely circumspect about what the PRSA code interpretation calls the "bona fide press event or tour" and "customary and reasonable hospitality," as well as about gifts of "nominal" value.

2. *Although public relations people may not be directly involved themselves, they should be alert to special favors or gifts given to*

members of publics by others within their business or organization. The kickback given in exchange for placing an order or giving a special low price is an instance of this. Such practices are not only unethical but almost always illegal as well. The lavish gift sent at Christmas may be just a subtle variation.

Summary

In your studies, discussions, or general reading, you may have encountered the terms "situation ethics" and "higher morality." Each is a key to a radically different school of ethical thought. This is germane for two reasons:

1. *These terms and the disagreements surrounding them should persuade you that there is a lot more to ethics generally, as well as to the ethics of public relations practice, than our brief discussion here can cover.* As a profession that has been put down and caricatured because of its ethical failings, because of its persistent P. T. Barnum associations, public relations needs people who are willing to give serious, sustained study to ethics and professional standards of conduct. Public relations practitioners should be communications experts, practical psychologists, and skilled administrators. They should also be careful students of ethics. Students who want to embark on a career in public relations should study journalism, economics and the other social sciences, and management. But they should also study the philosophy of human conduct.

If public relations is going to play an increasingly important role in resolving major economic, political and social issues, it must be practiced by people with great sensitivity to questions of right and wrong and to values like human dignity and individual freedom. Study will not be enough. There must also be personal commitment to ethical principles.

2. *The drafters of the PRSA and IABC professional codes of conduct have accepted the higher morality principle of ethics, even though they use appropriately secular terms.* The codes recognize "the fundamental value and dignity of the individual" and pledge that "[i]n serving the interest of clients and employers, we dedicate ourselves to. . .better communication, understanding and cooperation among the diverse individuals, groups and institutions of society." This is reinforced by mention of a "responsibility to the public" and a duty to "conduct. . .professional life in accord with the public interest." Clearly, "public" here refers to the general public or society at large.

Unless these are but empty high-sounding phrases, they mean

that the basis for deciding what is ethical conduct goes beyond situation ethics—decisions largely based on the needs and desires of the individuals directly involved in a particular situation. These code statements mean that the professional societies believe there is a more permanent and objective basis for deciding issues of right and wrong.

With their professional organizations embracing this principle, practitioners have strong support for unequivocally rejecting the notion that they can ever be "hired guns"—people whose loyalty and effort are sold to those who pay them. Practitioners will be able to lift their eyes beyond the immediate crisis or need to consider the full and long-range impact of what they do or counsel.

Exercises

1. Contact the public relations staff of a local business or organization to find out how it deals with mistakes in news releases it has sent out. Ask if the staff has established procedures for correcting errors in releases and in its own publications. If there are procedures, find out what they are and how they came to be developed.

2. Rewrite the script for the situation described on pages 398–399, where the university provost did not resign voluntarily but was removed by the president, advising the university public relations office how to handle it without losing credibility. Be practical and realistic as well as ethical in your advice.

3. See if you can obtain a copy of the Illinois Power Company videotape response to "60 Minutes." View it and discuss what parts of the "whole truth," if any, the network program omitted. (Copies may be available through PRSA or IABC chapters. The tape is entitled "'60 Minutes'/Our Reply.")

4. The "dirty tricks" mentioned on page 402 were an issue during the 1970s Watergate situation and the preceding presidential election. Read the part of the book *All the President's Men* to find out what political "dirty tricks" were involved and how effective they were as political public relations.

5. Discuss the situation mentioned on page 407, where a public relations agency faces a conflict of interest in taking on a promising new account if it retains a smaller account. Must the agency turn down the new account under the provisions of the PRSA code? If not, how can it sever relations with the older account gracefully? What considerations, besides the size of the new account and the conflict of interest, should the public relations agency weigh before making a final decision on how it will proceed?

Case study

Bovine Byproducts, Inc., operates manufacturing plants in the Chicago, Kansas City, and Fort Worth areas. At those sites, waste materials from nearby beef packing plants are recovered and used in the manufacture of a wide variety of glues and adhesives and, in recent years, a number of synthetics used as substitutes for petroleum-based plastics.

BB, however, has a long history of confrontation with state and federal government agencies over air and water pollution in the areas surrounding its plants. Faced by strong laws, BB has now met air and water standards required by the various levels of government. Of course, to perform satisfactorily, BB has to make major expenditures for filtering equipment and transport systems, which its public relations staff has emphasized in news releases for the past decade.

Now, however, communities in an area in the Southeast where solid wastes and spent chemicals from BB's manufacturing processes have been shipped are complaining that these materials are hazardous to children playing in these areas. Critics say that the materials are in containers that are deteriorating, so that eventually BB's pollution problems may simply resume far from the manufacturing plants.

BB's chief executive officer tells the vice-president for public relations, "We've spent 26 million dollars to end pollution. We got experts from across the country to design our solids disposal program, and we were assured that the materials and their containers would never again be a hazard. The Chamber of Commerce in one of those towns where they're complaining now had promoted the location of our operation there because it would help the local economy. I'm so sick and tired of this whole thing that I want you to issue a flat denial that our products are causing any hazard any place. And listen, those Chamber of Commerce directors down there owe our company something. Get in touch with them and see if you can talk them into issuing a statement condemning our critics and supporting our position. You might remind the president of the chamber that we keep quite a balance in his bank to meet our local payroll there. We could just as well send our checks right out of Chicago."

> • Does the vice-president for public relations face any problems of personal ethics in this situation? Explain.
> • What issues of professional practice ethics are raised by this situation?
> • Does this situation suggest that the vice-president for public relations must either act unethically or resign? What are the vice-president's ethical alternatives?

Suggested readings

Baker, Samm. *The Permissible Lie.* Boston: Beacon Press, 1968.

Barovick, Richard L. "Status Report: Code of Conduct for MNCs." *Public Relations Journal,* October 1979.

Dardenne, Peg. "Don't Rain on My Parade." *Public Relations Journal,* April 1980.

Golden, L. L. L. *Only by Public Consent.* New York: Hawthorn, 1968.

Merrill, John C., and Ralph D. Barney, eds. *Ethics and the Press: Readings in Mass Media Morality.* New York: Hastings House, 1976.

Moscowitz, Milton. "Trumpeting the New Values." *Communication World,* November 1983.

Nolan, Joseph. "Business Beware: Early Warning Signs in the Eighties." *Public Opinion,* April/May 1981.

Phelan, John M. *Disenchantment: Meaning and Morality in the Media.* New York: Hastings House, 1980.

Thayer, Lee, ed. *Ethics and Morality in the Media.* New York: Hastings House, 1980.

CODE OF PROFESSIONAL STANDARDS FOR THE PRACTICE OF PUBLIC RELATIONS
Public Relations Society of America

DECLARATION OF PRINCIPLES

Members of the Public Relations Society of America base their professional principles on the fundamental value and dignity of the individual, holding that the free exercise of human rights, especially freedom of speech, freedom of assembly and freedom of the press, is essential to the practice of public relations.

In serving the interests of clients and employers, we dedicate ourselves to the goals of better communication, understanding and cooperation among the diverse individuals, groups and institutions of society.

We pledge:

To conduct ourselves professionally, with truth, accuracy, fairness and responsibility to the public;

To improve our individual competence and advance the knowledge and proficiency of the profession through continuing research and education;

And to adhere to the articles of the Code of Professional Standards for the Practice of Public Relations as adopted by the governing Assembly of the Society.

ARTICLES OF THE CODE

These articles have been adopted by the Public Relations Society of America to promote and maintain high standards of public service and ethical conduct among its members.

1. A member shall deal fairly with clients or employers, past and present, with fellow practitioners and the general public.

2. A member shall conduct his or her professional life in accord with the public interest.

3. A member shall adhere to truth and accuracy and to generally accepted standards of good taste.

4. A member shall not represent conflicting or competing interests without the express consent of those involved, given after a full disclosure of the facts, nor place himself or herself in a position where the member's interest is or may be in conflict with a duty to a client, or others, without a full disclosure of such interests to all involved.

5. A member shall safeguard the confidences of both present and former clients or employers and shall not accept retainers or employment which may involve the disclosure or use of these confidences to the disadvantage or prejudice of such clients or employers.

6. A member shall not engage in any practice which tends to corrupt the integrity of channels of communication or the processes of government.

7. A member shall not intentionally communicate false or misleading information and is obligated to use care to avoid communication of false or misleading information.

8. A member shall be prepared to identify publicly the name of the client or employer on whose behalf any public communication is made.

9. A member shall not make use of any individual or organization purporting to serve or represent an announced cause, or purporting to be independent or unbiased, but actually serving an undisclosed special or private interest of a member, client or employer.

10. A member shall not intentionally injure the professional reputation or practice of another practitioner. However, if a member has evidence that another member has been guilty of unethical, illegal or unfair practices, includ-

ing those in violation of this Code, the member shall present the information promptly to the proper authorities of the Society for action in accordance with the procedure set forth in Article XIII of the Bylaws.

11. A member called as a witness in a proceeding for the enforcement of this Code shall be bound to appear, unless excused for sufficient reason by the Judicial Panel.

12. A member, in performing services for a client or employer, shall not accept fees, commissions or any other valuable consideration from anyone other than the client or employer in connection with those services without the express consent of the client or employer, given after a full disclosure of the facts.

13. A member shall not guarantee the achievement of specified results beyond the member's direct control.

14. A member shall, as soon as possible, sever relations with any organization or individual if such relationship requires conduct contrary to the articles of this Code.

CODE OF ETHICS
International Association of Business Communicators

COMMUNICATION AND INFORMATION DISSEMINATION

1. Communication professionals will uphold the credibility and dignity of their profession by encouraging the practice of honest, candid and timely communication.

The highest standards of professionalism will be upheld in all communication. Communicators should encourage frequent communication and messages that are honest in their content, candid, accurate and appropriate to the needs of the organization and its audiences.

2. Professional communicators will not use any information that has been generated or appropriately acquired by a business for another business without permission. Further, communicators should attempt to identify the source of information to be used.

When one is changing employers, information developed at the previous position will not be used without permission from that employer. Acts of plagiarism and copyright infringement are illegal acts; material in the public domain should have its source attributed, if possible. If an organization grants permission to use its information and requests public acknowledgment, it will be made in a place appropriate to the material used. The material will be used only for the purpose for which permission was granted.

STANDARDS OF CONDUCT

3. Communication professionals will abide by the spirit and letter of all laws and regulations governing their professional activities.

All international, national and local laws and regulations must be observed, with particular attention to those pertaining to communication, such as copyright law. Industry and organizational regulations will also be observed.

4. Communication professionals will not condone any illegal or unethical act related to their professional activity, their organization and its business or the public environment in which it operates.

It is the personal responsibility of professional communicators to act honestly, fairly and with integrity at all times in all professional activities. Looking the other way while others act illegally tacitly condones such acts whether or not the communicator has committed them. The communicator should speak with the individual involved, his or her supervisor or appropriate authorities—depending on the context of the situation and one's own ethical judgment.

CONFIDENTIALITY/DISCLOSURE

5. Communication professionals will respect the confidentiality and right-to-privacy of all individuals, employers, clients and customers.

Communicators must determine the ethical balance between right-to-privacy and need-to-know. Unless the situation involves illegal or grossly unethical acts, confidences should be maintained. If there is a conflict between right-to-privacy and need-to-know, a communicator should first talk with the source and negotiate the need for the information to be communicated.

6. Communication professionals will not use any confidential information gained as a result of professional activity for personal benefit or for that of others.

Confidential information can be used to give inside advantage to stock transactions, gain favors from outsiders, assist a competing company for whom one is going to work, assist companies in developing a marketing advantage, achieve a publishing advantage or otherwise act to the detriment of an organization. Such information must remain confidential during and after one's employment period.

PROFESSIONALISM

7. Communication professionals should uphold IABC's standards for ethical conduct in all professional activity, and should use IABC and its designation of accreditation (ABC) only for purposes that are authorized and fairly represent the organization and its professional standards.

IABC recognizes the need for professional integrity within any organization, including the association. Members should acknowledge that their actions reflect on themselves, their organizations and their profession.

A SYSTEM OF ENACTMENT

To guide communication professionals in ethical matters and assure professional consistency, an ethical philosophy and code must have a means of enactment. The code must reinforce the observance of all civil and criminal laws and regulations, yet be flexible enough for situational considerations and for seeking reform through legitimate channels.

Therefore, the following steps should be undertaken to enact the IABC Code of Ethics:

Communication

The code should be published, along with supplementary materials and a brief reference bibliography, in a folder given to each member on a one-time basis. New members should automatically receive a Code on joining.

Include a sentence on all application and annual renewal forms stating "I have reviewed and pledge to uphold IABC's code of ethics and standards of professional communication."

In all IABC application materials and introductory brochures, include the principles of the code.

Communication World should run an article on a topic of professional ethics relevant to IABC's philosophy at least annually. A variety of themes can be chosen from the code's principles and explanations. Different approaches and case examples can increase editorial options.

At least one session about ethics should be scheduled at the IABC annual conference to assist newer professionals in developing and refining their communication ethics, education and professional development. Ethics should also be supported in IABC's professional development seminar series and sessions at district conferences. Names of speakers on ethics should be made available and shared among districts and local chapters.

IABC ethics must be participatory. In the development of a communication ethos, two-way communication is essential; therefore, the proposed IABC ethics documents should be submitted for review by all chapters with feedback collected and discussed by the districts and sent to IABC. Clarification, specific questions and concerns with accompanying recommendations are important in developing a document that fairly and honestly represents the ethical perspective of its membership. Above all, the opinions and concerns of members in *all* countries must be given full consideration.

Review Committee

Establish an ethics review committee of at least three accredited members. Non-accredited members may be appointed upon special approval by the IABC Executive Committee and the director representing ethics on the Executive Board.

The first function should be to offer an IABC member service in assisting with general ethical questions related to the profession. The committee would not provide legal opinions. Opinions on questions would be solicited from an additional two accredited members and one member at random, and these would be factored into the review committee's summary opinion. Names of those requesting and giving opinions would be confidential.

The second function of the review committee would be the professional development of members on the subject of ethics, working in conjunction with IABC's professional development committee. Efforts should be made to inform and educate membership on matters of ethics, focusing on helping individuals develop ethical decision-making skills that are interdependent with IABC policy.

The third function should be to review and sanction violations of ethical conduct among members as they reflect on IABC and the communication profession. If a member's conduct is deemed by the director responsible for ethics to violate IABC's ethical code in a way that jeopardizes the credibility of the organization and profession, then the matter would first be discussed with the individual to determine the facts of the situation. Then, if circumstances warrant, the matter would be taken up by the ethics review committee. The individual's name would be kept confidential. In addition to the committee's deliberation, at least three additional opinions would be sought in any decision. Two opinions would be solicited at random from the pool of accredited members and one from a member-at-large. The IABC director representing ethics on the Executive Board would be an ex-officio member of the process.

Members of the ethics review committee would serve staggered, three-year consecutive terms to ensure internal consistency. They may serve more than one term but not consecutively. Members of the committee will be IABC accredited as a means of objective evidence that they have a working knowledge of communication ethics which meets the organization's standards of professionalism. Non-accredited members may be appointed upon special approval by the IABC Executive Committee and the director representing ethics on the Executive Board.

SANCTIONS

It is recognized that while the code may apply to communication professionals generally, sanctions would apply only to IABC members.

For a first violation, unless criminal activity is involved, the sanctions would be informative and educational. They would share concern over the situation, rendering opinions with the intent to help guide the member toward more professional performance.

A second violation for the same or related offense would bring a warning, again with the intent of information and education.

A third or subsequent violation could involve a further warning, or if the situation were flagrant without serious commitment of improvement, an alternative sanction of suspension for up to one year could be given. *Any decision of suspension or reinstatement must be reviewed and approved by the IABC Executive Committee and the executive board director responsible.*

Index

419